井上雄彦

Takehiko Inoue

I'VE WORKED ON THIS FOR SIX YEARS, BUT ONLY FOUR MONTHS HAVE GONE BY IN THE STORY... BUT WE'VE REACHED THE END FOR NOW. THANK YOU FOR STICKING IT OUT THROUGH THE FINAL VOLUME.

I THINK I'M GONNA READ SOME BOOKS, SEE SOME MOVIES, WATCH SOME VIDEOS, WATCH SOME BASKETBALL, PLAY SOME BASKETBALL, TAKE A TRIP... I'VE GOT A LOT TO CATCH UP ON!

Takehiko Inoue's *Slam Dunk* is one of the most popular manga of all time, having sold over 100 million copies worldwide. He followed that series up with two titles lauded by critics and fans alike—*Vagabond*, a fictional account of the life of Miyamoto Musashi, and *Real*, a manga about wheelchair basketball.

SLAM DUNK
Vol. 31: Shohoku High School Basketball Team

SHONEN JUMP Manga Edition

STORY AND ART BY TAKEHIKO INOUE

English Adaptation/Stan!
Translation/Joe Yamazaki
Touch-up Art & Lettering/James Gaubatz
Cover & Graphic Design/Matt Hinrichs
Editor/Mike Montesa

© 1990 - 2013 Takehiko Inoue and I.T. Planning, Inc.
Originally published in Japan in 1996 by Shueisha
Inc., Tokyo. English translation rights arranged with
I.T. Planning, Inc. All rights reserved.

Printed in Canada

Published by VIZ Media, LLC
P.O. Box 77010
San Francisco, CA 94107

10 9 8 7 6 5 4 3 2 1
First printing, December 2013

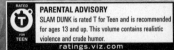

THE WORLD'S
MOST POPULAR MANGA

www.shonenjump.com

SLAM DUNK

Vol. 31: Shohoku High School Basketball Team

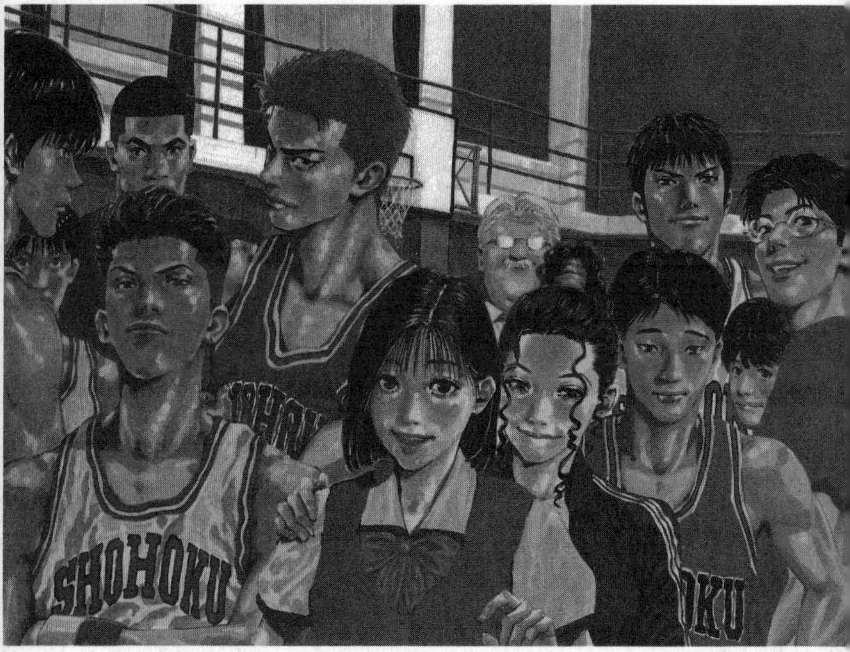
SHOHOKU
KU

STORY AND ART BY
TAKEHIKO INOUE

Character Introduction

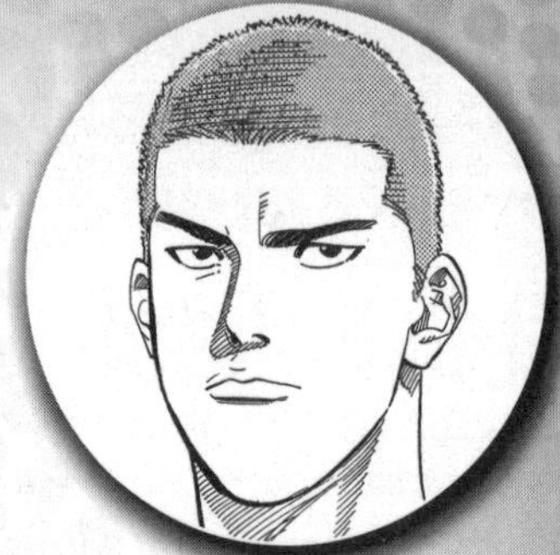

Hanamichi Sakuragi
A first-year at Shohoku High School, Sakuragi is in love with Haruko Akagi.

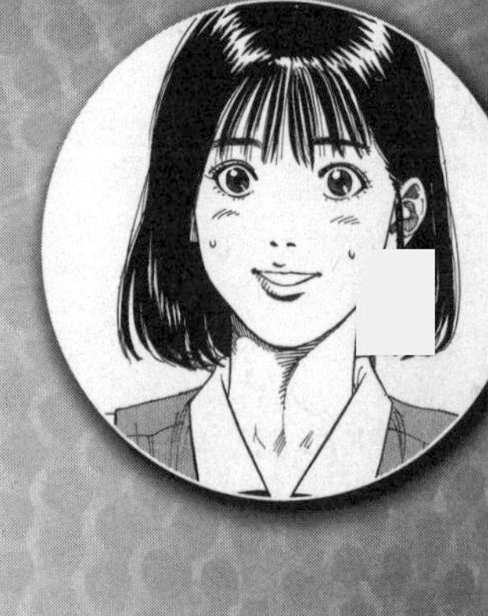

Haruko Akagi
Also a first-year at Shohoku, Takenori Akagi's little sister has a crush on Kaede Rukawa.

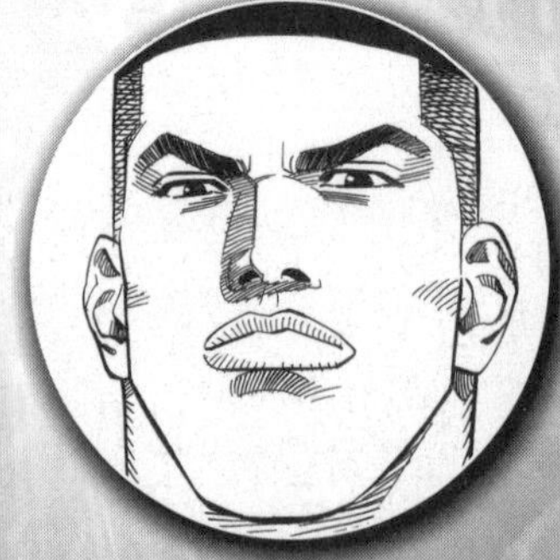

Takenori Akagi
A third-year and the basketball team's captain, Akagi has an intense passion for his sport.

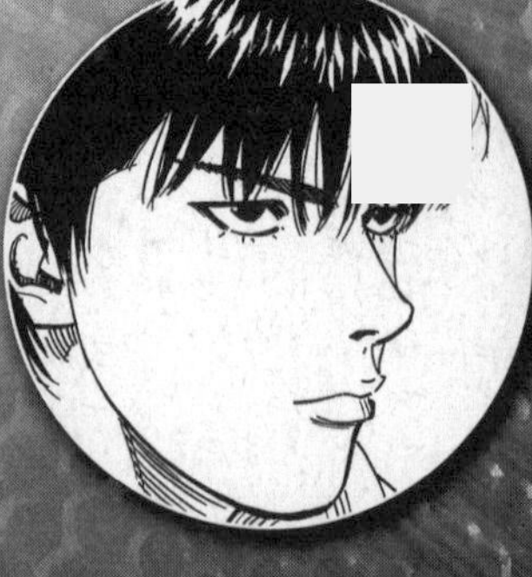

Kaede Rukawa
The object of Haruko's affection (and that of many of Shohoku's female students!), this first-year has been a star player since junior high.

Sawakita

Fukatsu

Kawata

Ryota Miyagi
A problem child with
a thing for Ayako.

Ayako
Basketball Team
Manager

Hisashi Mitsui
An MVP during
junior high.

Our Story Thus Far

Hanamichi Sakuragi is rejected by close to 50 girls during his three years
in junior high. He joins the basketball team to be closer to Haruko Akagi,
but his frustration mounts when all he does is practice day after day.

Shohoku advances through the Prefectural Tournament and earns a spot in
the Nationals and makes it to the second round to face Sannoh Kogyo, last
year's national champions and considered by most to be the best team in
the country.

Overwhelmed by Sannoh's players, led by their ace Sawakita, Shohoku
manages to stay in the game thanks to Rukawa's brilliant performance.
With Shohoku staging an amazing comeback, Sakuragi suddenly injures his

Vol. 31:
Shohoku High School Basketball Team

Table of Contents

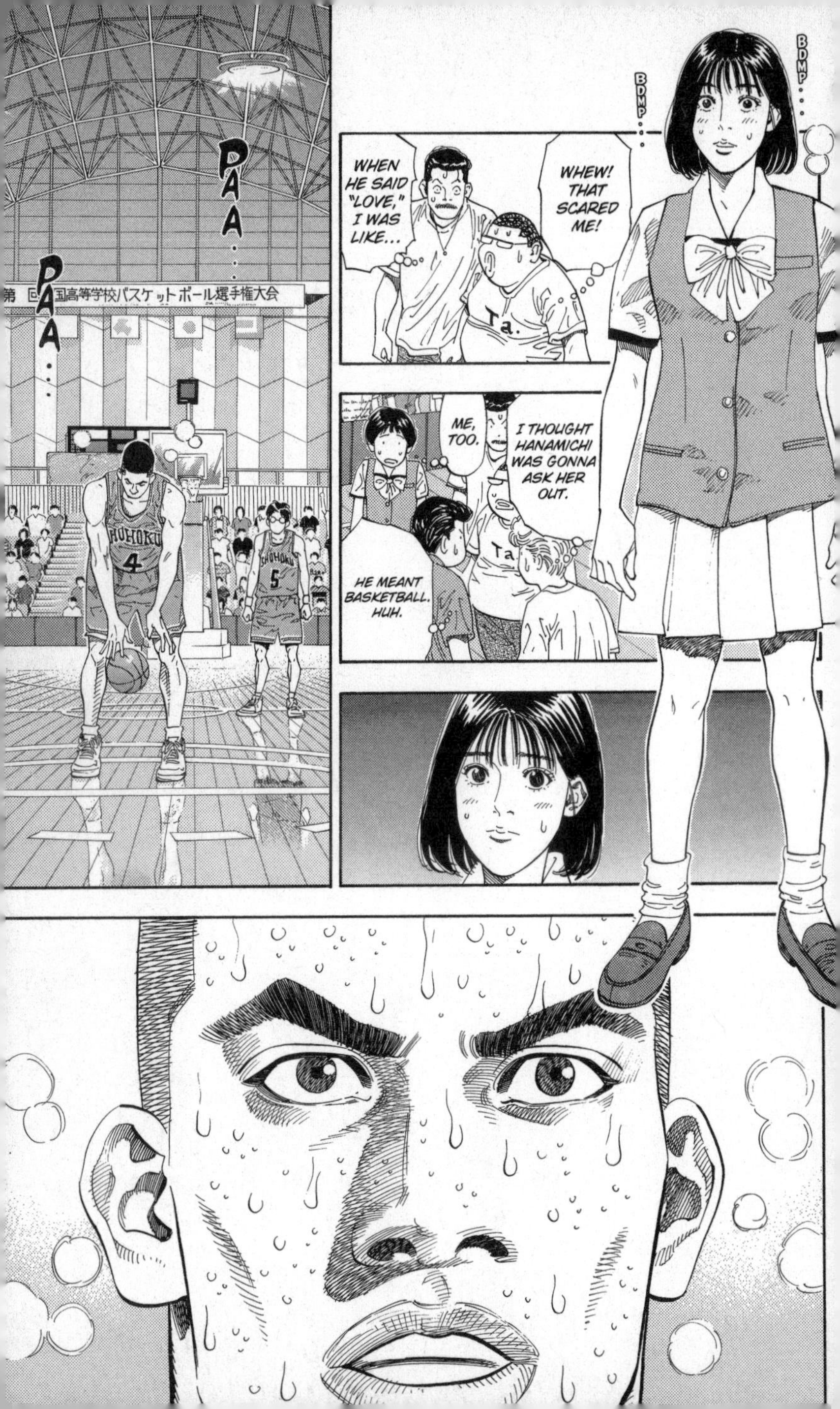
BDMP...
BDMP...
WHEW! THAT SCARED ME!
WHEN HE SAID "LOVE," I WAS LIKE...
I THOUGHT HANAMICHI WAS GONNA ASK HER OUT.
ME, TOO.
HE MEANT BASKETBALL. HUH.
PAA...
PAA...
第 回 国高等学校バスケットボール選手権大会
SHOHOKU 4
SHOHOKU 5
Ta.

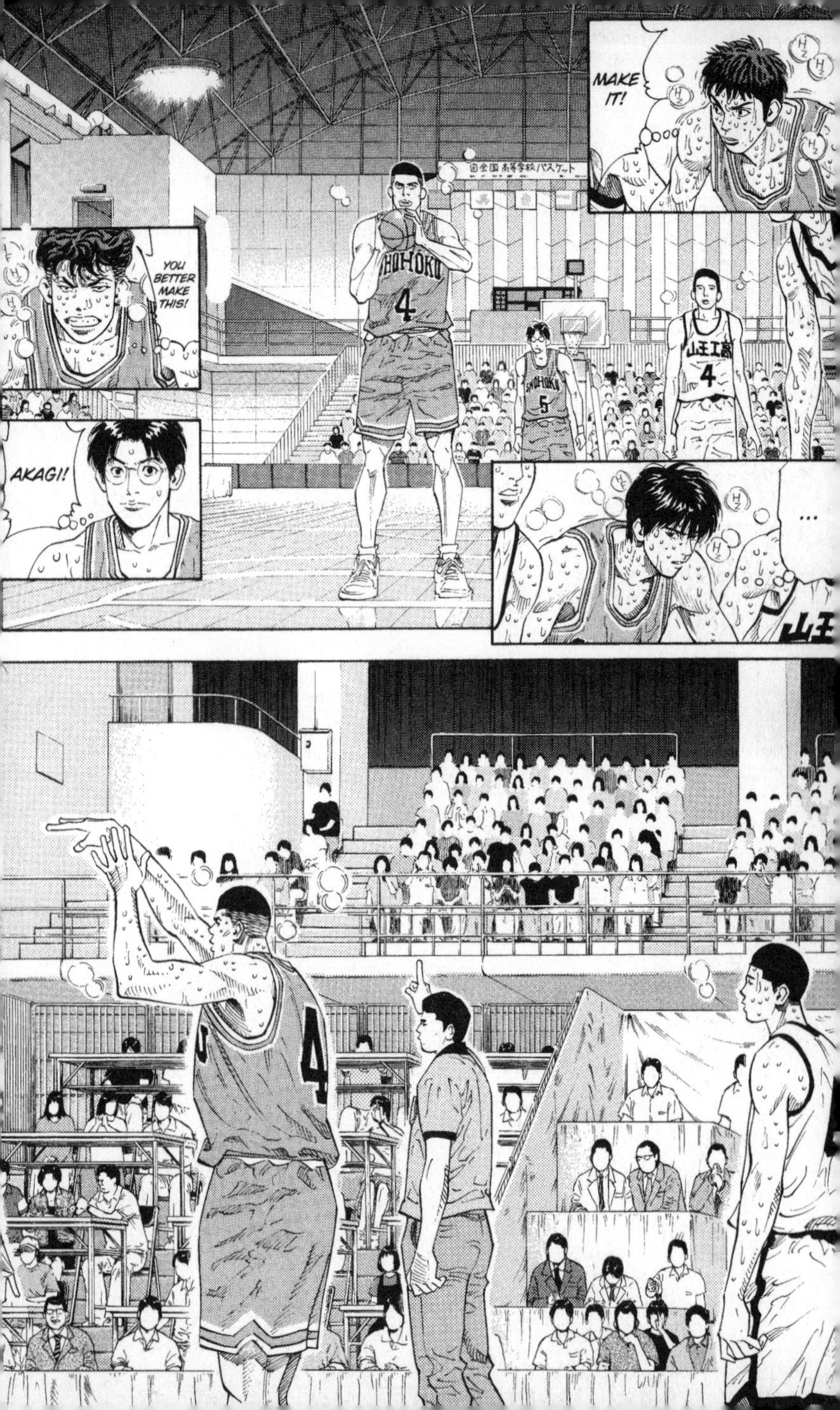
MAKE IT!
...
YOU BETTER MAKE THIS!
AKAGI!

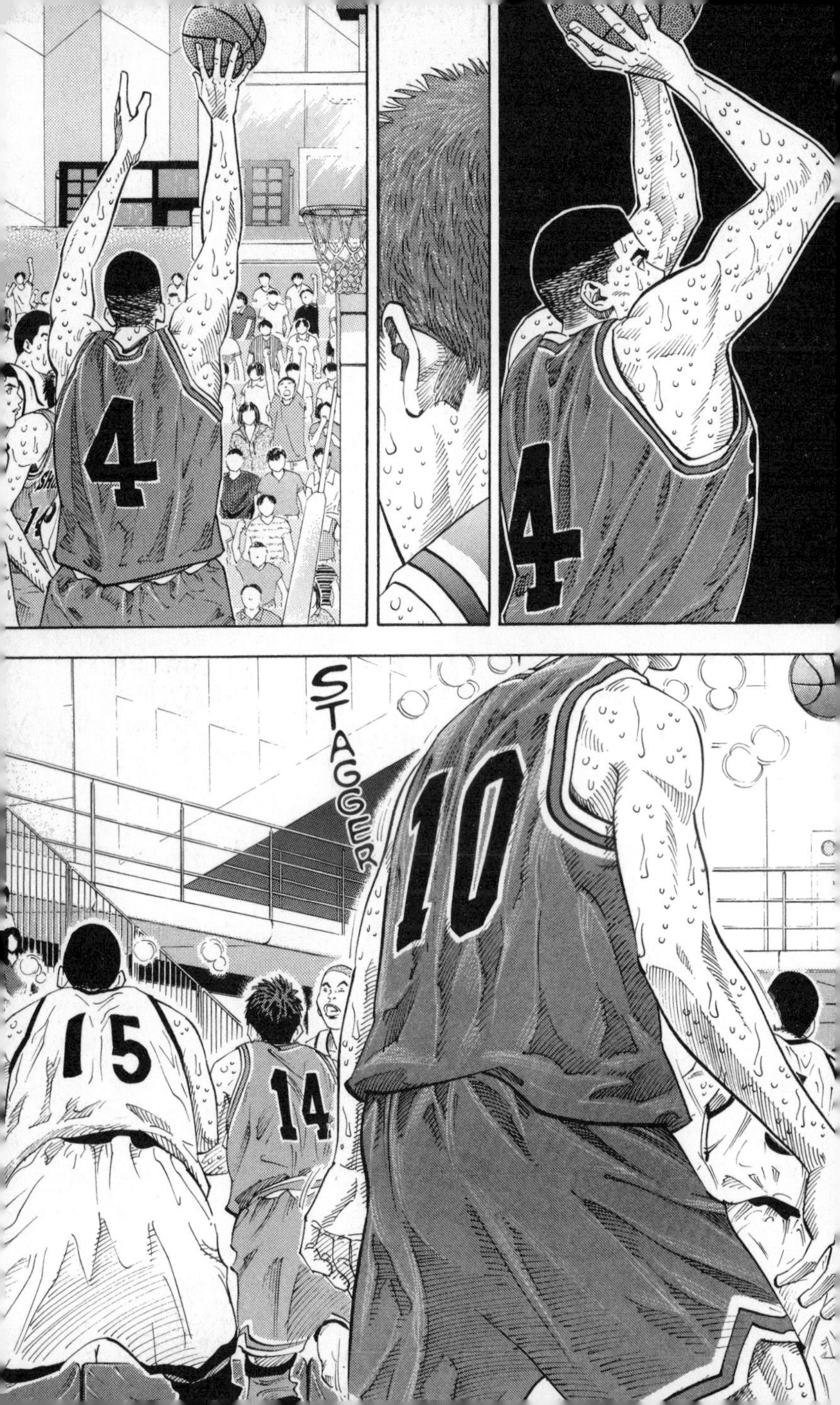
STAGGER

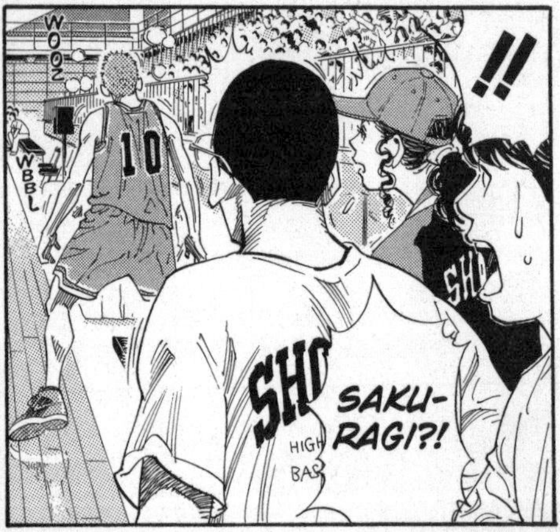
WOOZ
WBBL
!!
SAKU-
RAGI?!
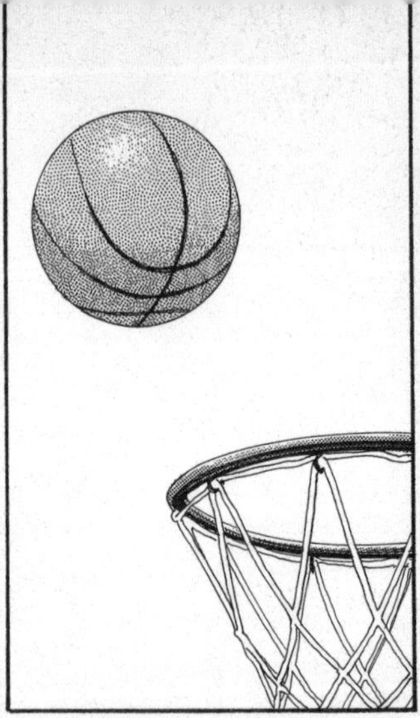
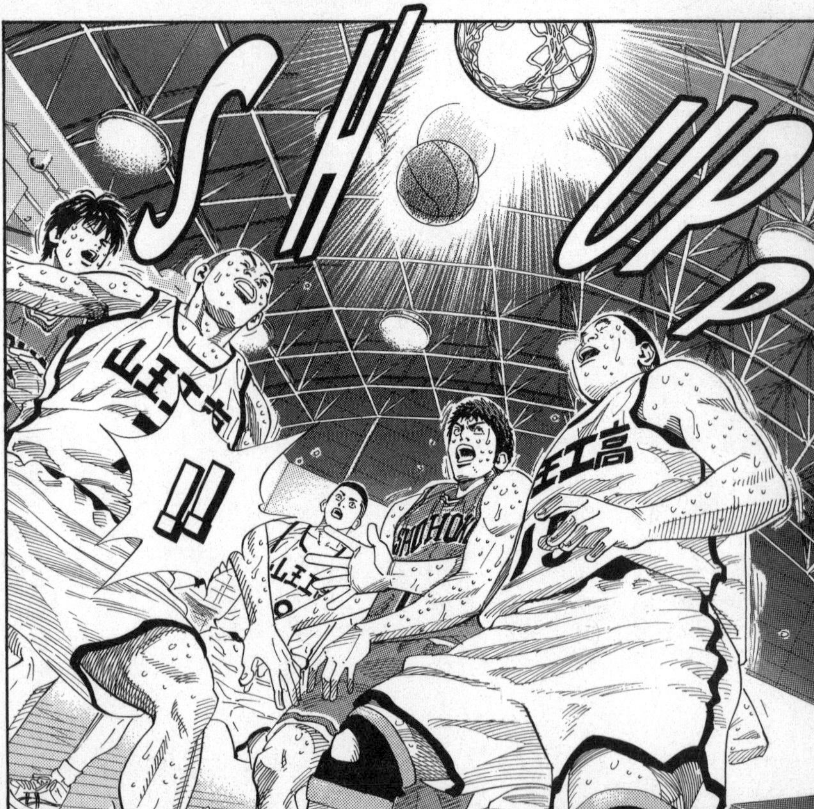
SHUPP
!!

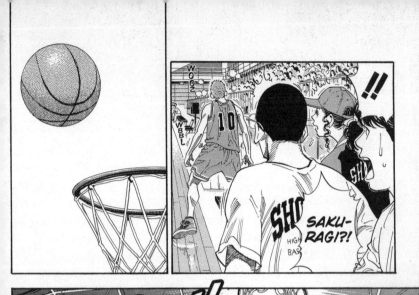

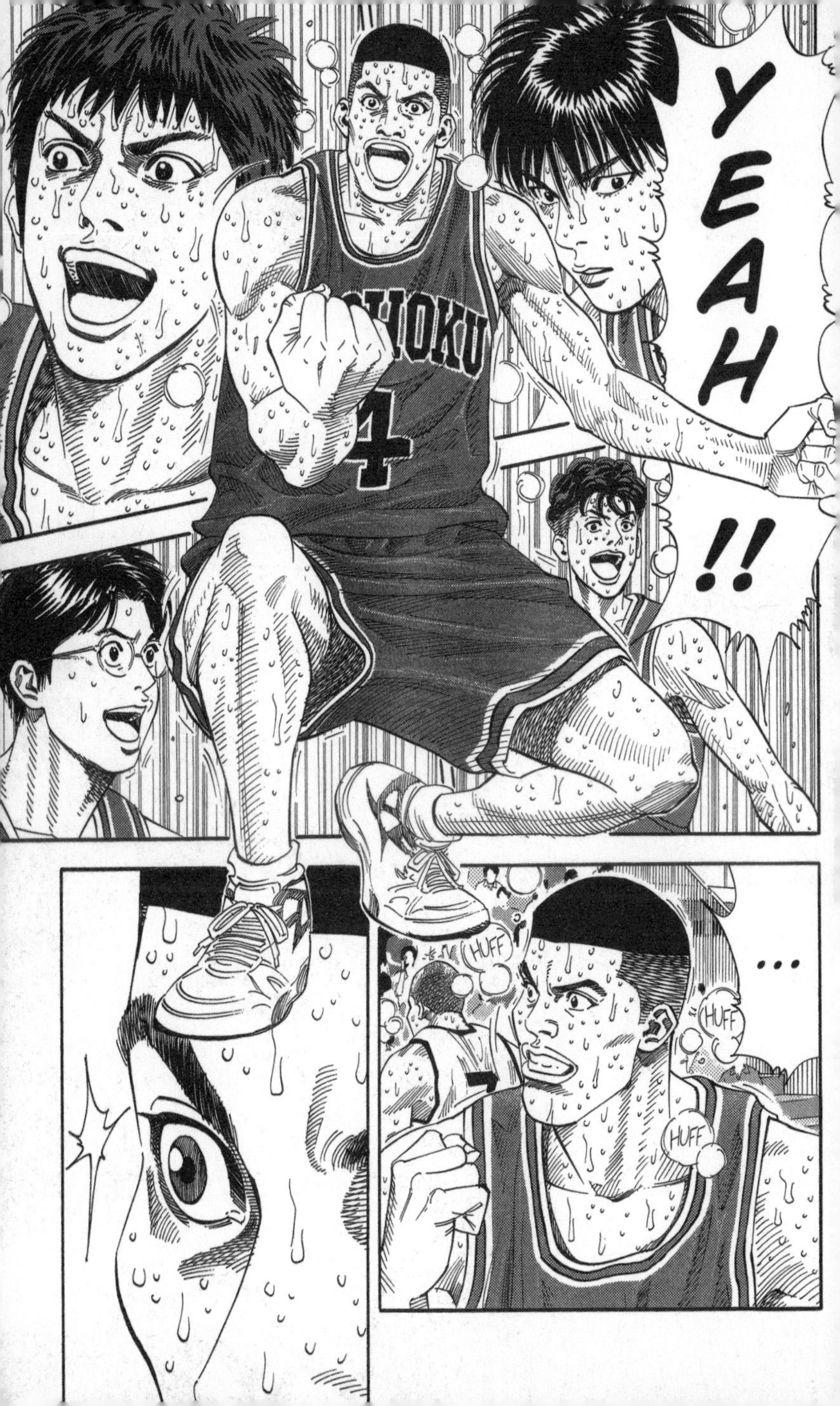
YEAH!!
SHOHOKU
4
...
HUFF
HUFF
HUFF

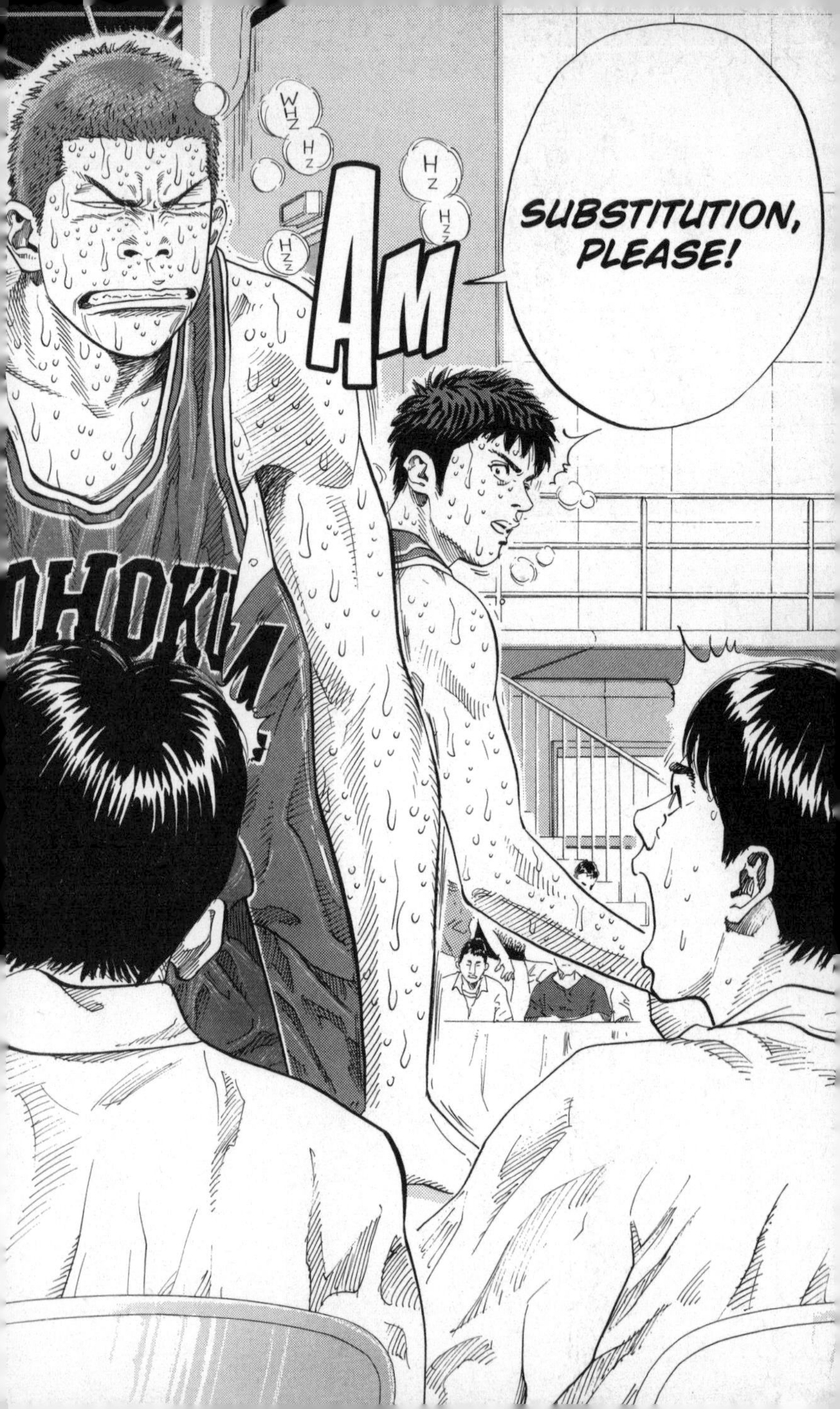
SUBSTITUTION, PLEASE!
AM
WHZ HZ
HZ HZZ
HZZ
SHOHOKU

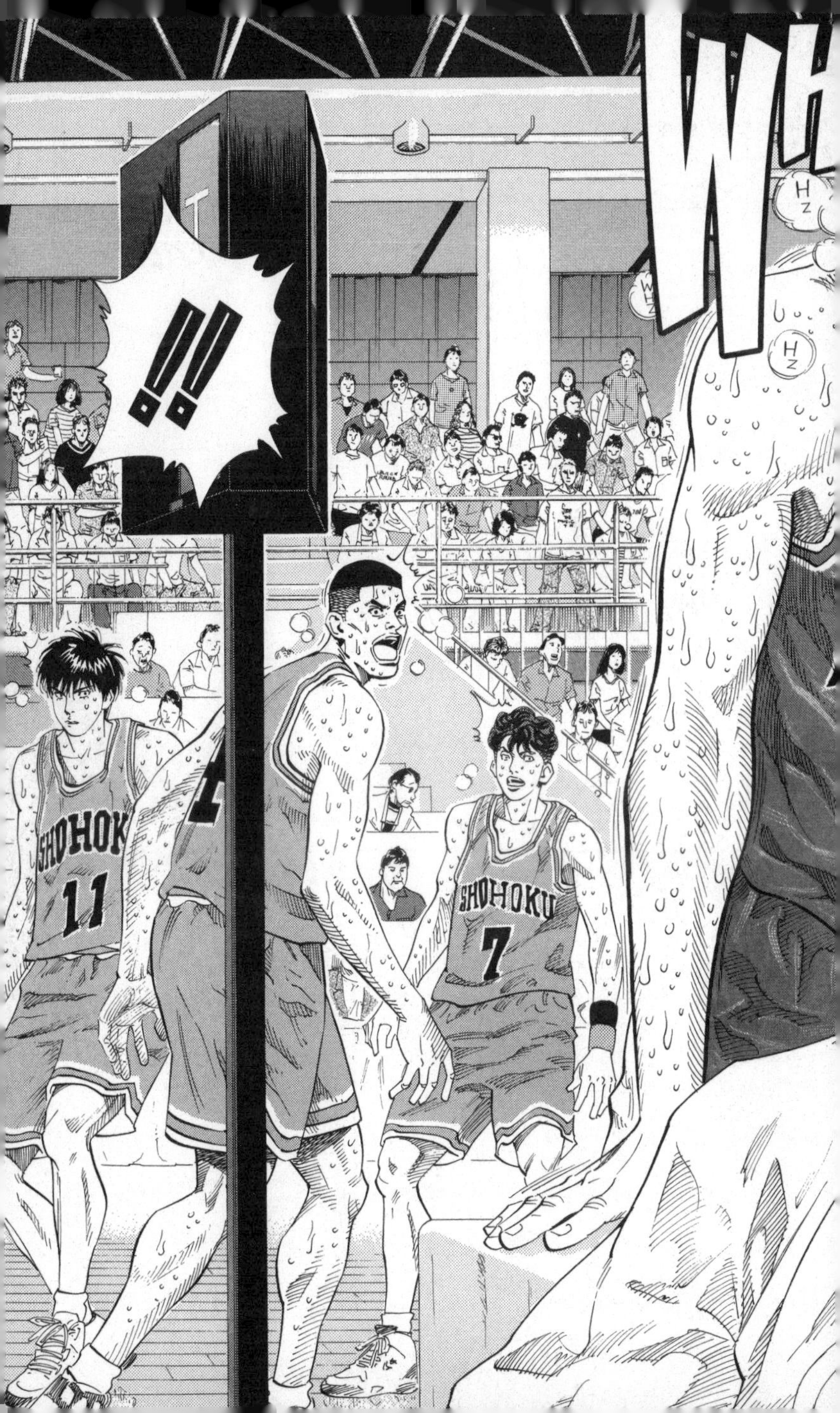
!!

HA-HANA-MICHI!!
HEY!!
SAKU-RAGI!!
WHAD-DAYA THINK YOU'RE DOING?!
SAKU-RAGI!!
SAKU-RAGI!
GLARE
...
!!
ZING
Hz
WHZ
Hzz
Hzz
WHZ
GORI...

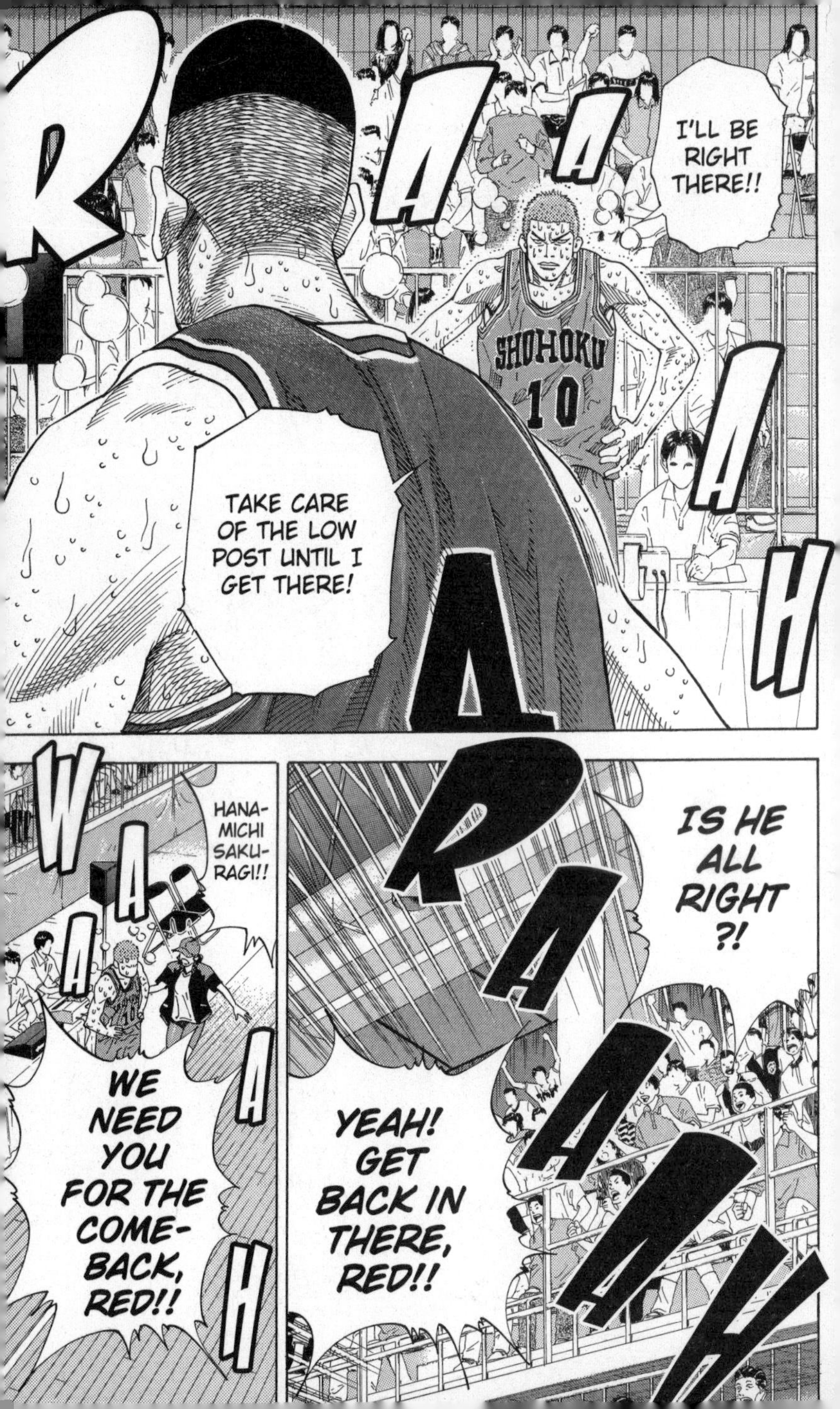
RAAAAH
TAKE CARE OF THE LOW POST UNTIL I GET THERE!
I'LL BE RIGHT THERE!!
IS HE ALL RIGHT?!
YEAH! GET BACK IN THERE, RED!!
RAAAAH
HANA-MICHI SAKU-RAGI!!
WE NEED YOU FOR THE COME-BACK, RED!!
WAAAAH

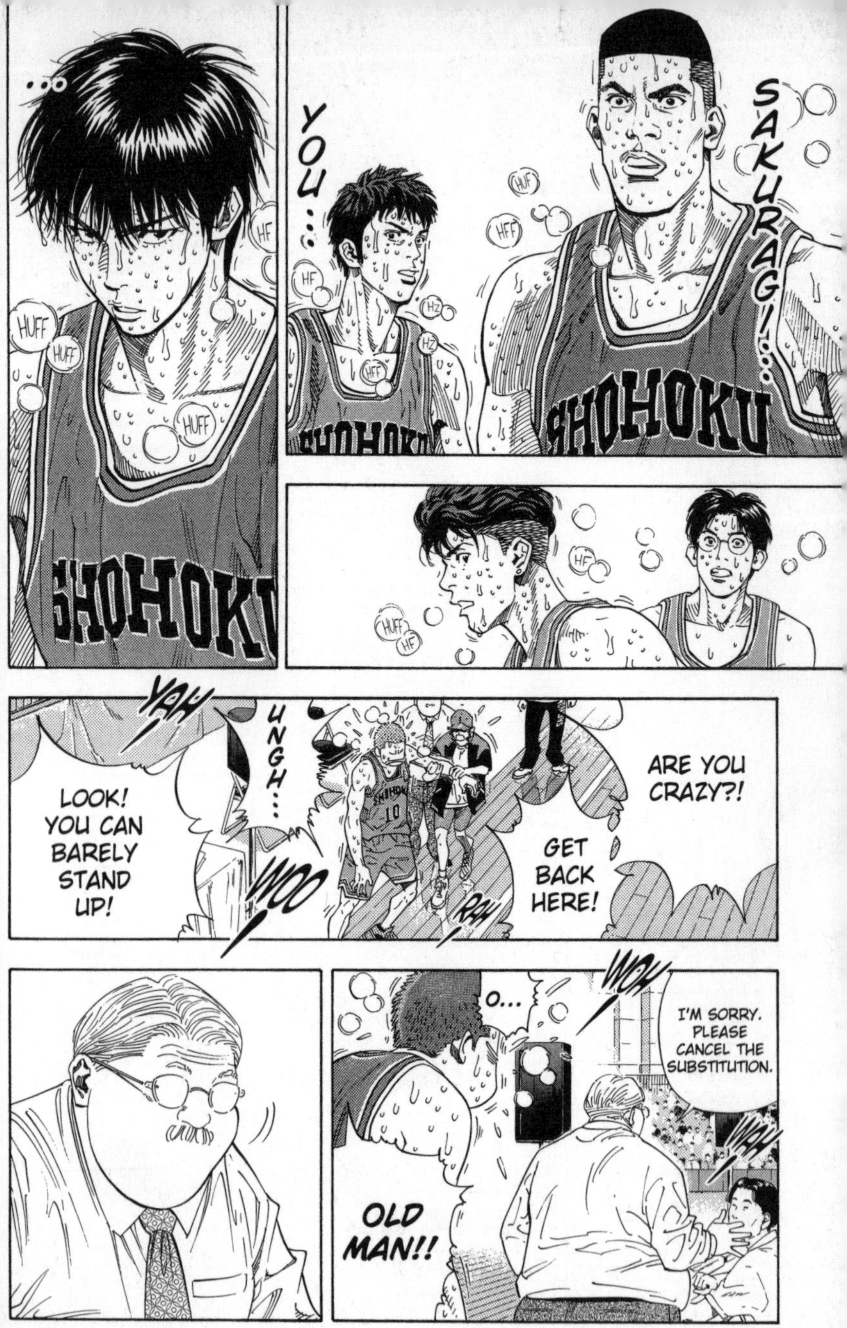
SAKURAGI...
HUFF
HFF
YOU...
HF
HZ
HZ
HFF
HF
HUFF
HF
...
HF
HUFF
HUFF
HUFF
ARE YOU CRAZY?!
GET BACK HERE!
UNGH...
YAH
WOO
RAH
LOOK! YOU CAN BARELY STAND UP!
WOW
I'M SORRY. PLEASE CANCEL THE SUBSTITUTION.
O...
WAH
OLD MAN!!

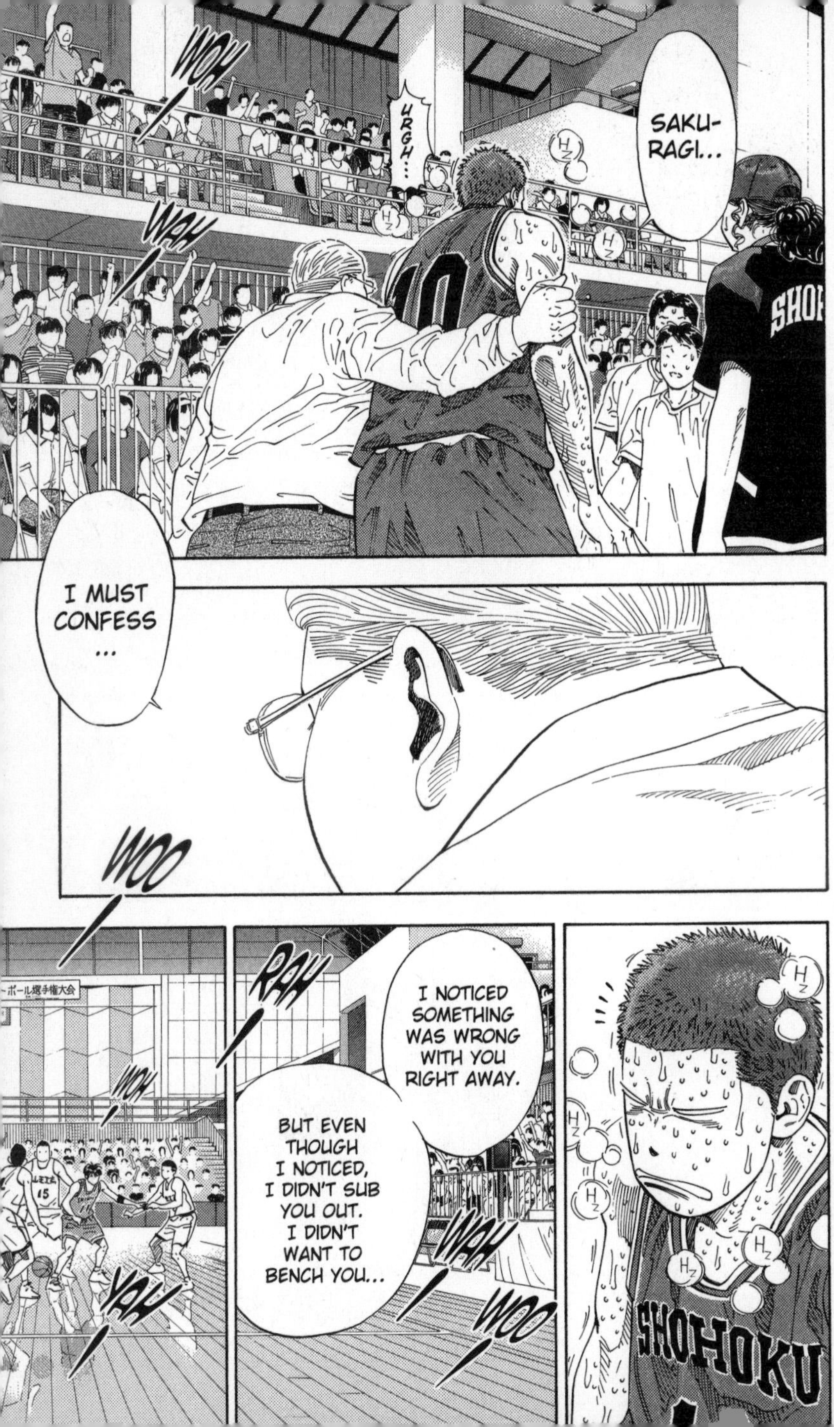
SAKU-RAGI...
URGH...
WOH
WAH
I MUST CONFESS...
WOO
I NOTICED SOMETHING WAS WRONG WITH YOU RIGHT AWAY.
BUT EVEN THOUGH I NOTICED, I DIDN'T SUB YOU OUT. I DIDN'T WANT TO BENCH YOU...
RAH
WAH
WOO
ーボール選手権大会
WOH
YAH
SHOHOKU

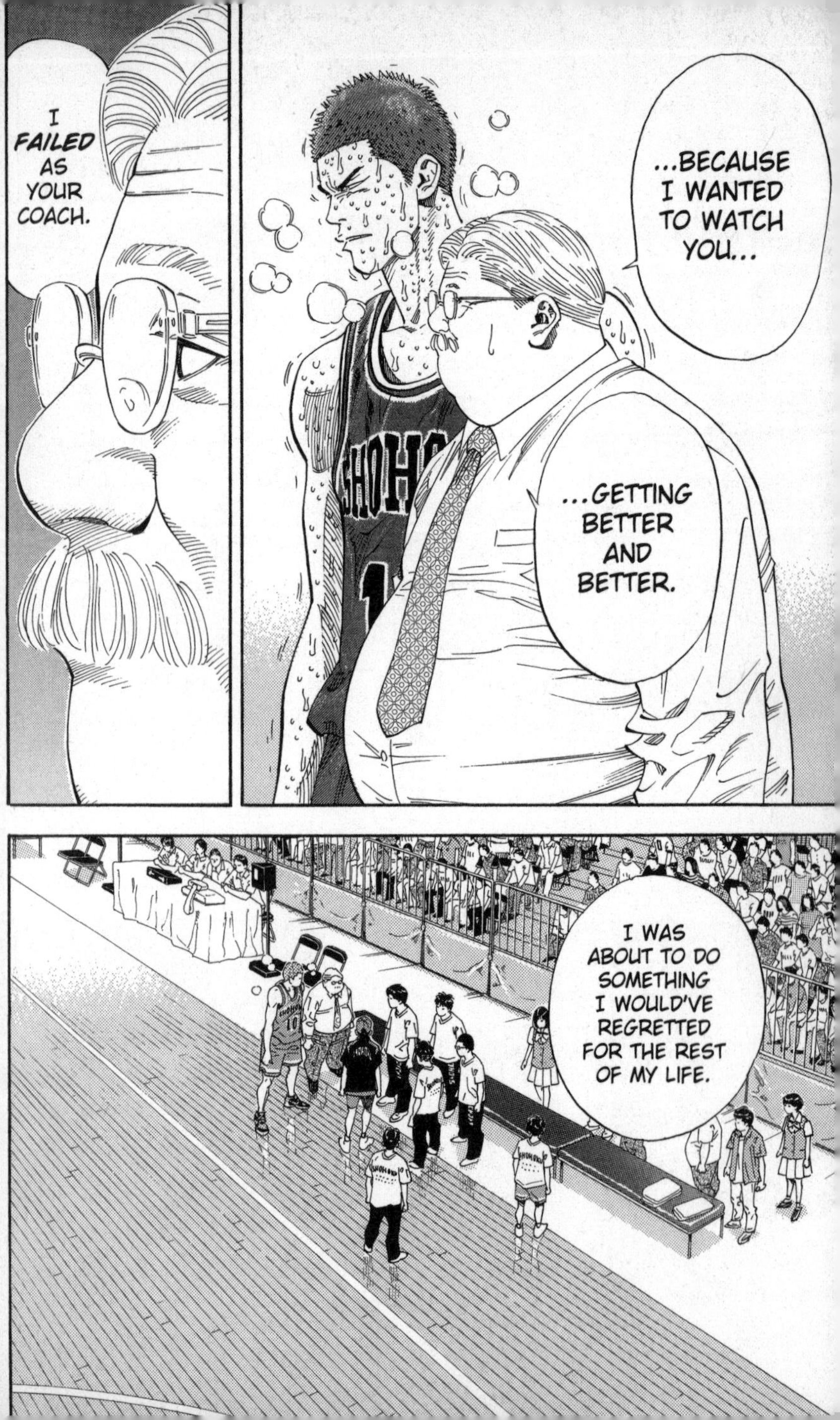
...BECAUSE I WANTED TO WATCH YOU...
...GETTING BETTER AND BETTER.
I *FAILED* AS YOUR COACH.
I WAS ABOUT TO DO SOMETHING I WOULD'VE REGRETTED FOR THE REST OF MY LIFE.

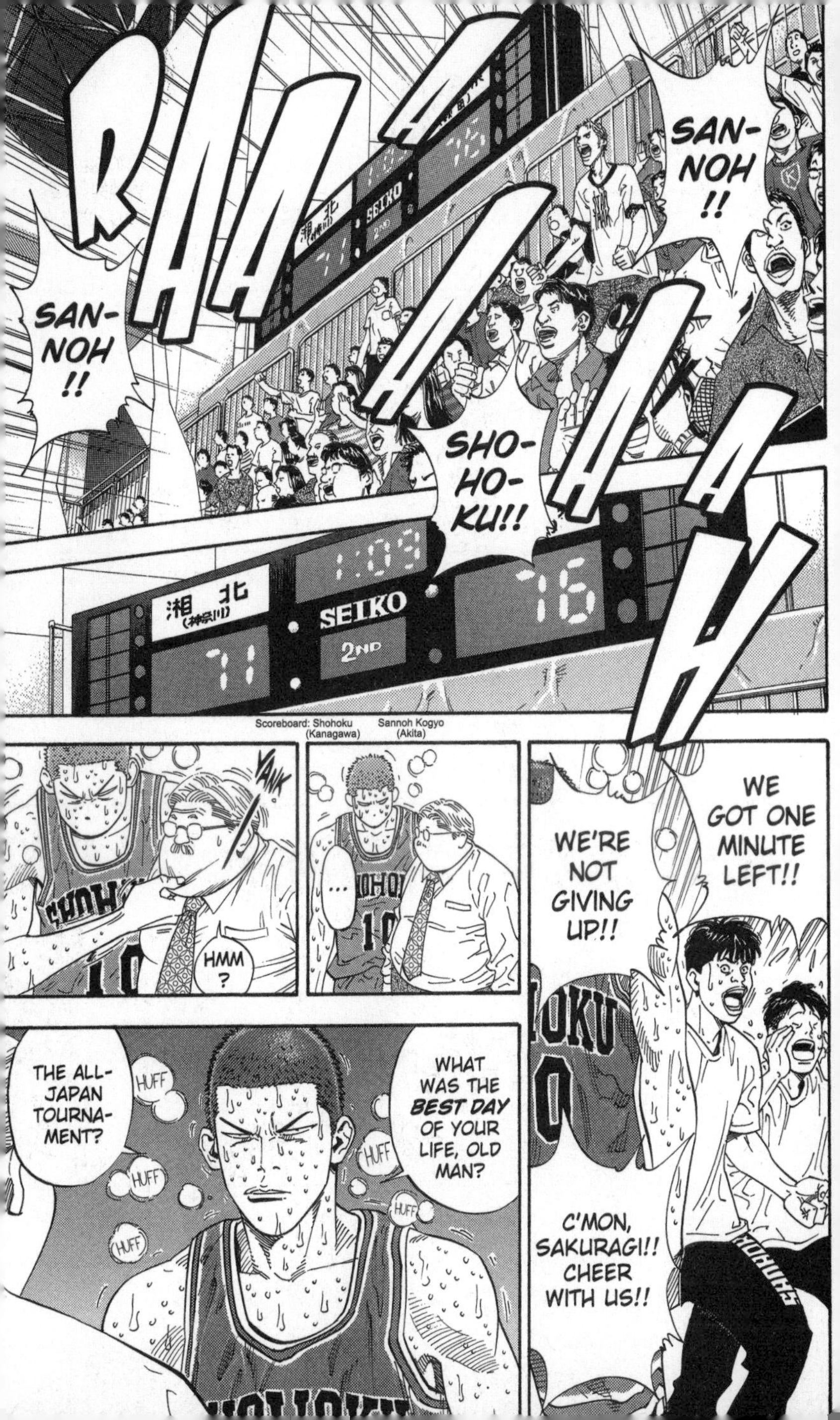

RAAAAAAAH
SAN-NOH!!
SHO-HO-KU!!
SAN-NOH!!
湘北 (神奈川)
1:09
SEIKO
2ND
71
76
Scoreboard: Shohoku (Kanagawa) Sannoh Kogyo (Akita)
WE GOT ONE MINUTE LEFT!!
WE'RE NOT GIVING UP!!
C'MON, SAKURAGI!! CHEER WITH US!!
...
YANK
HMM?
WHAT WAS THE *BEST DAY* OF YOUR LIFE, OLD MAN?
HUFF
HUFF
THE ALL-JAPAN TOURNAMENT?
HUFF
HUFF
HUFF

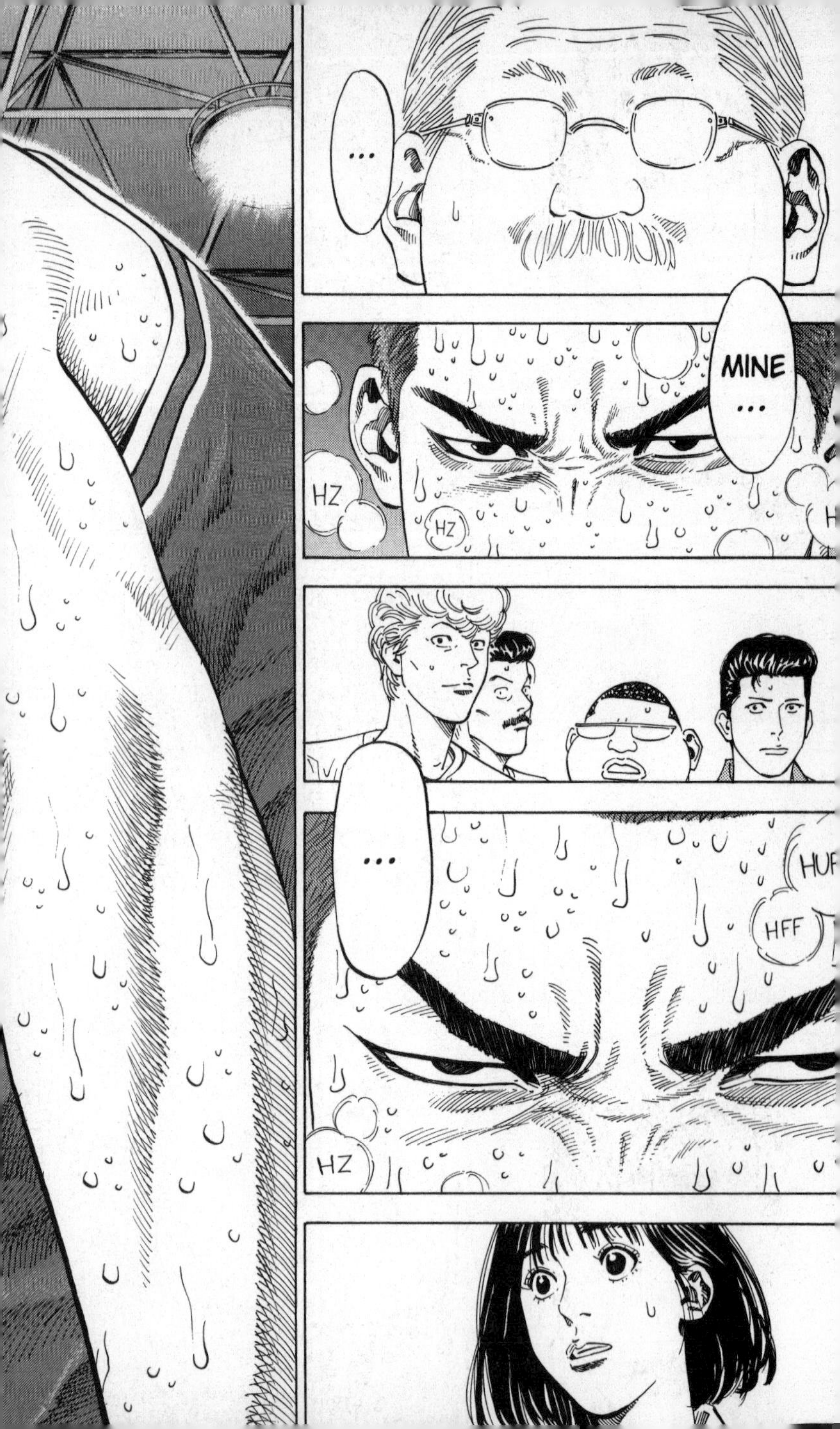
...
MINE
...
HZ
HZ
...
HUF
HFF
HZ

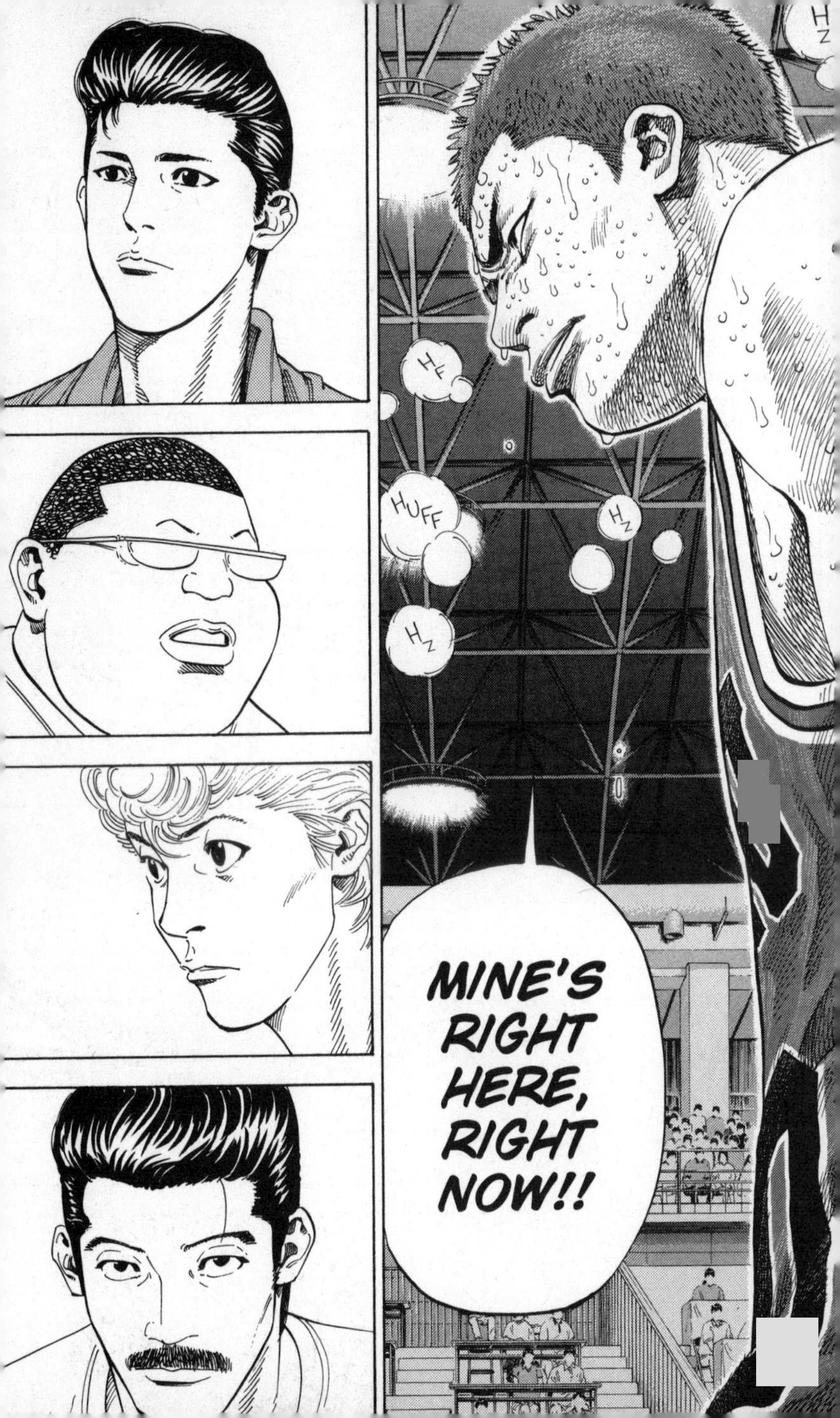
HZ
HUFF
HZ
HZ
MINE'S RIGHT HERE, RIGHT NOW!!

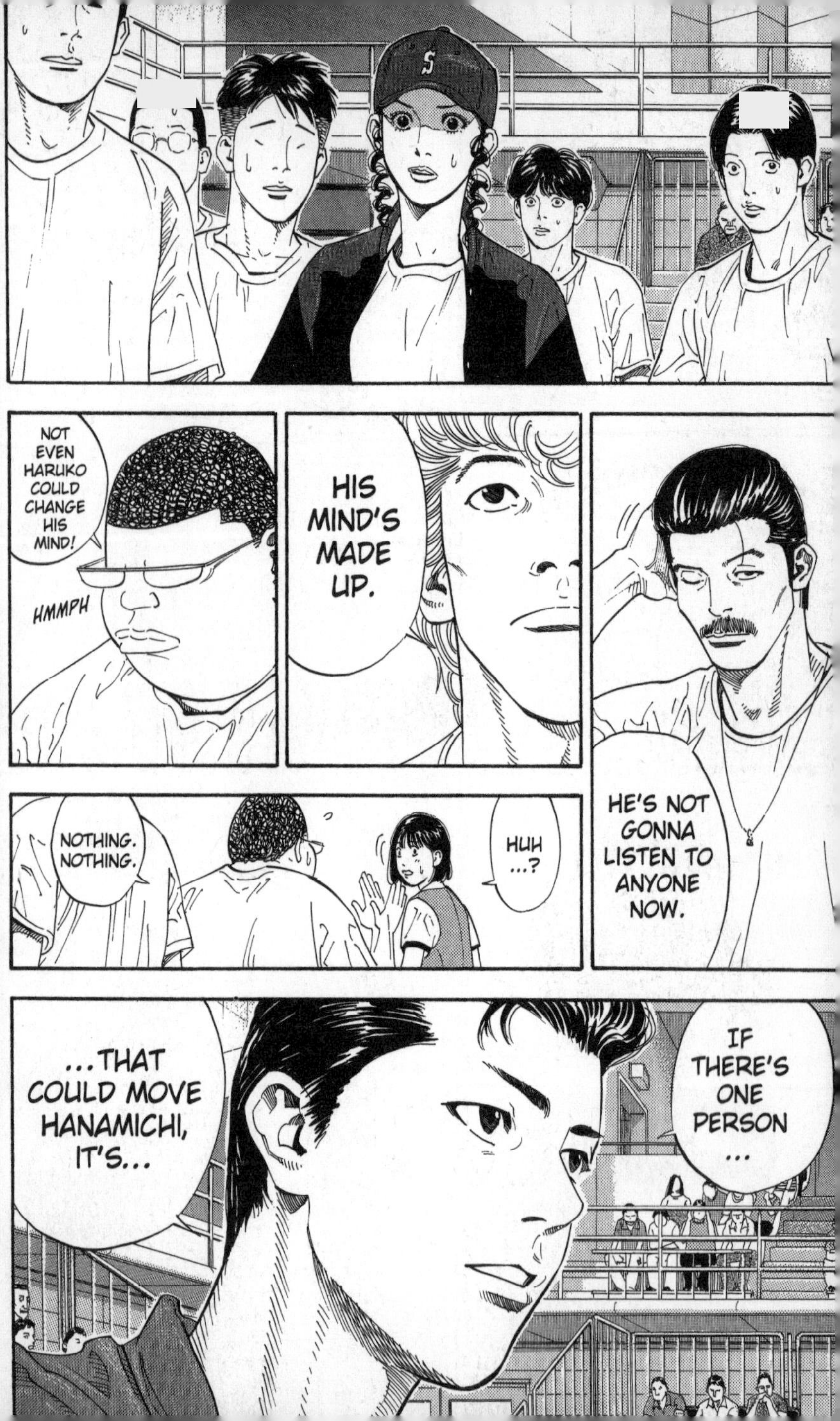
HE'S NOT GONNA LISTEN TO ANYONE NOW.
HIS MIND'S MADE UP.
NOT EVEN HARUKO COULD CHANGE HIS MIND!
HMMPH
HUH ...?
NOTHING. NOTHING.
IF THERE'S ONE PERSON ...
...THAT COULD MOVE HANAMICHI, IT'S...

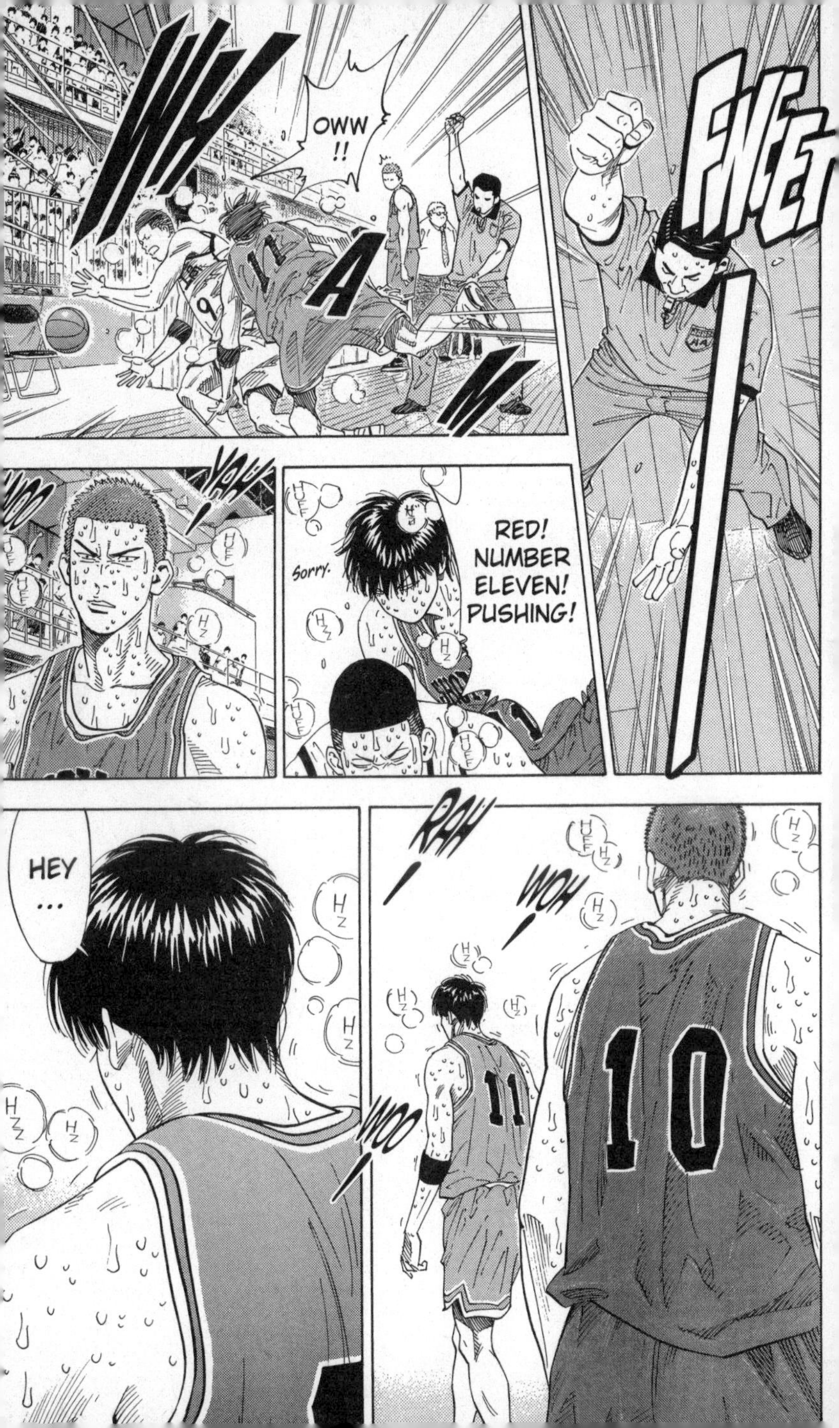
FWEET
WHAM
OWW !!
RED! NUMBER ELEVEN! PUSHING!
Sorry.
HUFF
RAH
WOH
WOO
HEY ...

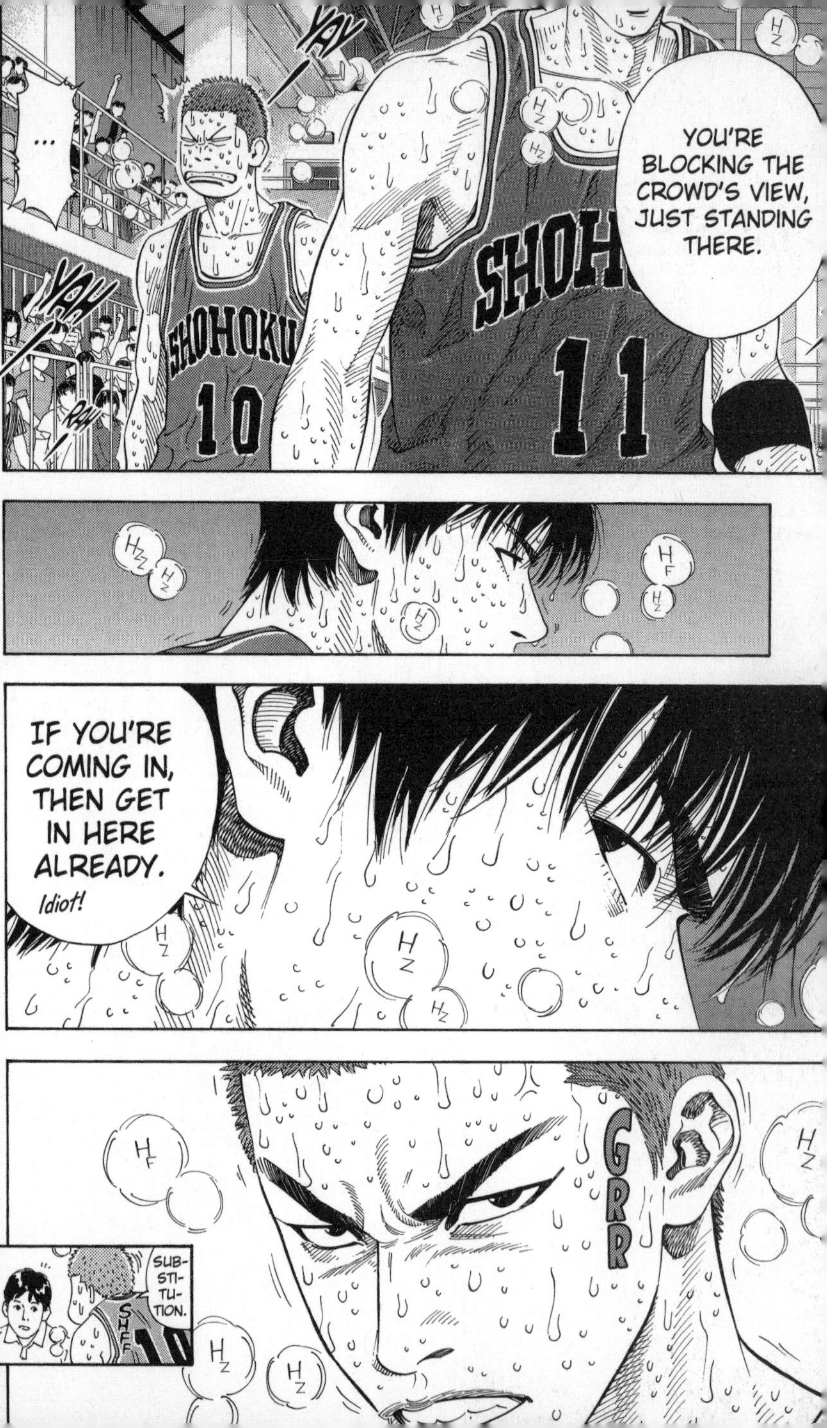
YOU'RE BLOCKING THE CROWD'S VIEW, JUST STANDING THERE.
YAY
...
YAH
RAH
IF YOU'RE COMING IN, THEN GET IN HERE ALREADY.
Idiot!
GRR
SUB-STI-TU-TION.
SHFF

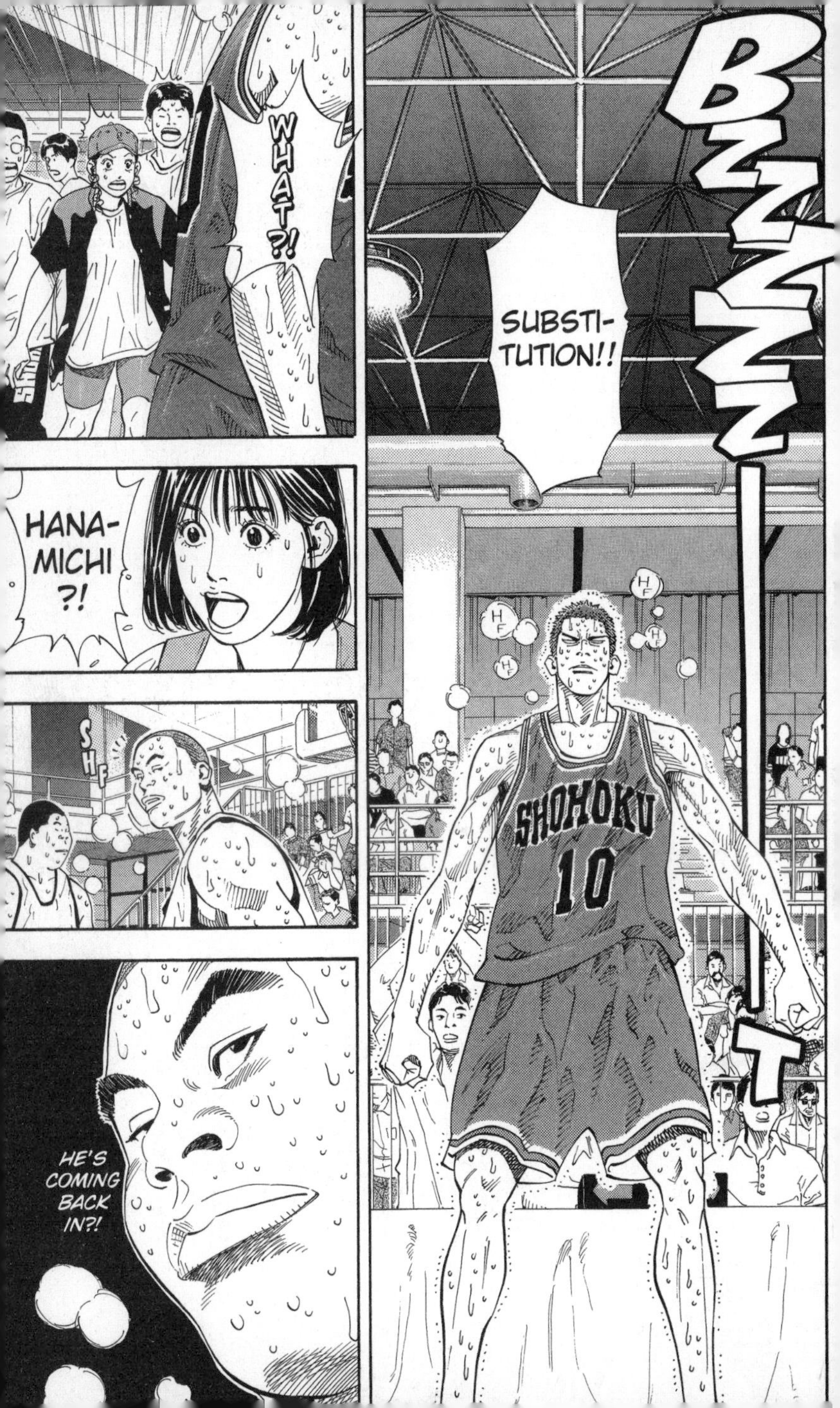
BZZZZT
SUBSTI-TUTION!!
WHAT?!
HANA-MICHI?!
HE'S COMING BACK IN?!

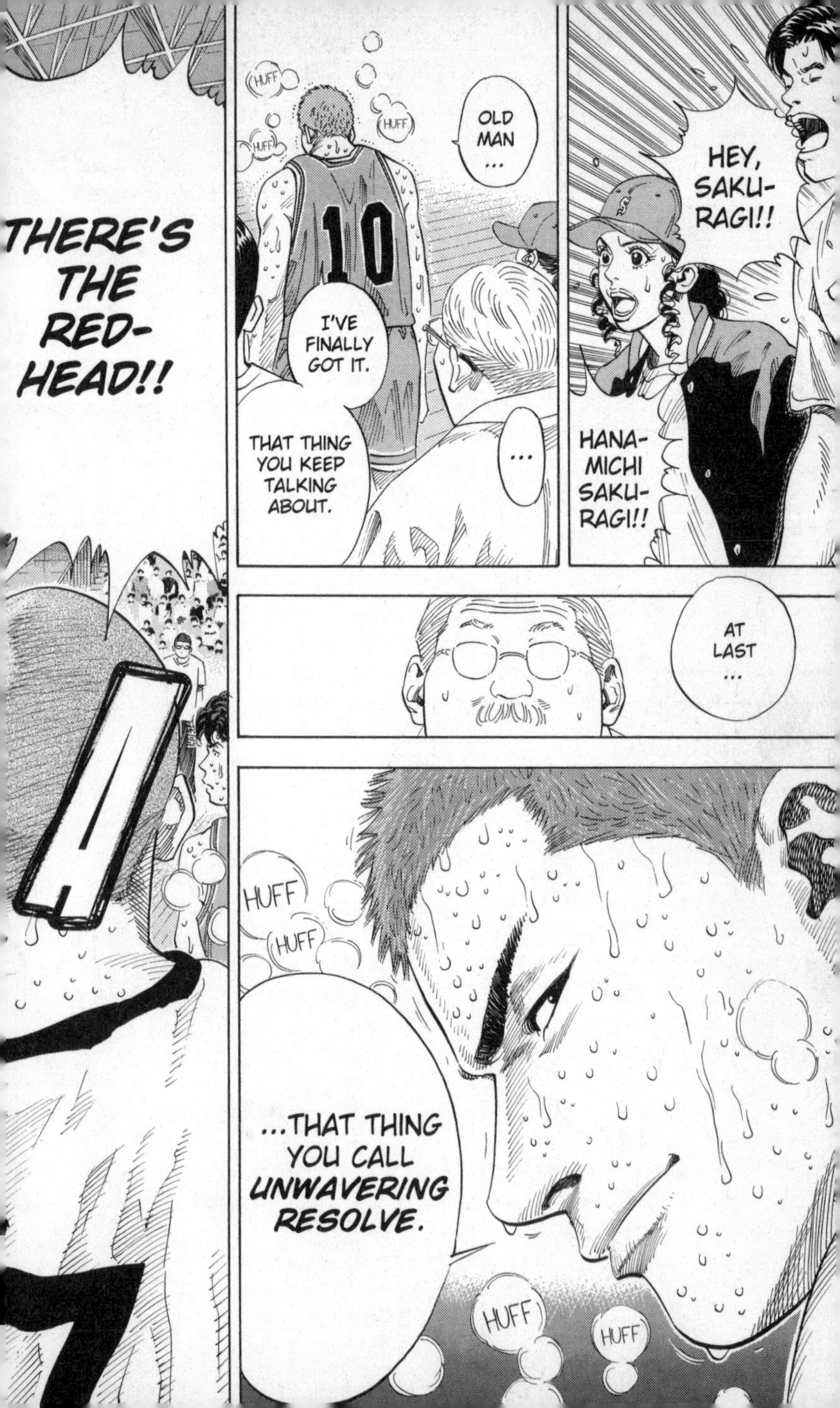
HEY, SAKURAGI!!
HANAMICHI SAKURAGI!!
HUFF
HUFF
HUFF
OLD MAN ...
I'VE FINALLY GOT IT.
THAT THING YOU KEEP TALKING ABOUT.
...
AT LAST ...
HUFF
HUFF
...THAT THING YOU CALL ***UNWAVERING RESOLVE.***
HUFF
HUFF
THERE'S THE RED-HEAD!!

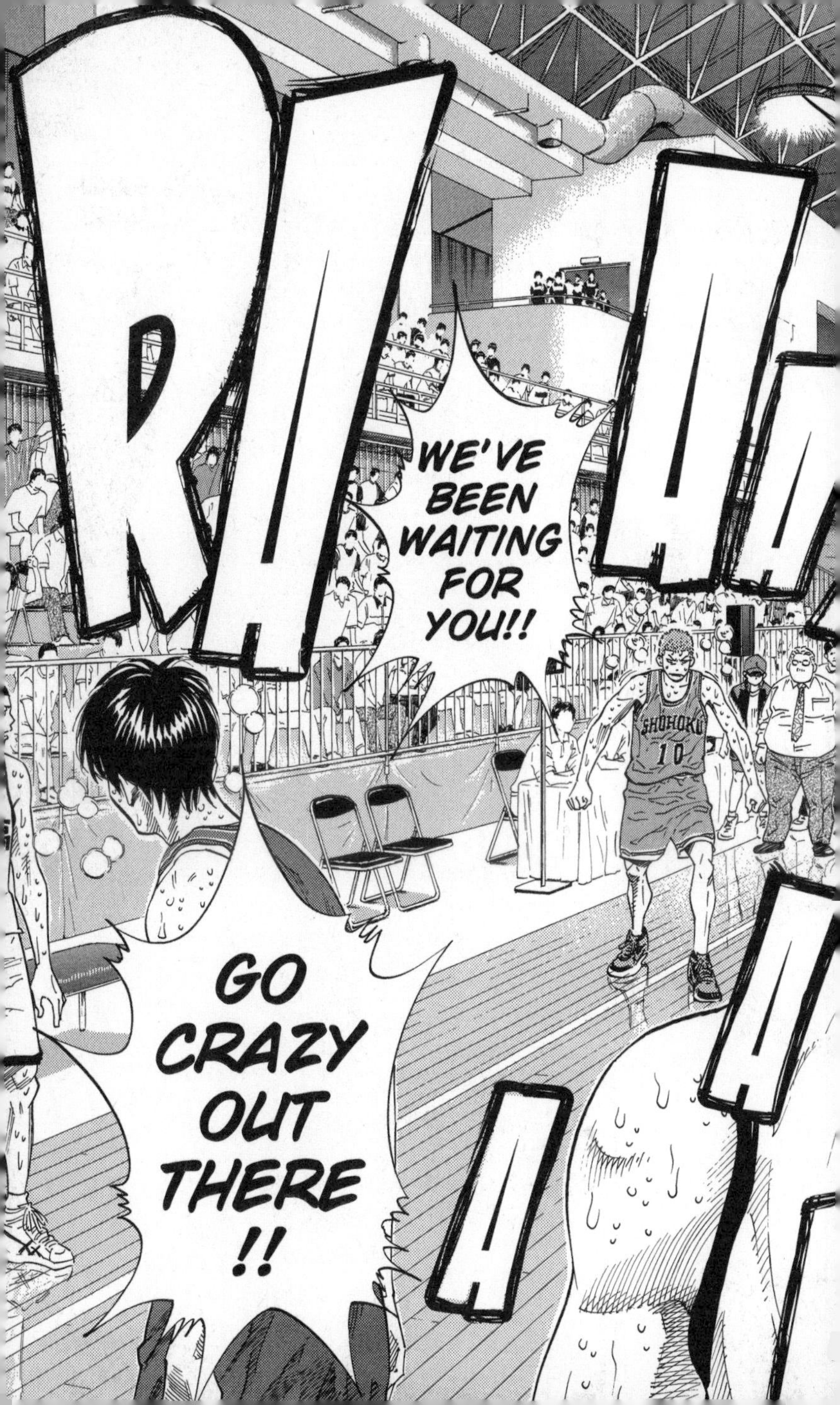
WE'VE BEEN WAITING FOR YOU!!
GO CRAZY OUT THERE!!

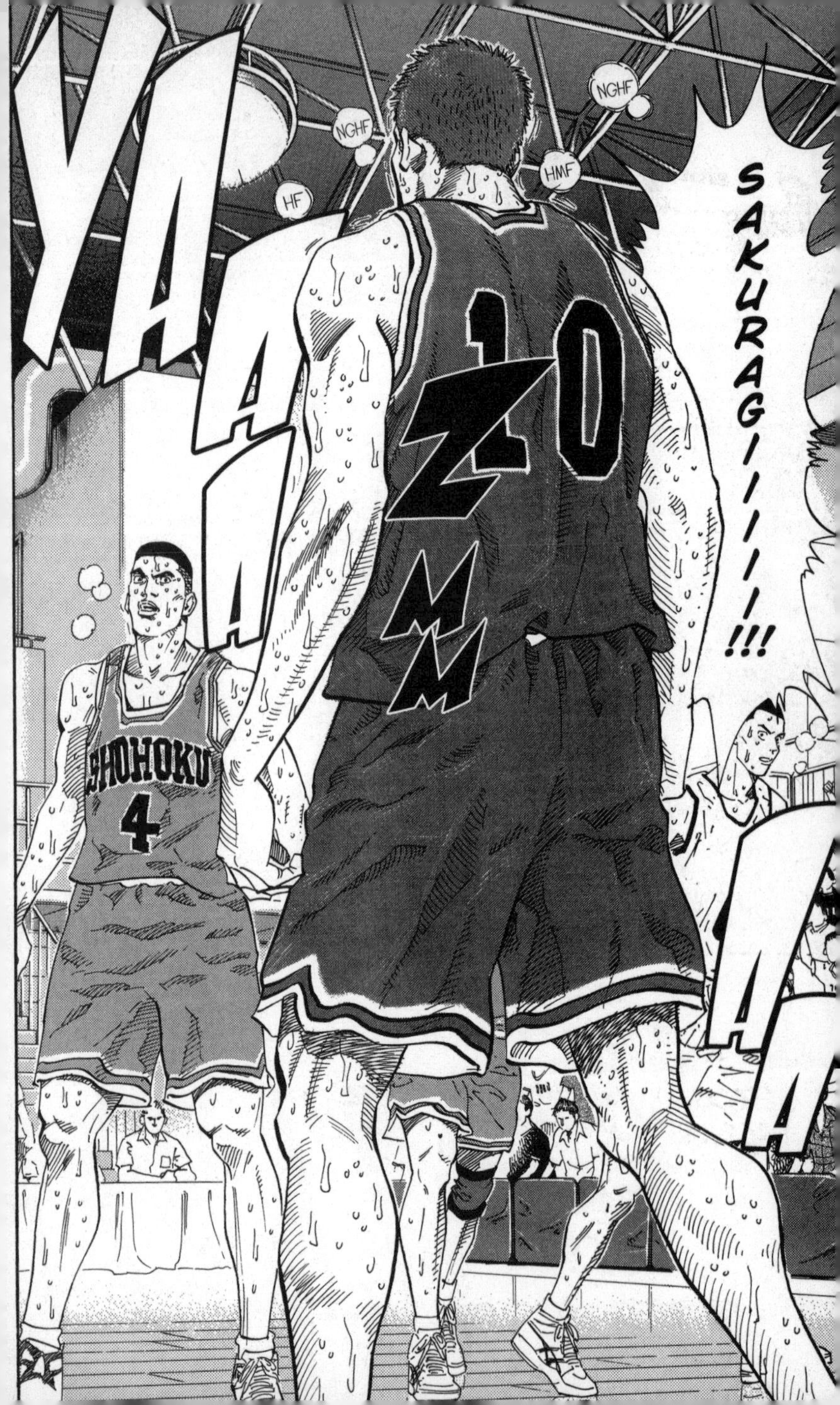
SAKURAGI!!!!!!!!
NGHF
HMF
NGHF
HF
ZMMM
SHOHOKU
4

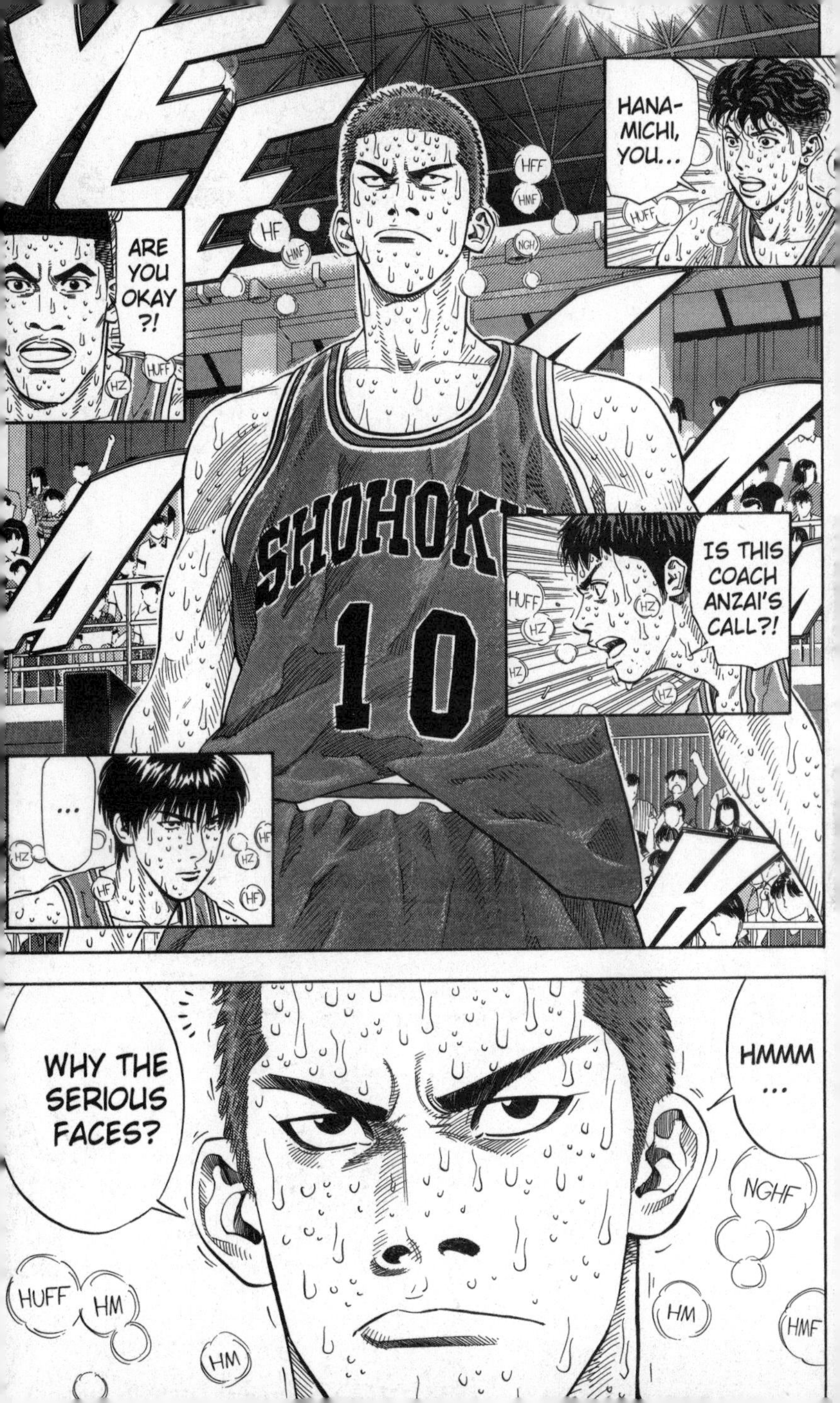
HANA-MICHI, YOU...
HUFF
ARE YOU OKAY?!
HUFF
HZ
HFF
HMF
HF
HMF
NGH
IS THIS COACH ANZAI'S CALL?!
HUFF
HZ
HZ
HZ
HZ
...
HZ
HZ
HF
HF
HF
HMMM ...
NGHF
HM
HMF
WHY THE SERIOUS FACES?
HUFF
HM
HM

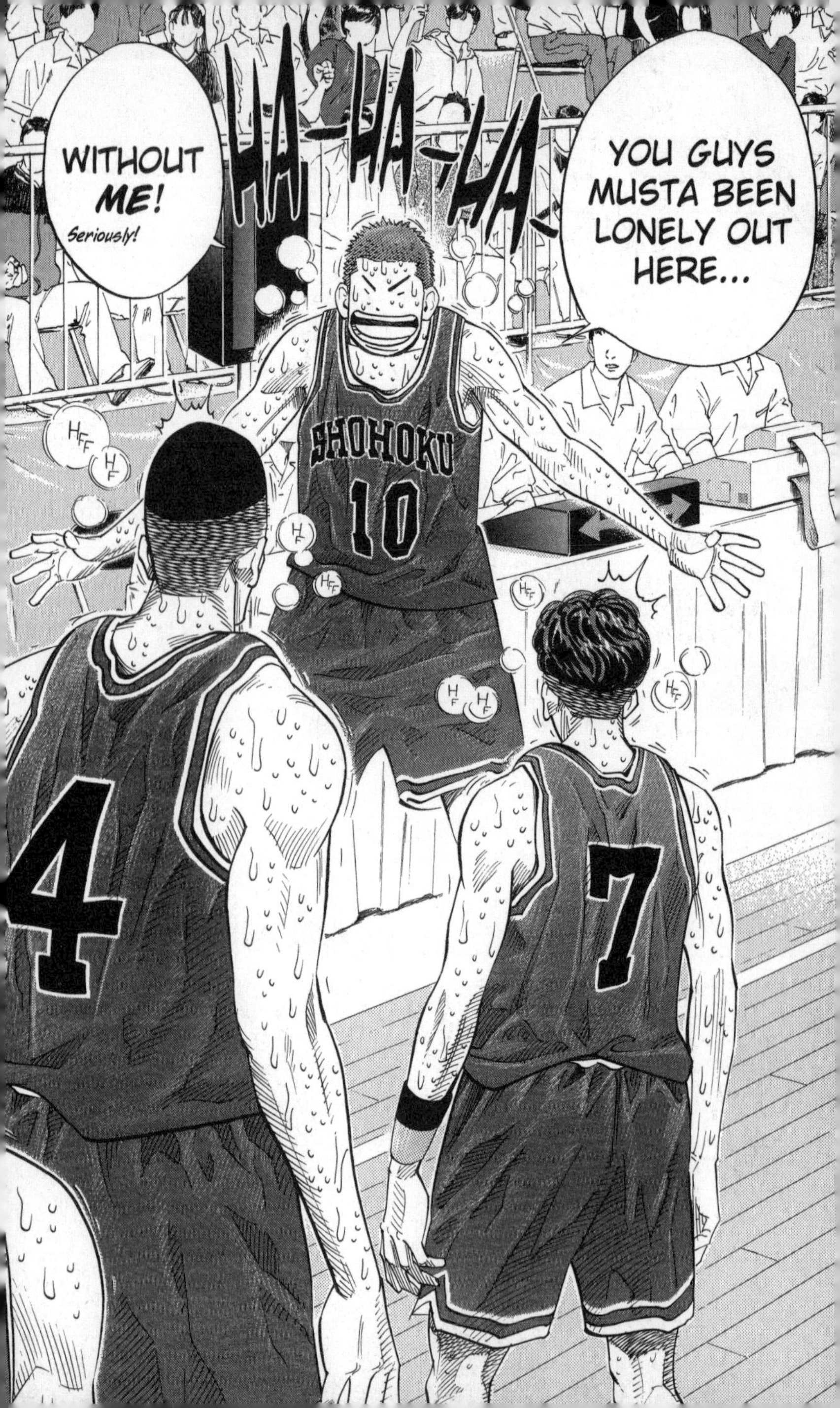
YOU GUYS MUSTA BEEN LONELY OUT HERE...
HA-HA-HA
WITHOUT ME!
Seriously!
HFF
HF
HF
HFF
HFF
HFF
HF
HF
HFF

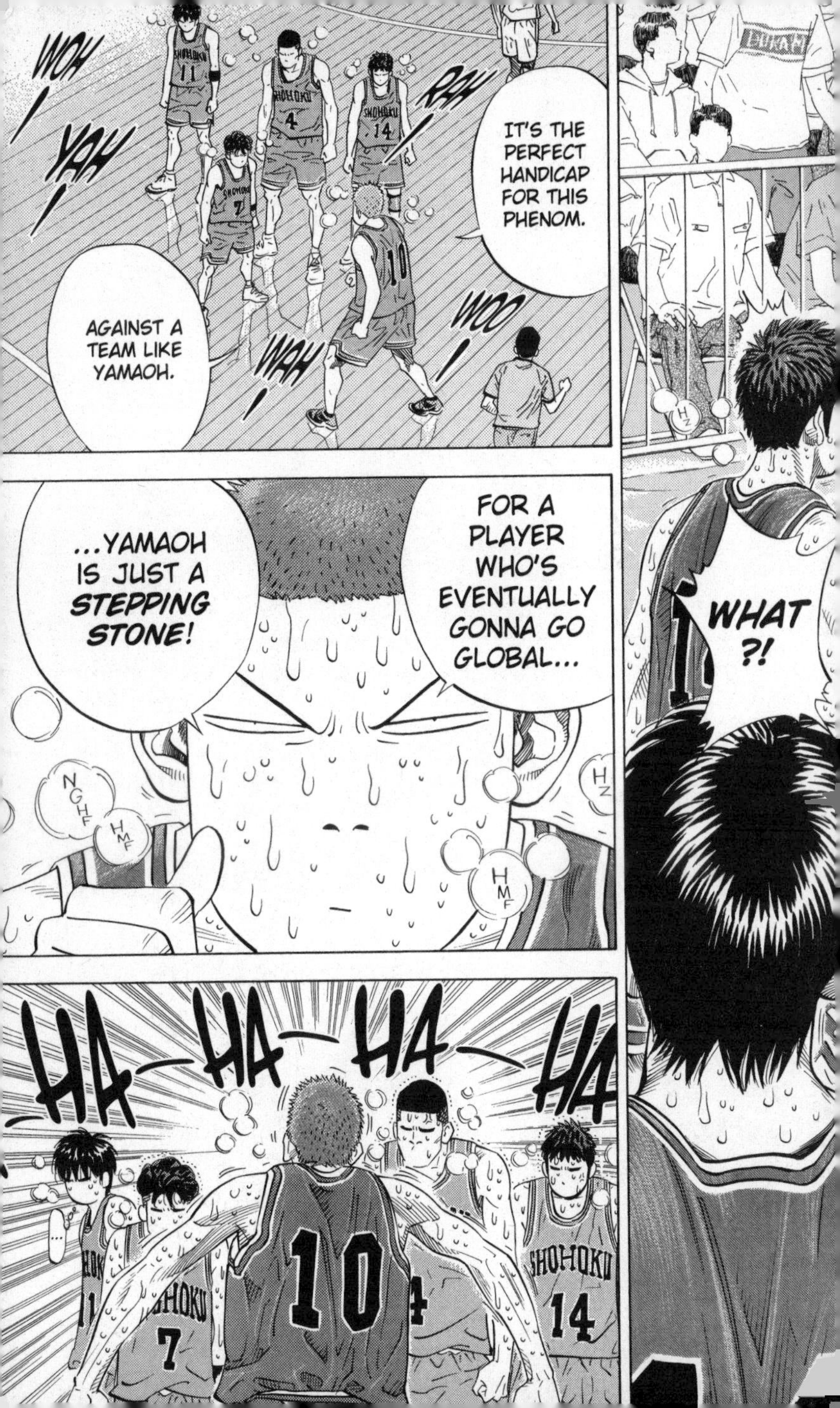
RAH
WOH-YAH
IT'S THE PERFECT HANDICAP FOR THIS PHENOM.
AGAINST A TEAM LIKE YAMAOH.
WOO-WAH
HZ
FOR A PLAYER WHO'S EVENTUALLY GONNA GO GLOBAL...
...YAMAOH IS JUST A ***STEPPING STONE!***
HZ
NGHF
HMF
HMF
WHAT ?!
HA-HA-HA-HA
...

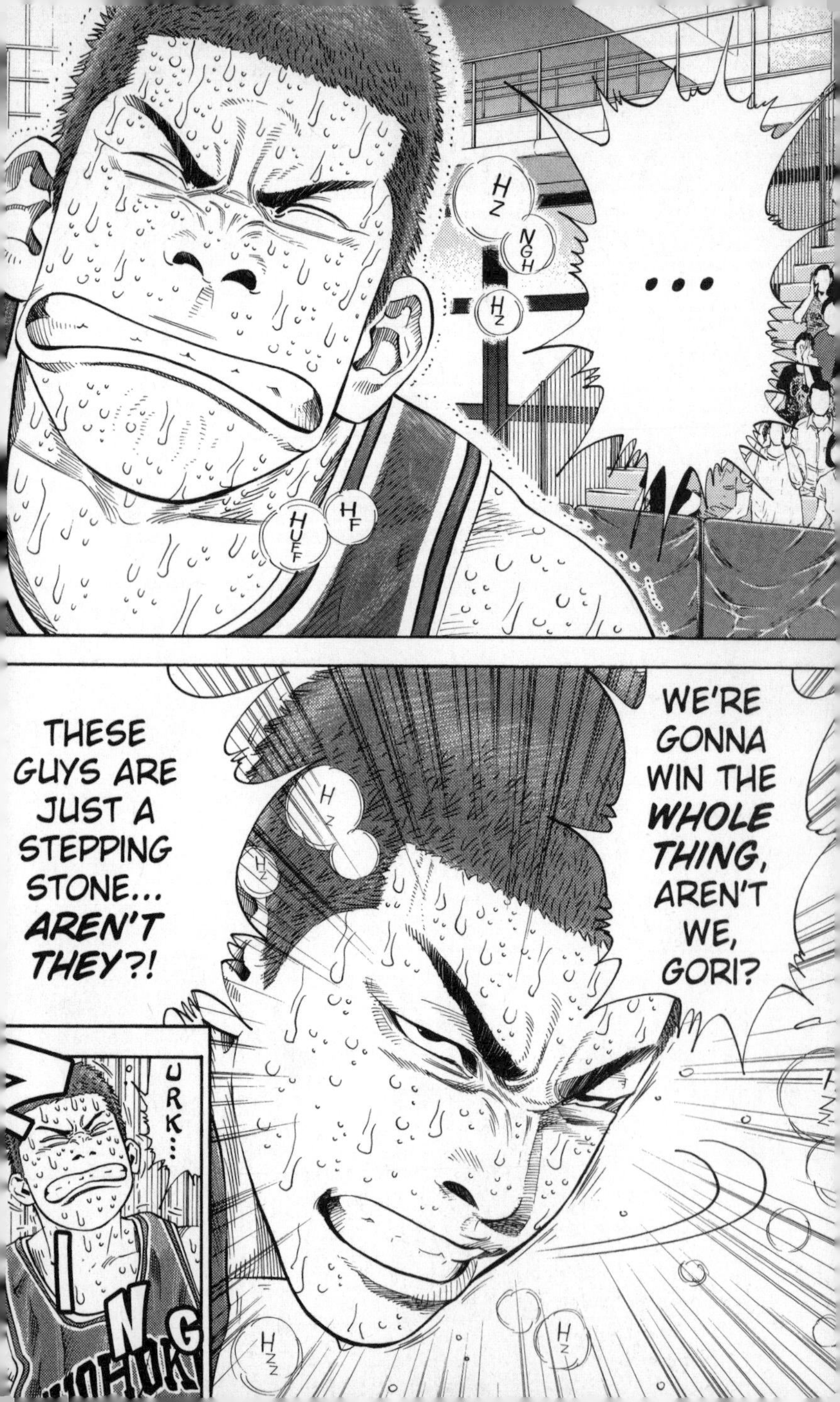
HZ
NGH
HZ
...
HF
HUFF
WE'RE GONNA WIN THE ***WHOLE THING***, AREN'T WE, GORI?
THESE GUYS ARE JUST A STEPPING STONE... ***AREN'T THEY?!***
HZ
HZ
URK...
HZZ
HZ

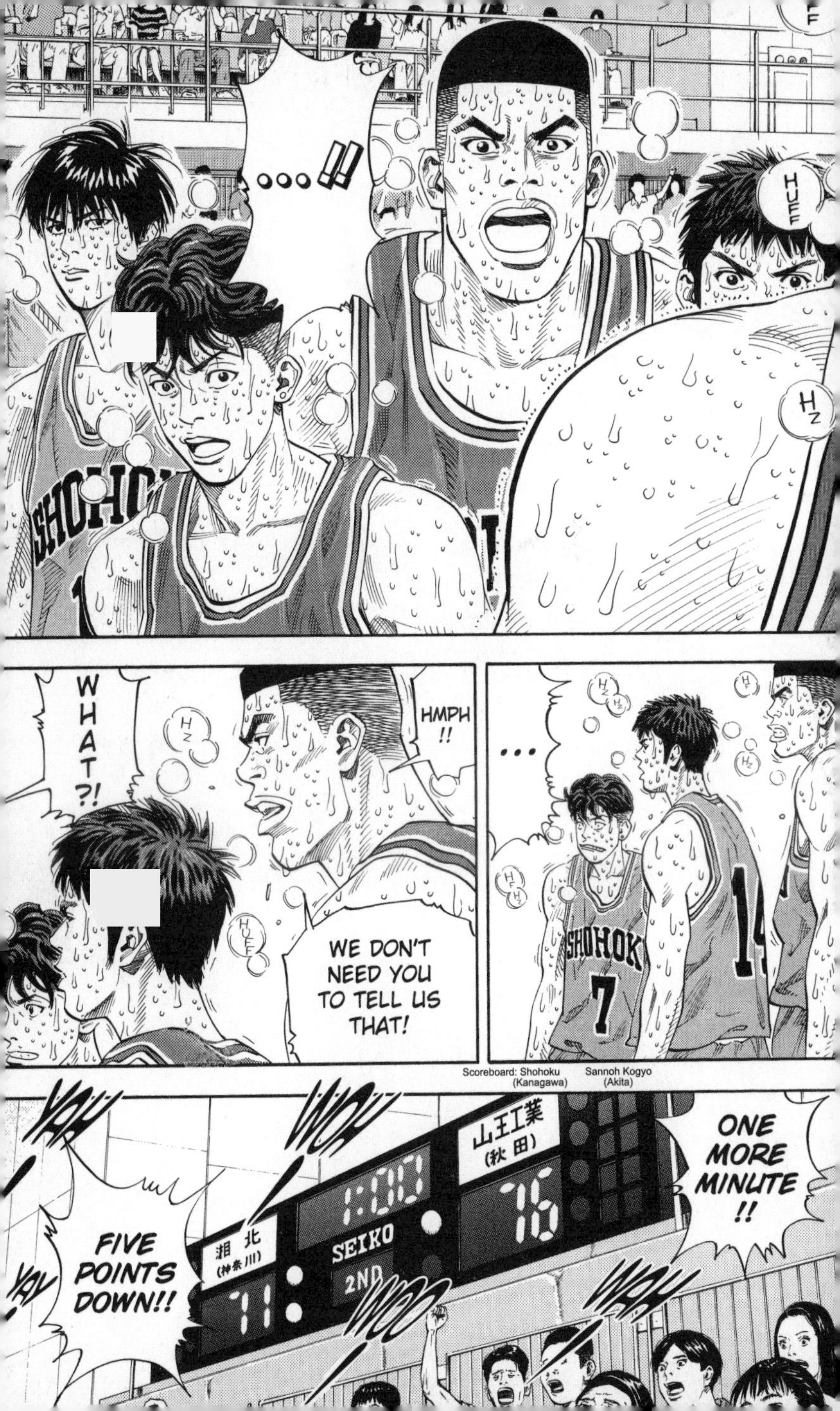
...!!
HUFF
Hz
...
WHAT?!
HMPH!!
HUFF
WE DON'T NEED YOU TO TELL US THAT!
Scoreboard: Shohoku (Kanagawa) Sannoh Kogyo (Akita)
ONE MORE MINUTE!!
WOH
山王工業 (秋田)
76
1:00
SEIKO
2ND
湘北 (神奈川)
71
FIVE POINTS DOWN!!
WOH
WOH
YAY

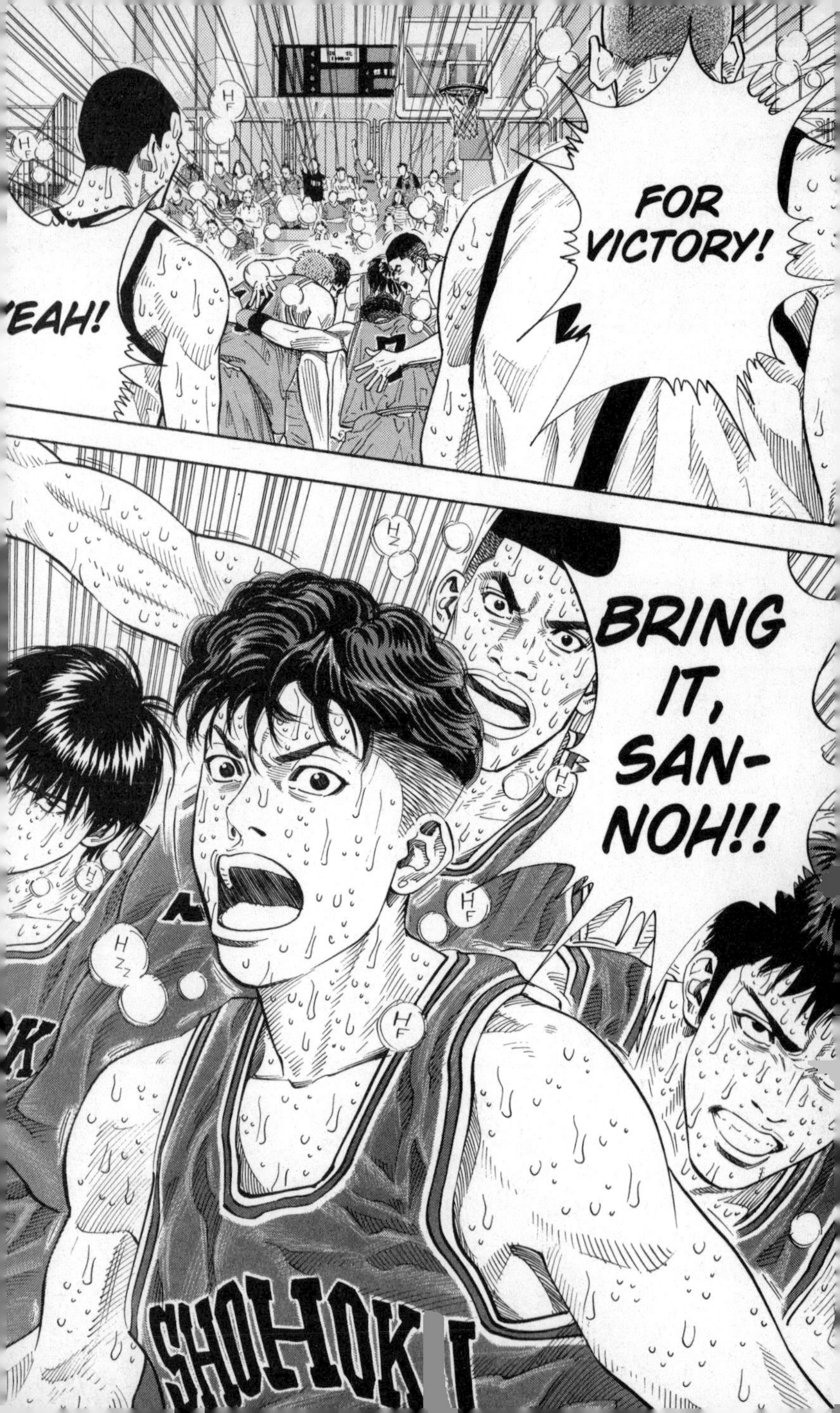
FOR VICTORY!
YEAH!
BRING IT, SAN-NOH!!
SHOHOKU

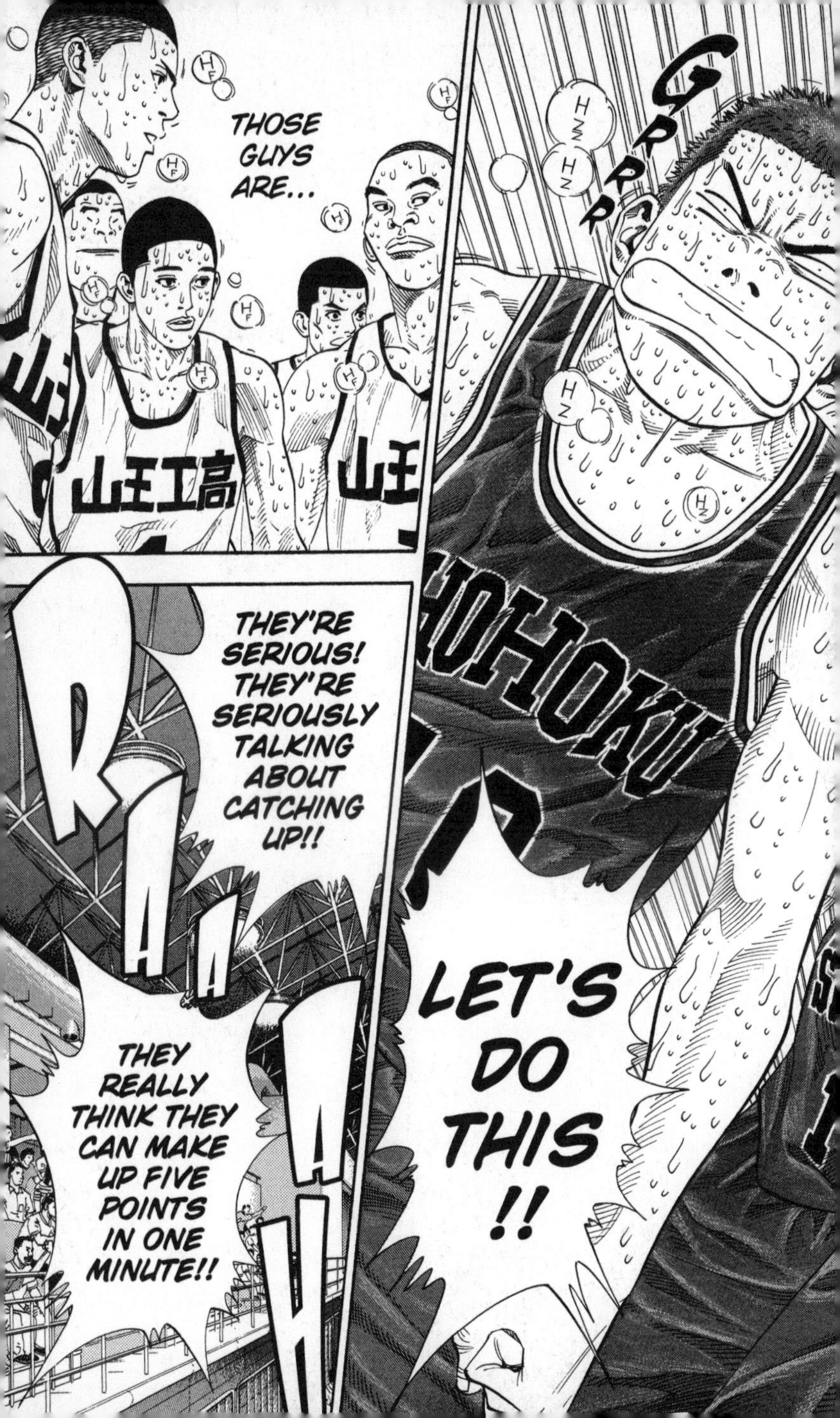
GRRRR
LET'S DO THIS!!
THOSE GUYS ARE...
山王工高
THEY'RE SERIOUS! THEY'RE SERIOUSLY TALKING ABOUT CATCHING UP!!
RAAAH
THEY REALLY THINK THEY CAN MAKE UP FIVE POINTS IN ONE MINUTE!!

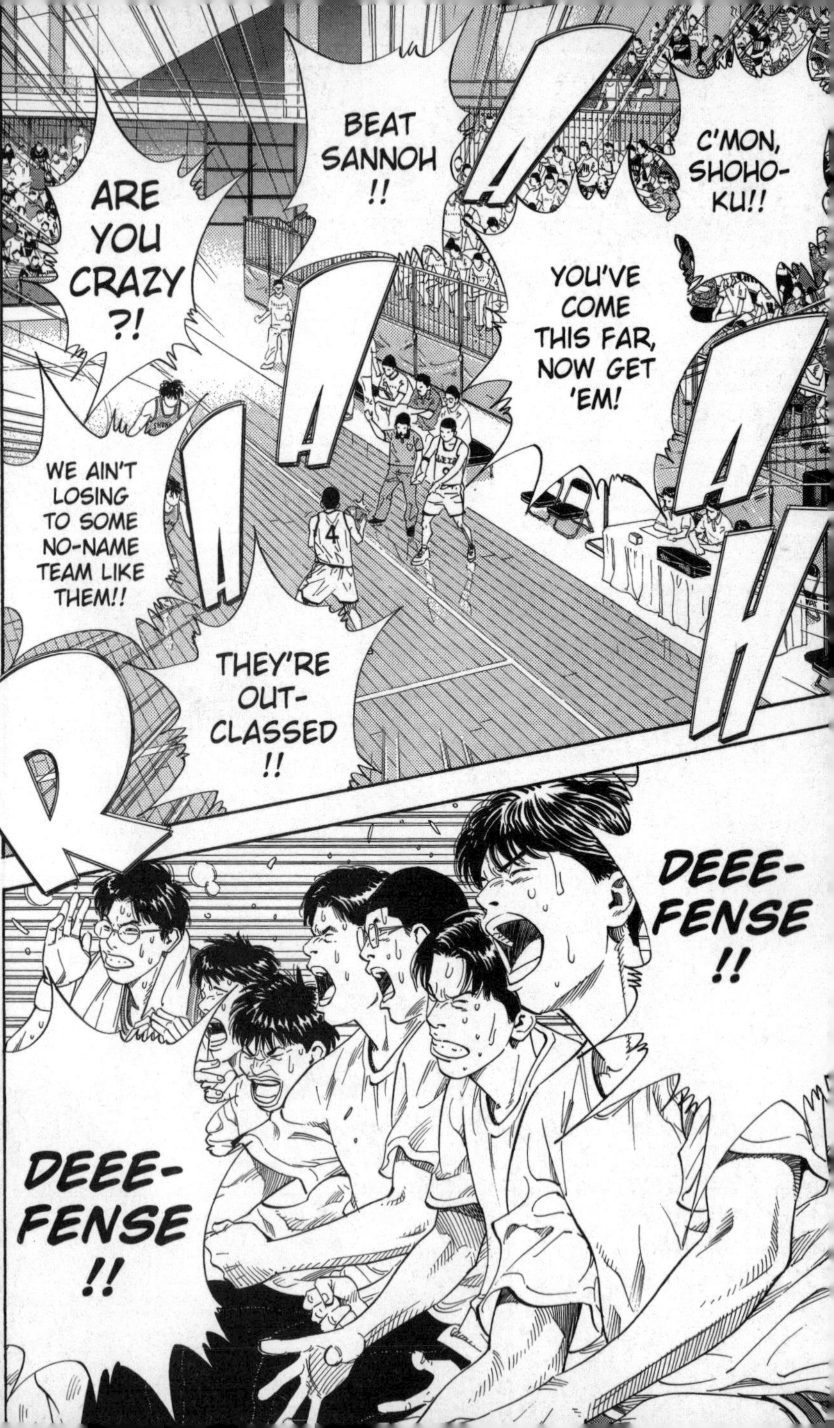
C'MON, SHOHO-KU!!
BEAT SANNOH !!
ARE YOU CRAZY ?!
YOU'VE COME THIS FAR, NOW GET 'EM!
WE AIN'T LOSING TO SOME NO-NAME TEAM LIKE THEM!!
THEY'RE OUT-CLASSED !!
DEEE-FENSE !!
DEEE-FENSE !!

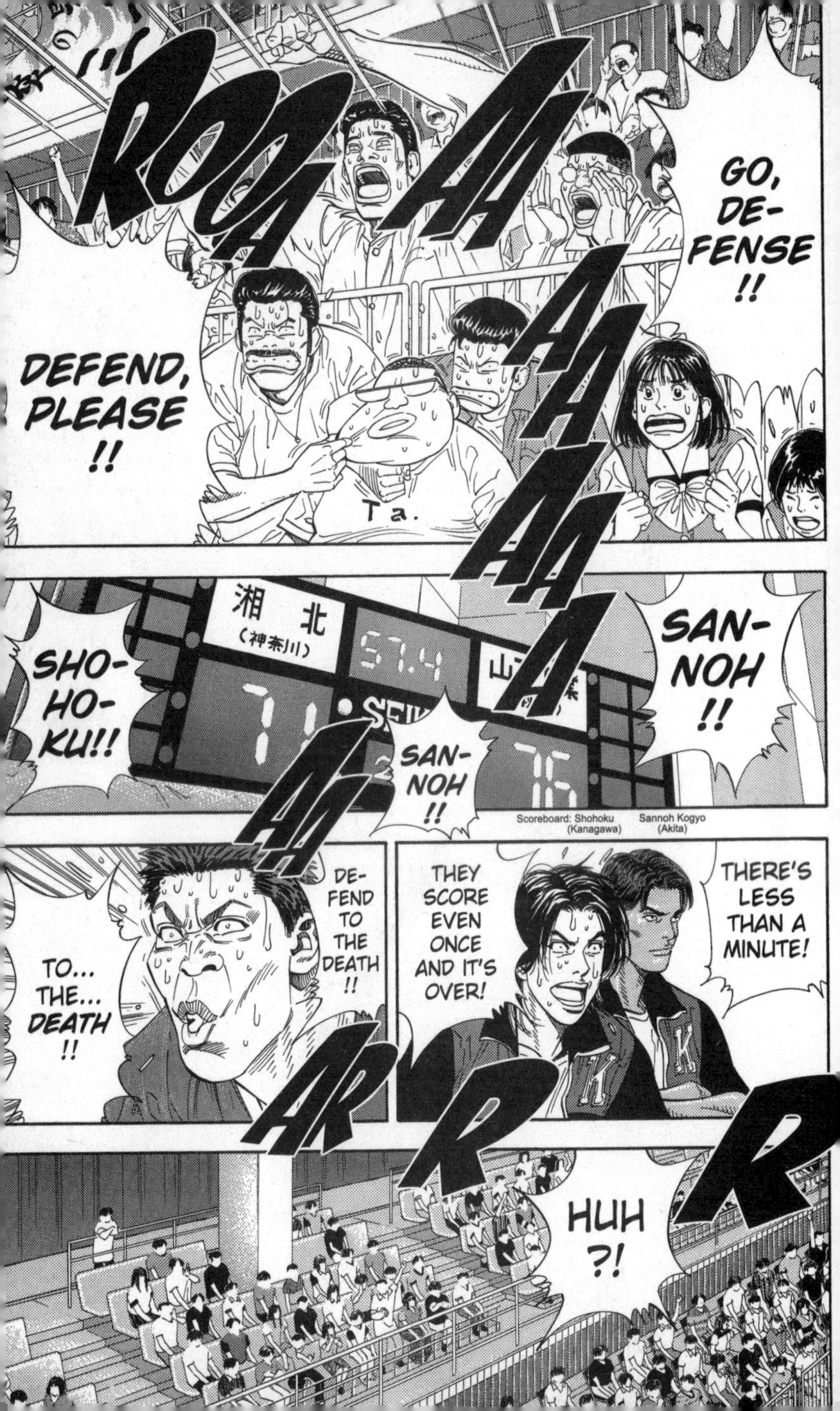
ROAAAAAAAAAAARRR
GO, DE-FENSE!!
DEFEND, PLEASE!!
Ta.
SAN-NOH!!
湘北
(神奈川)
57.4
SAN-NOH!!
SHO-HO-KU!!
Scoreboard: Shohoku (Kanagawa) Sannoh Kogyo (Akita)
THERE'S LESS THAN A MINUTE!
THEY SCORE EVEN ONCE AND IT'S OVER!
DE-FEND TO THE DEATH!!
TO... THE... DEATH!!
HUH?!

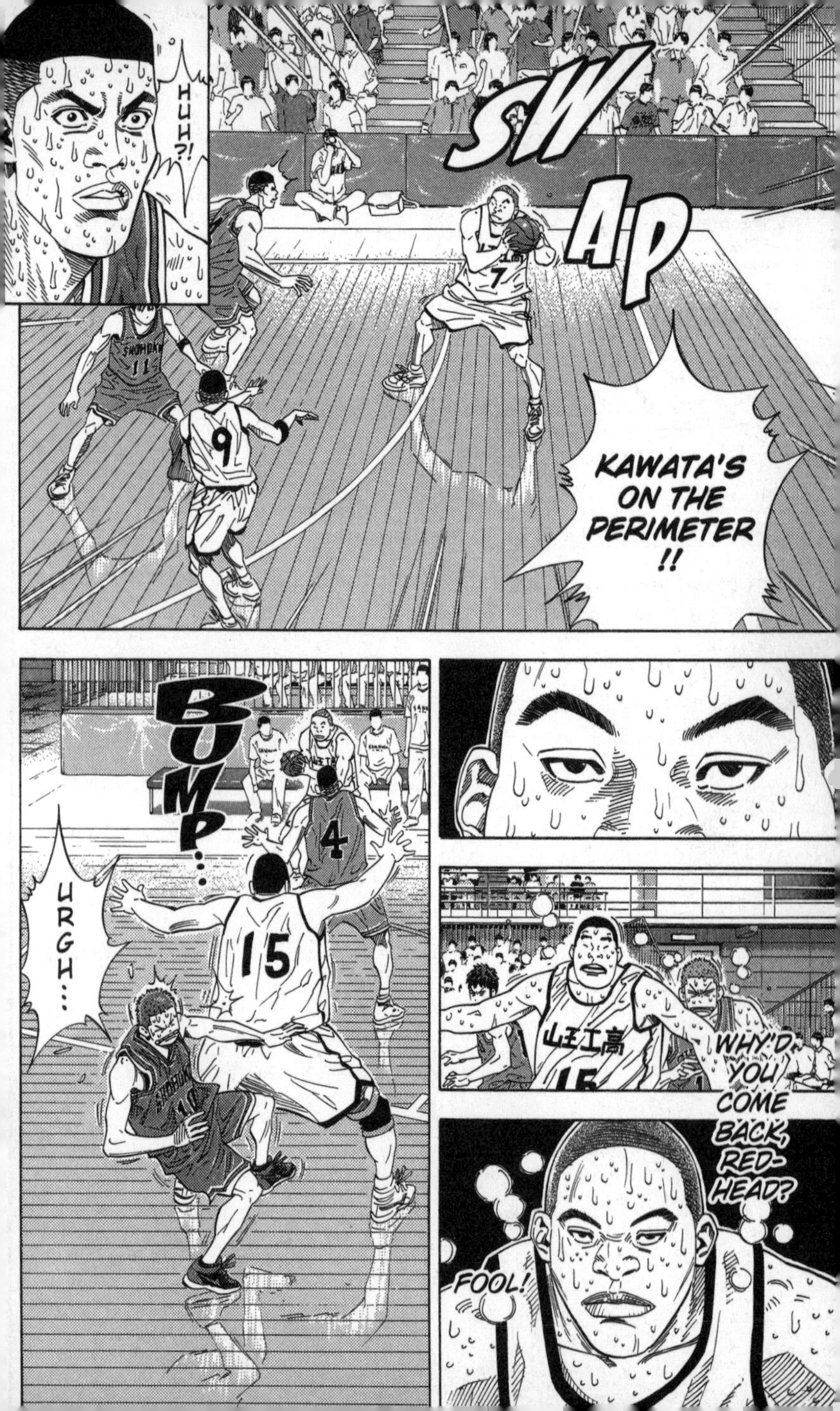
SWAP
HUH?!
KAWATA'S ON THE PERIMETER !!
WHY'D YOU COME BACK, RED-HEAD?
FOOL!
BUMP...
URGH...

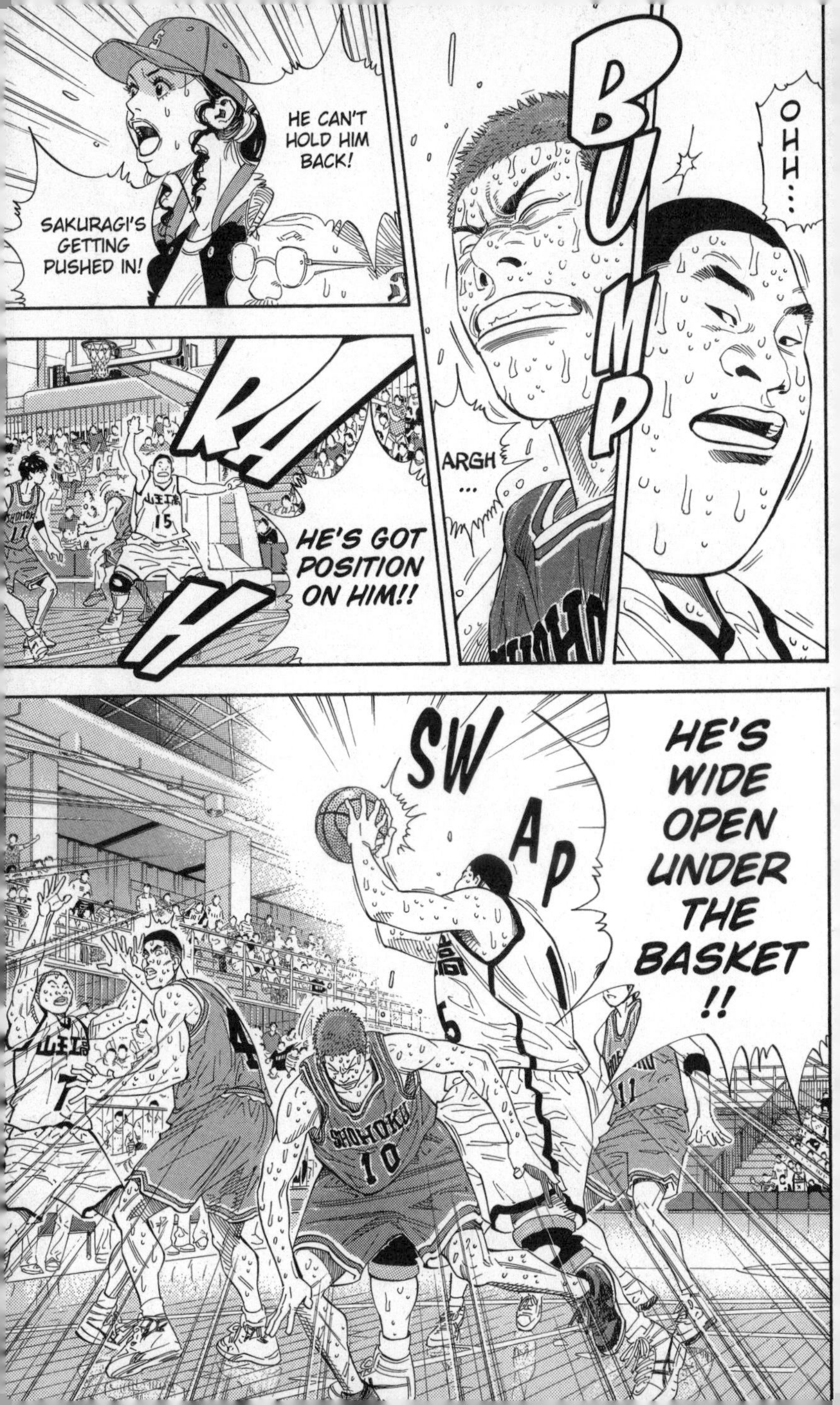
OHH...
BUMP
ARGH...
HE CAN'T HOLD HIM BACK!
SAKURAGI'S GETTING PUSHED IN!
WHAM
HE'S GOT POSITION ON HIM!!
HE'S WIDE OPEN UNDER THE BASKET!!
SWAP

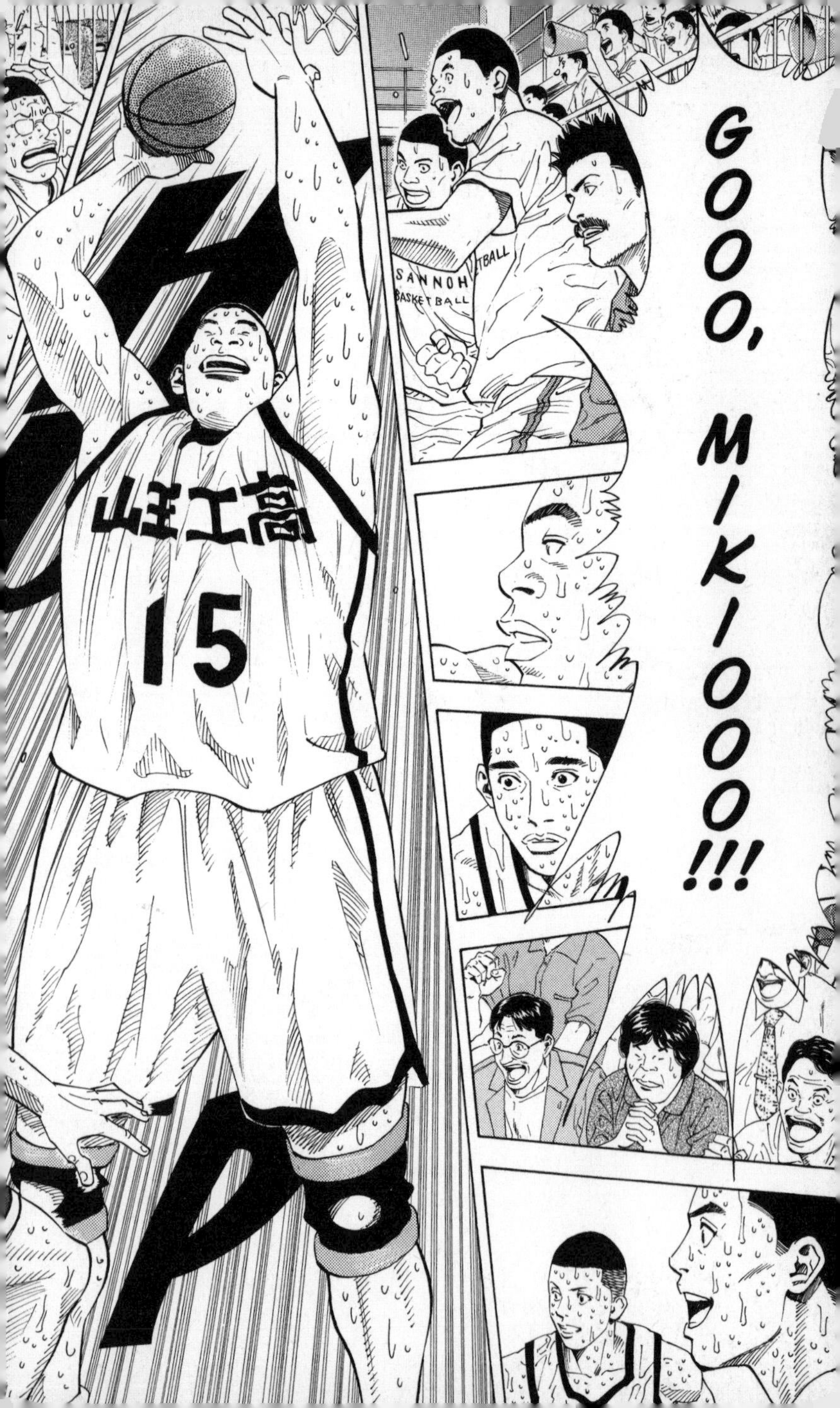
GOOO, MIKIOOOO!!!
SANNOH BASKETBALL
山王工高
15

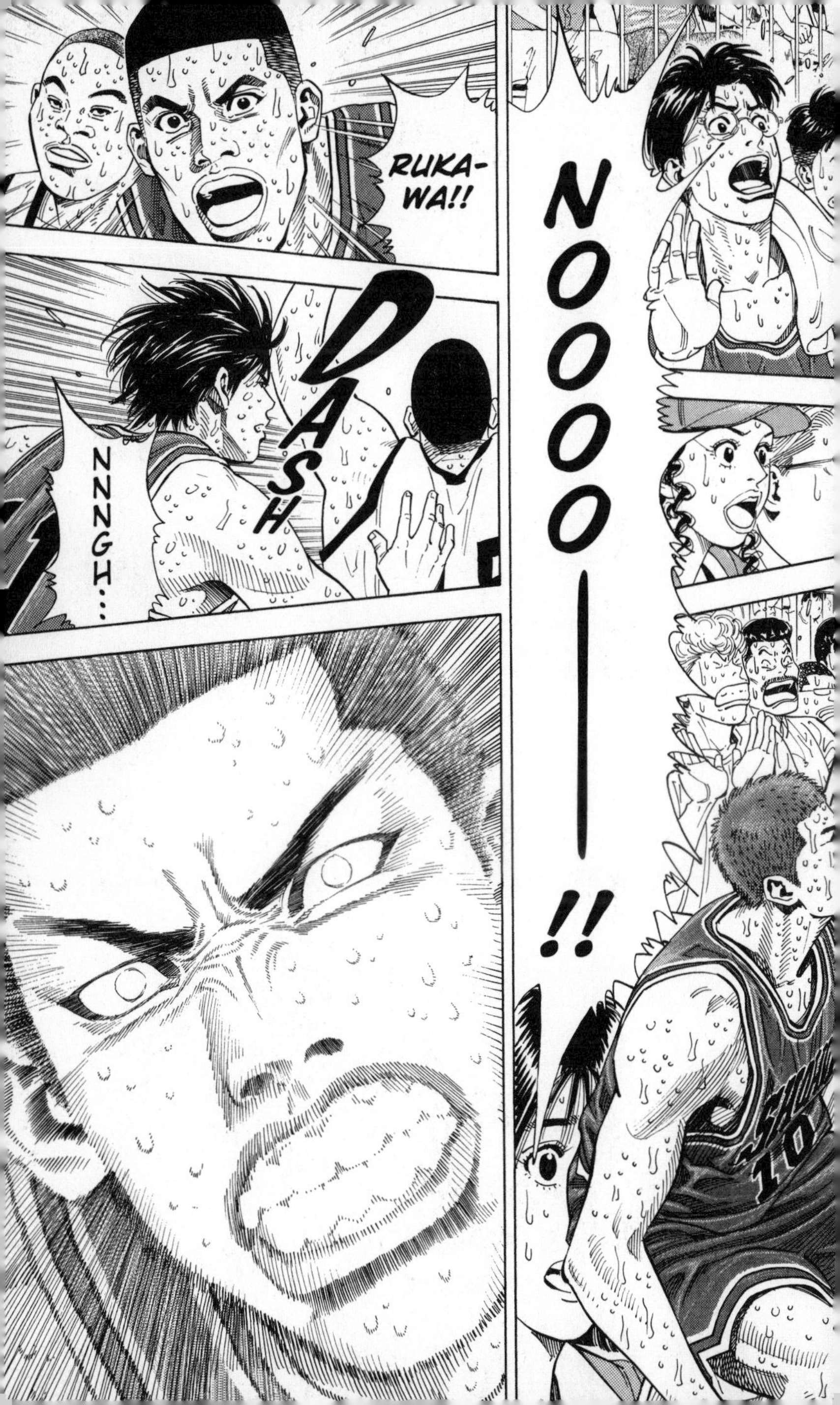
NOOOO—!!
RUKA-WA!!
DASH
NNNGH...

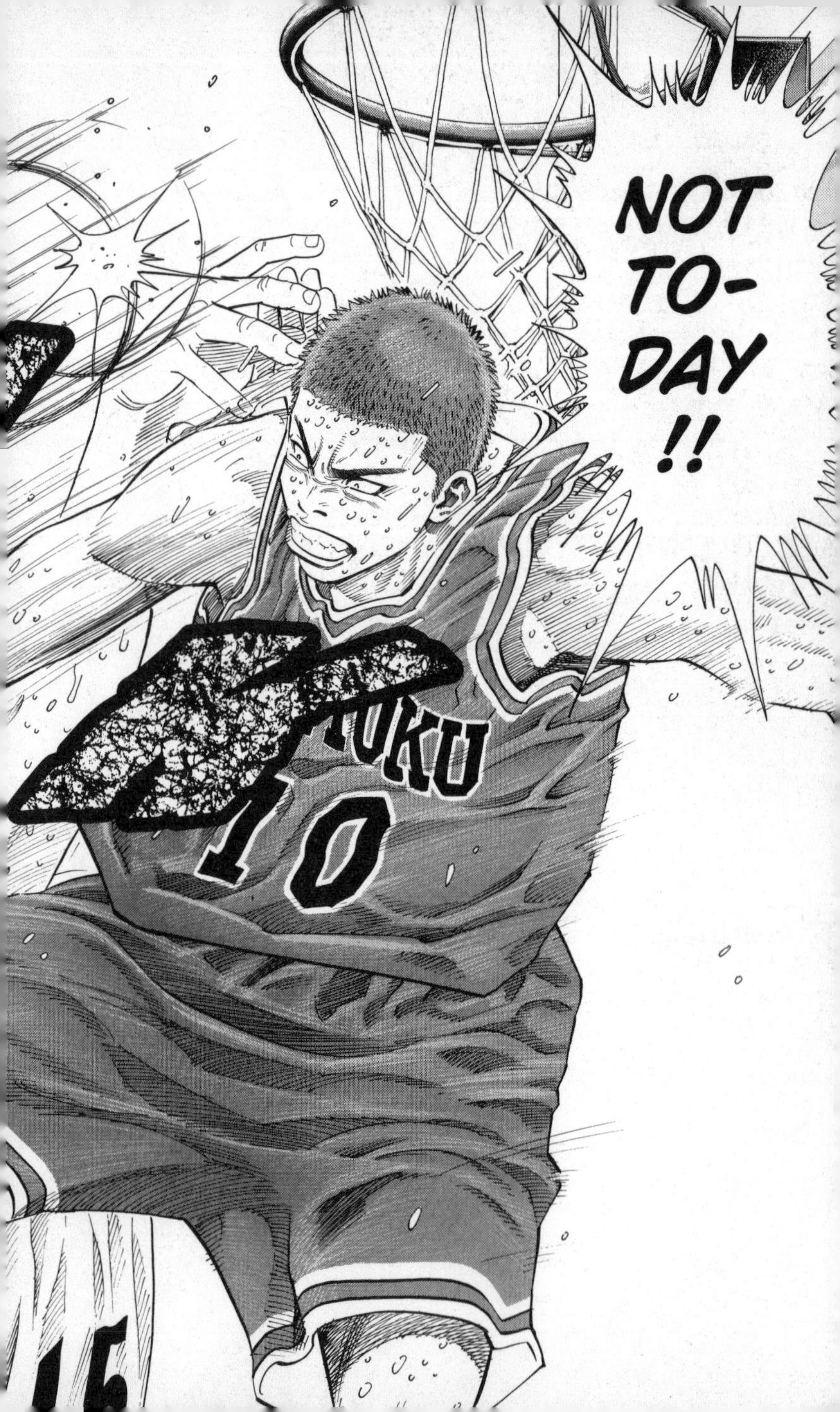
NOT TO-DAY!!

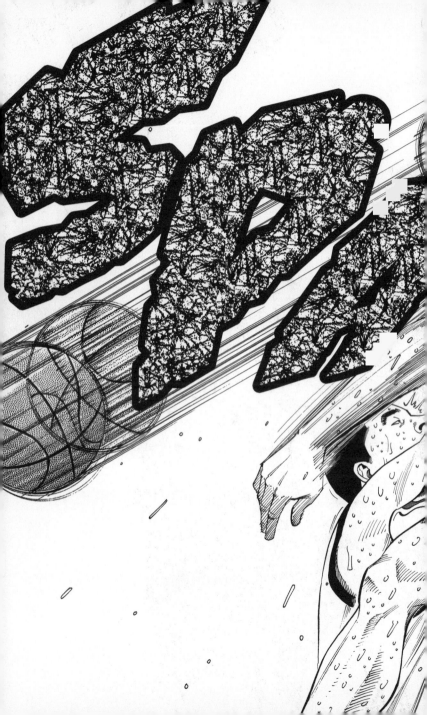

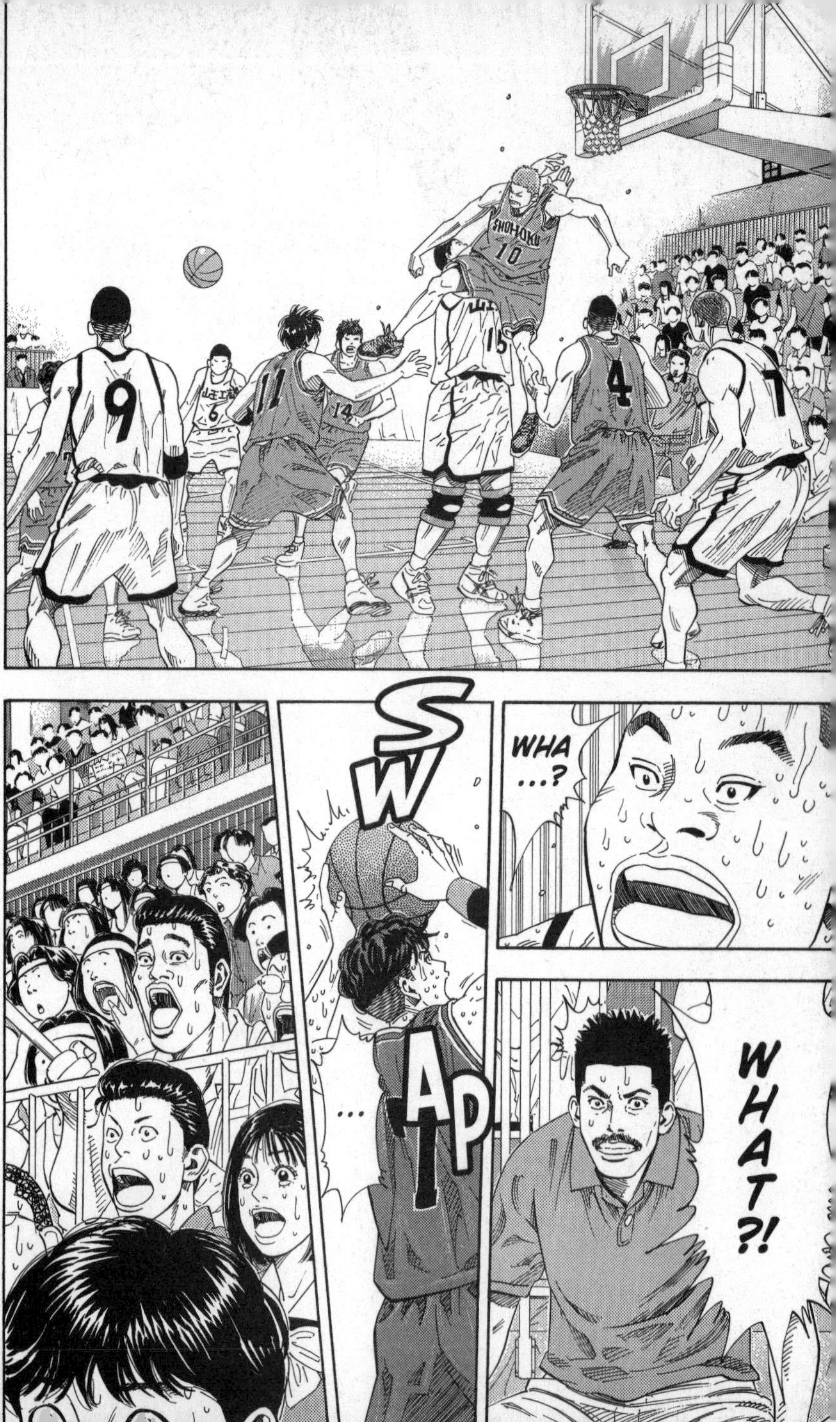
WHA ...?
WHAT?!
SW
...
AP

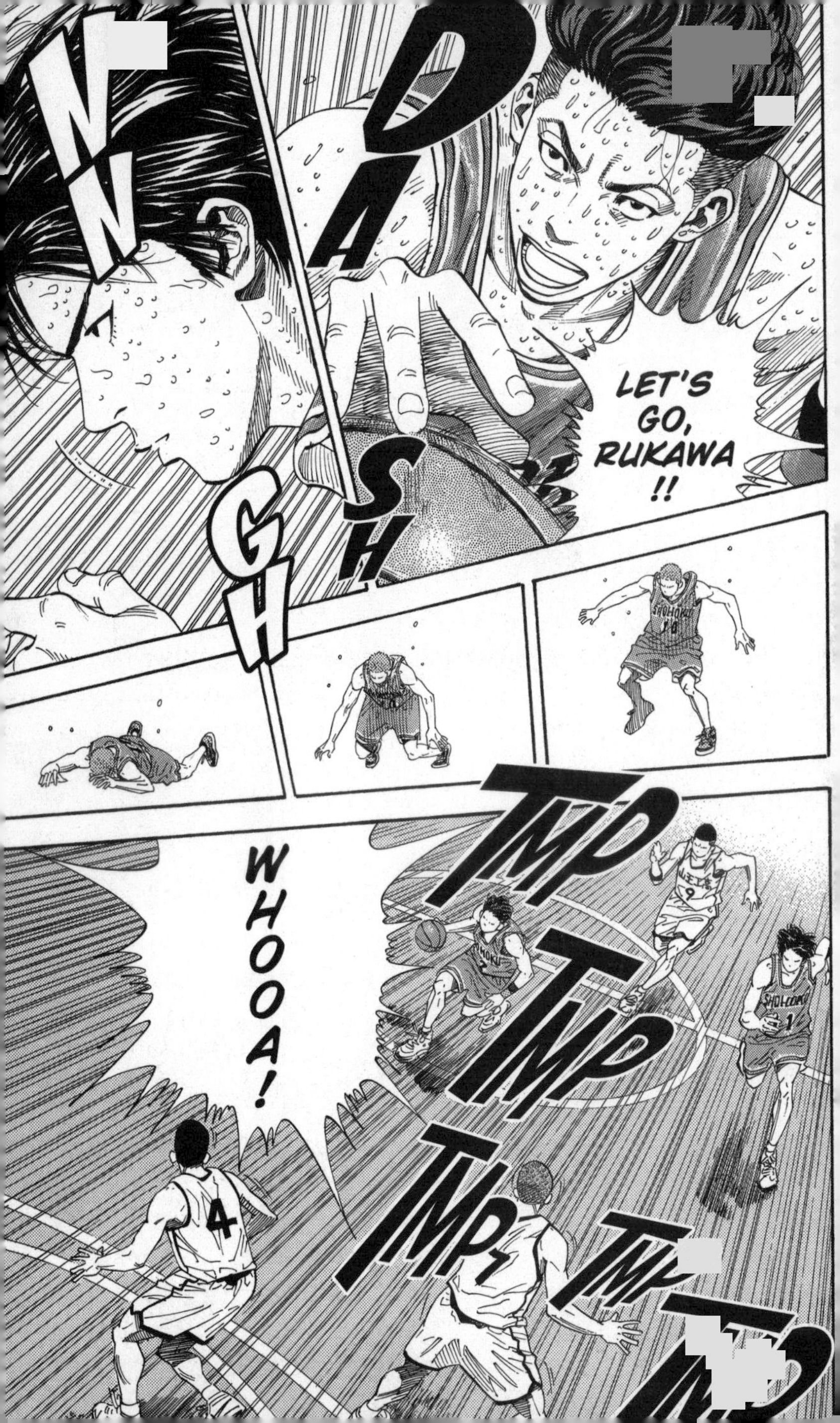

DA
LET'S GO, RUKAWA !!
SH
NN
GH
TMP
TMP
TMP
TMP
WHOOOA!

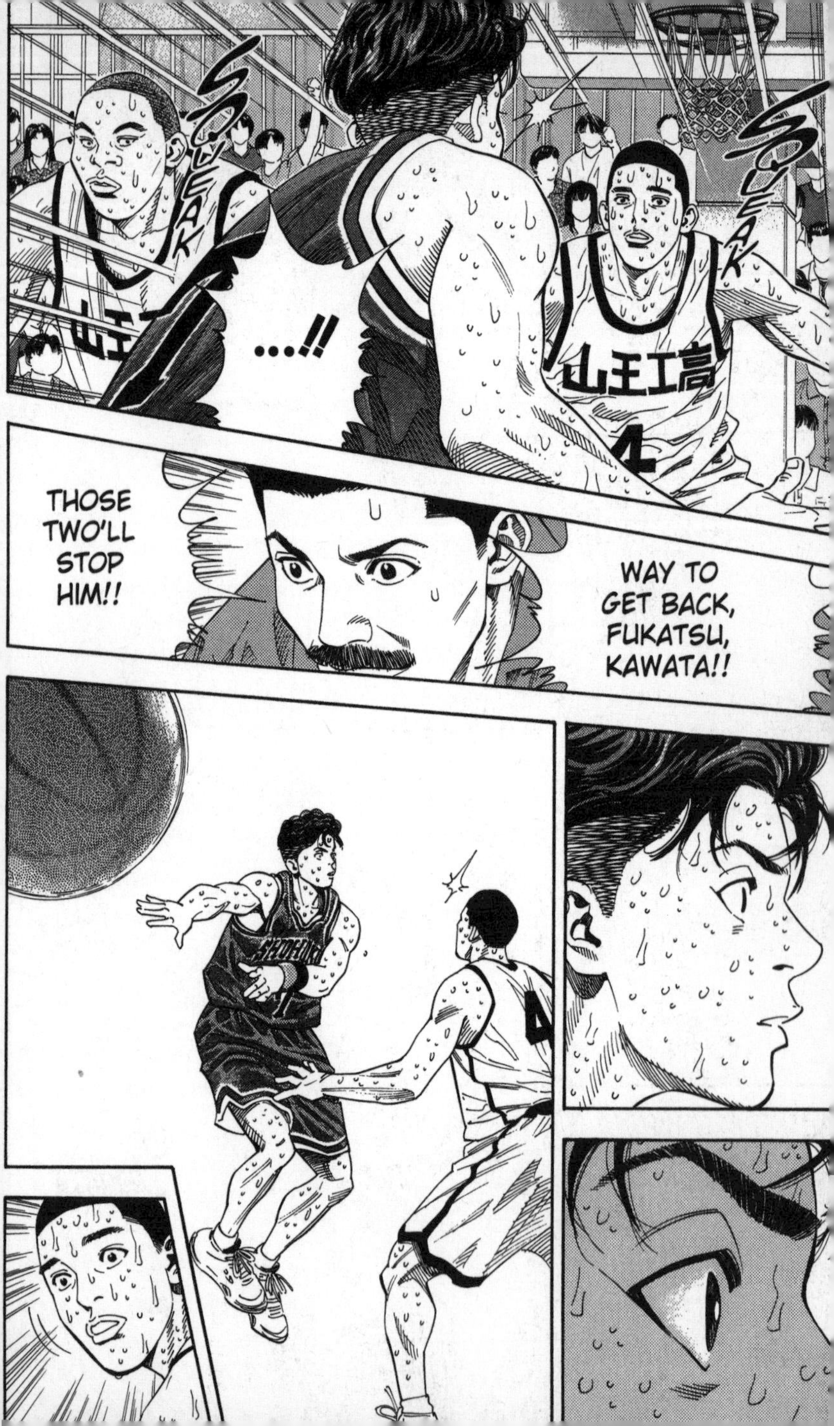
SQUEAK
SQUEAK
...!!
山王工高
WAY TO GET BACK, FUKATSU, KAWATA!!
THOSE TWO'LL STOP HIM!!
SHOHOKU

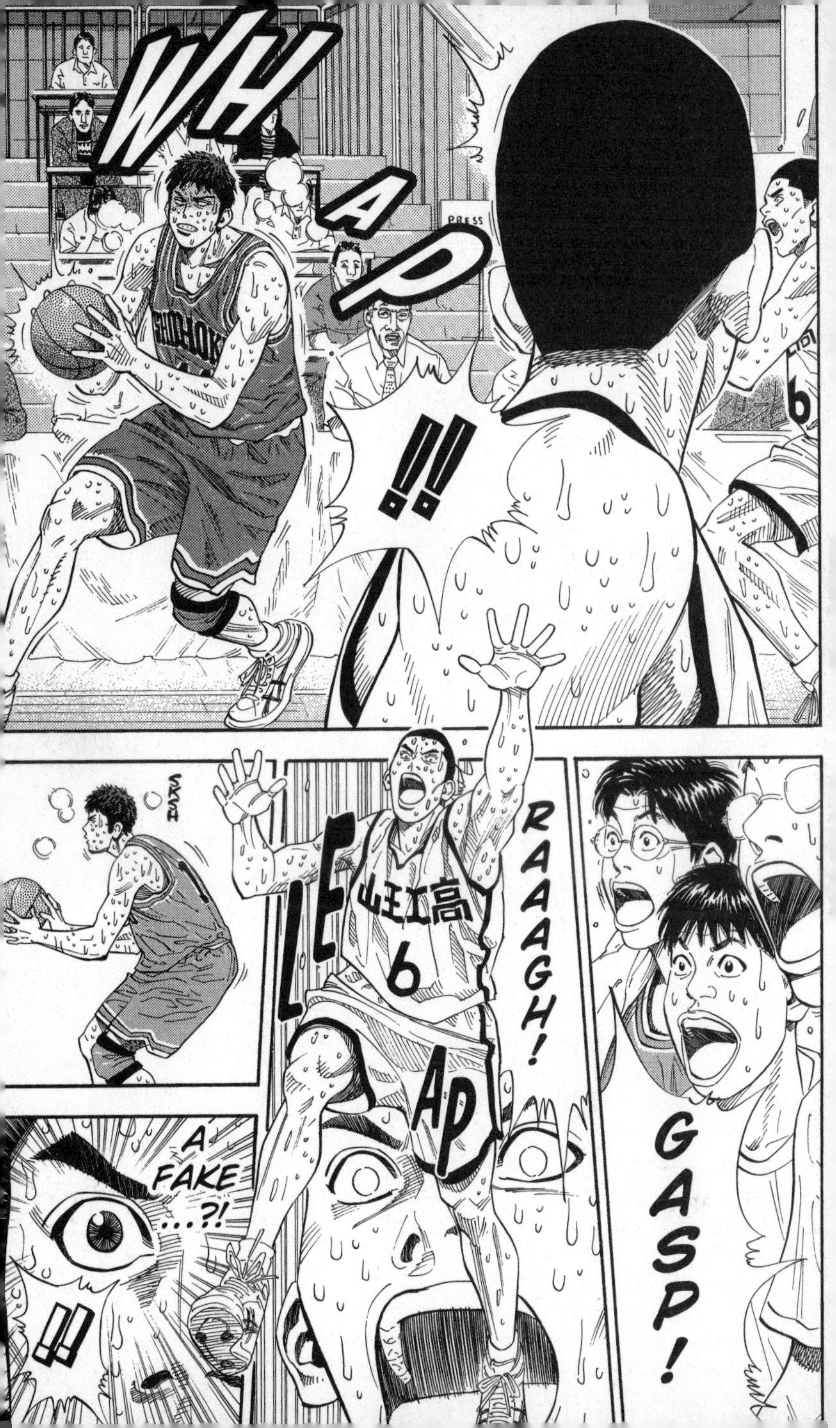
WHAP
!!
GASP!
RAAAGH!
LEAP
A FAKE ...?!
!!

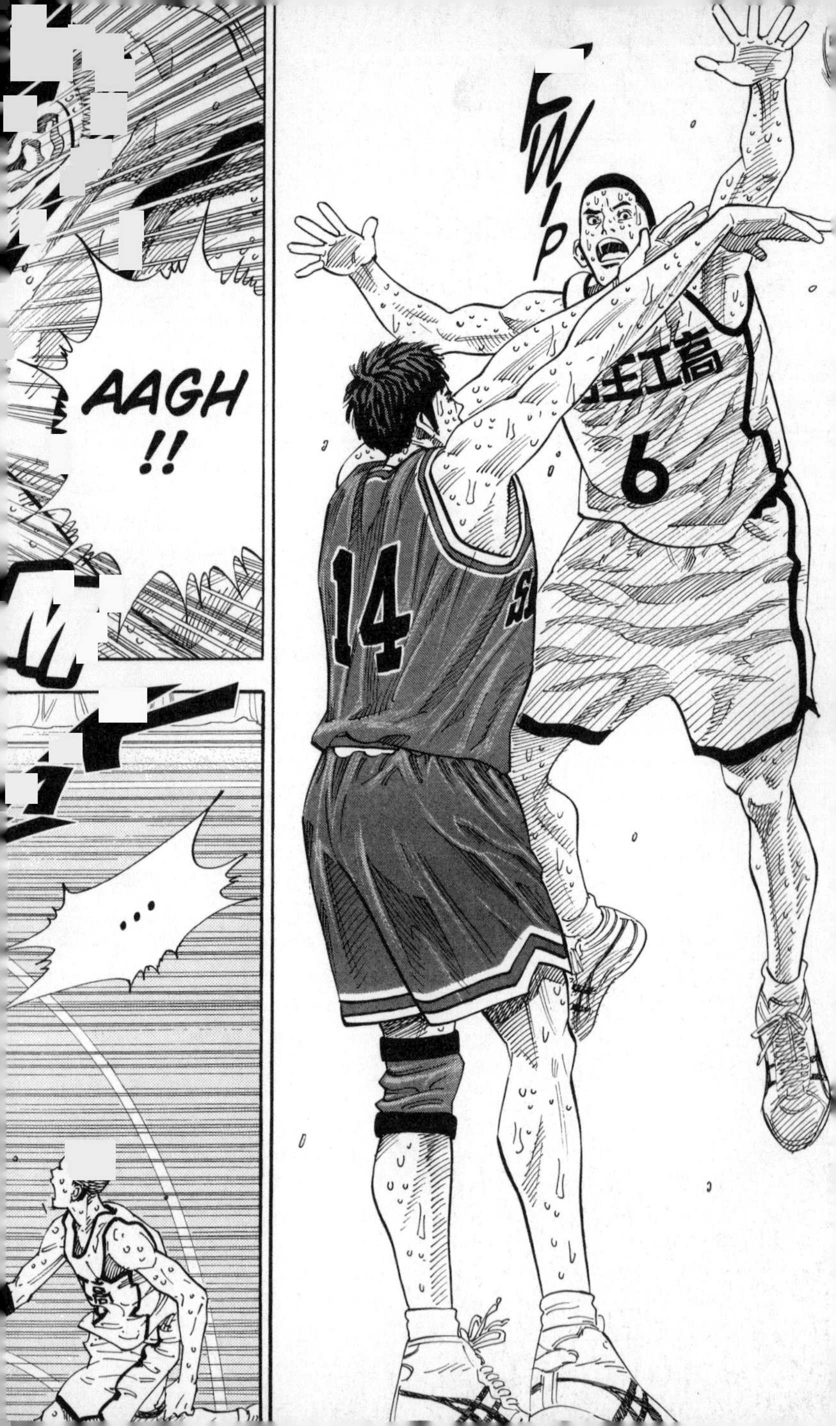
WIP
AAGH !!
...

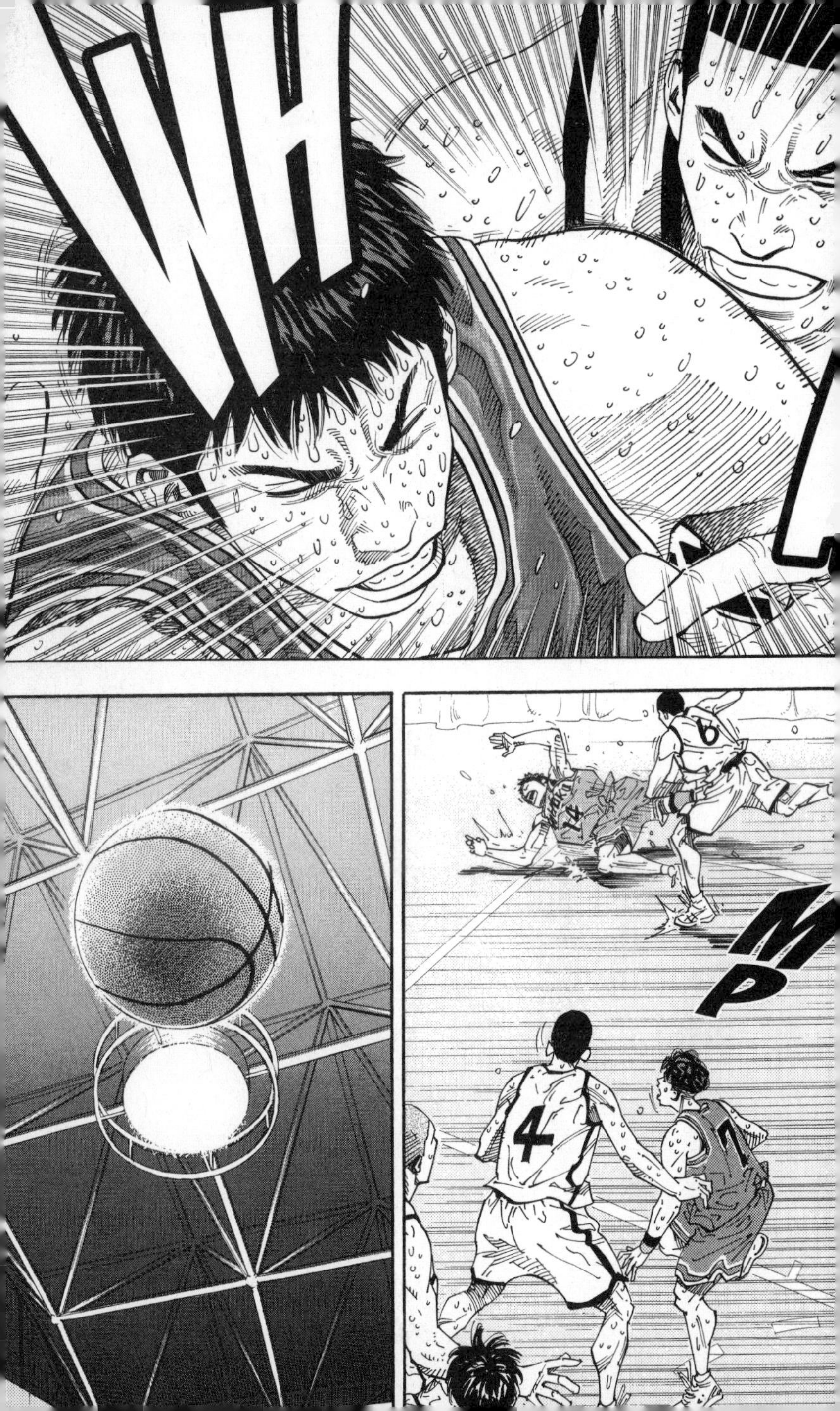
WH
MP

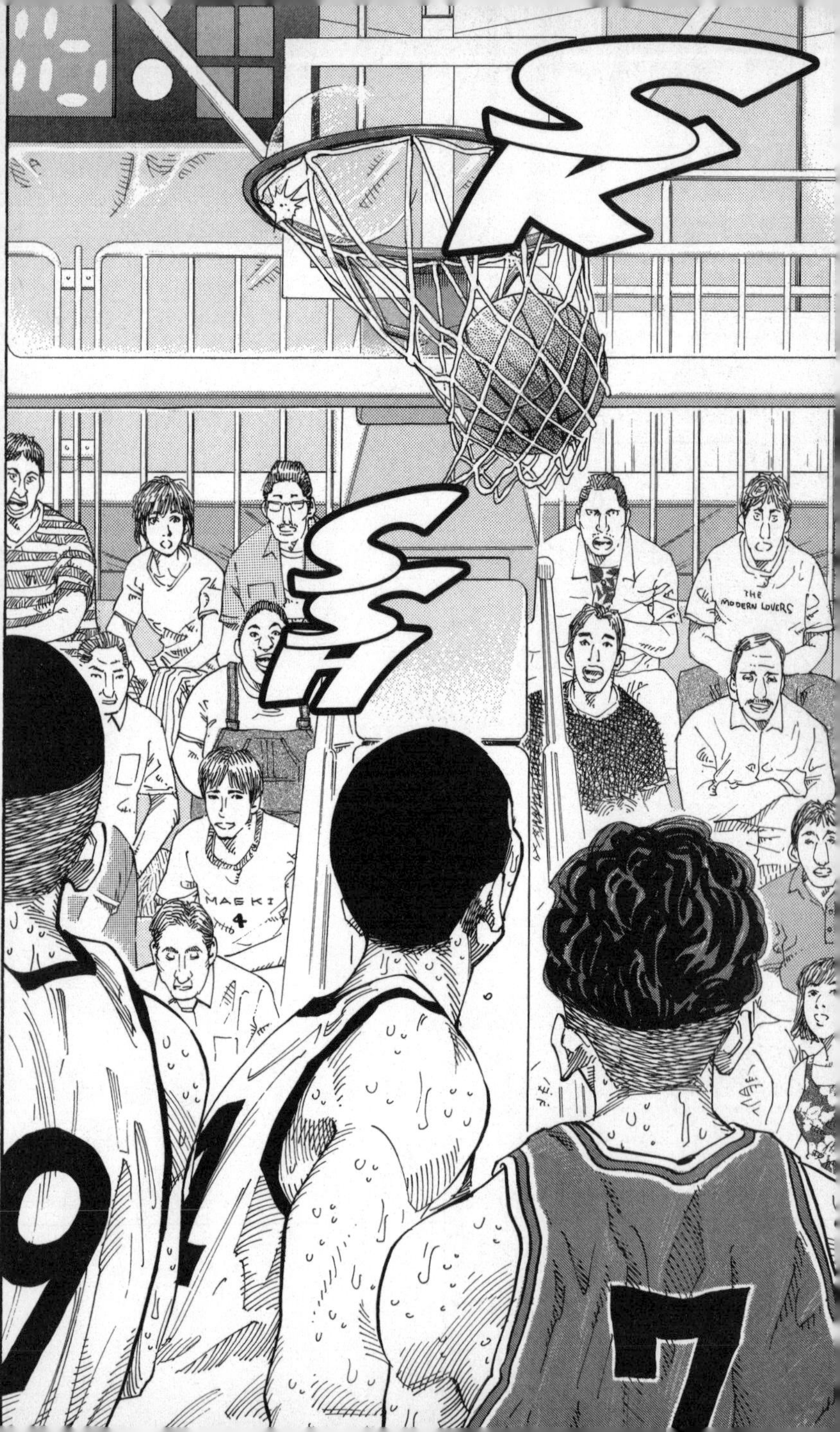
THE MODERN LOVERS
MAGKI
4

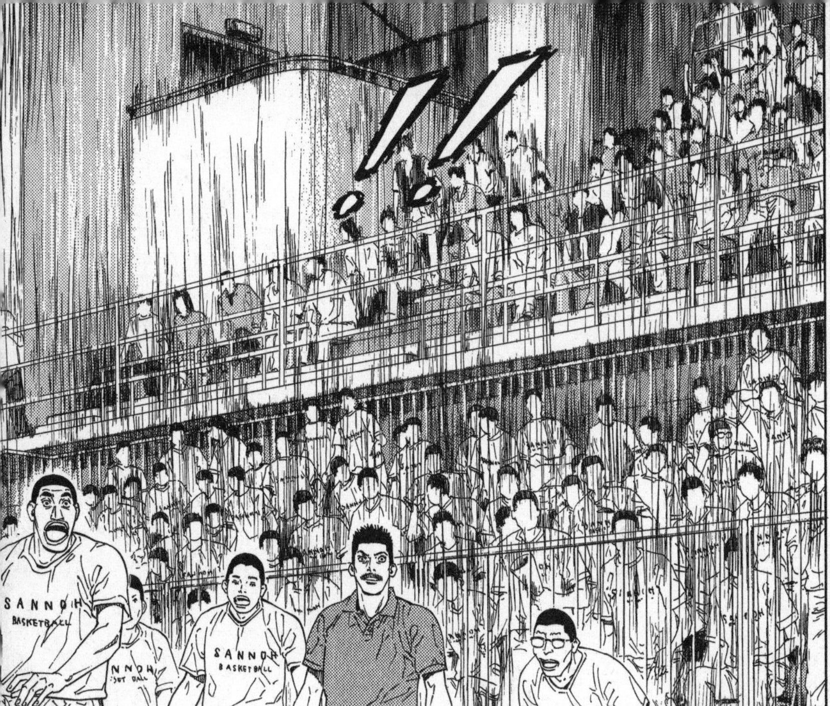
!!
SANNOH
BASKETBALL

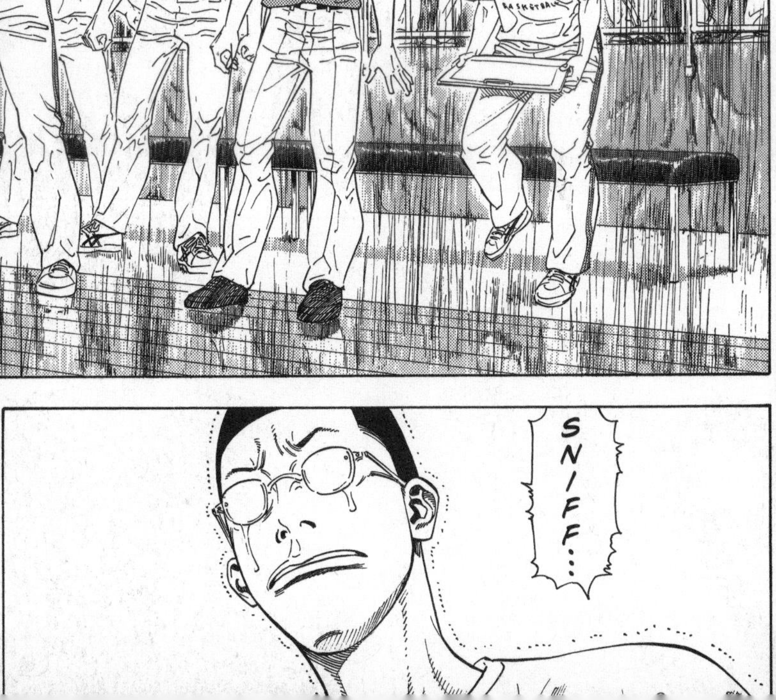
SNIFF...

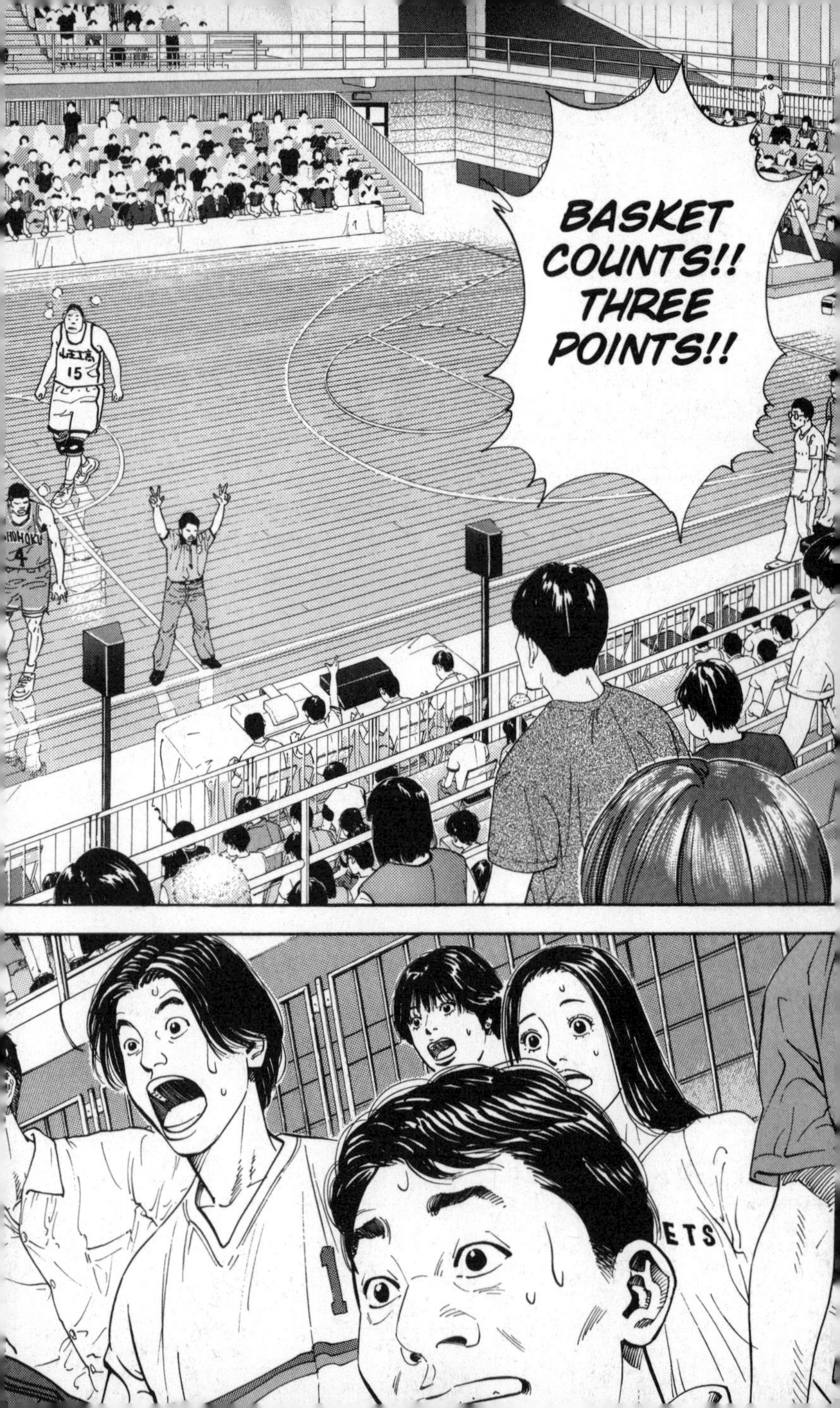
BASKET COUNTS!! THREE POINTS!!
SHOHOKU
4
15
ETS

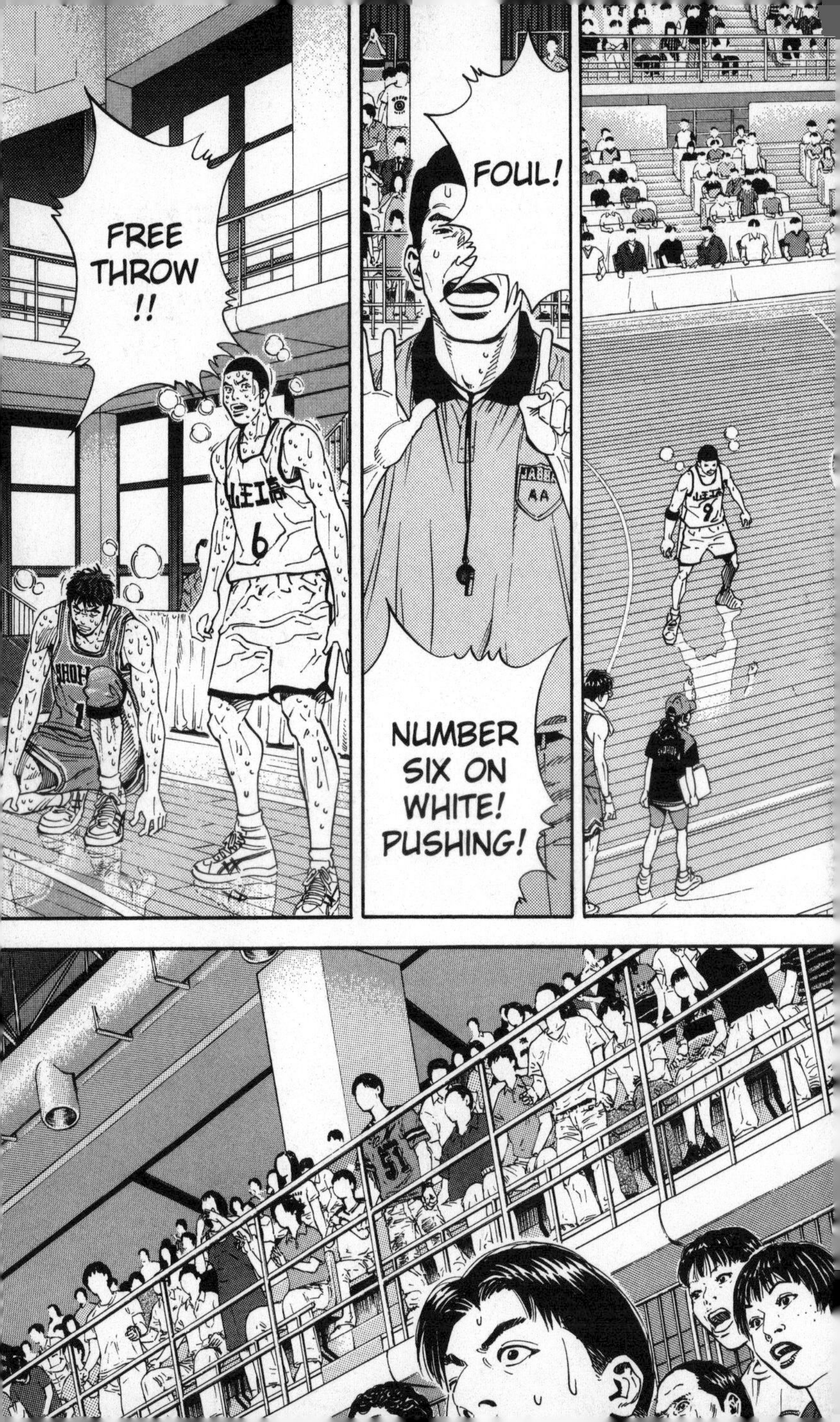
FOUL!
NUMBER SIX ON WHITE! PUSHING!
FREE THROW !!

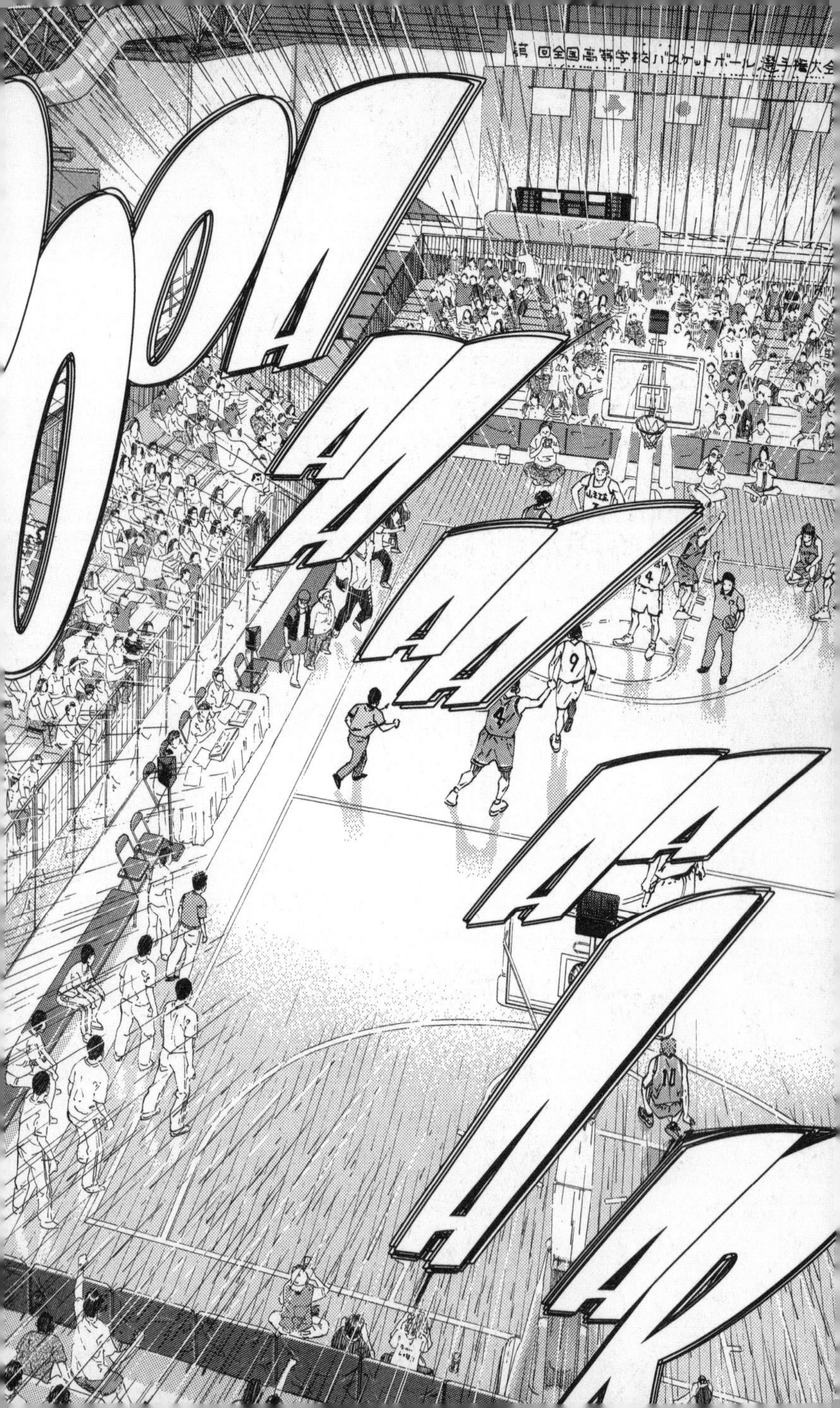
第 回全国高等学校バスケットボール選手権大会

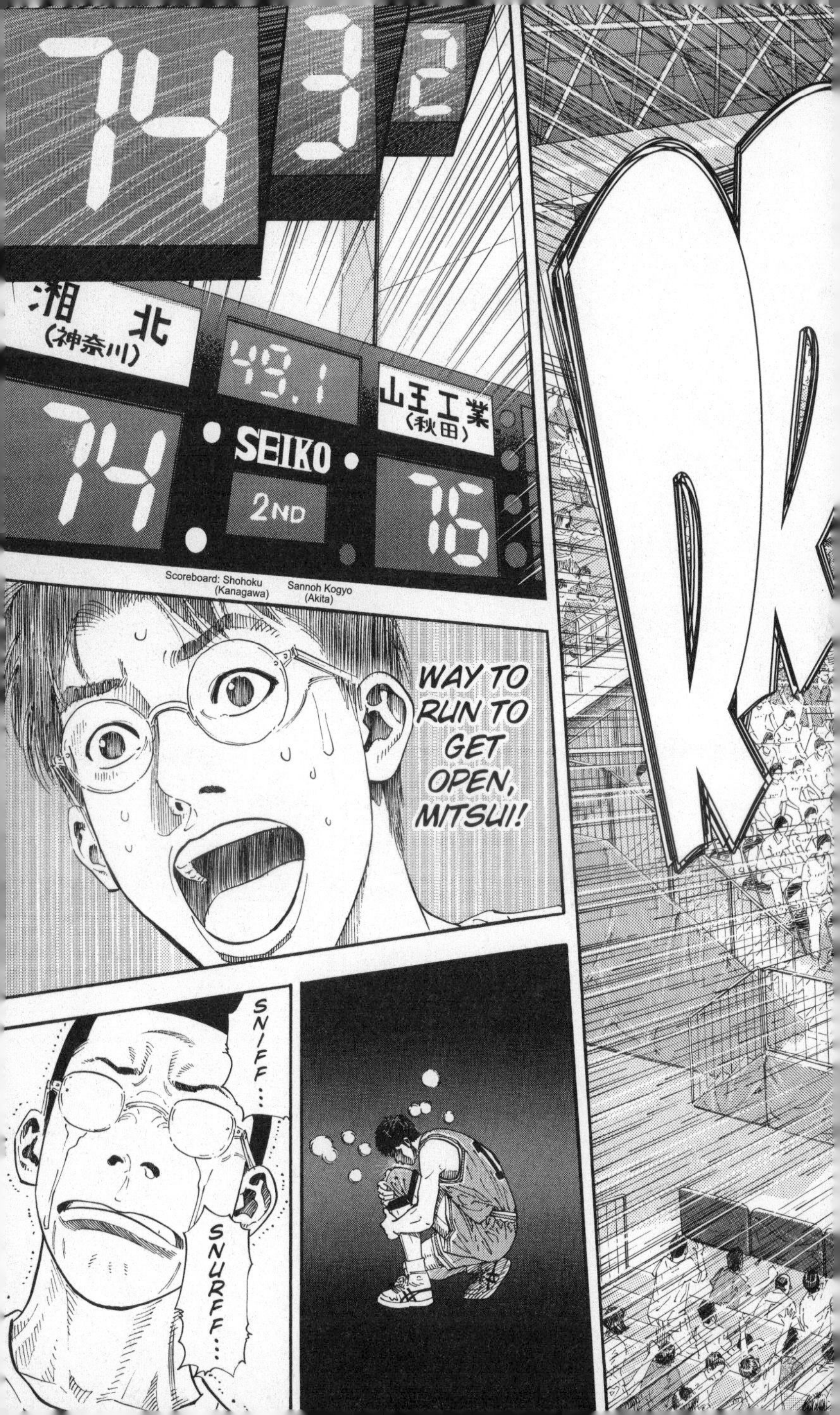
74
32
湘北
〈神奈川〉
49.1
山王工業
〈秋田〉
SEIKO
74
2ND
76
Scoreboard: Shohoku (Kanagawa) Sannoh Kogyo (Akita)
WAY TO RUN TO GET OPEN, MITSUI!
SNIFF...
SNURFF...

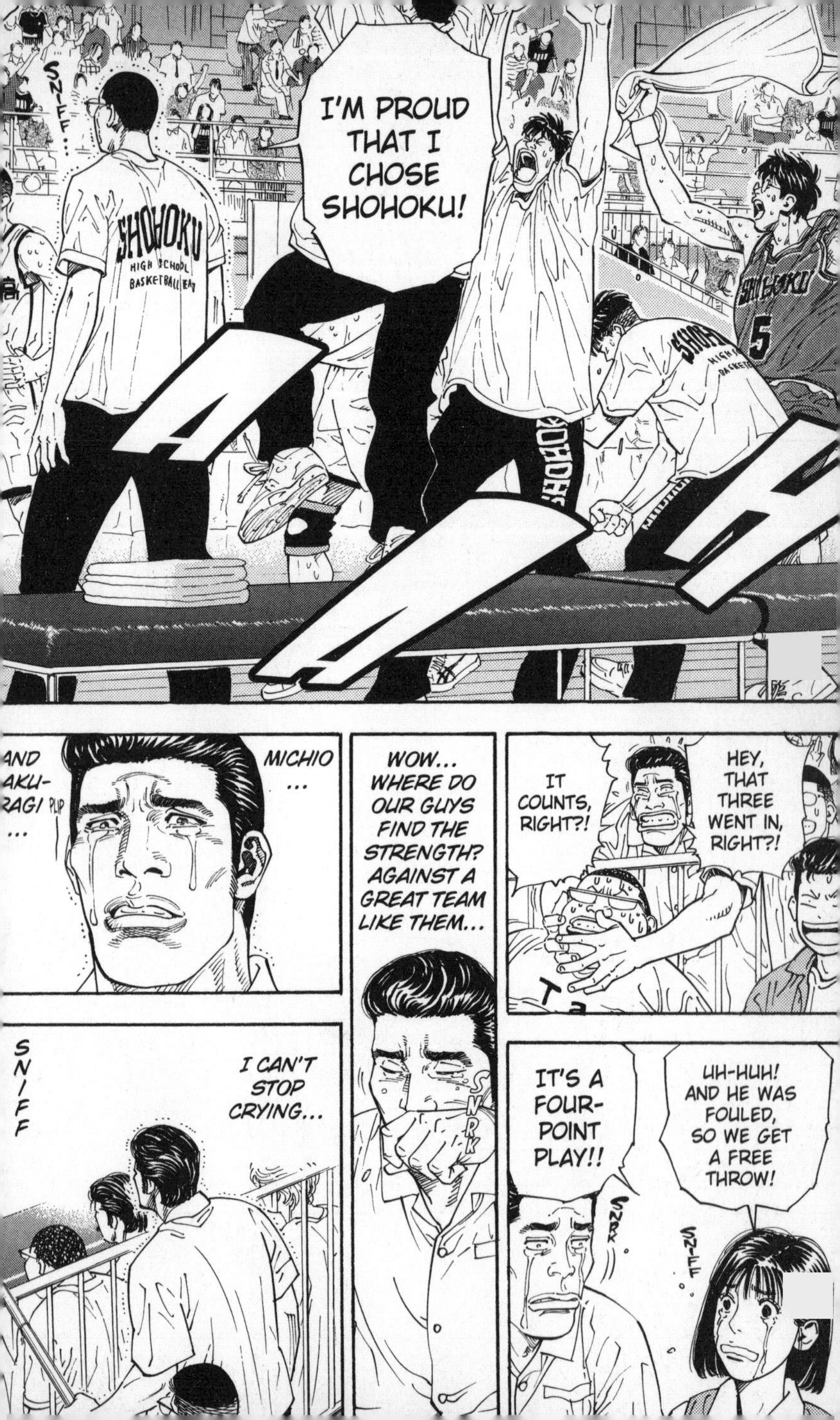
I'M PROUD THAT I CHOSE SHOHOKU!
SNIFF...
HEY, THAT THREE WENT IN, RIGHT?!
IT COUNTS, RIGHT?!
WOW... WHERE DO OUR GUYS FIND THE STRENGTH? AGAINST A GREAT TEAM LIKE THEM...
MICHIO ...
AND AKU-RAGI ...
PLIP
UH-HUH! AND HE WAS FOULED, SO WE GET A FREE THROW!
SNIFF
IT'S A FOUR-POINT PLAY!!
SNRK
SNRK
I CAN'T STOP CRYING...
SNIFF

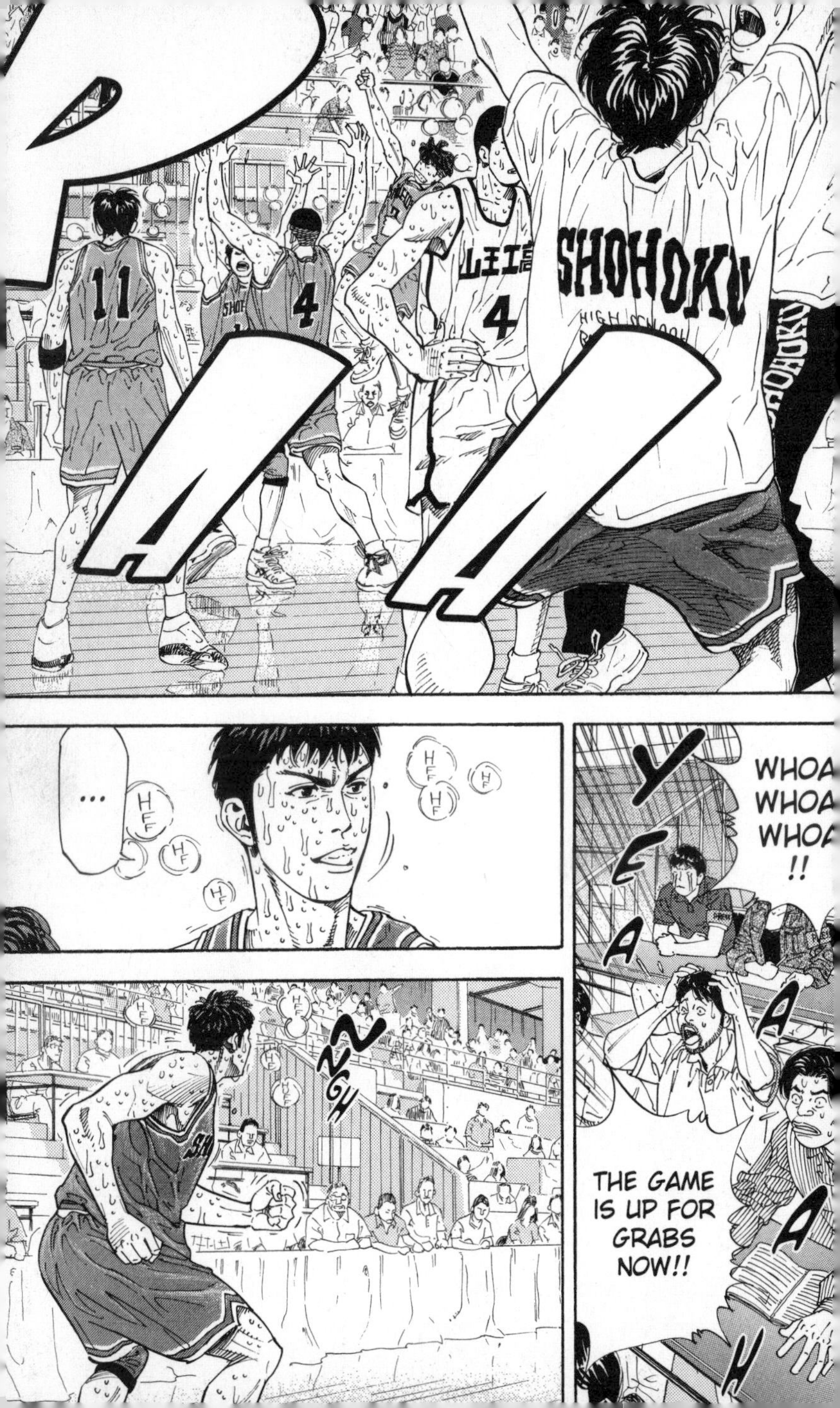
YEAAAAH
WHOA WHOA WHOA!!
THE GAME IS UP FOR GRABS NOW!!
...
HF HF HF HF HF
HF HF HUFF
NNGH

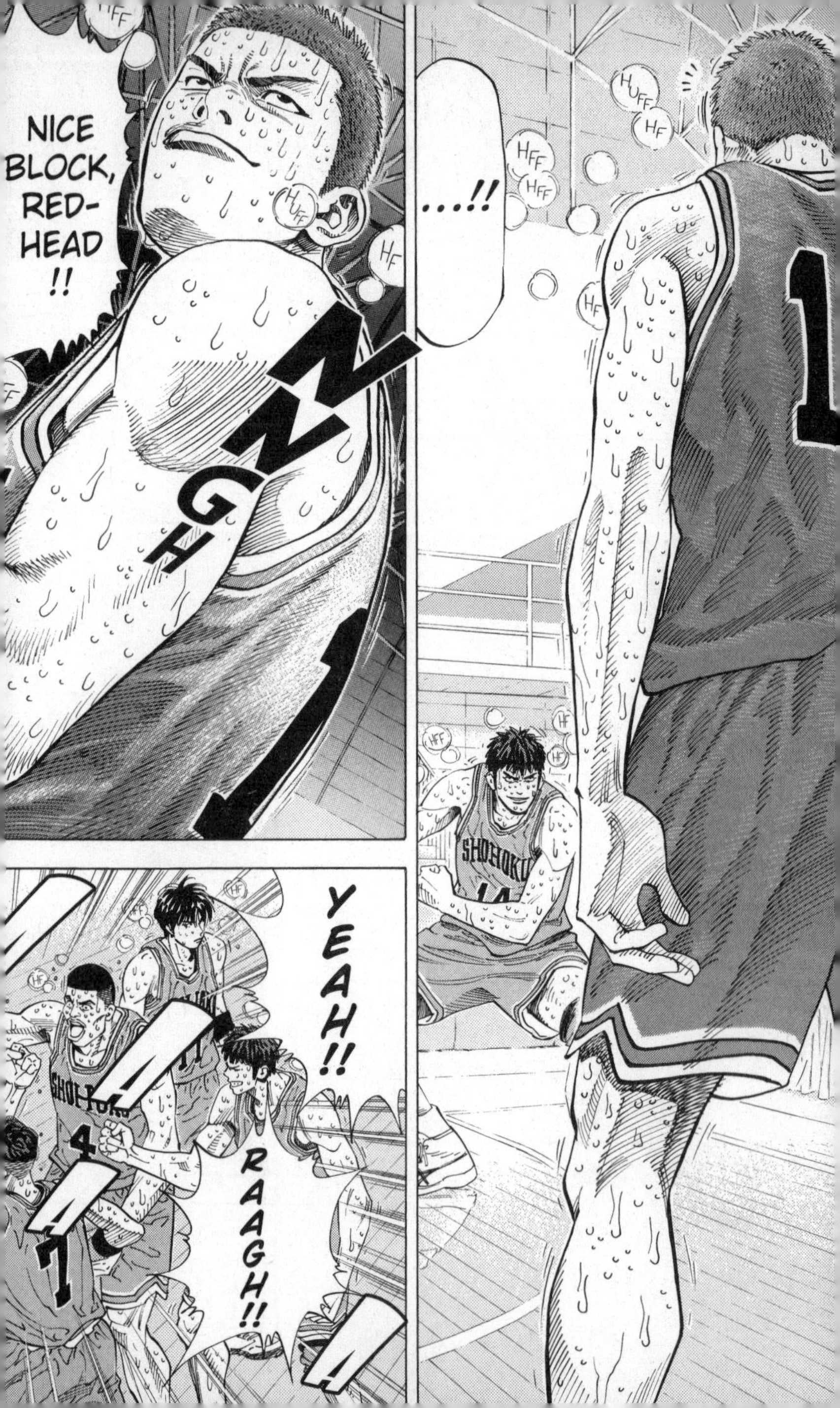
HUFF
HF
HFF
HFF
...!!
HUFF
HF
HFF
NICE BLOCK, RED-HEAD!!
NNGH
HF
HFF
HF
YEAH!!
RAAGH!!

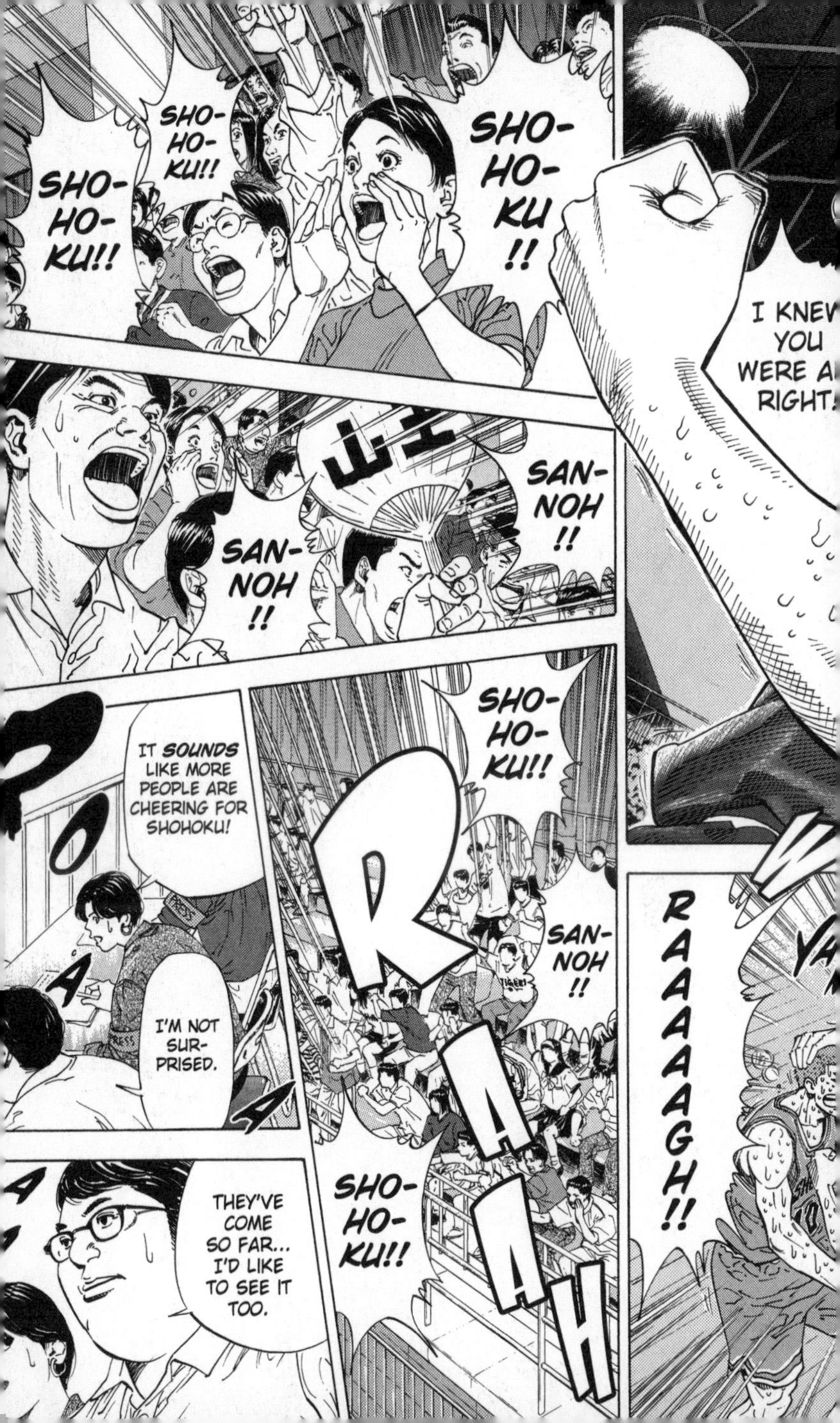
I KNEW YOU WERE A RIGHT.
SHO-HO-KU!!
SHO-HO-KU!!
SHO-HO-KU!!
SAN-NOH!!
SAN-NOH!!
SHO-HO-KU!!
SAN-NOH!!
RAAAH
IT SOUNDS LIKE MORE PEOPLE ARE CHEERING FOR SHOHOKU!
I'M NOT SUR-PRISED.
THEY'VE COME SO FAR... I'D LIKE TO SEE IT TOO.
SHO-HO-KU!!
RAAAAAAAGH!!

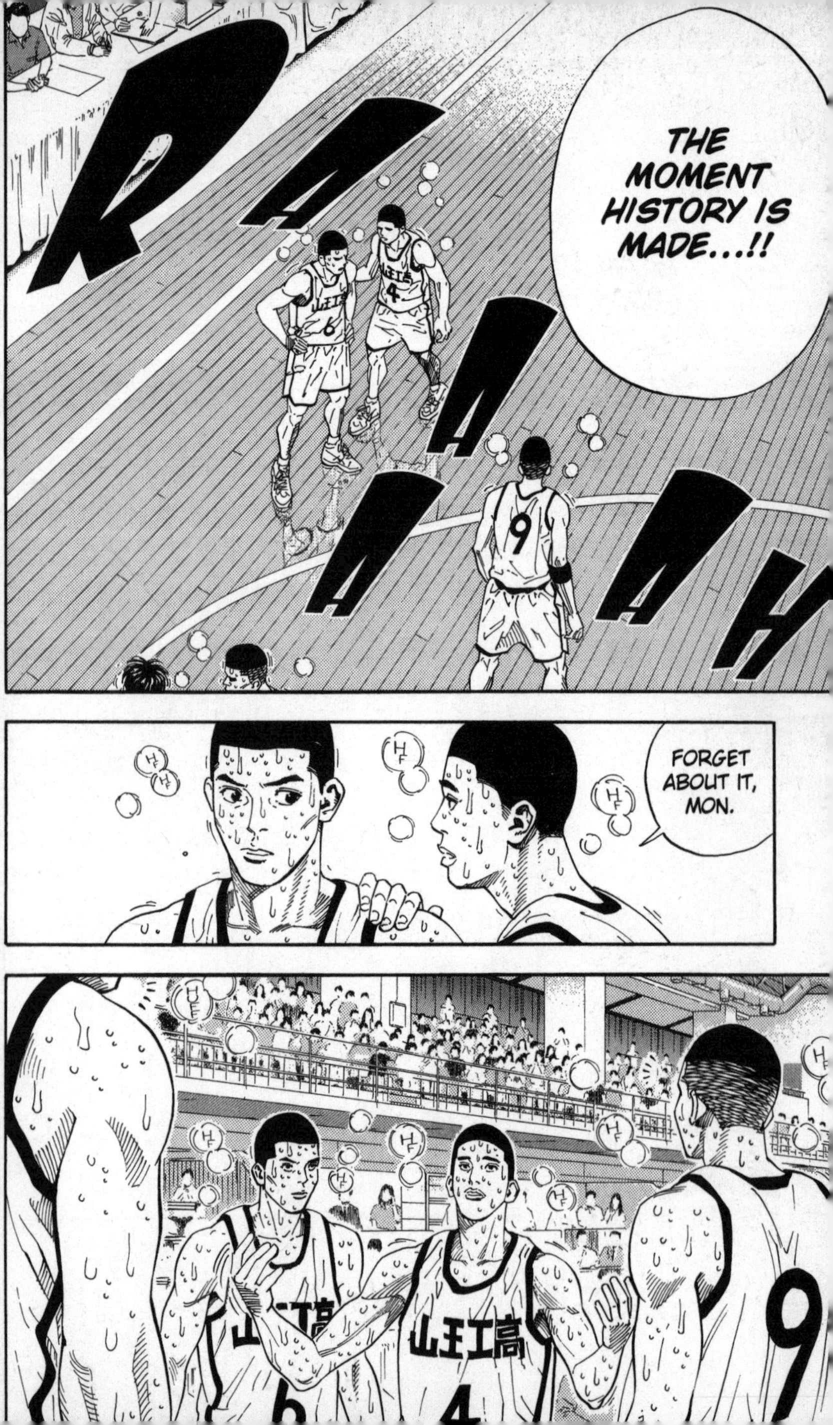
THE MOMENT HISTORY IS MADE...!!
RAAAAH
FORGET ABOUT IT, MON.
山王工高
山王工高

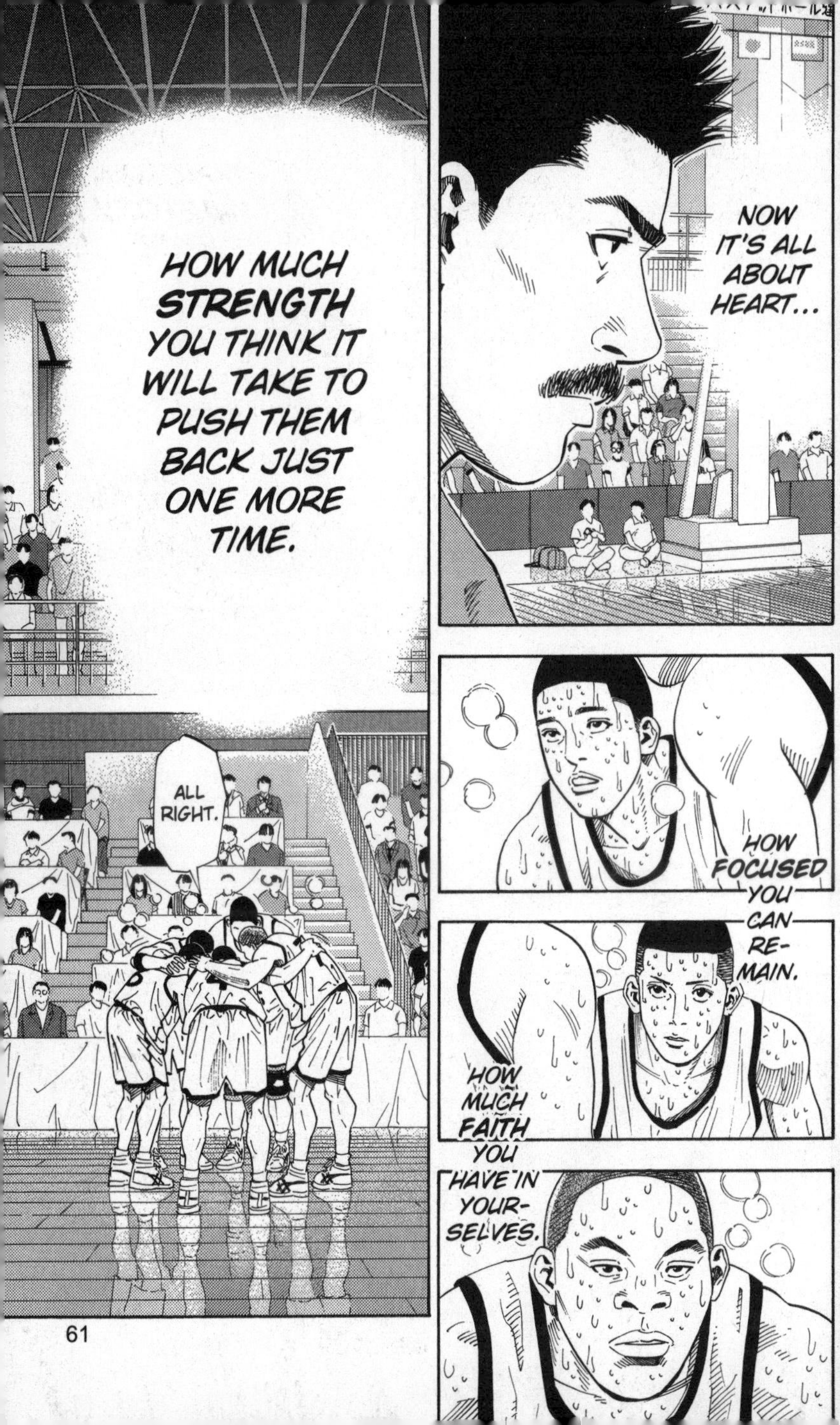
NOW IT'S ALL ABOUT HEART...
HOW FOCUSED YOU CAN RE-MAIN.
HOW MUCH FAITH YOU HAVE IN YOUR-SELVES.
HOW MUCH STRENGTH YOU THINK IT WILL TAKE TO PUSH THEM BACK JUST ONE MORE TIME.
ALL RIGHT.

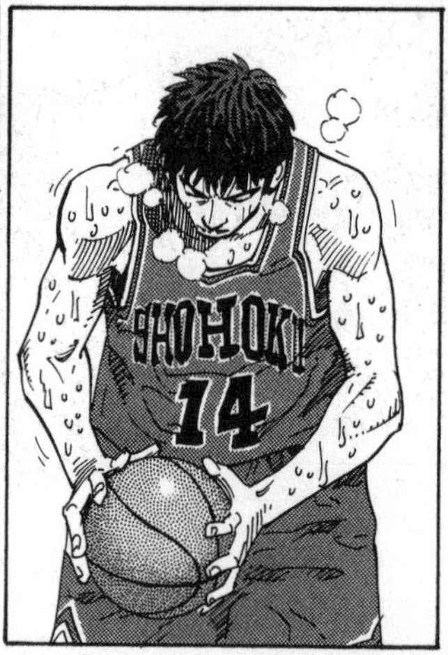
SHOHOKU
14
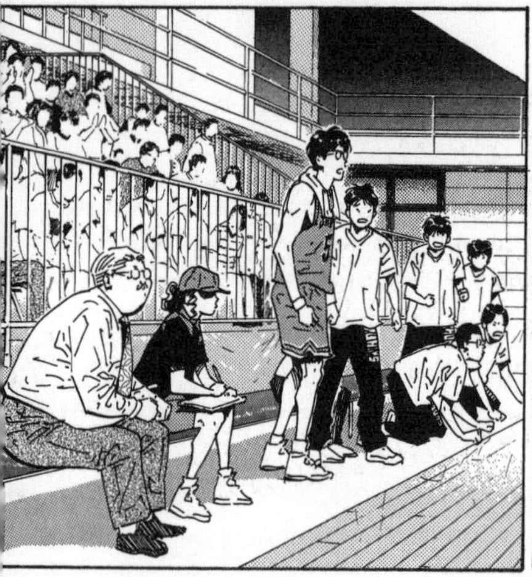
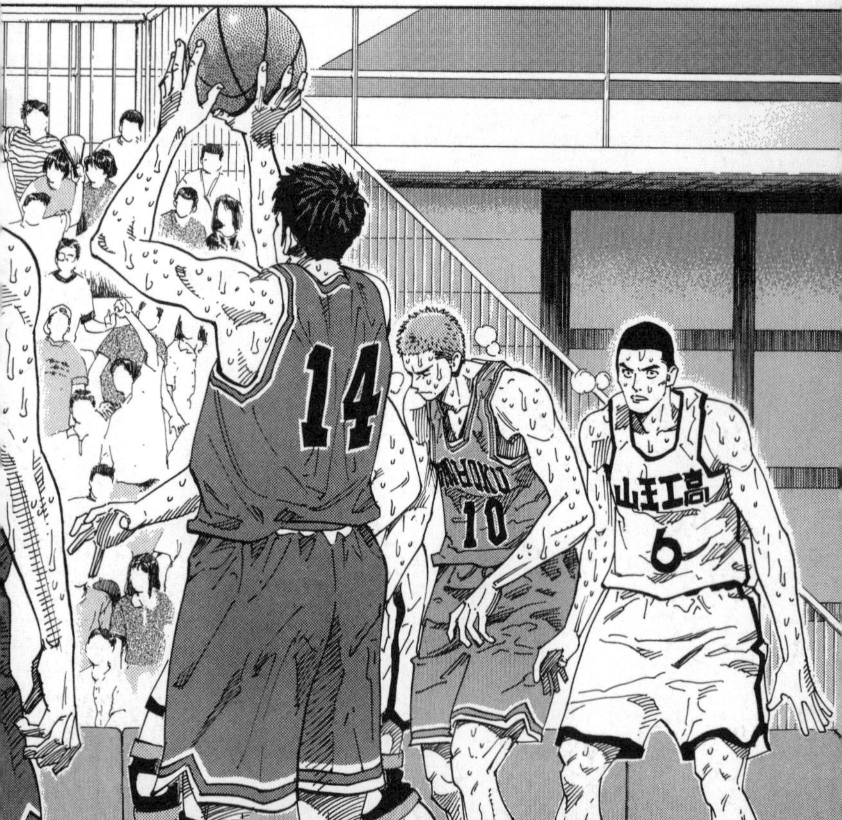
14
10
山王工高
6

READ THIS WAY

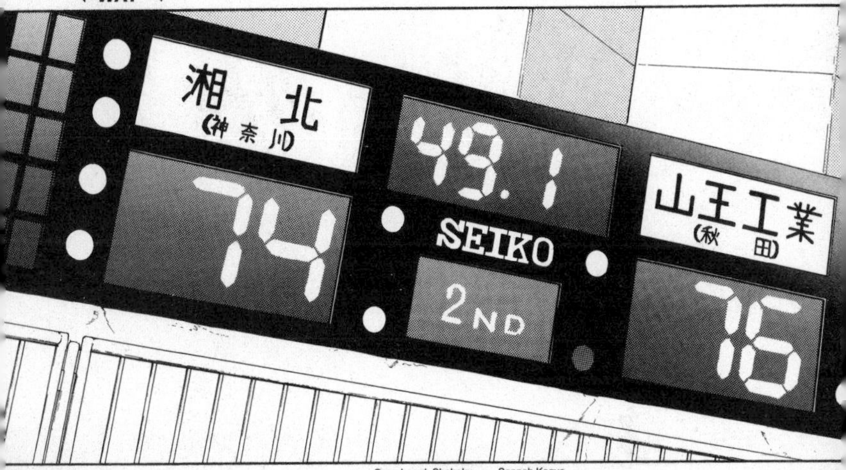
湘北
(神奈川)
74
49.1
SEIKO
2ND
山王工業
(秋田)
76

Scoreboard: Shohoku (Kanagawa) Sannoh Kogyo (Akita)

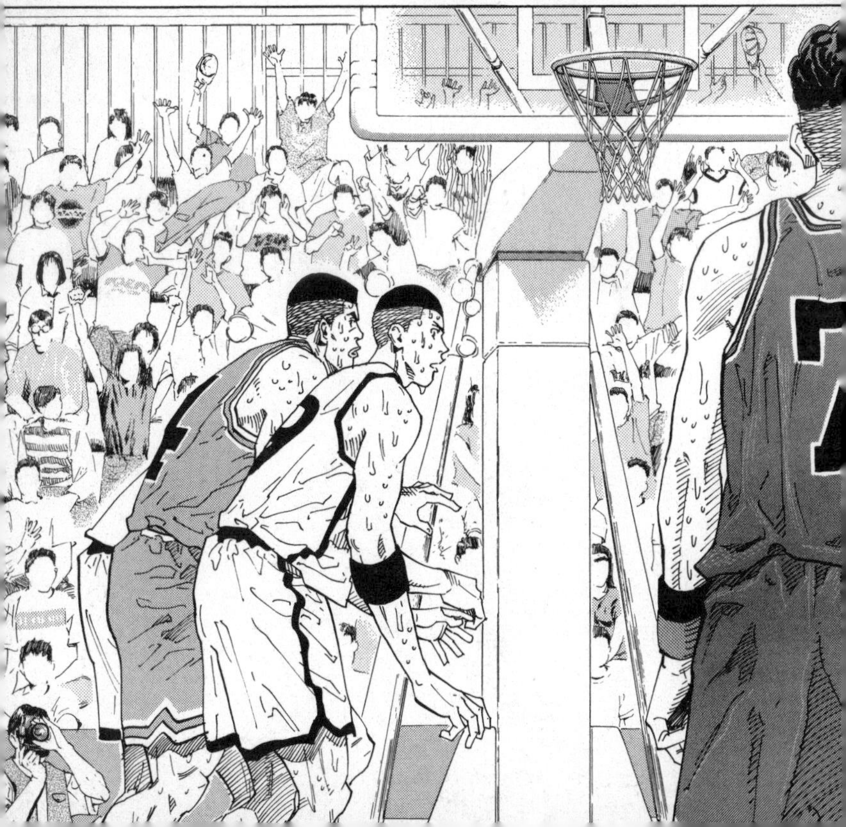

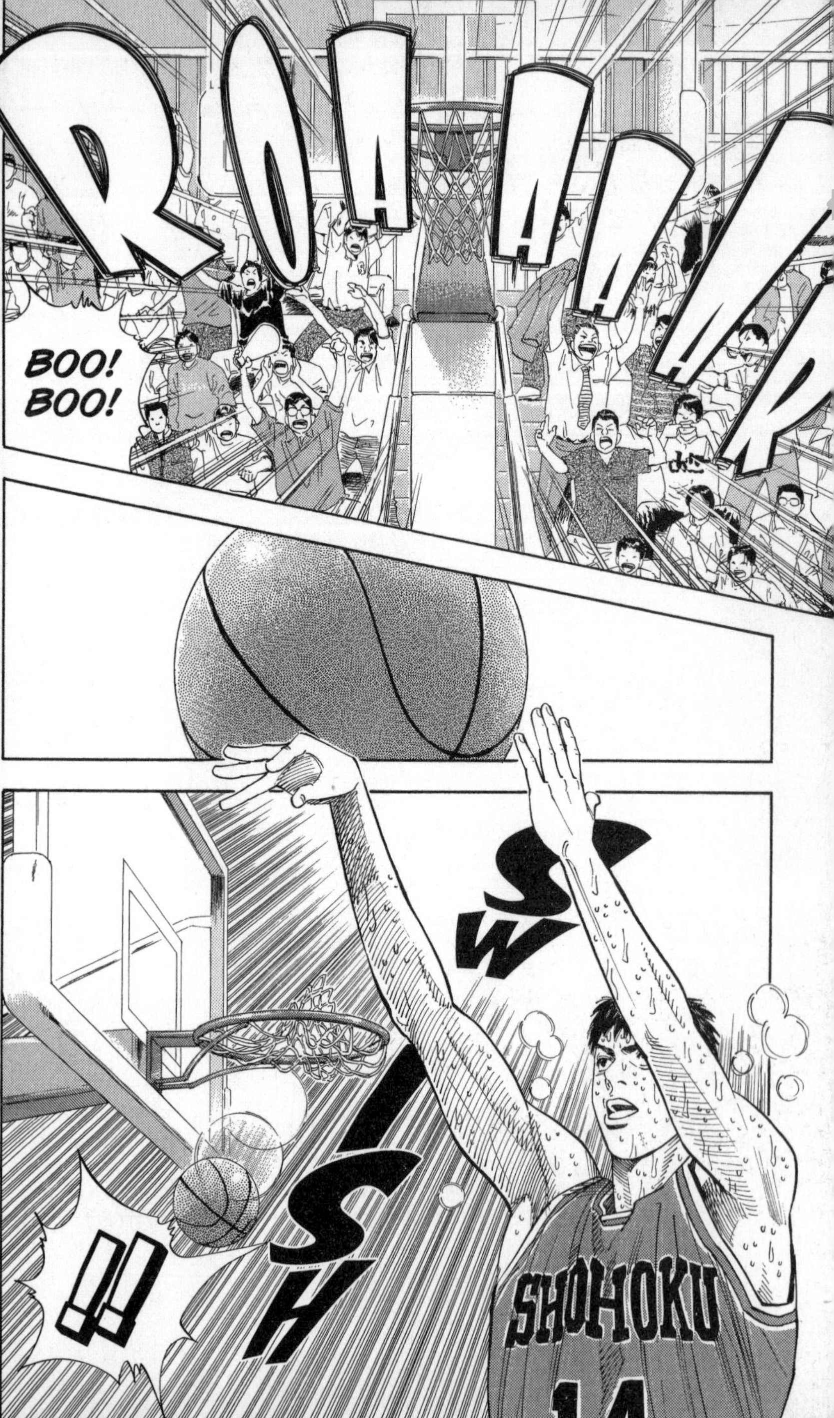
ROAAAR
BOO!
BOO!
SWISH
!!
SHOHOKU

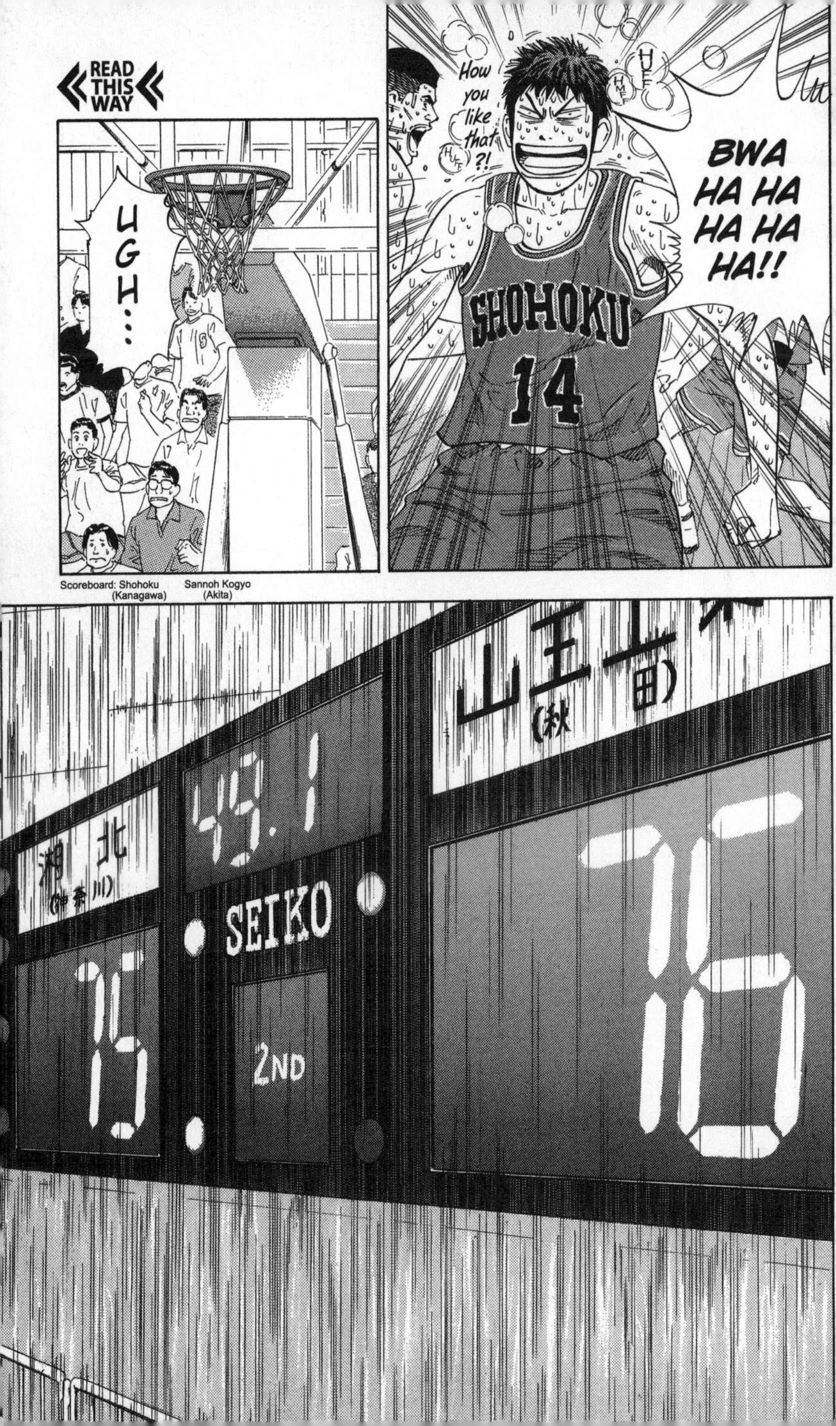
READ THIS WAY
How you like that?!
HUF HMF HUF
BWA HA HA HA HA HA!!
UGH...
Scoreboard: Shohoku (Kanagawa) Sannoh Kogyo (Akita)
SEIKO
2ND

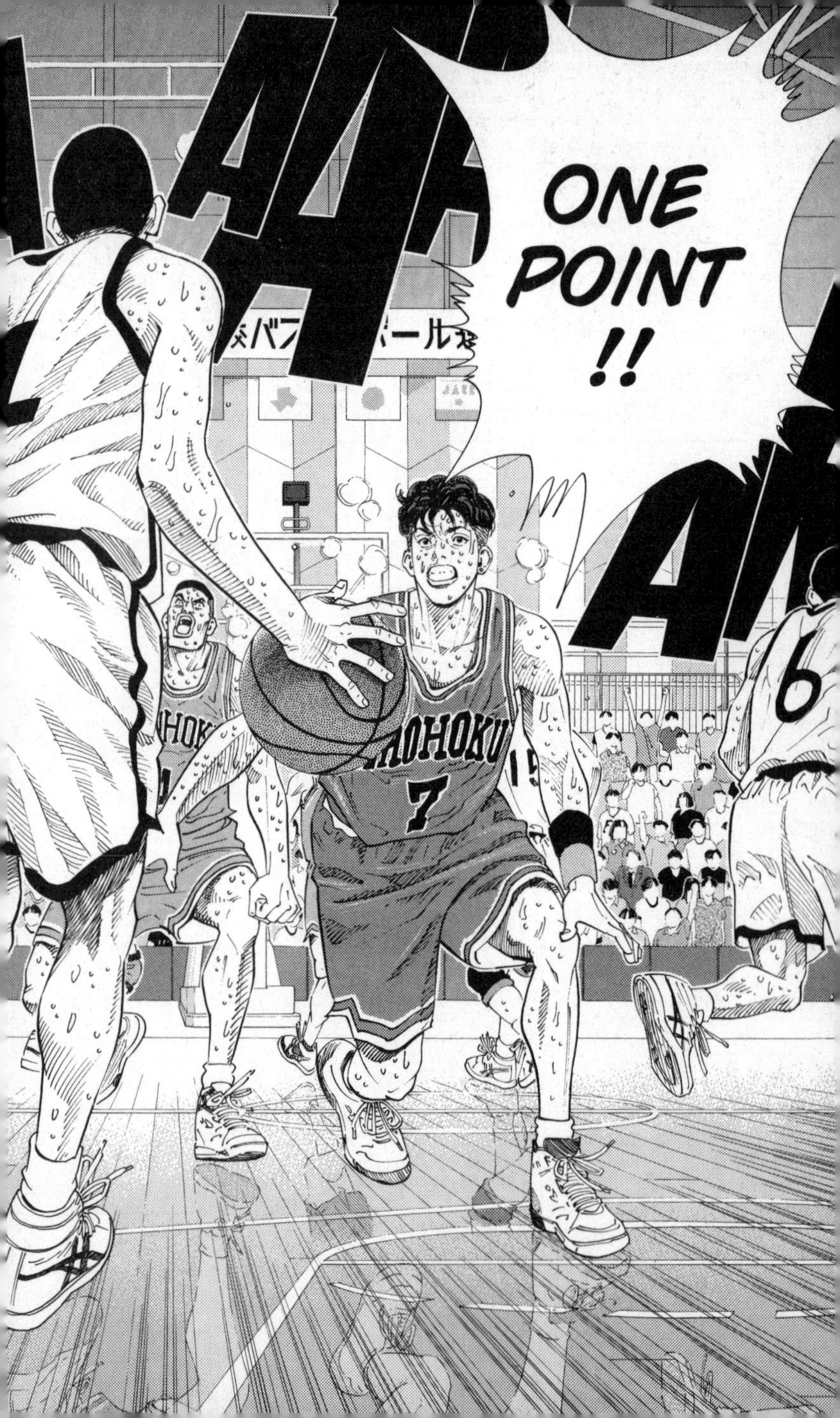
ONE POINT !!

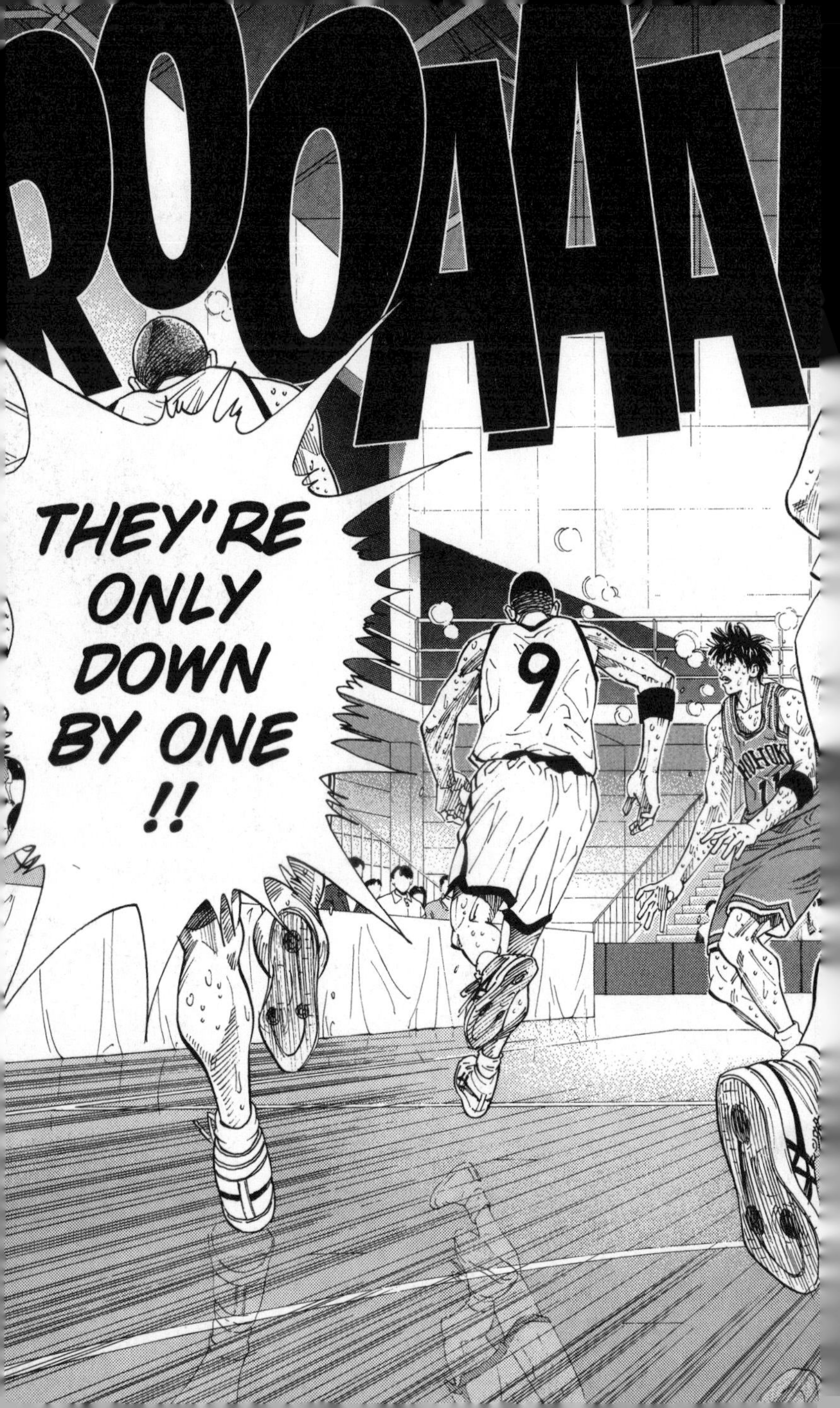
ROOAAA
THEY'RE ONLY DOWN BY ONE !!

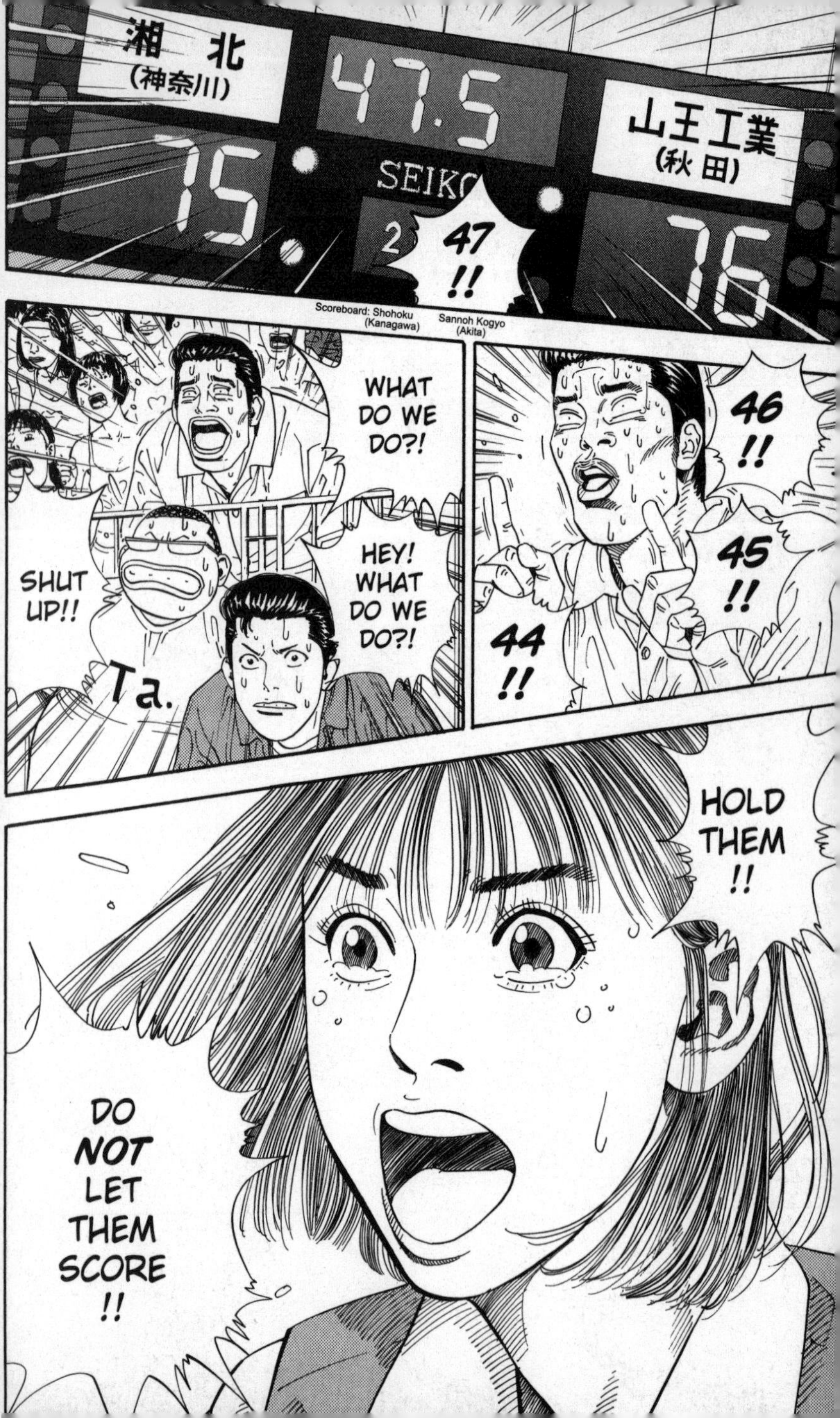
湘北
(神奈川)
47.5
山王工業
(秋田)
75
SEIKO
2
76
47 !!
Scoreboard: Shohoku (Kanagawa) Sannoh Kogyo (Akita)
46 !!
45 !!
44 !!
WHAT DO WE DO?!
HEY! WHAT DO WE DO?!
SHUT UP!!
Ta.
HOLD THEM !!
DO NOT LET THEM SCORE !!

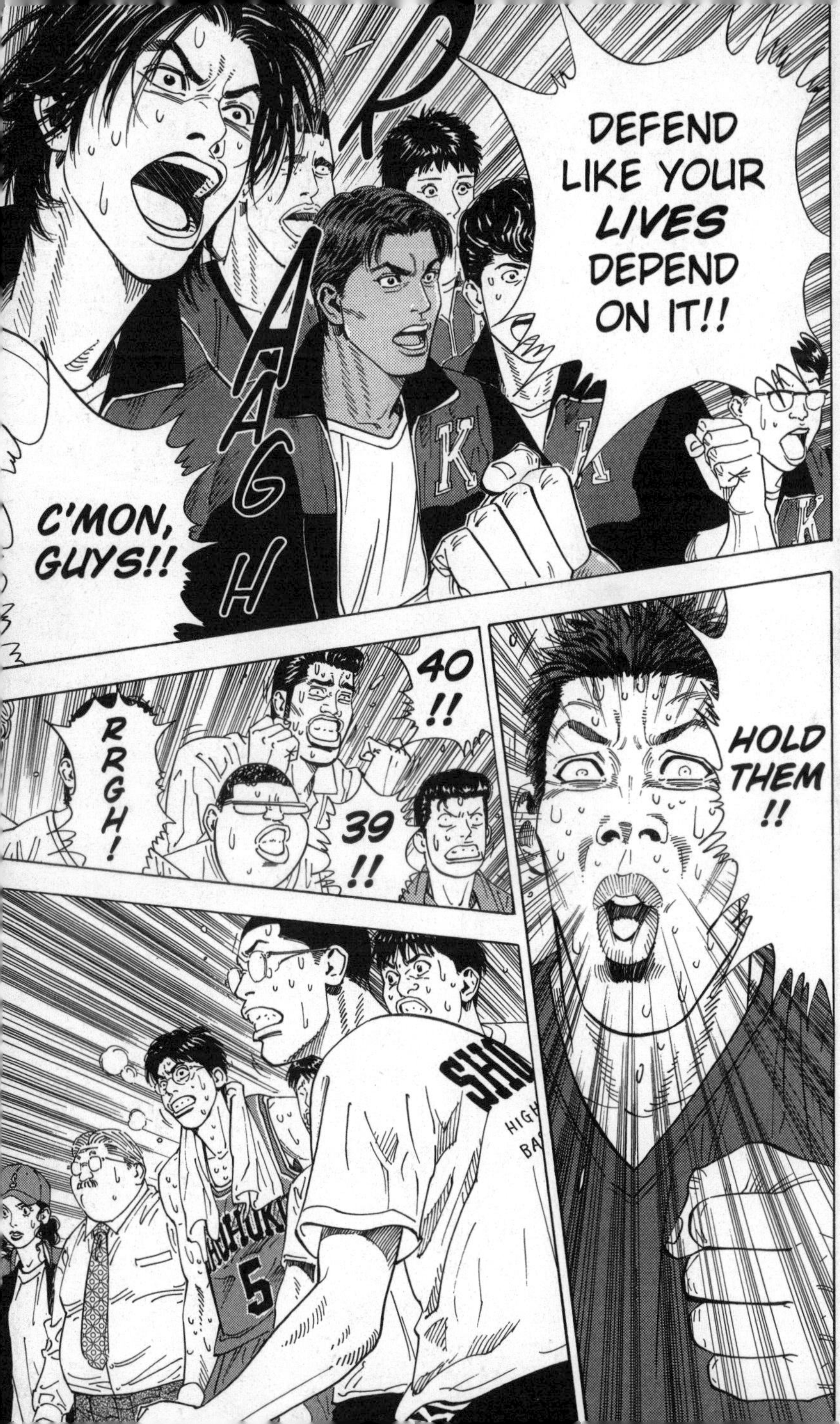
DEFEND LIKE YOUR LIVES DEPEND ON IT!!
RAAGH
C'MON, GUYS!!
HOLD THEM!!
40!!
RRGH!
39!!

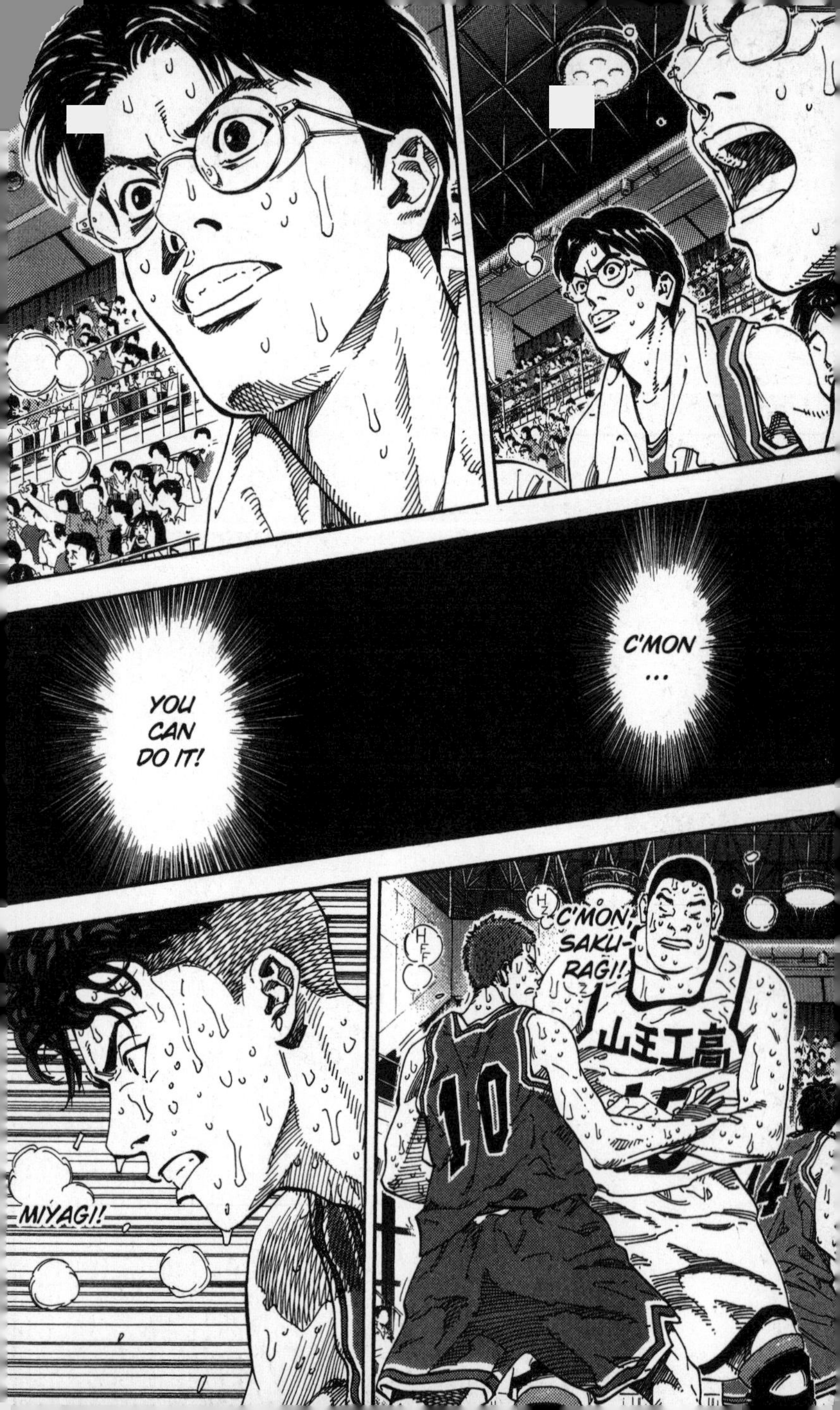
C'MON...
YOU CAN DO IT!
HFF
C'MON, SAKU-RAGI!!
山王工高
MIYAGI!

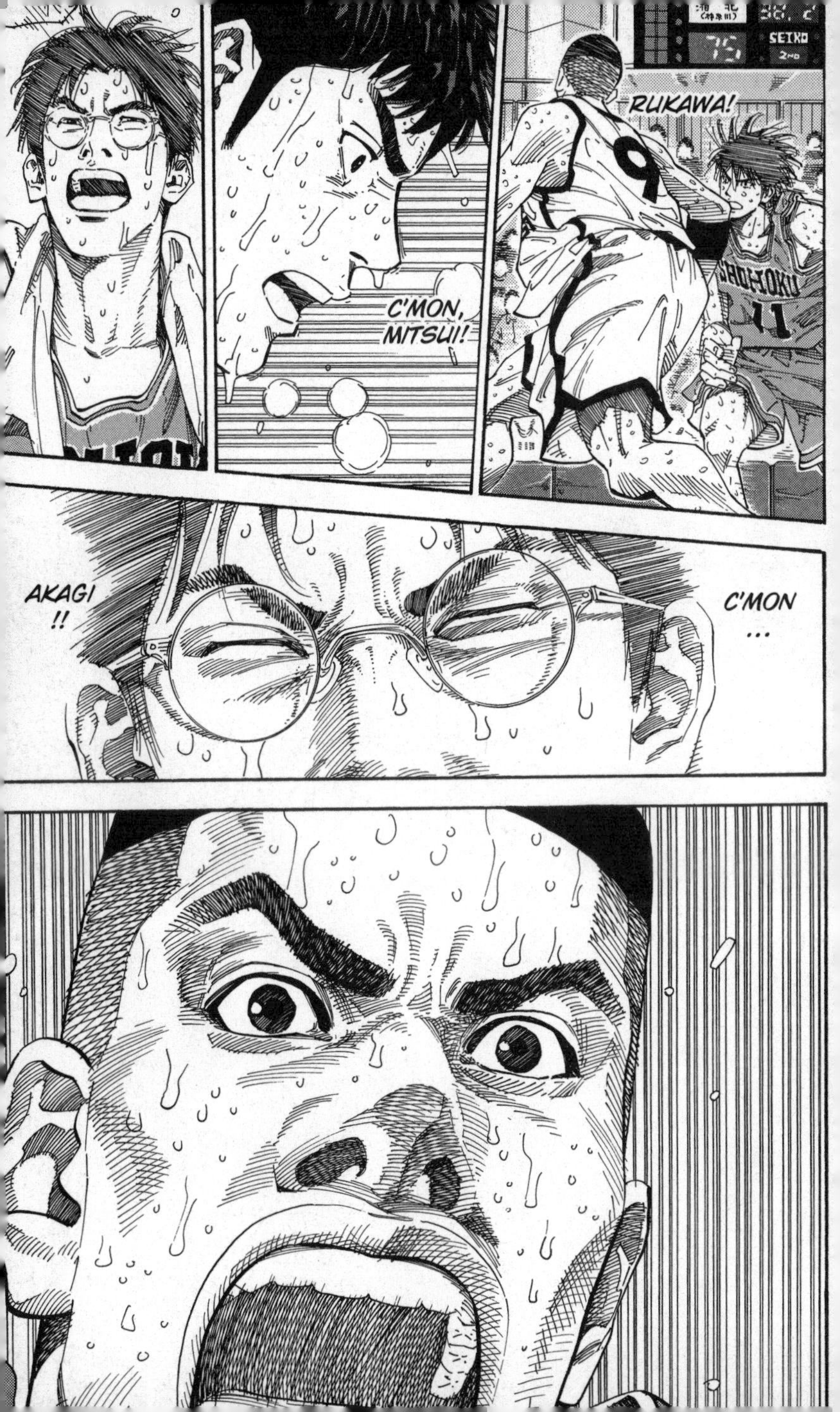
RUKAWA!
C'MON, MITSUI!
C'MON ...
AKAGI !!

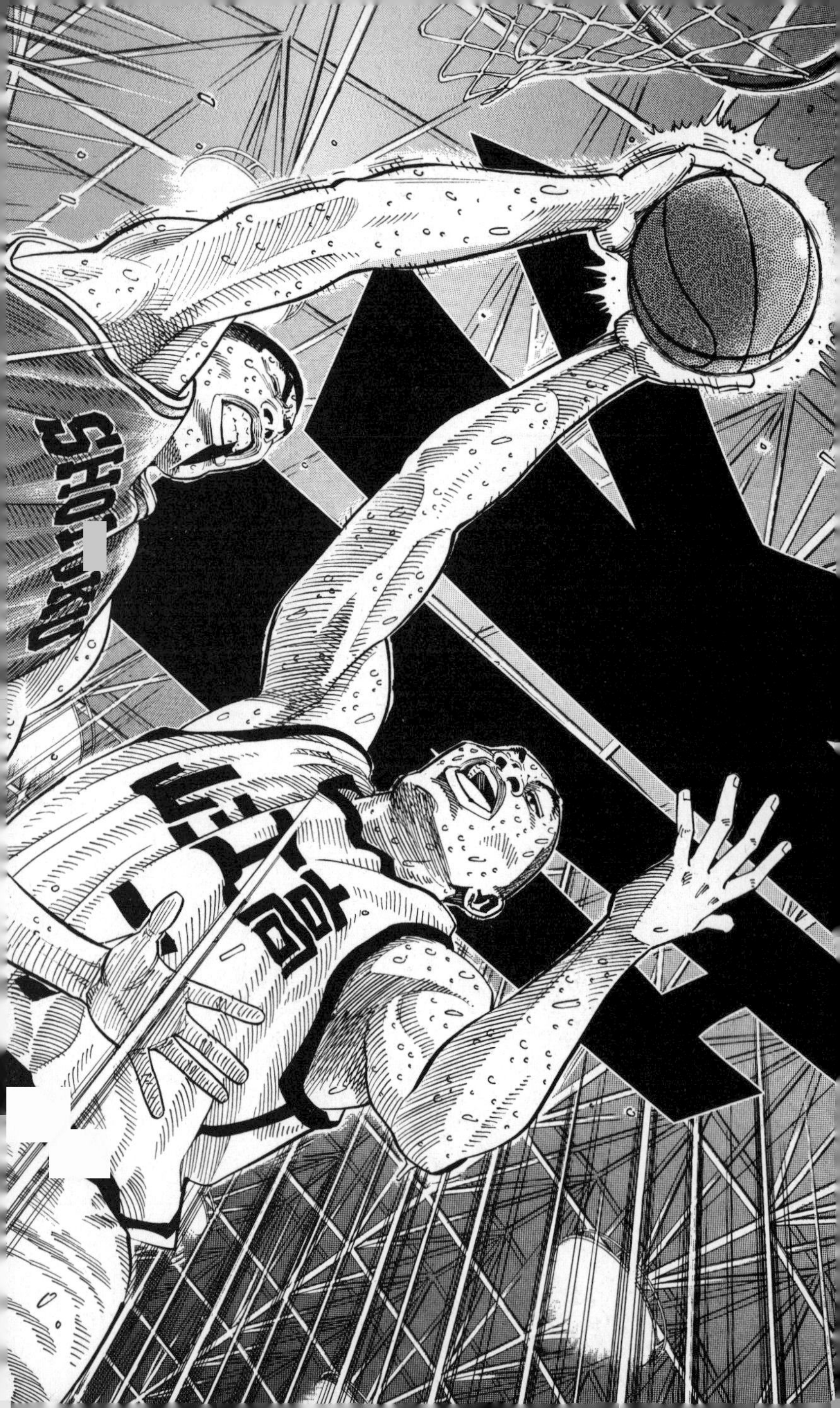

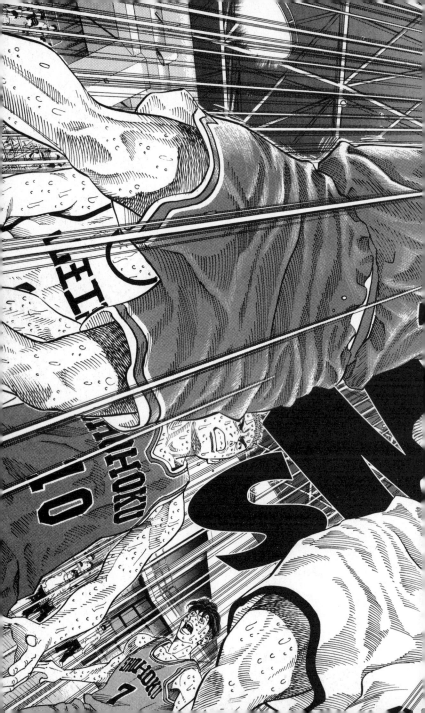

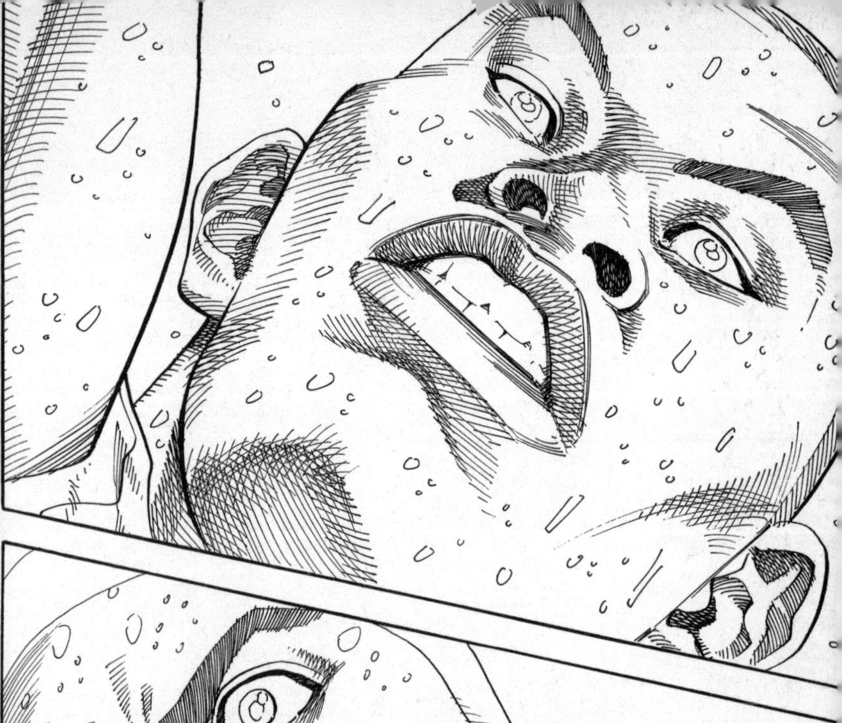
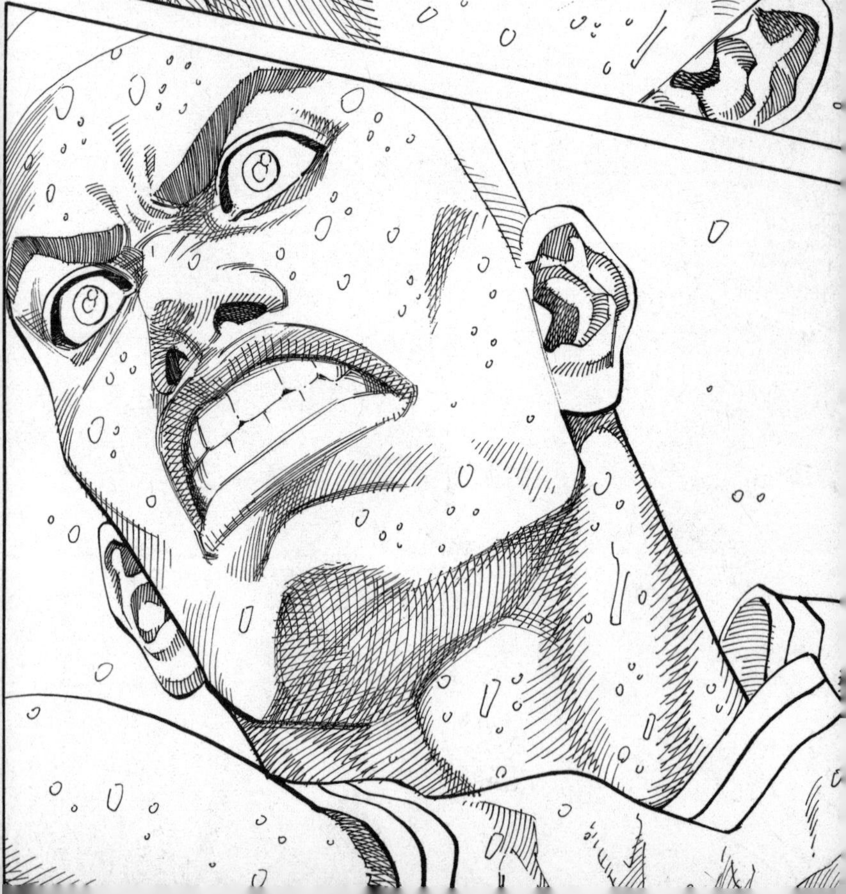

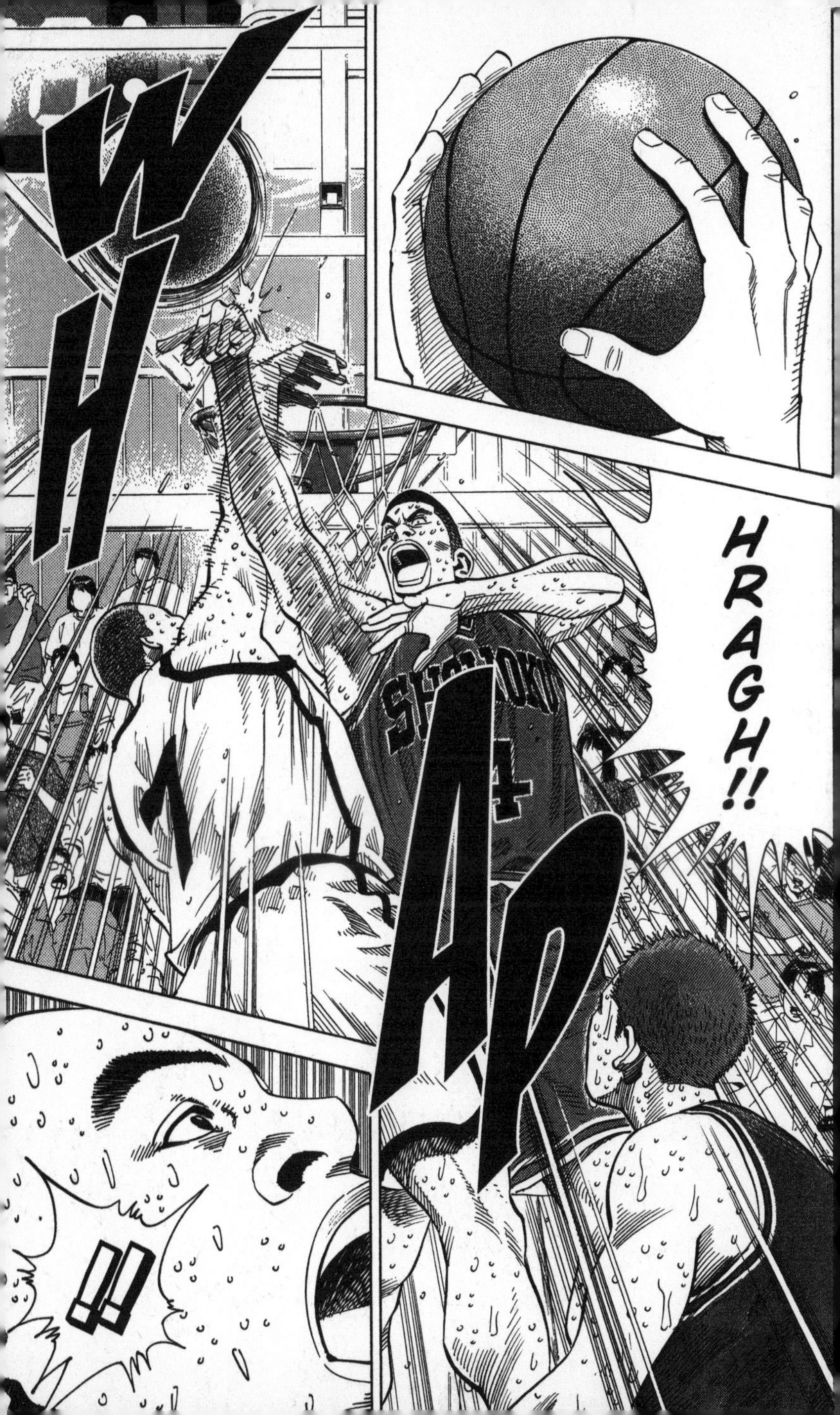
HRAGH!!
!!

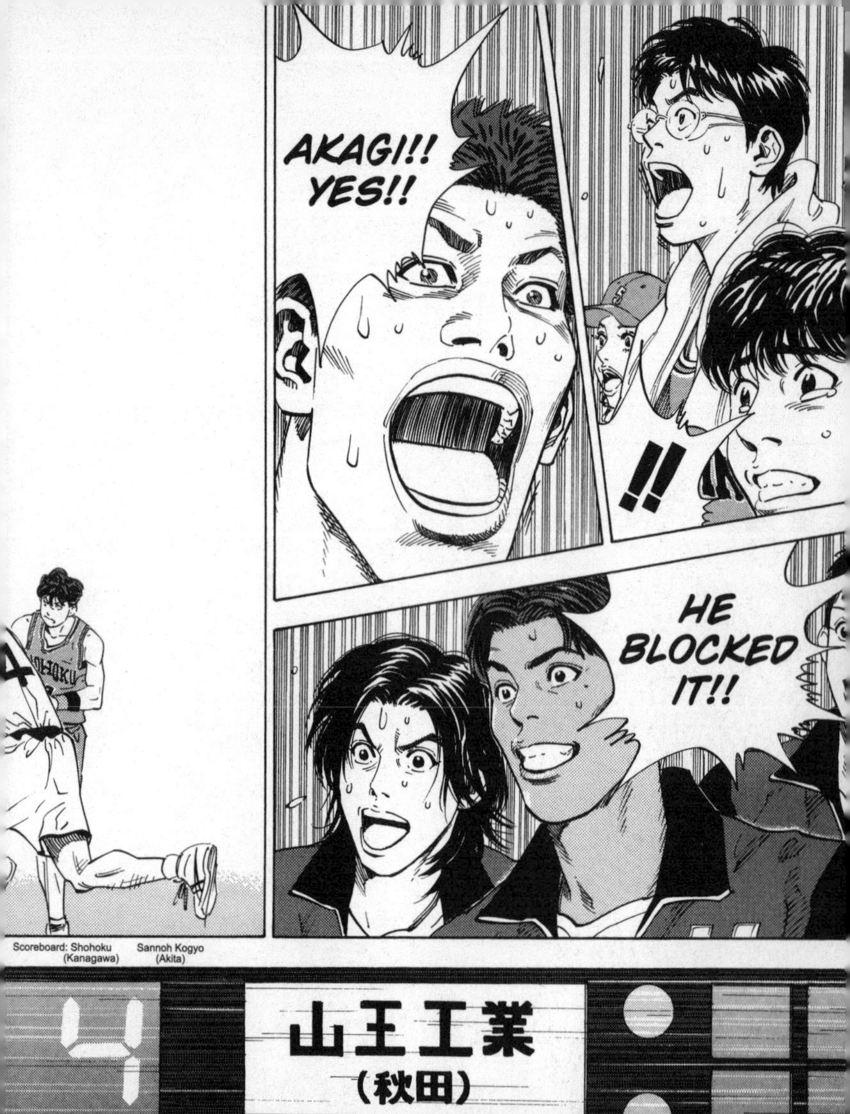
!!
AKAGI!! YES!!
HE BLOCKED IT!!

Scoreboard: Shohoku (Kanagawa) Sannoh Kogyo (Akita)

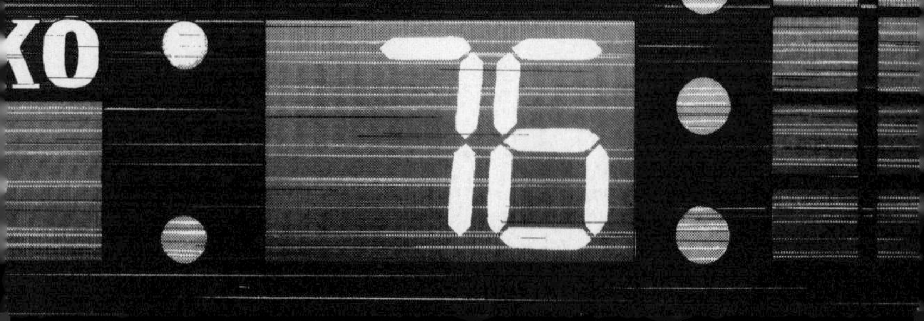
山王工業
(秋田)
76

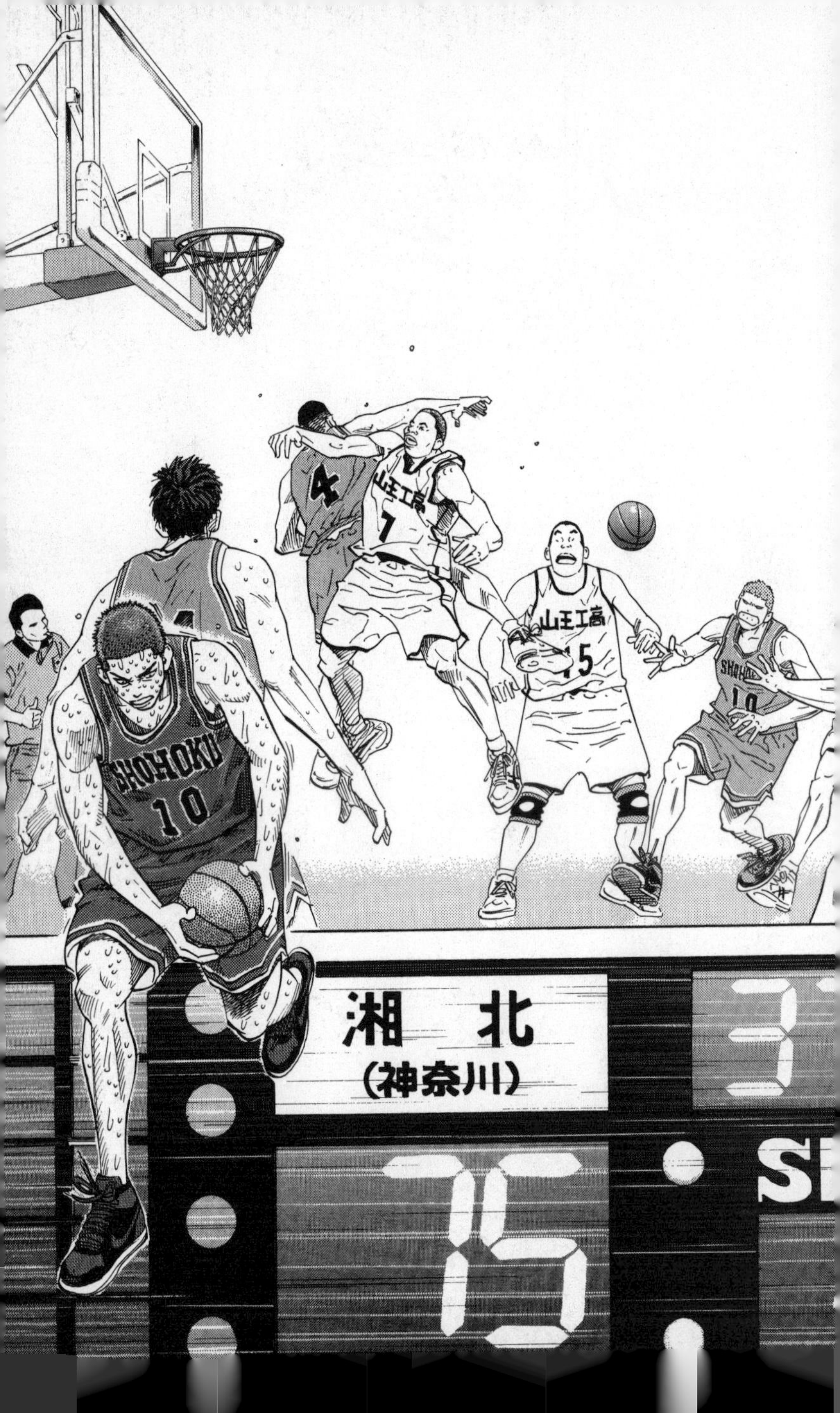
山王工高
山王工高
SHOHOKU
湘北
(神奈川)
75

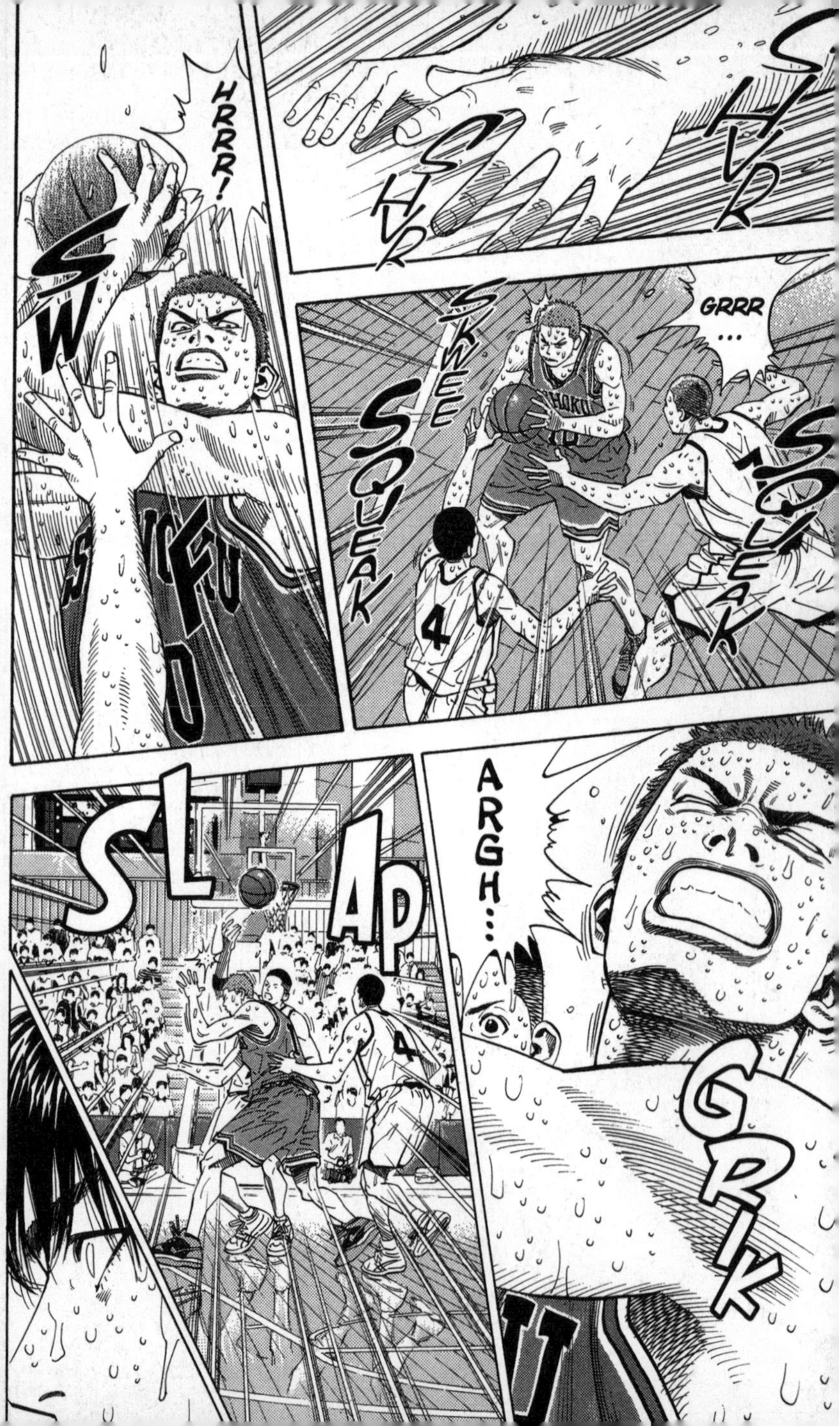

SHVR
SHVR
HRRR!
SW
GRRR ...
SQUEAK
SKWEE
SQUEAK
ARGH...
GRIK
SL
AP

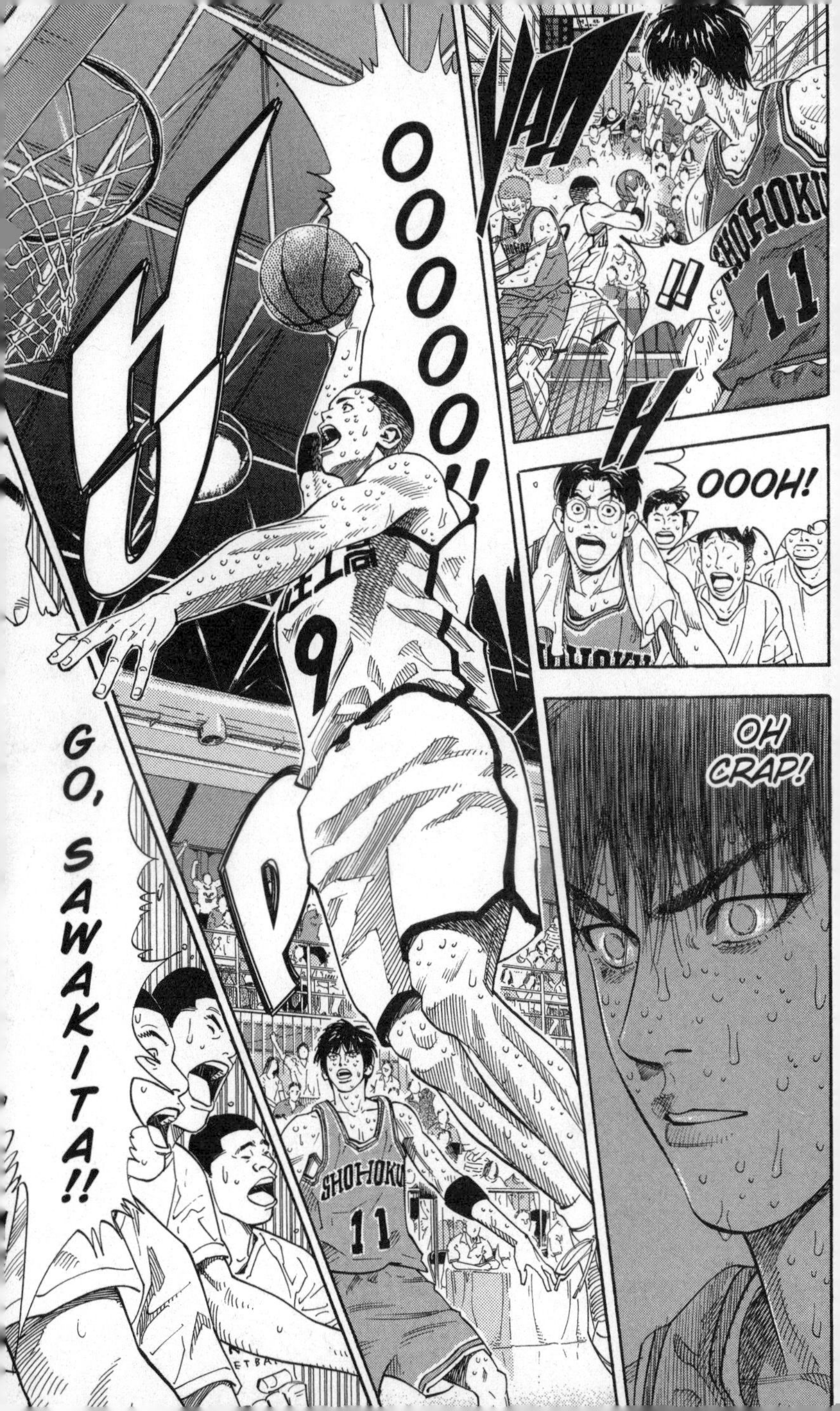

!!
OOOH!
OH CRAP!
OOOOOO!!
GO, SAWAKITA!!

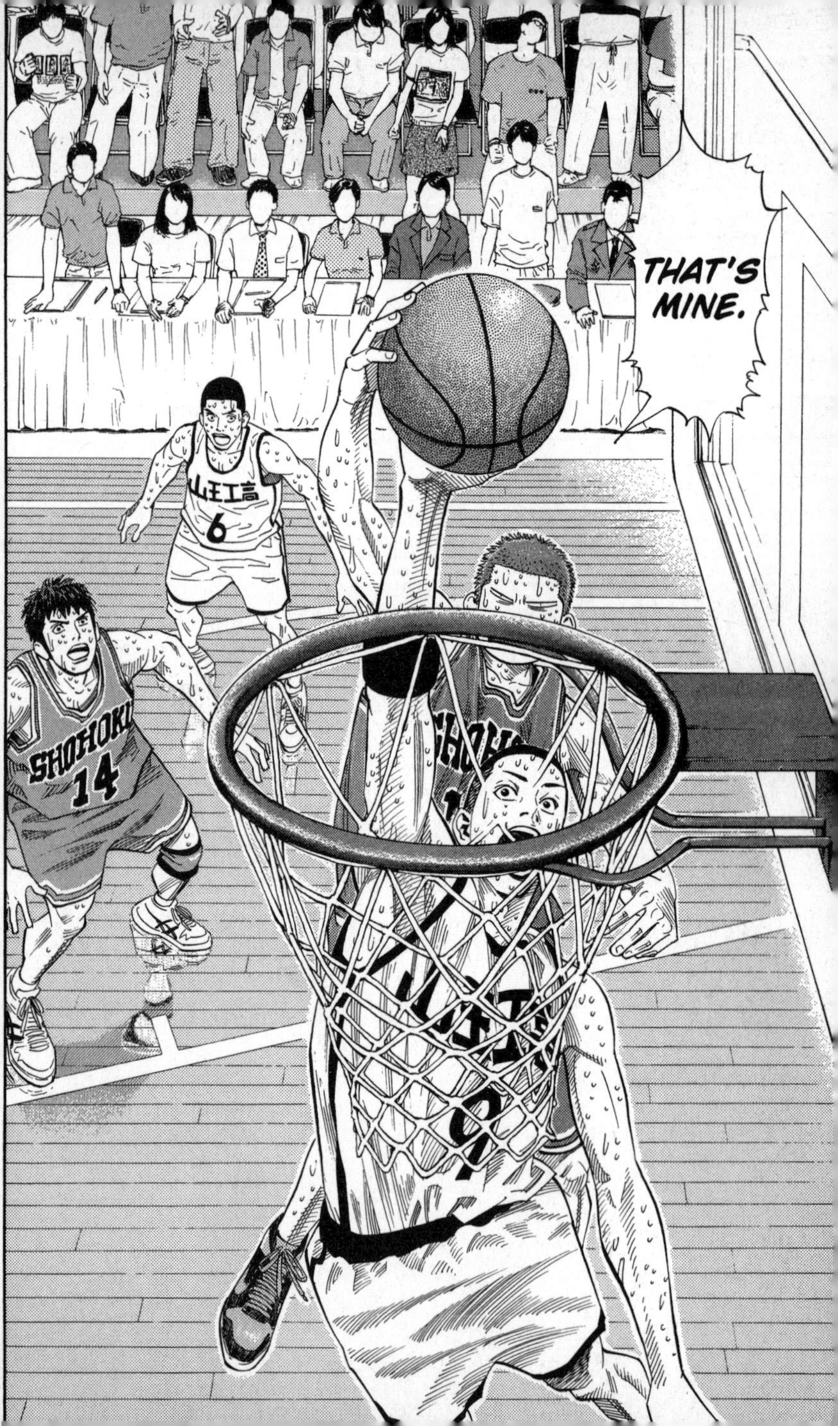
THAT'S
MINE.
山王工高
6
SHOHOKU
14

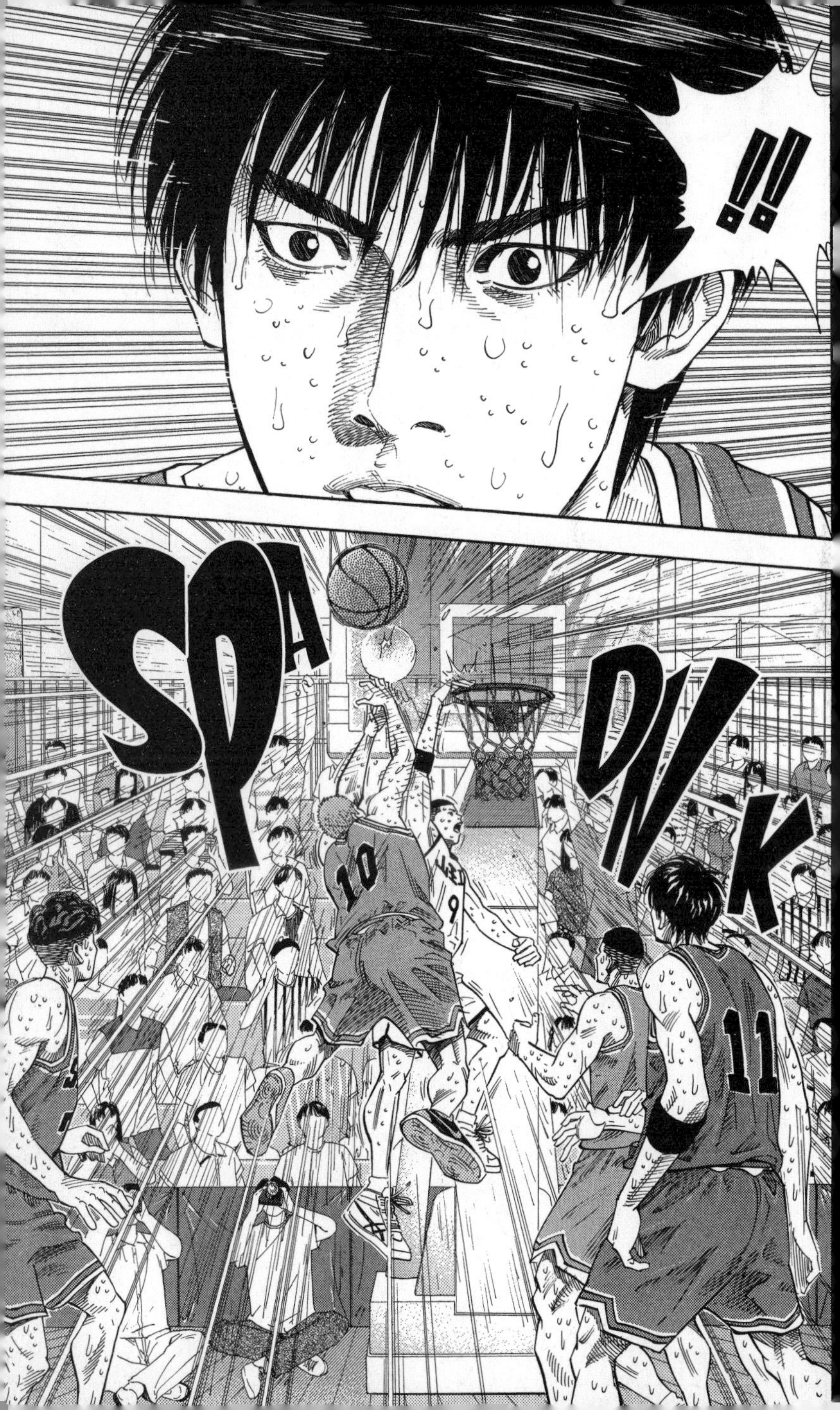
!!
SPA
DUNK

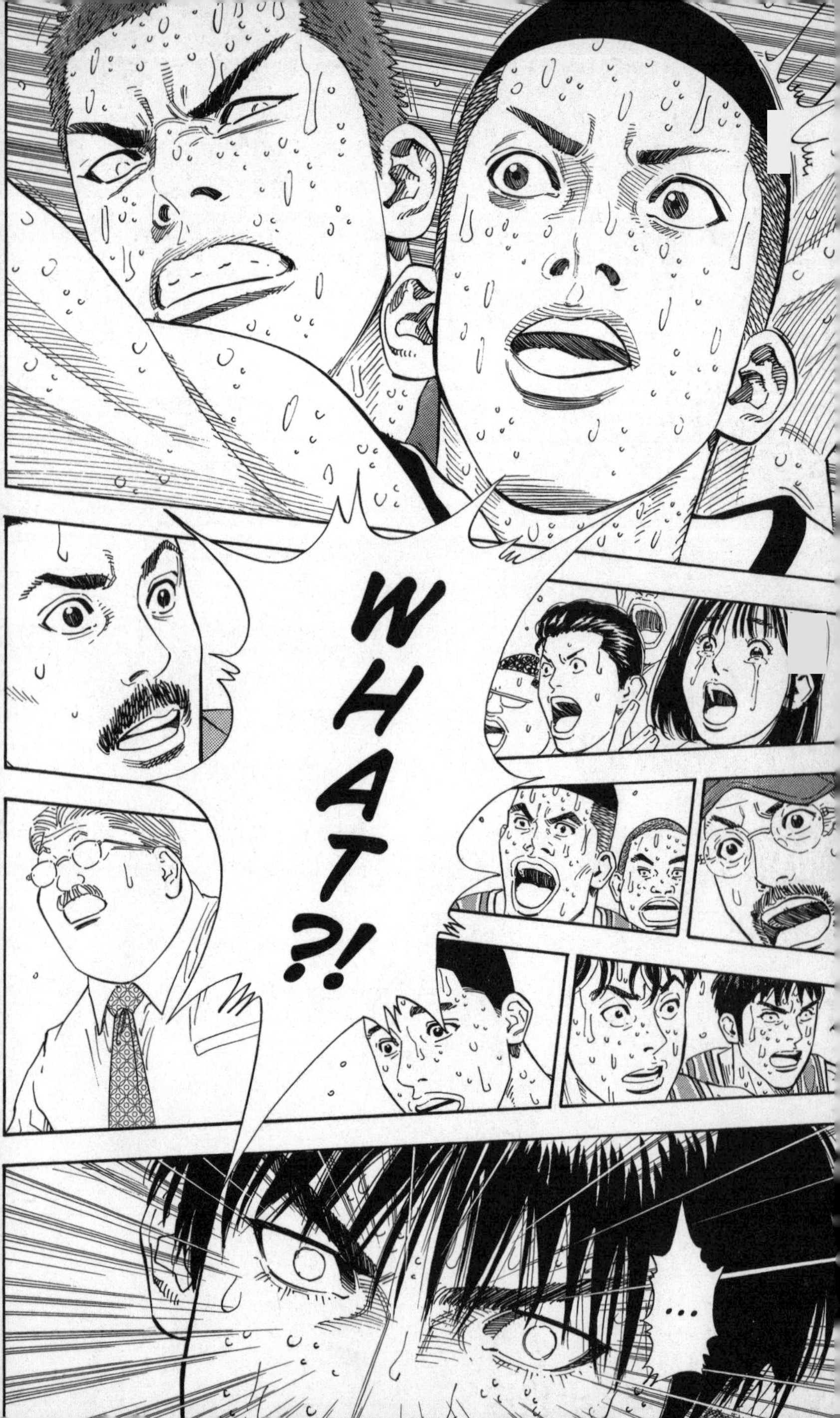
WHAT?!
...

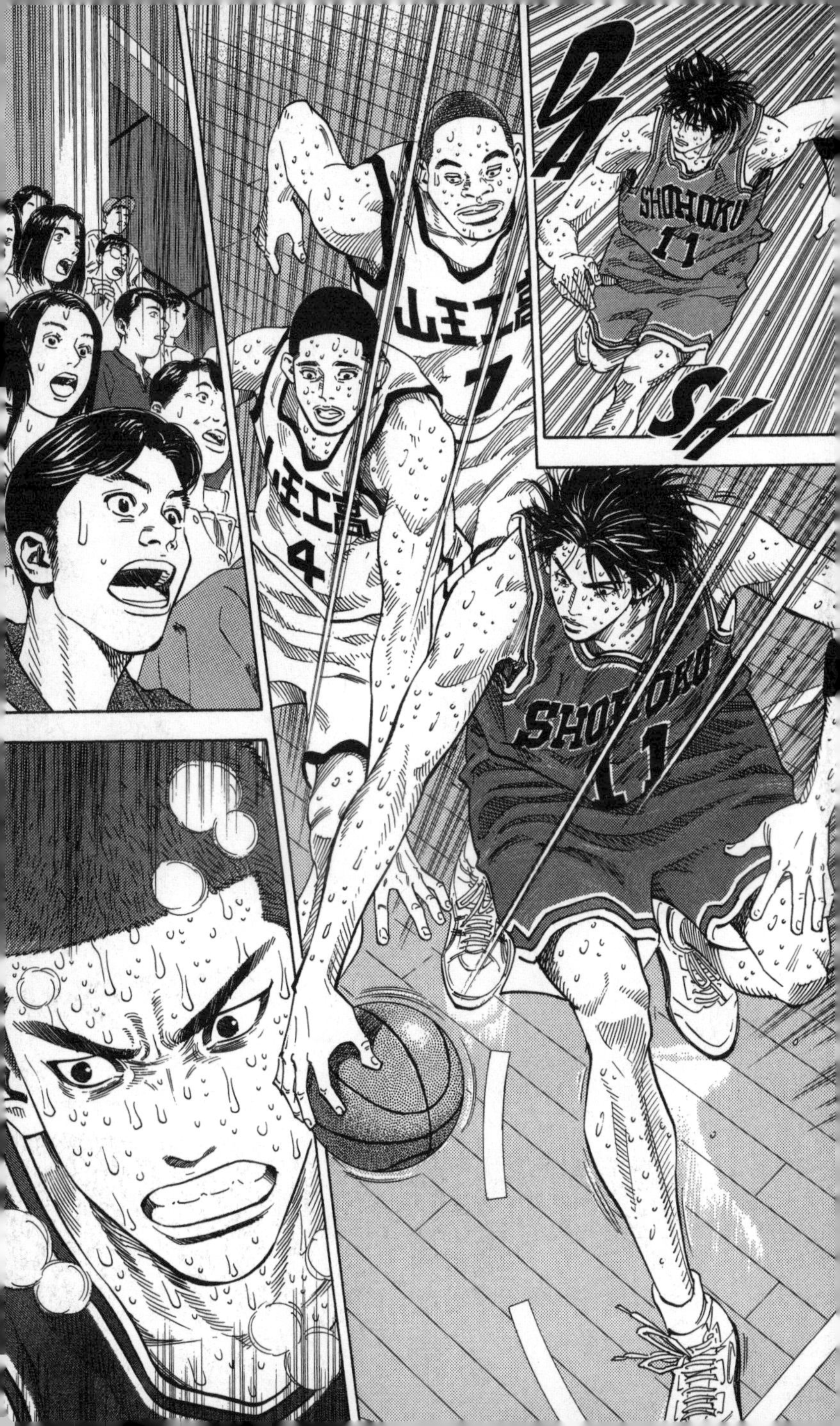
DA
SH

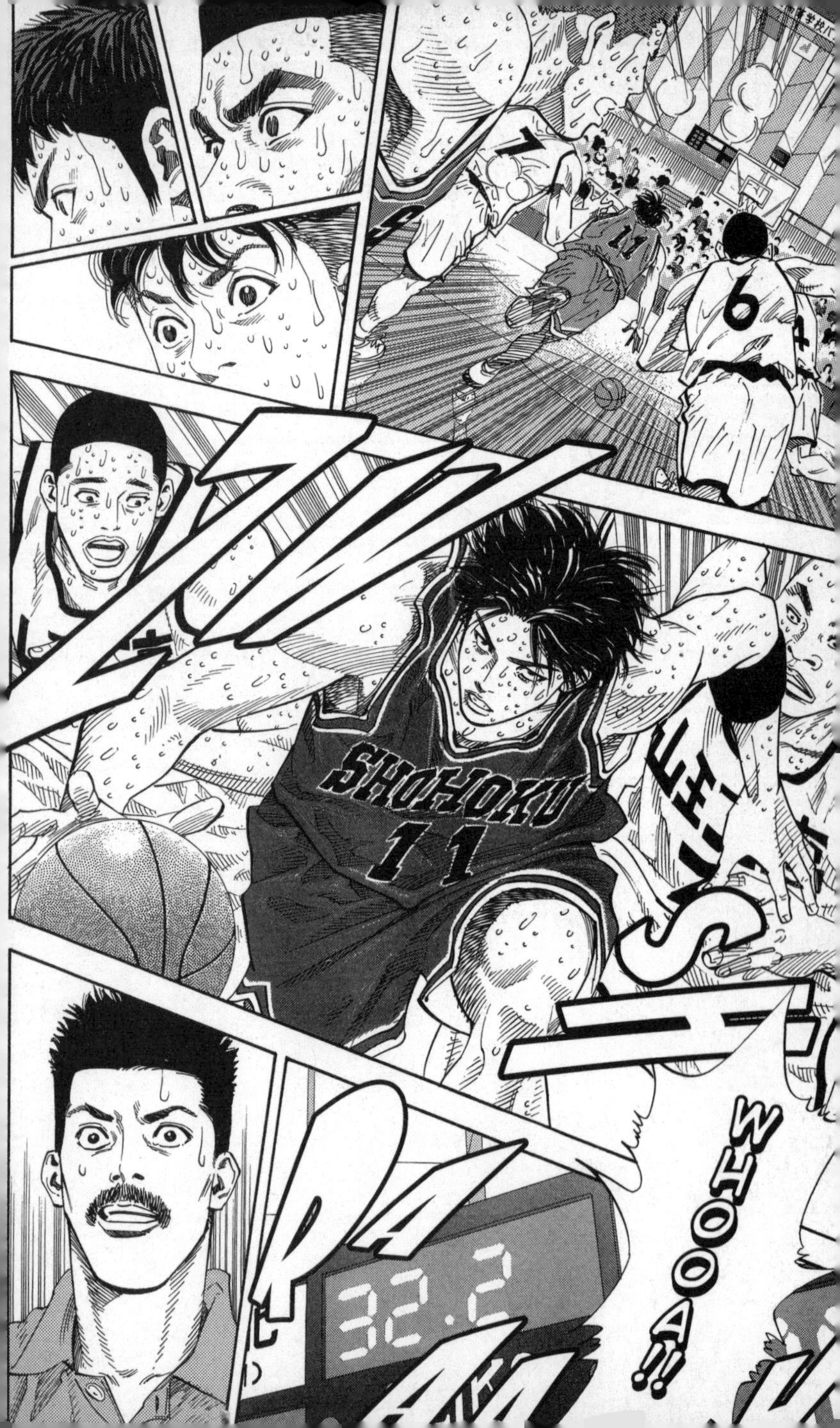
SHOHOKU
11
32.2
WHOOOA!!

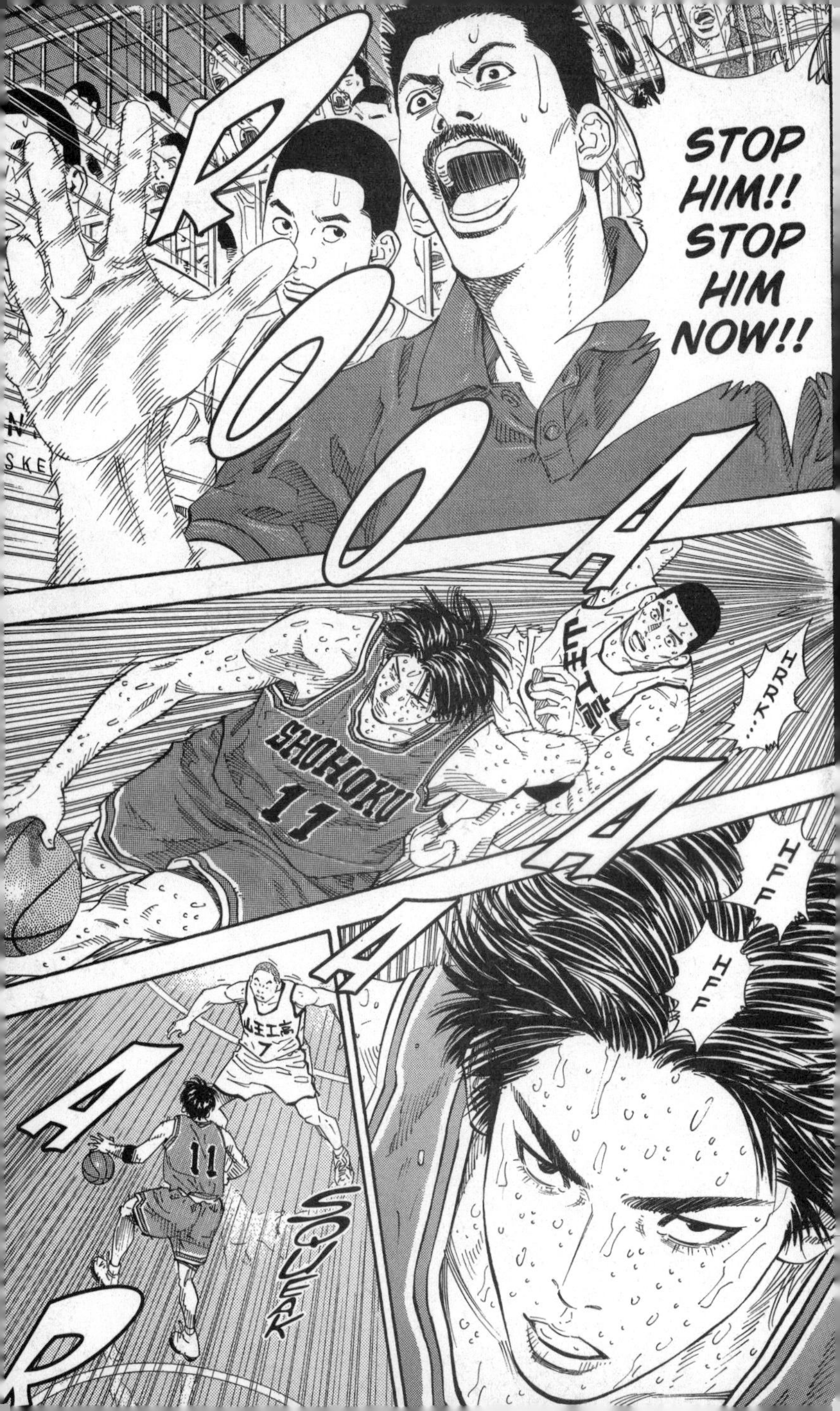
STOP HIM!! STOP HIM NOW!!
ROOAAAA
SHOHOKU
11
HRRK...
HFF HFF
山王工高
7
11
SQUEAK
R

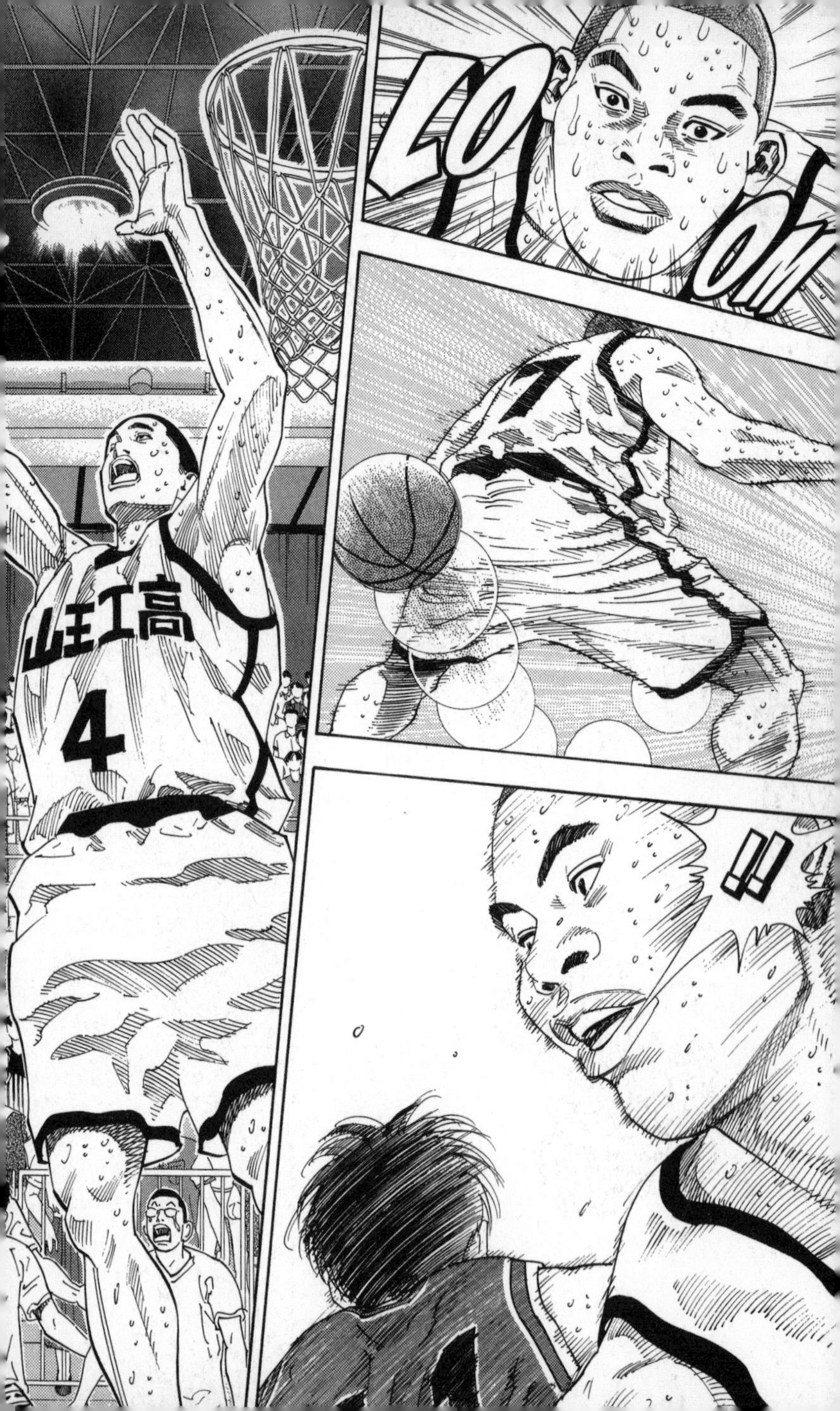
山王工高

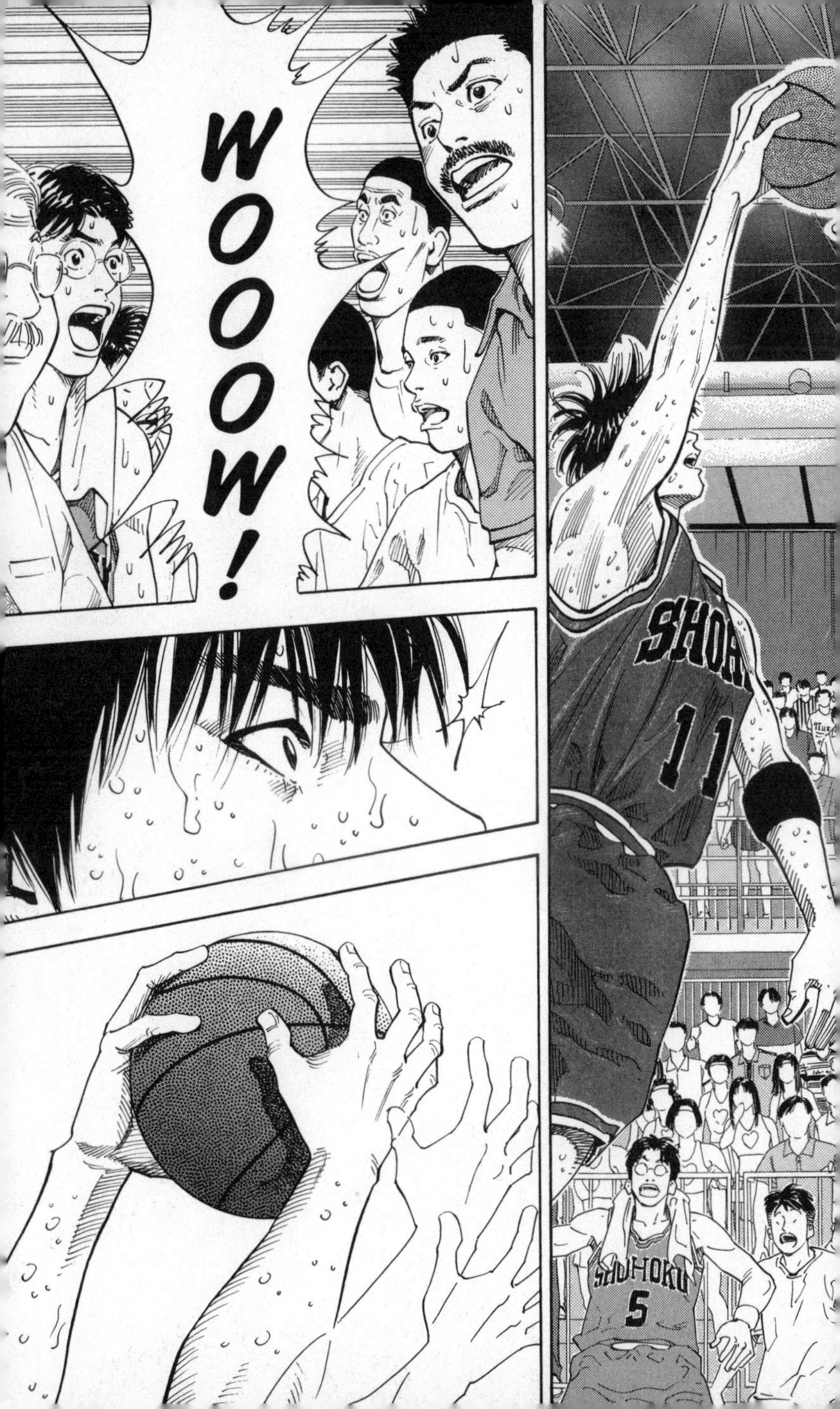

WOOOW!

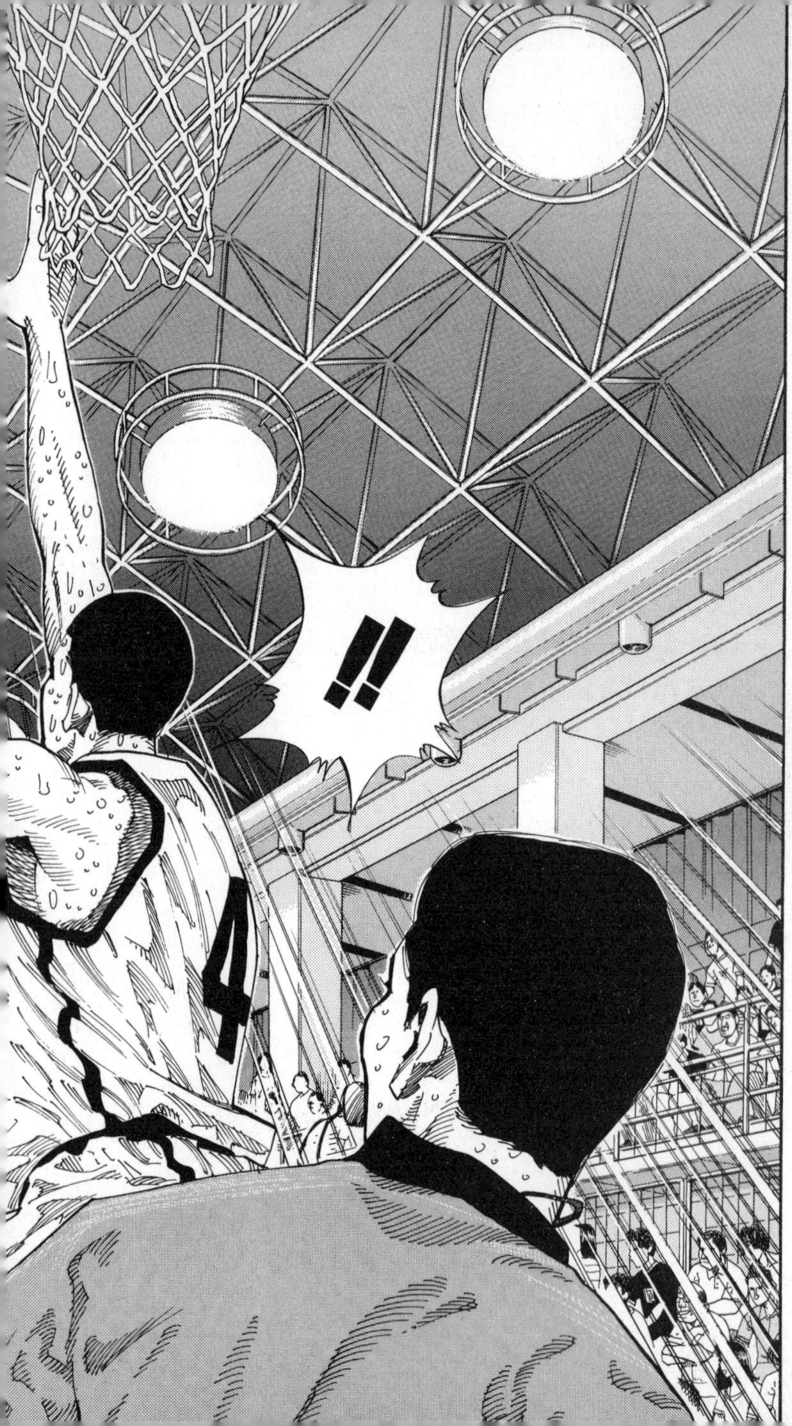
!!

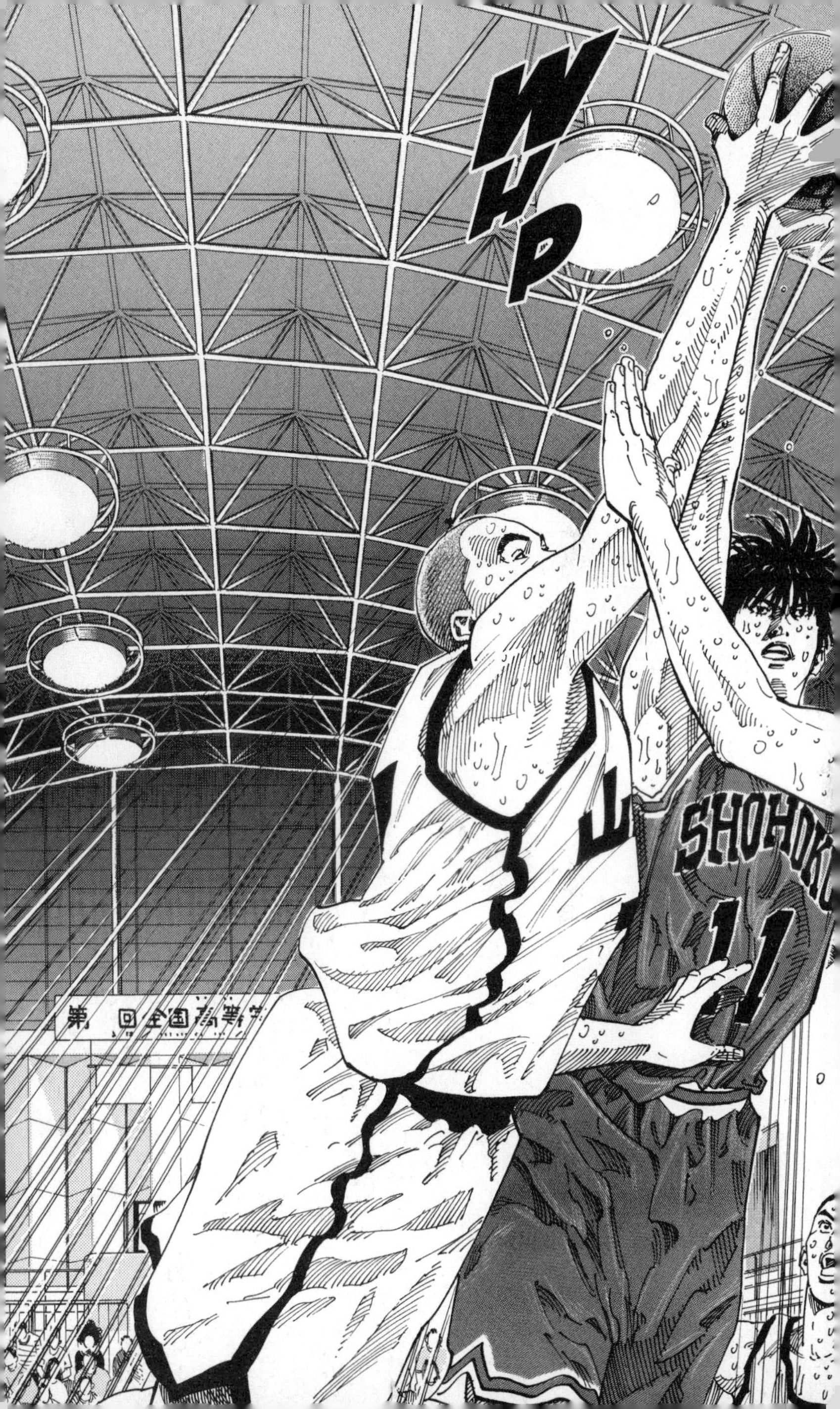
WHIP
SHOHOKU
11

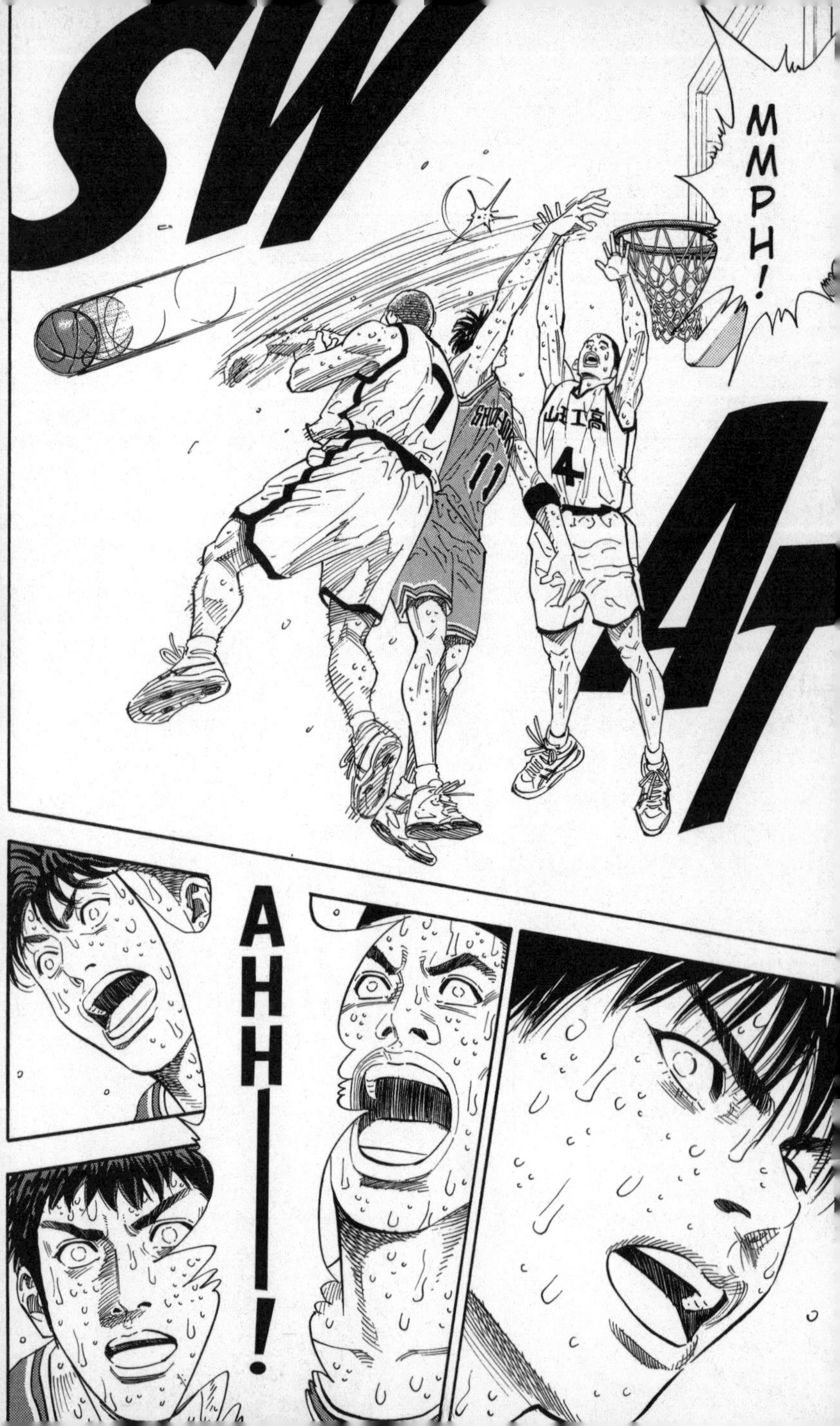SWAT
MMPH!
AHH!!

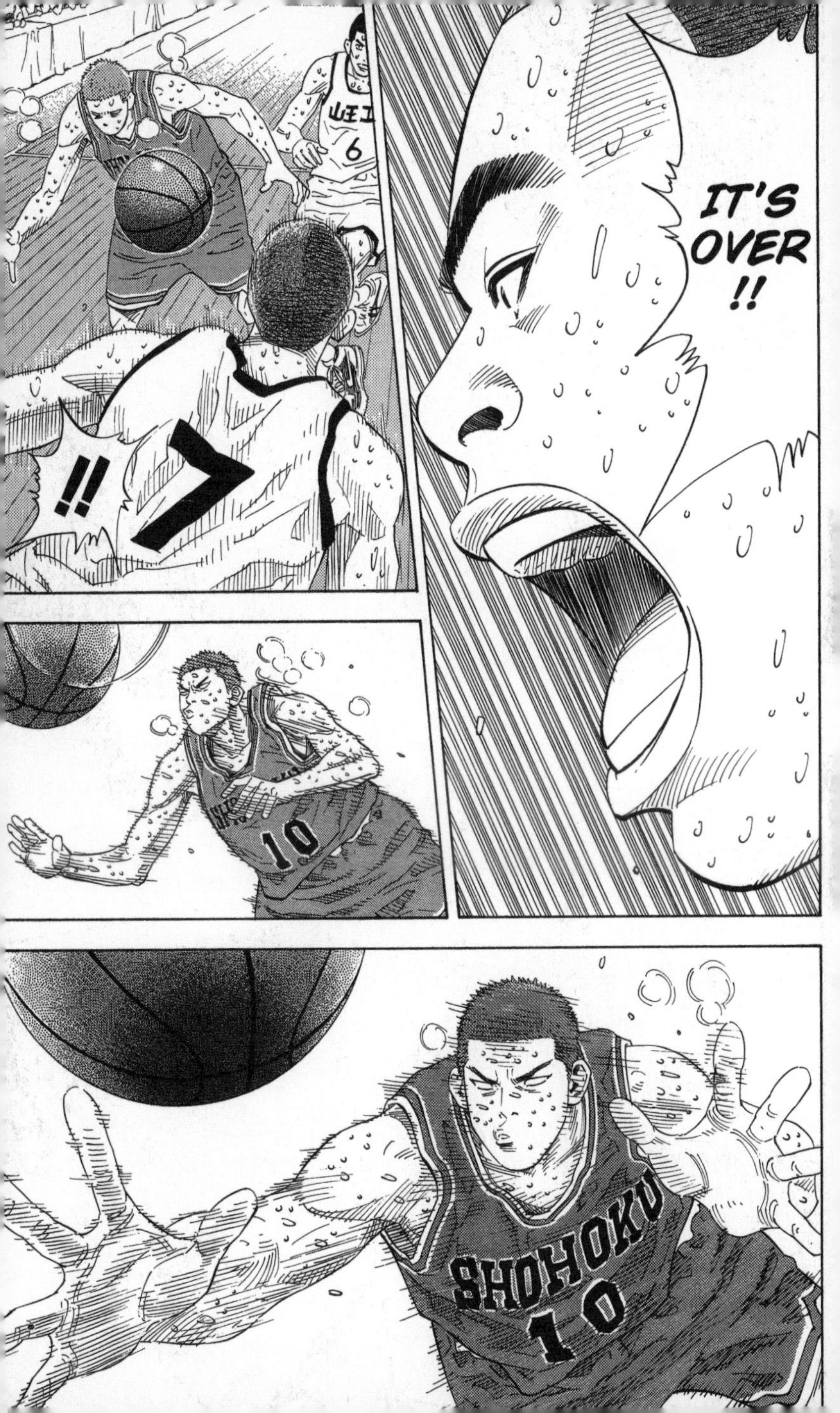
IT'S OVER !!
!!

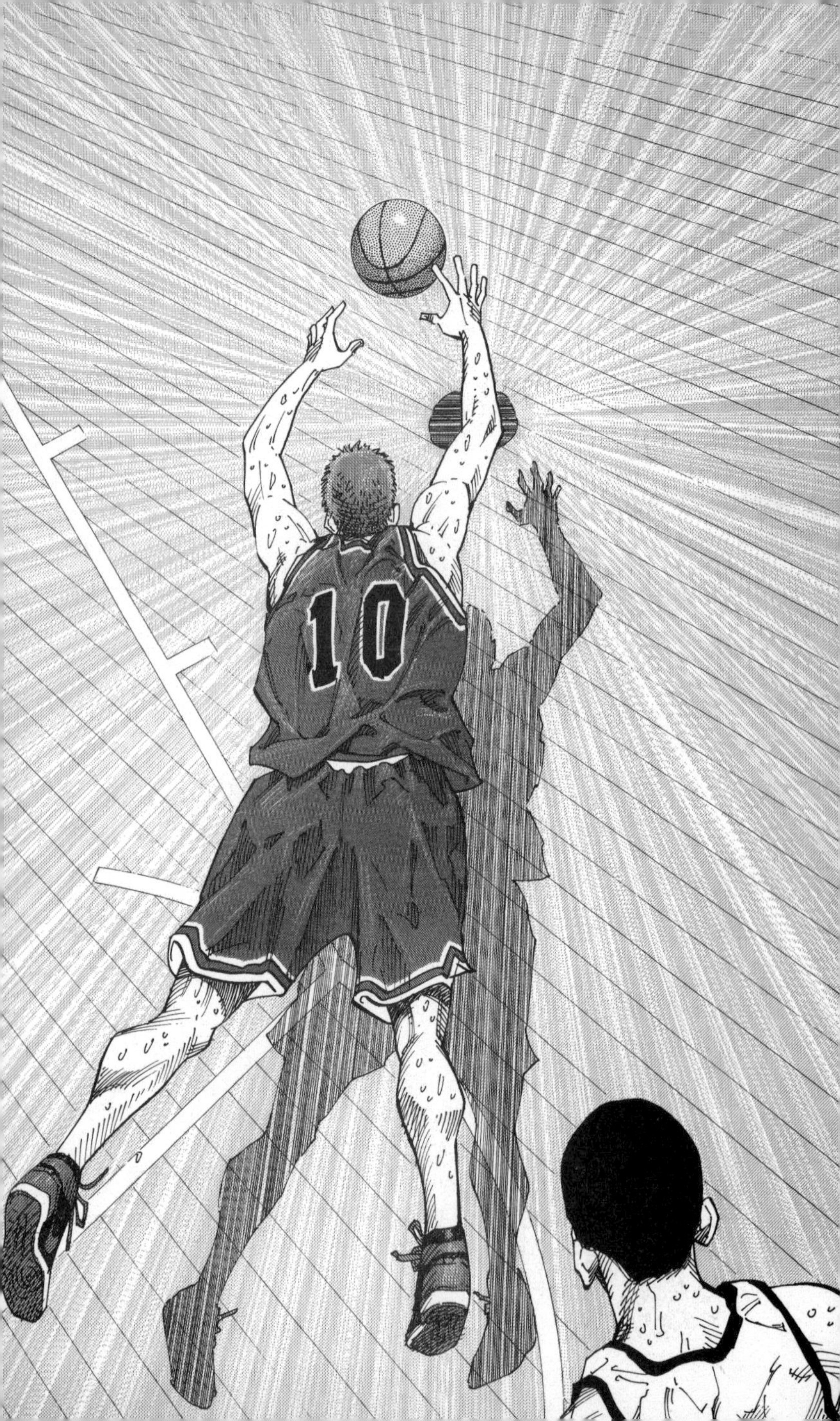

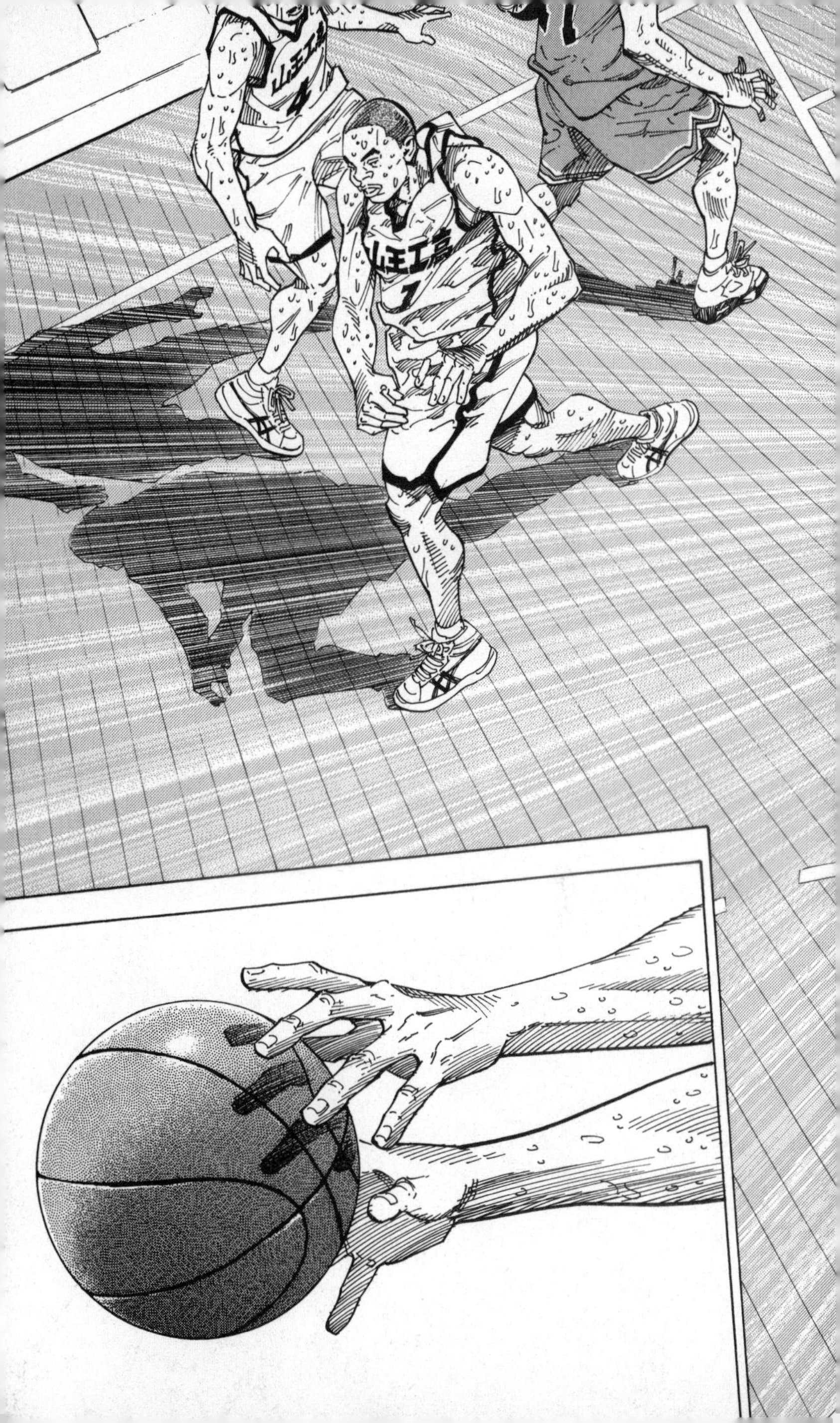

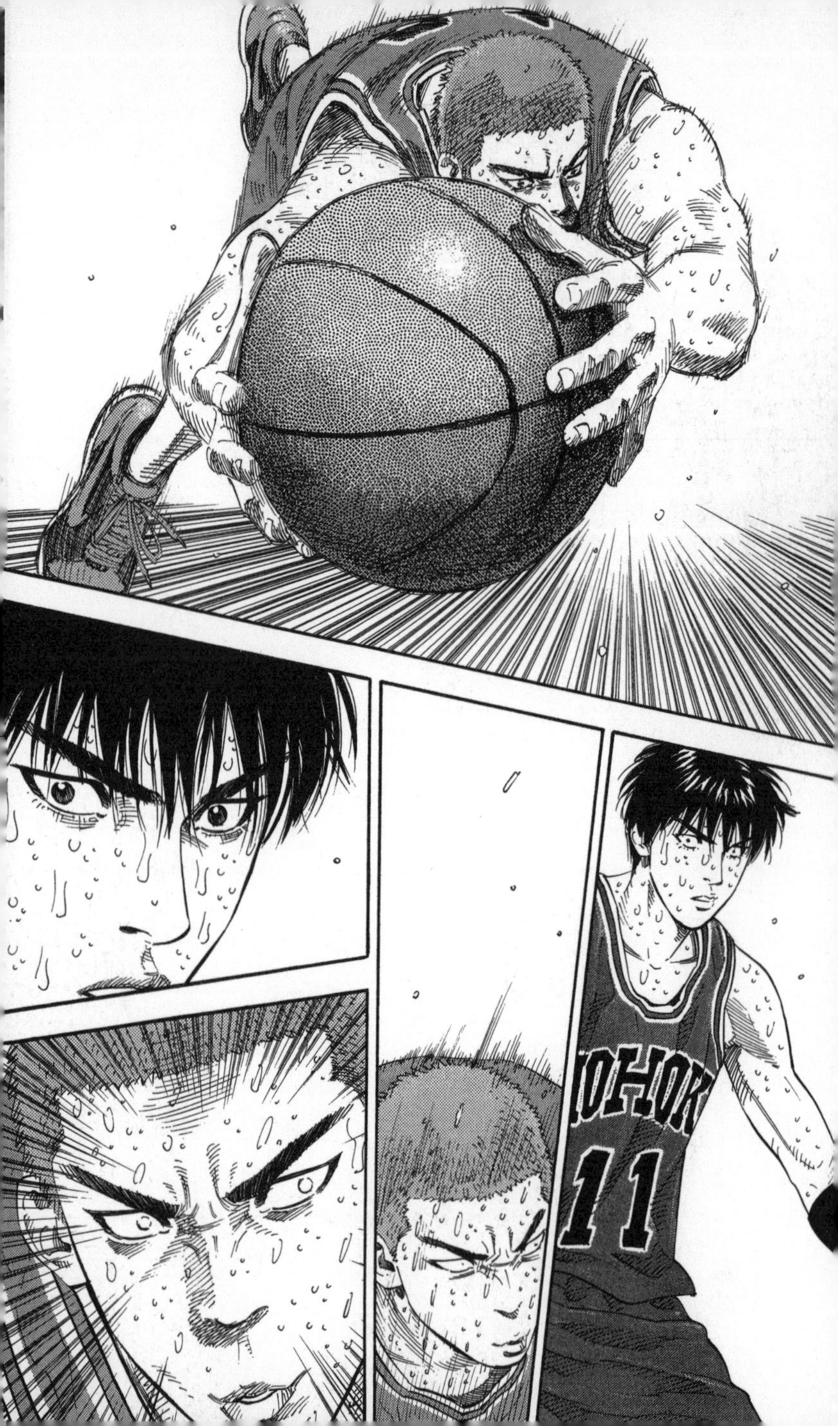

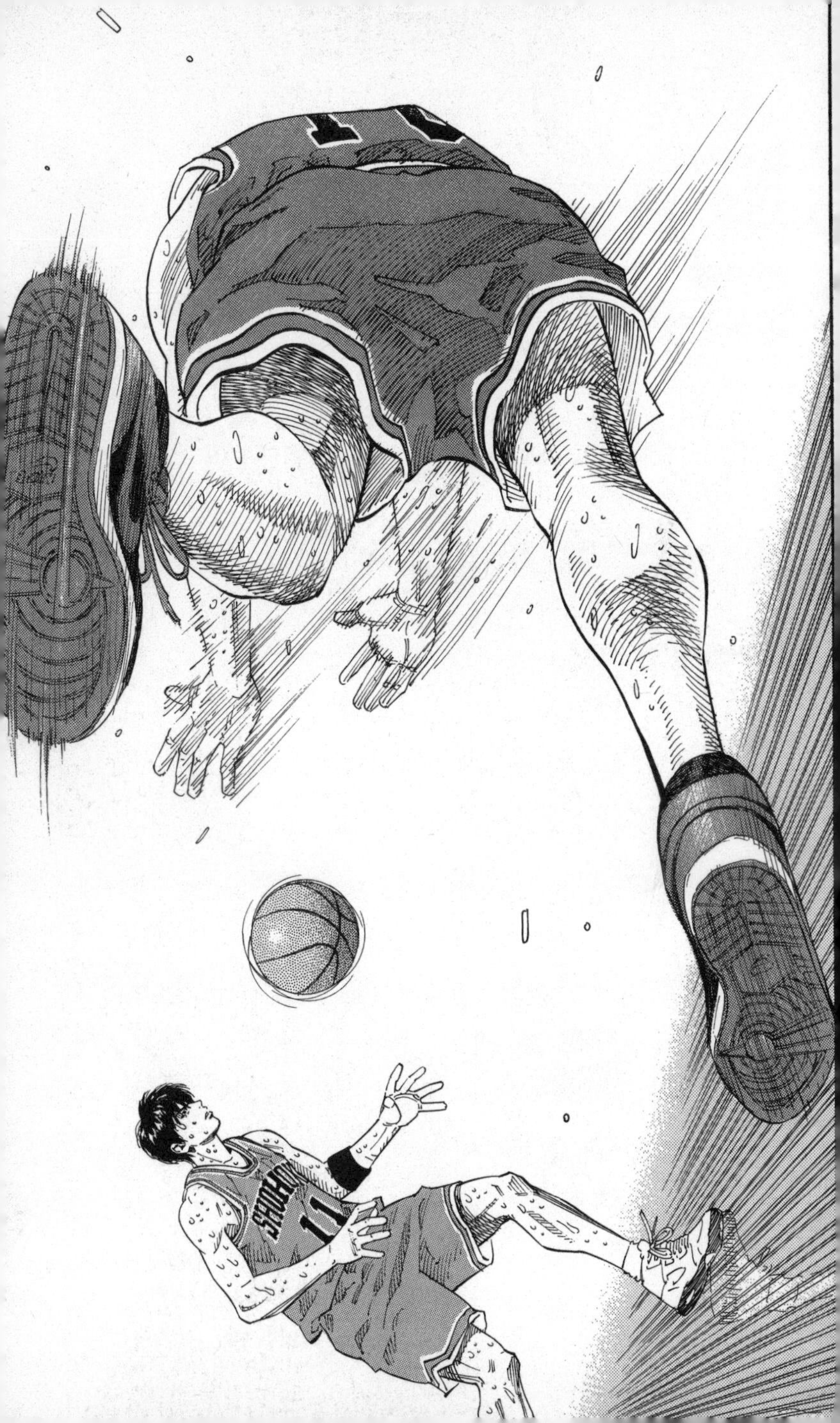

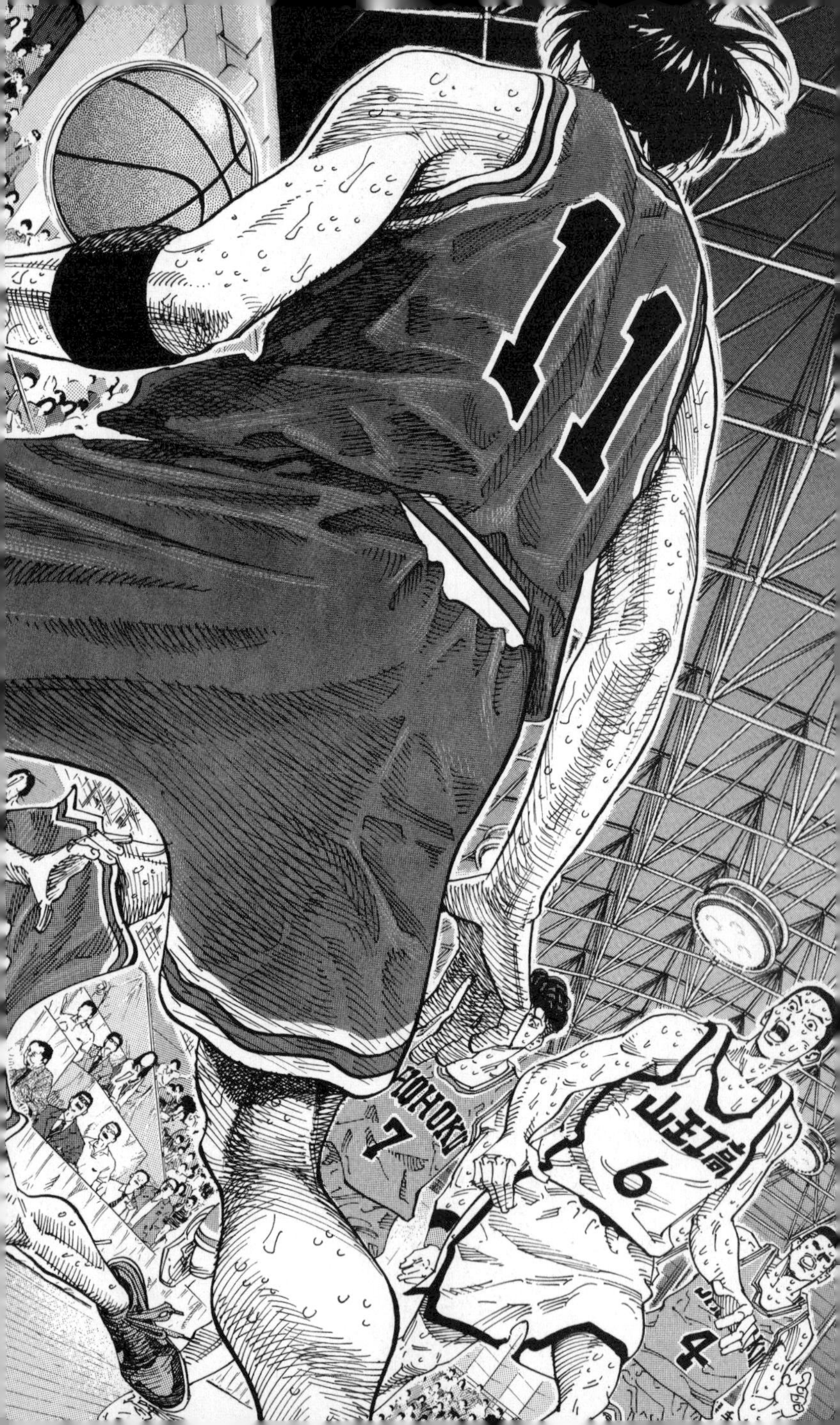
HOHOKU
7
山王工高
6
4

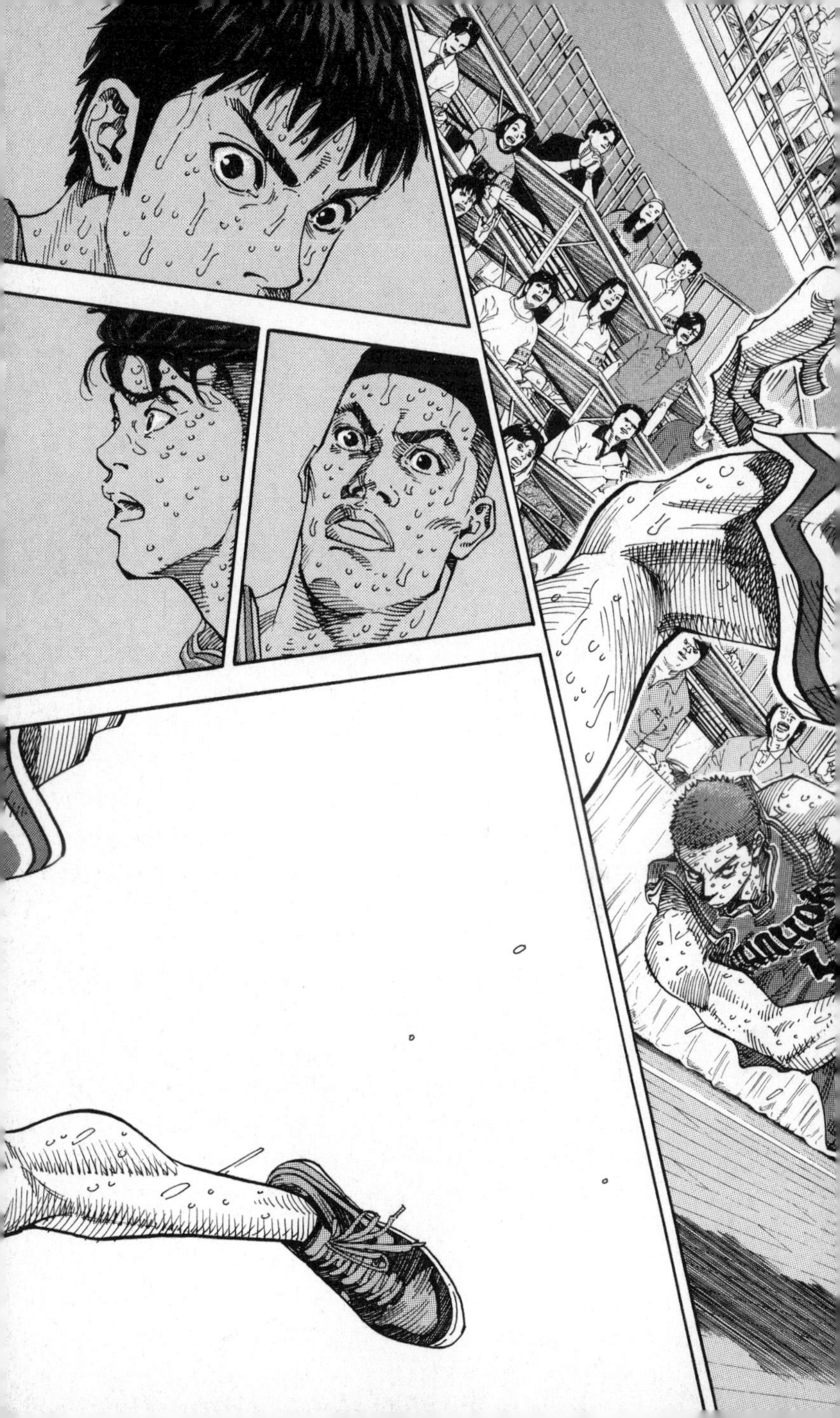

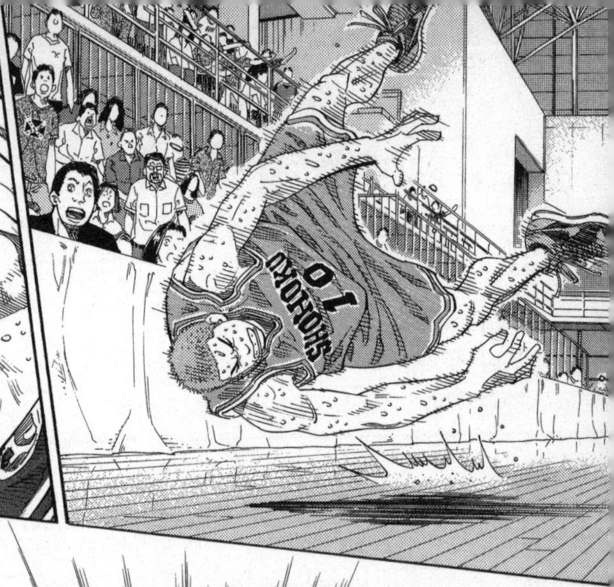
SHOHOKU
10
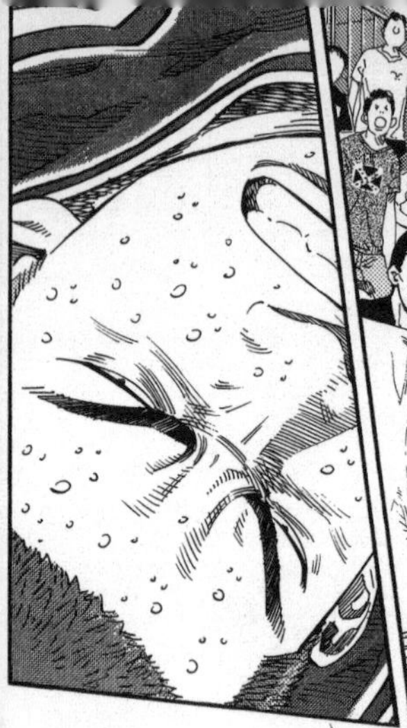
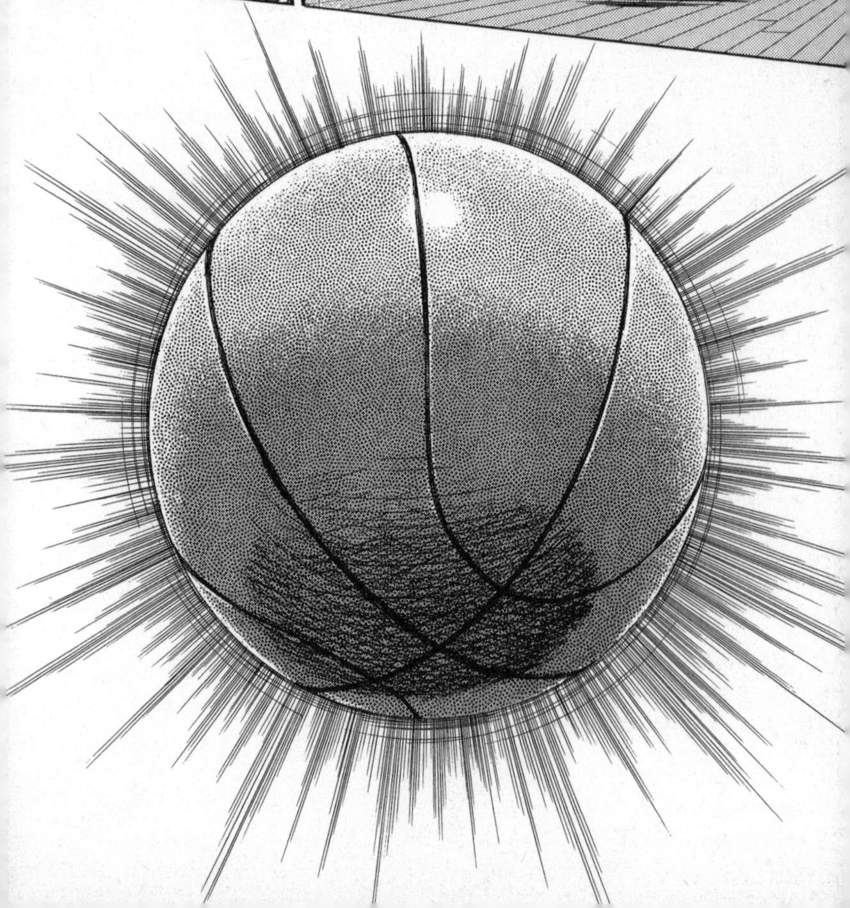

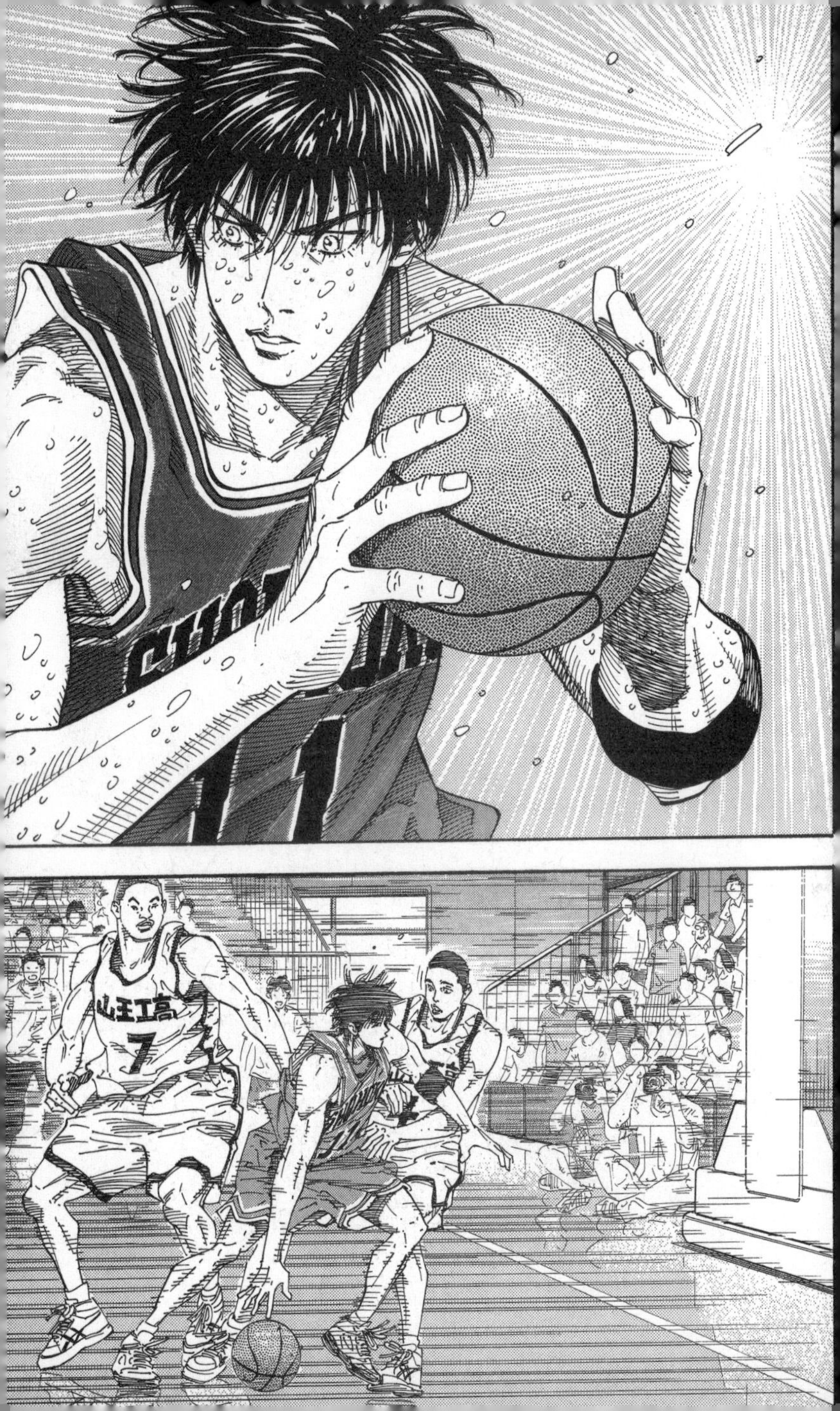
山王工高

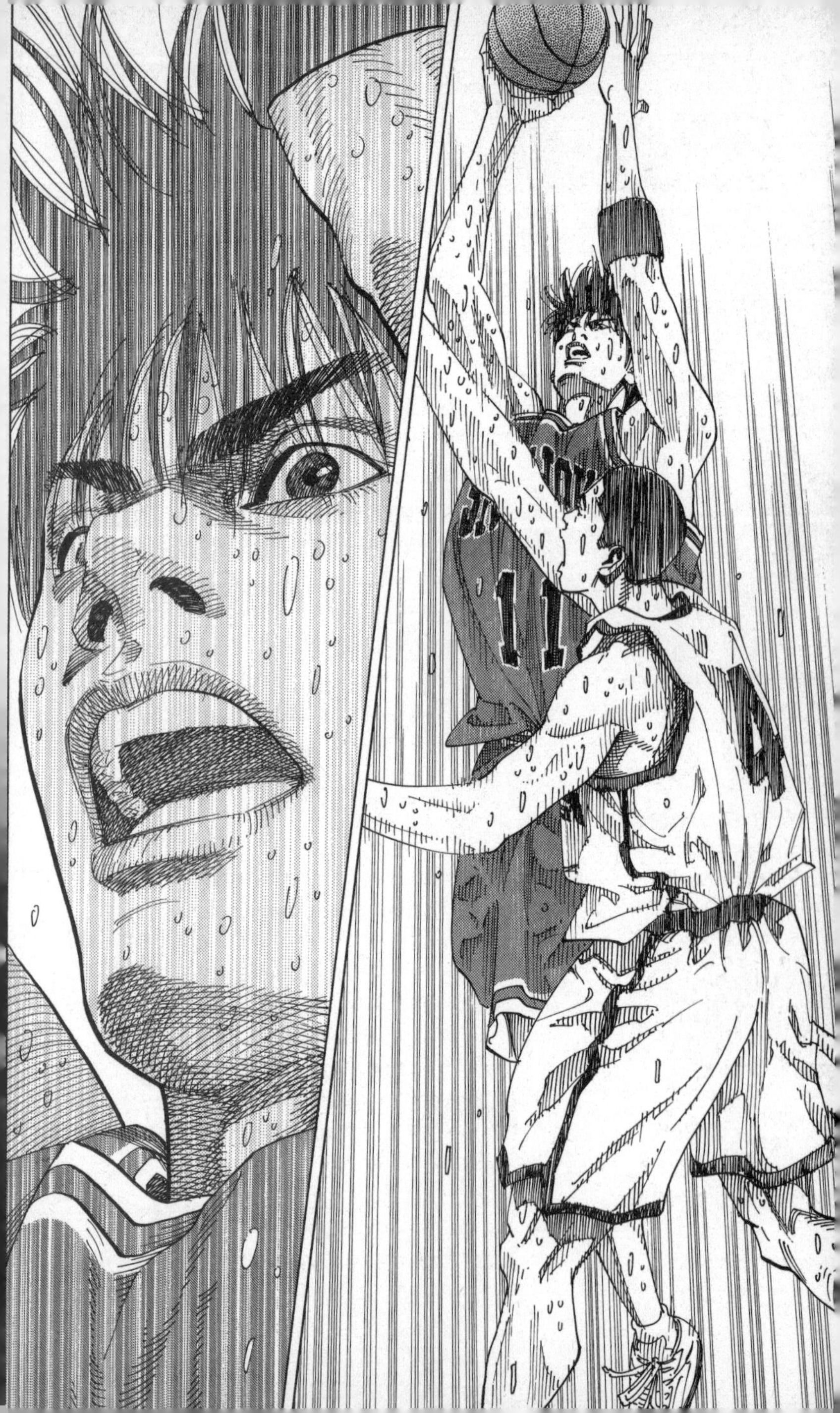
11

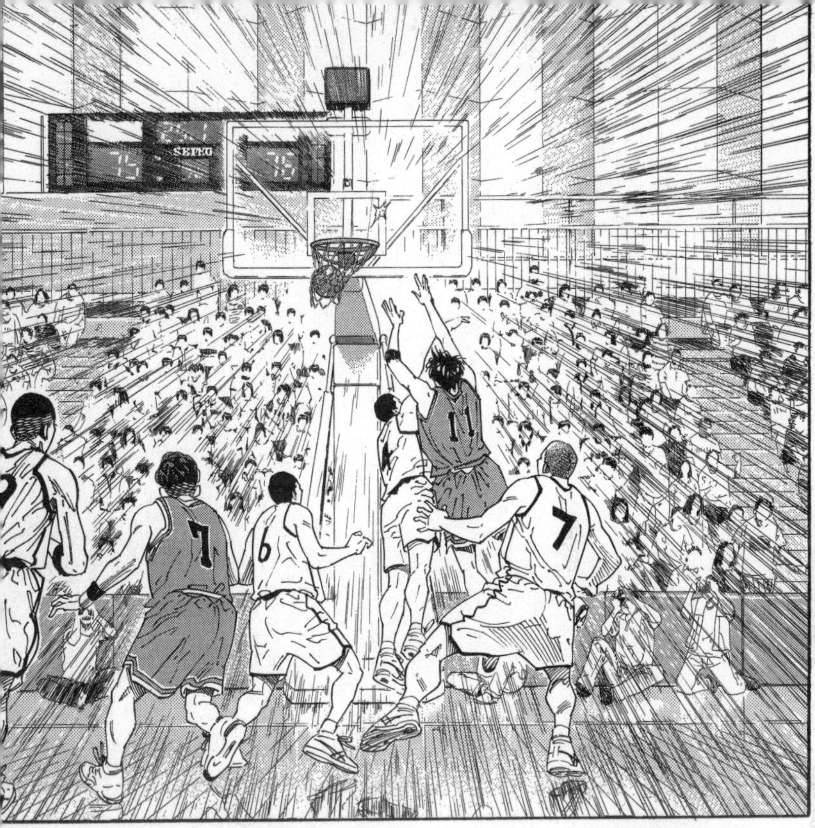
75
SEIKO
75
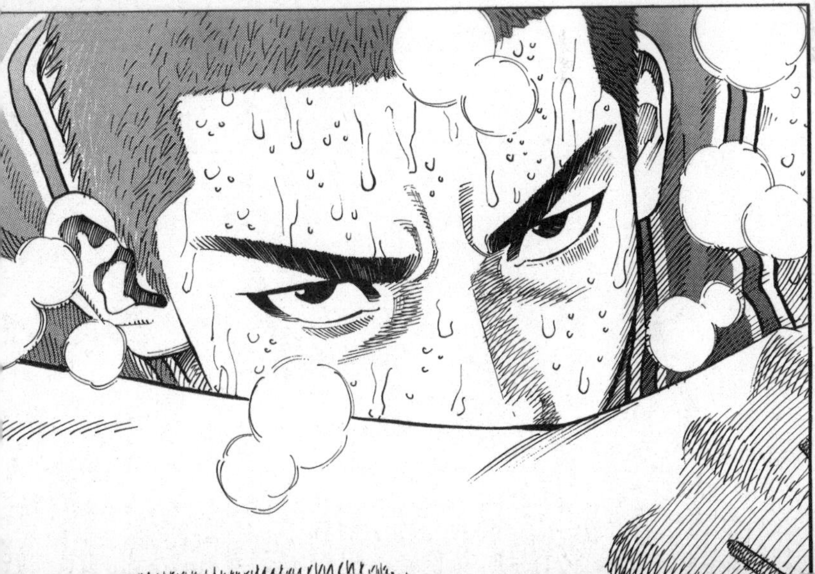

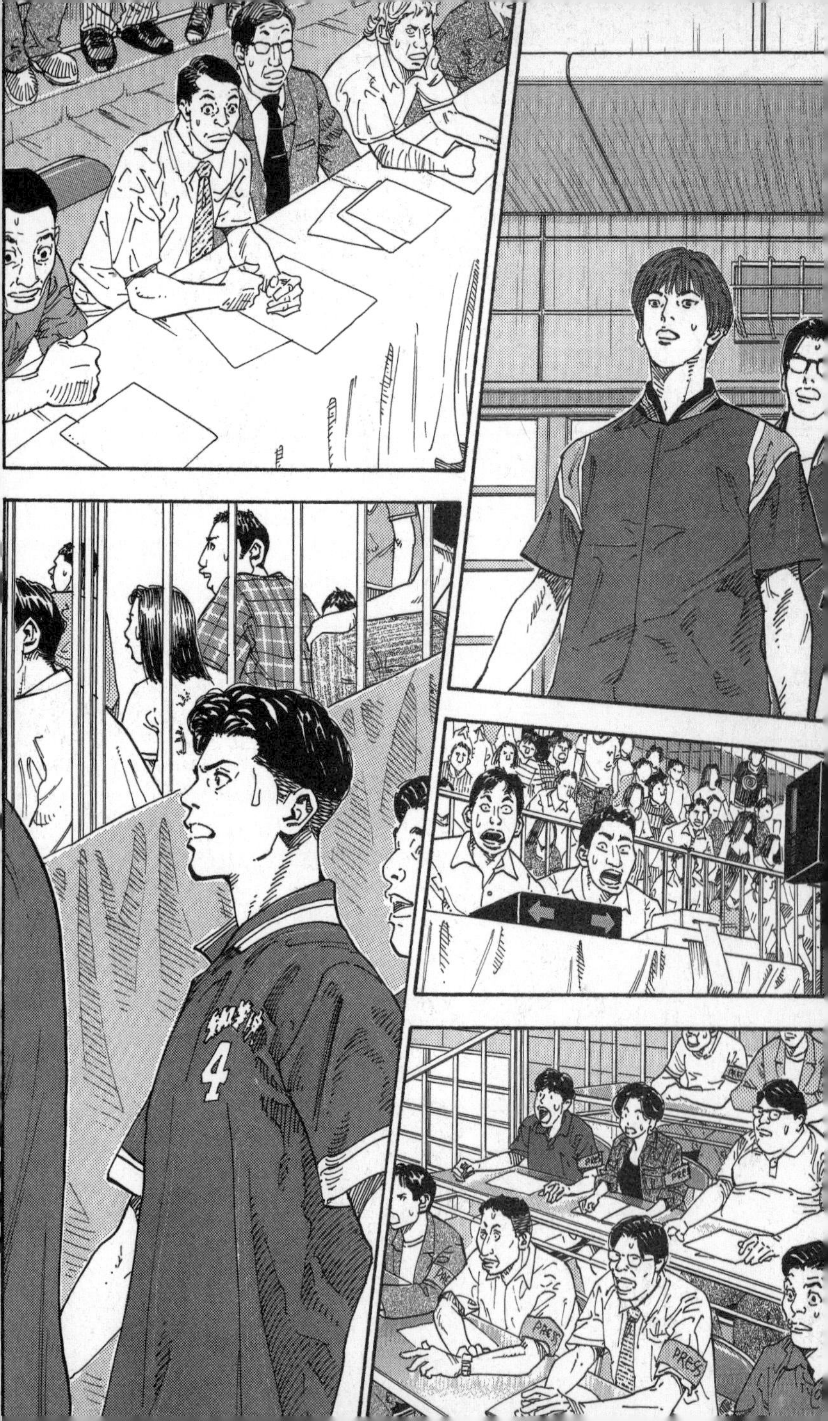
PRESS

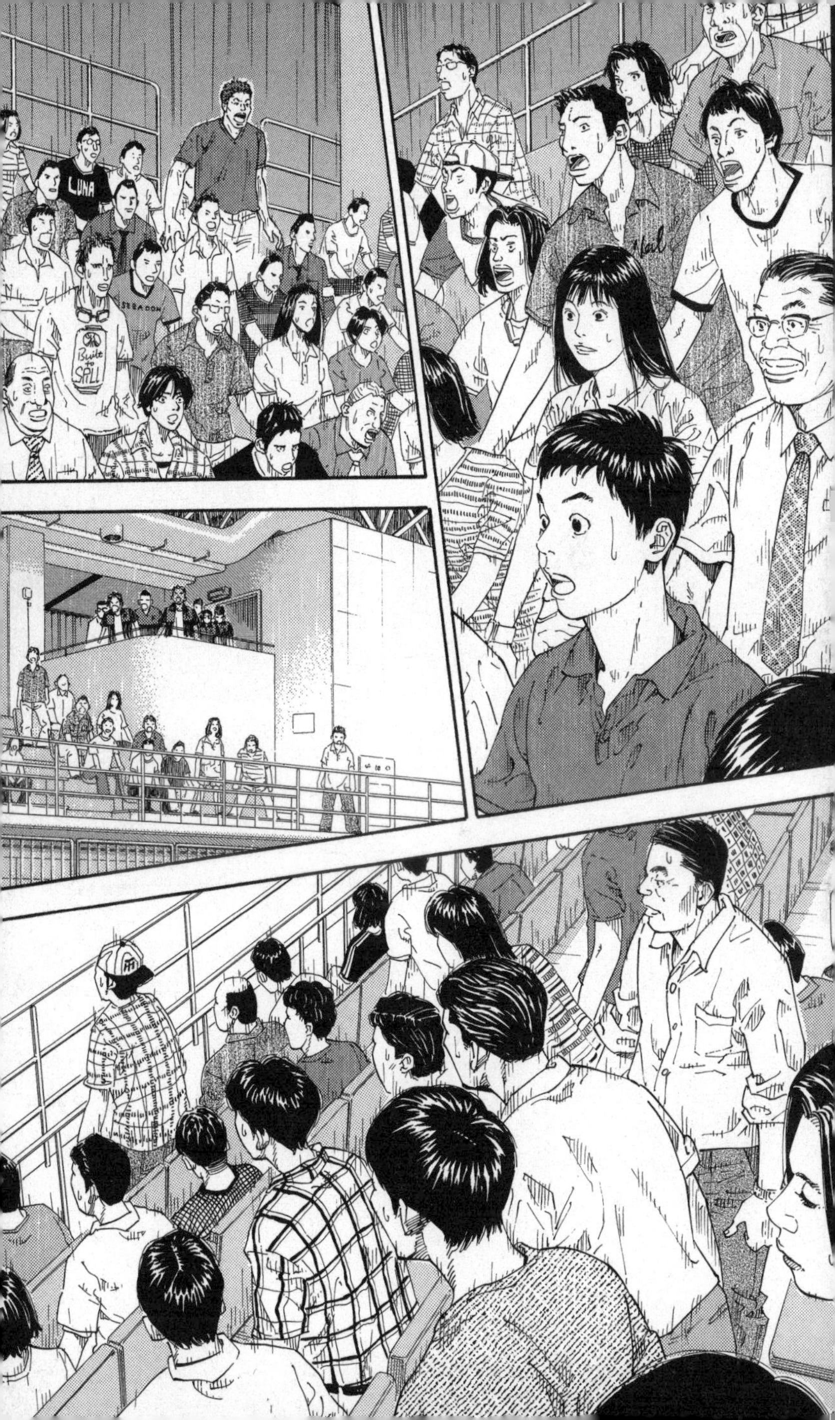
LUNA
Built to SPILL

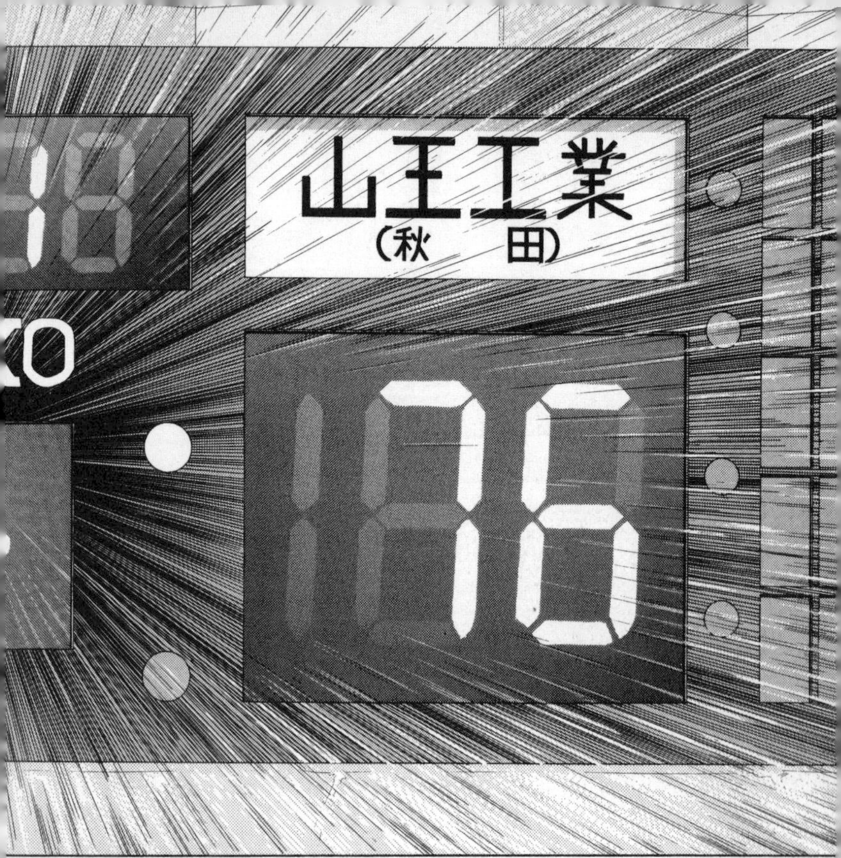
山王工業
(秋　田)
76

Scoreboard: Shohoku (Kanagawa) Sannoh Kogyo (Akita)

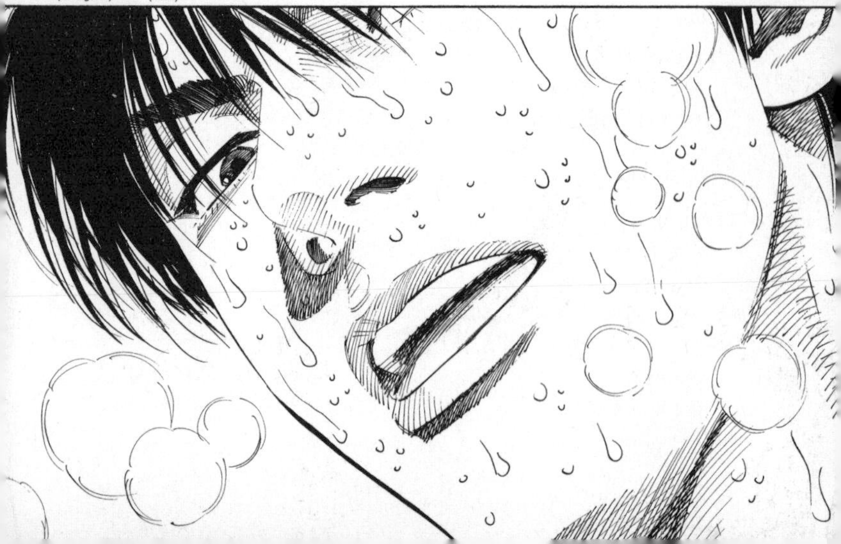

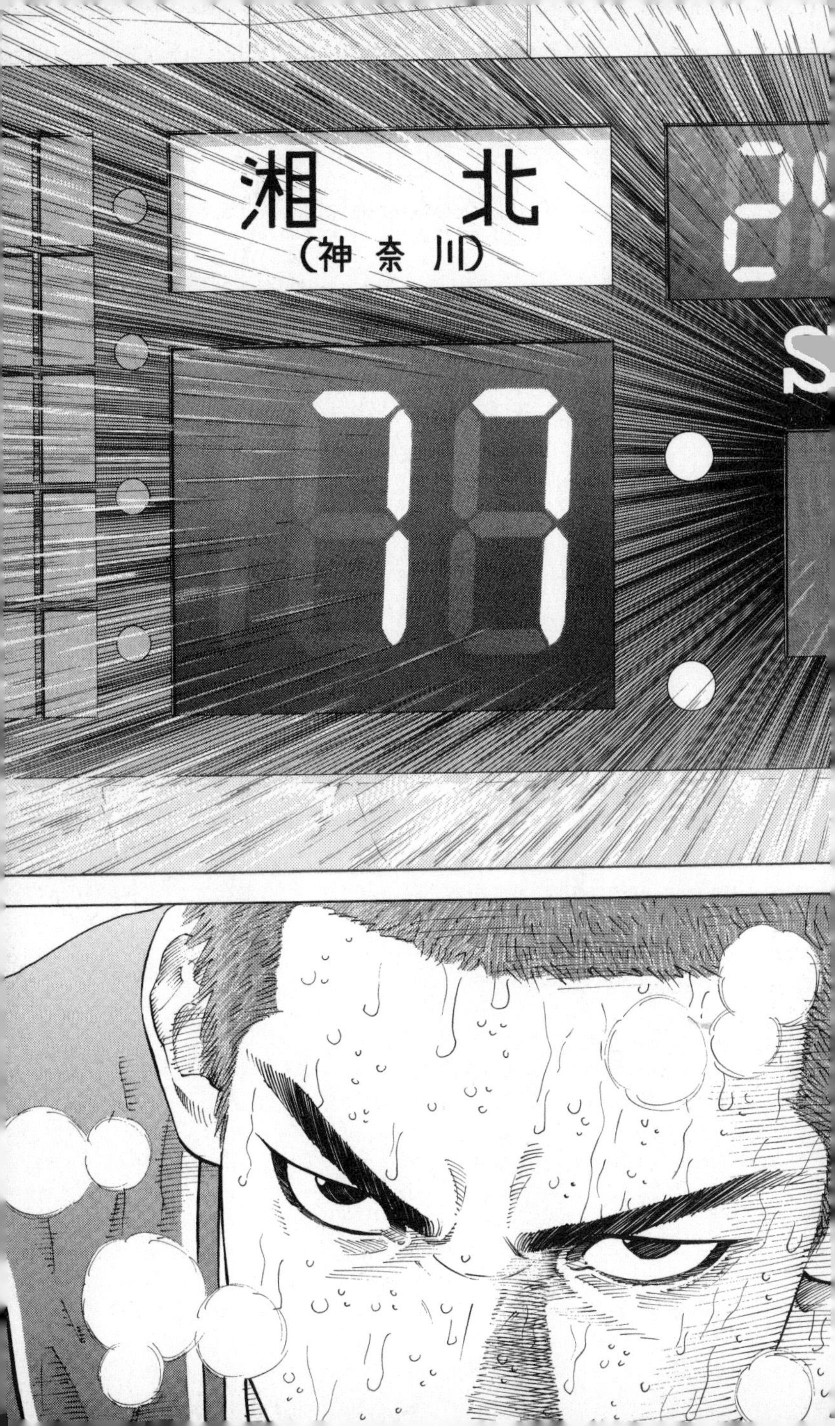
湘北
(神奈川)
71

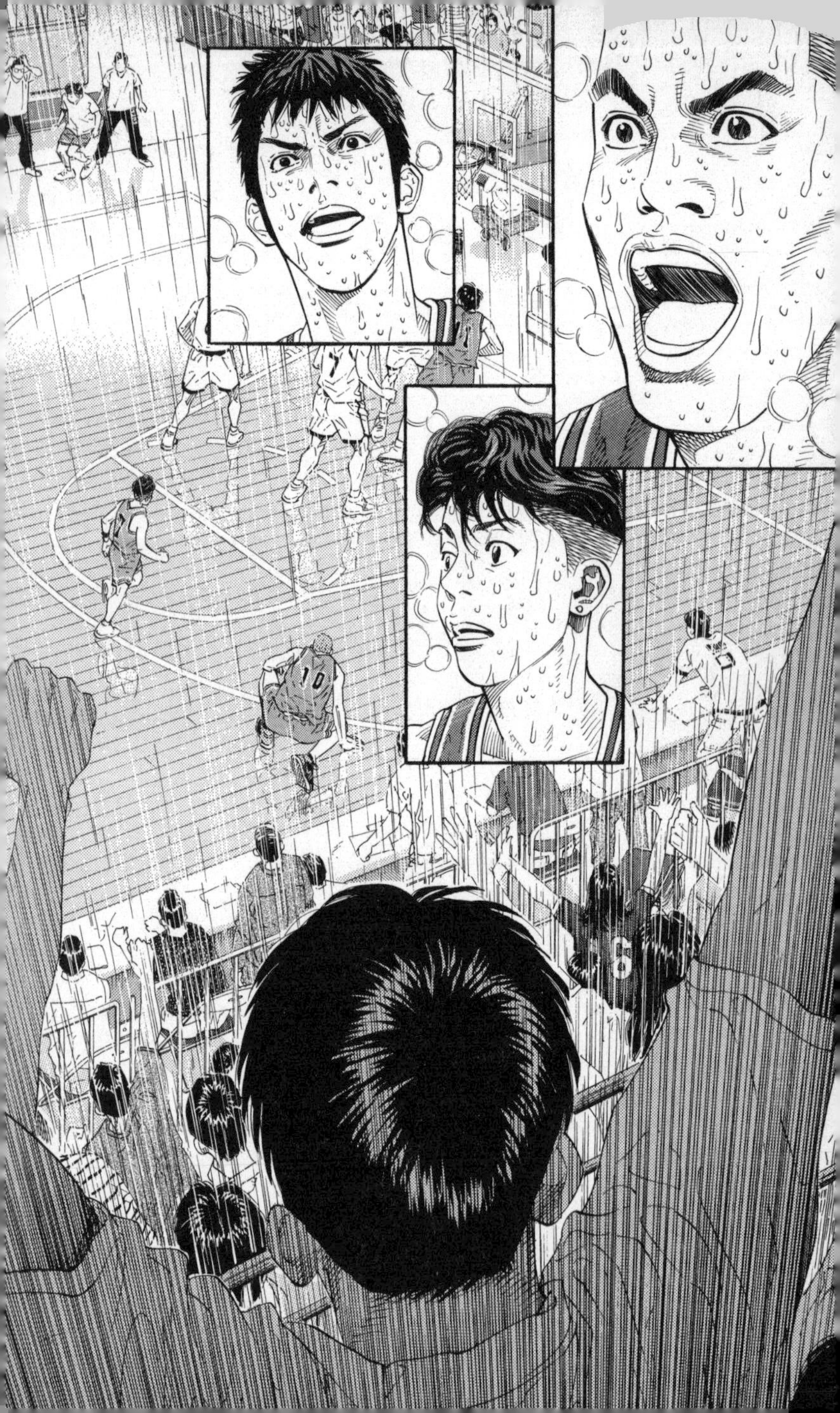

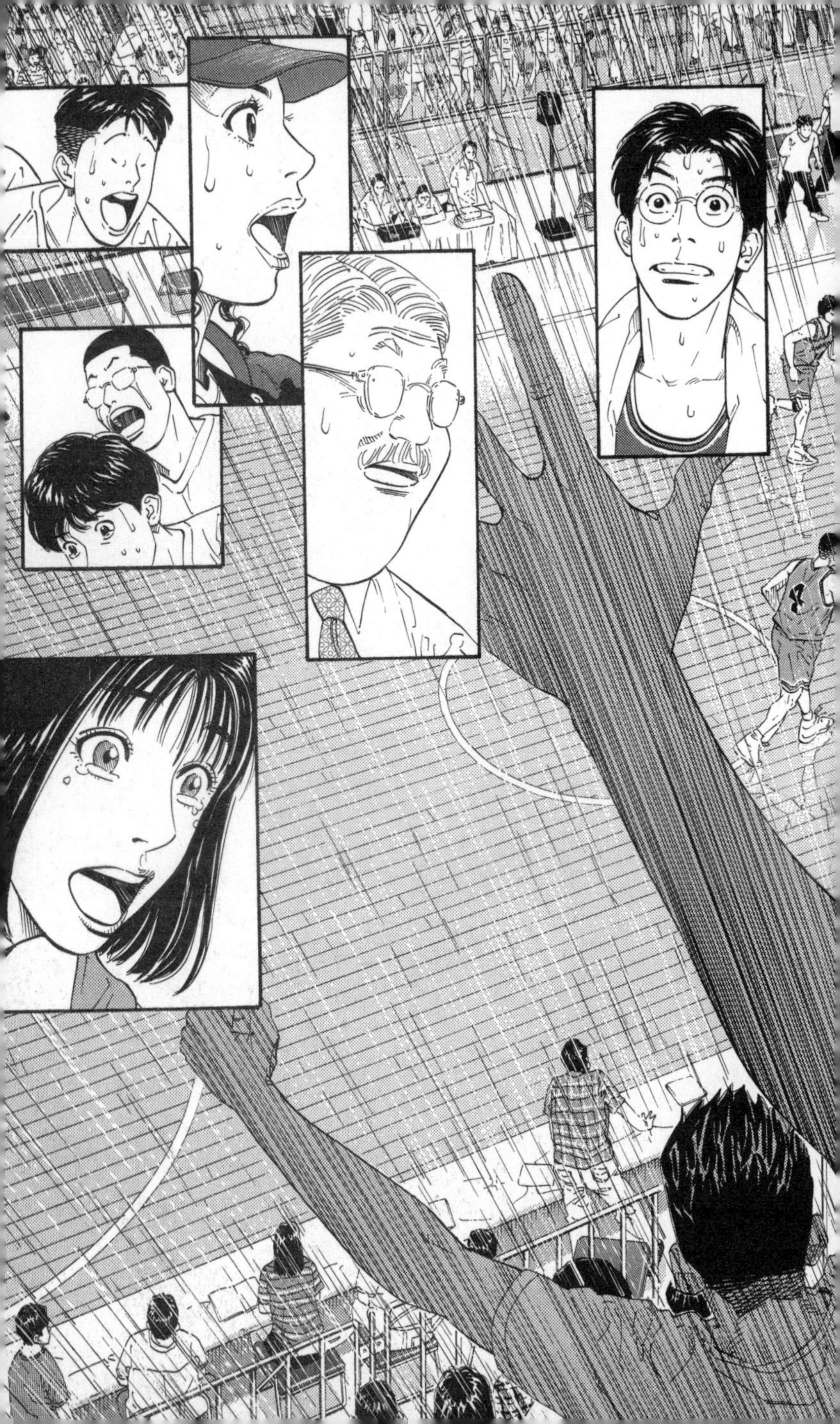

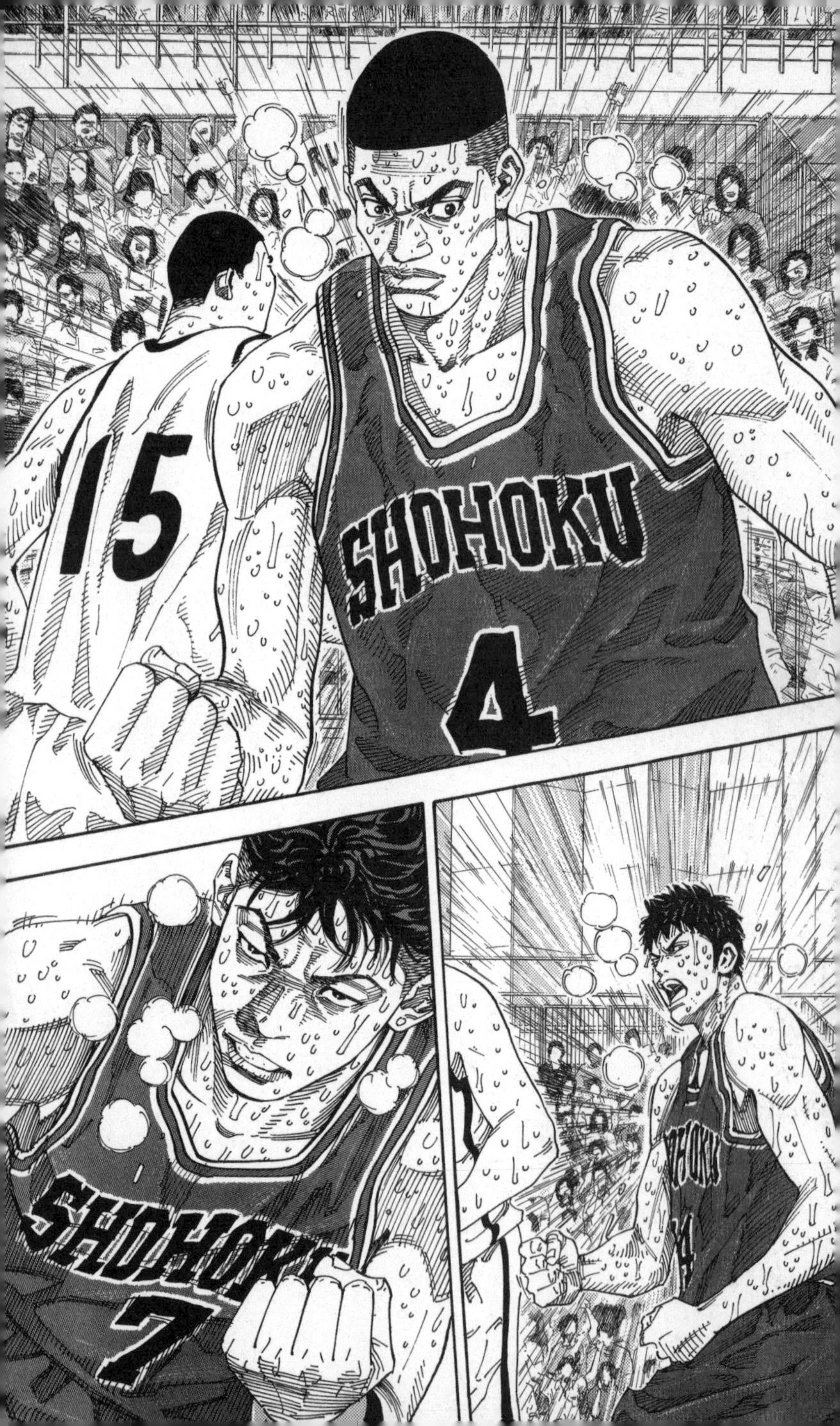
SHOHOKU

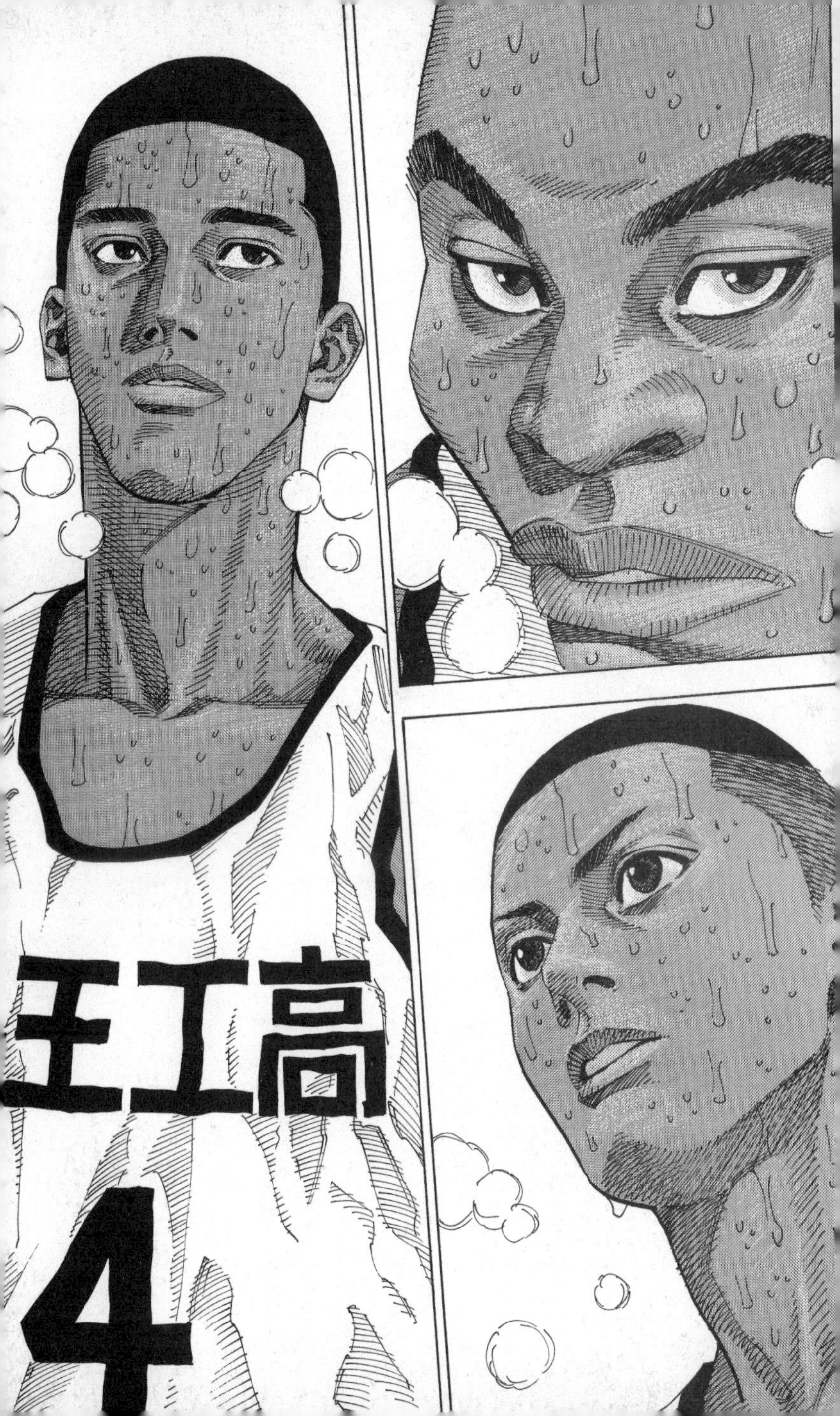

王工高
4

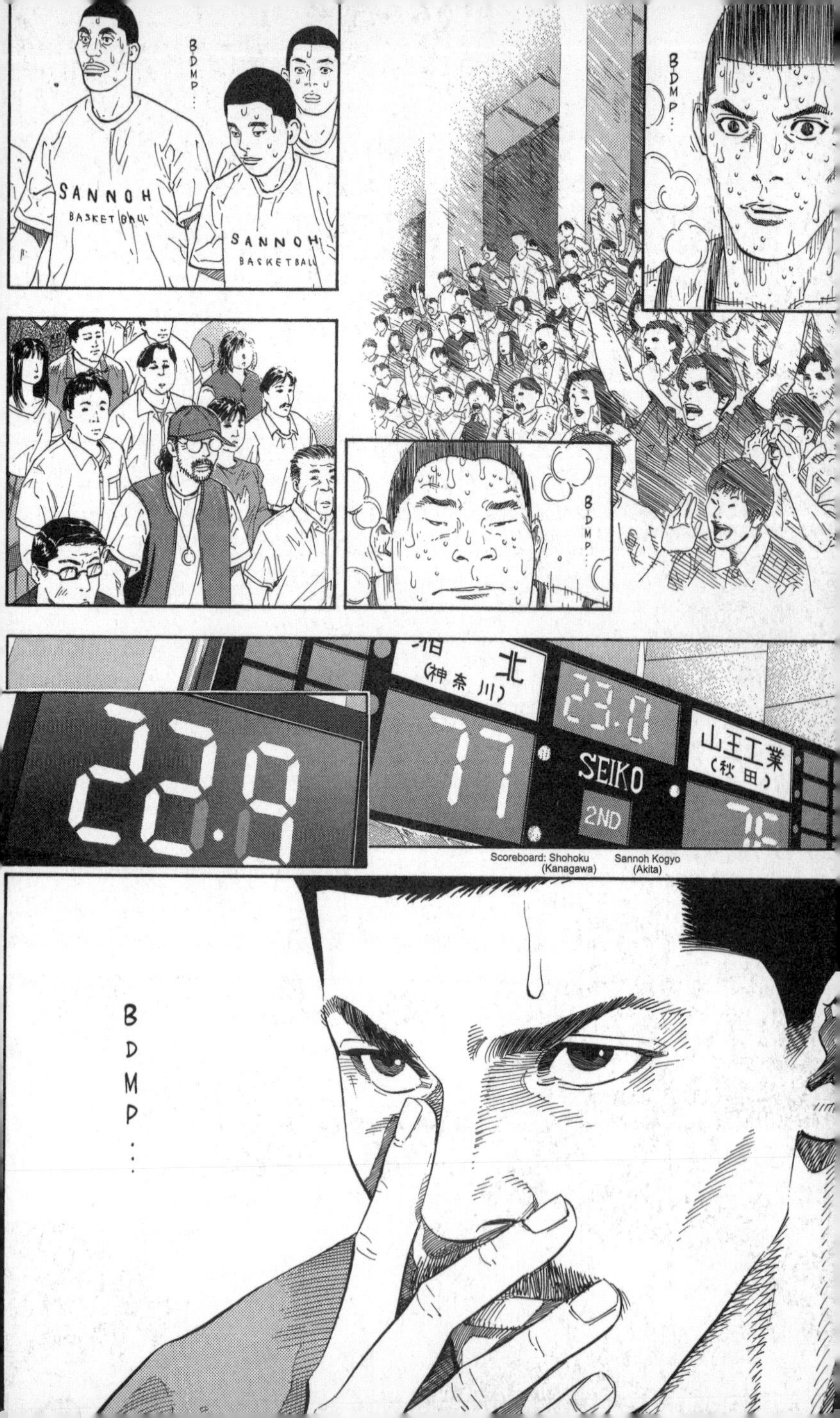
BDMP...
BDMP...
BDMP...
湘北
(神奈川)
23.0
山王工業
(秋田)
77
SEIKO
2ND
22.9
BDMP...
Scoreboard: Shohoku (Kanagawa) Sannoh Kogyo (Akita)

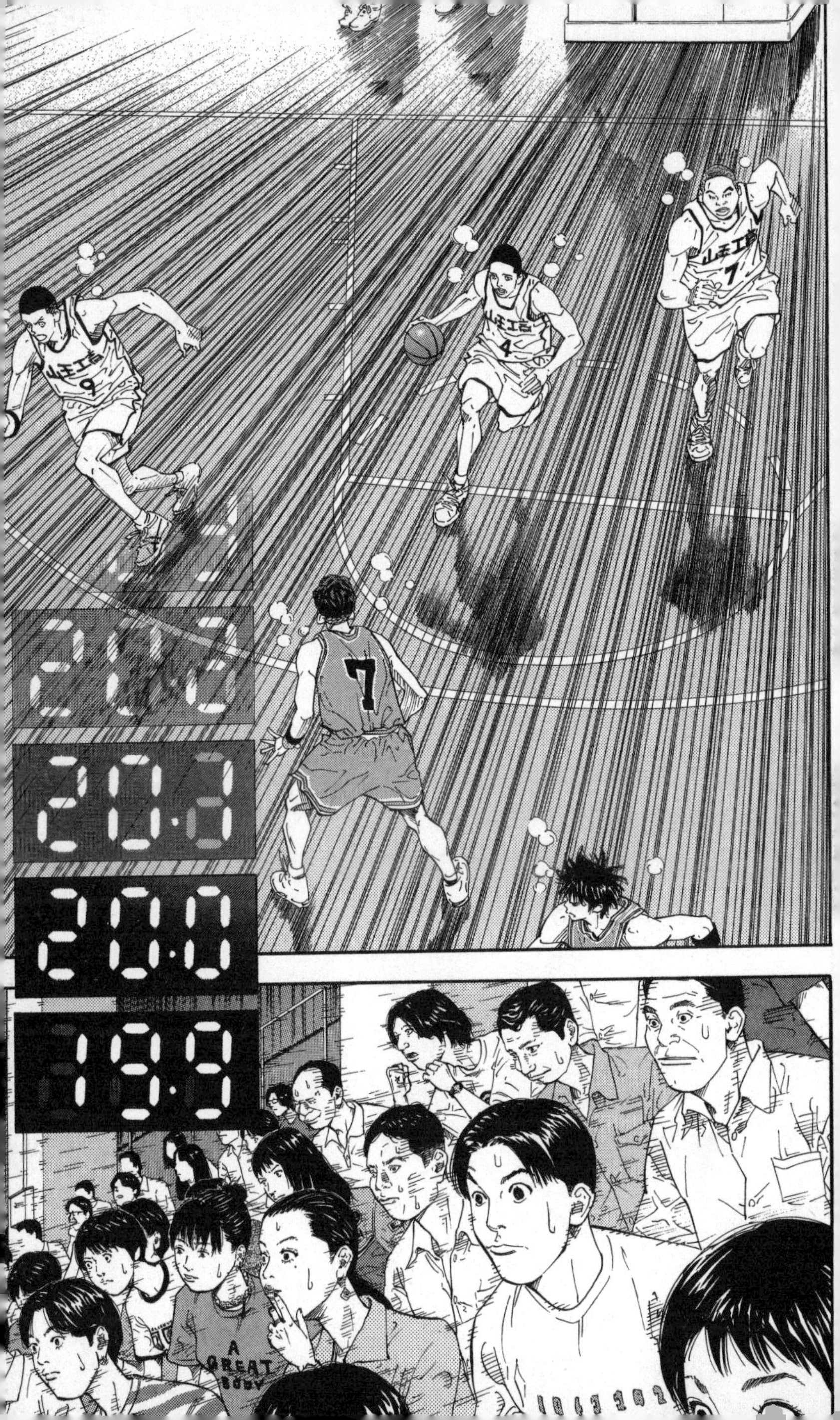
20.2
20.1
20.0
19.9
A GREAT BODY

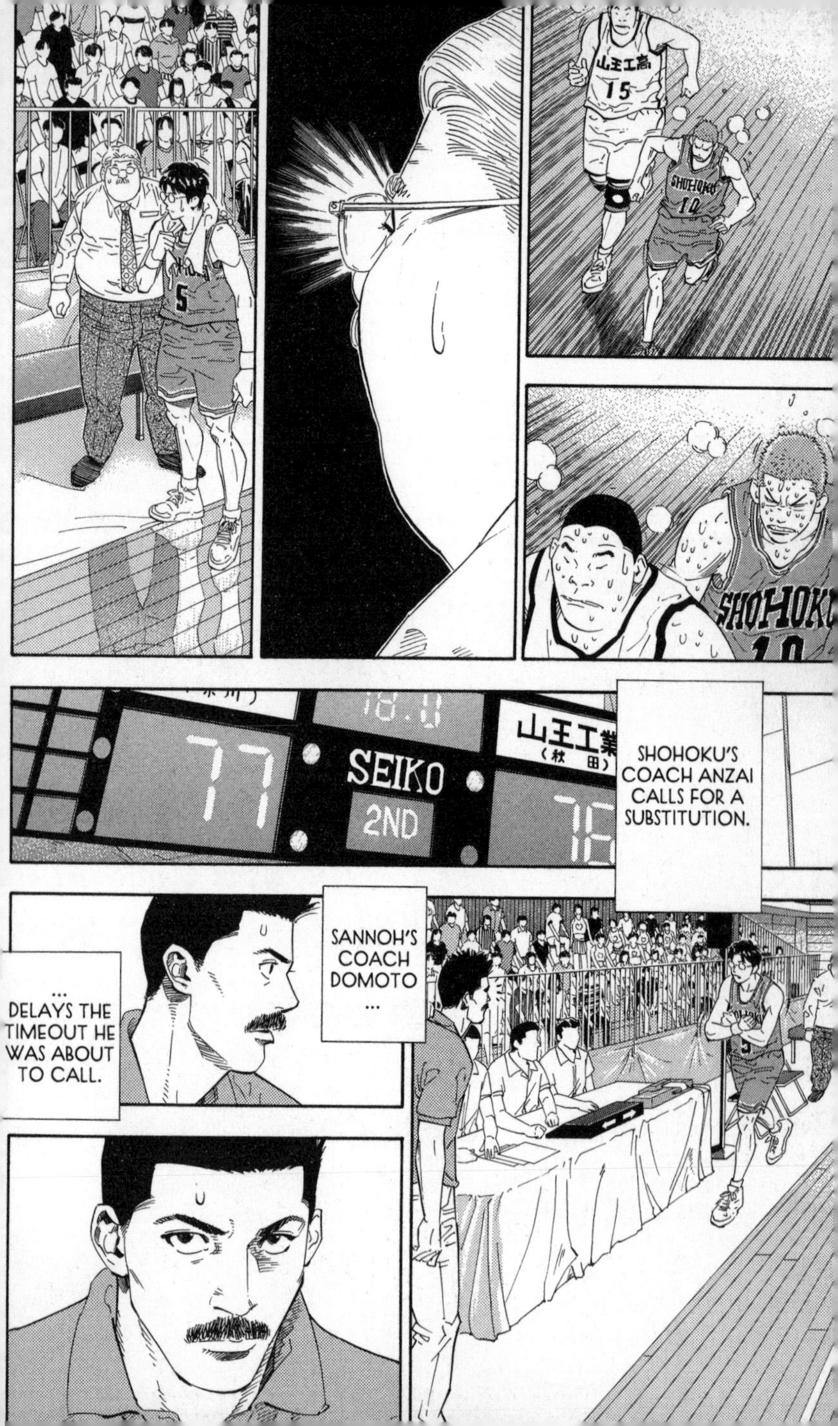
SHOHOKU
山王工業
(秋田)
77
SEIKO
2ND
SHOHOKU'S COACH ANZAI CALLS FOR A SUBSTITUTION.
SANNOH'S COACH DOMOTO ...
... DELAYS THE TIMEOUT HE WAS ABOUT TO CALL.

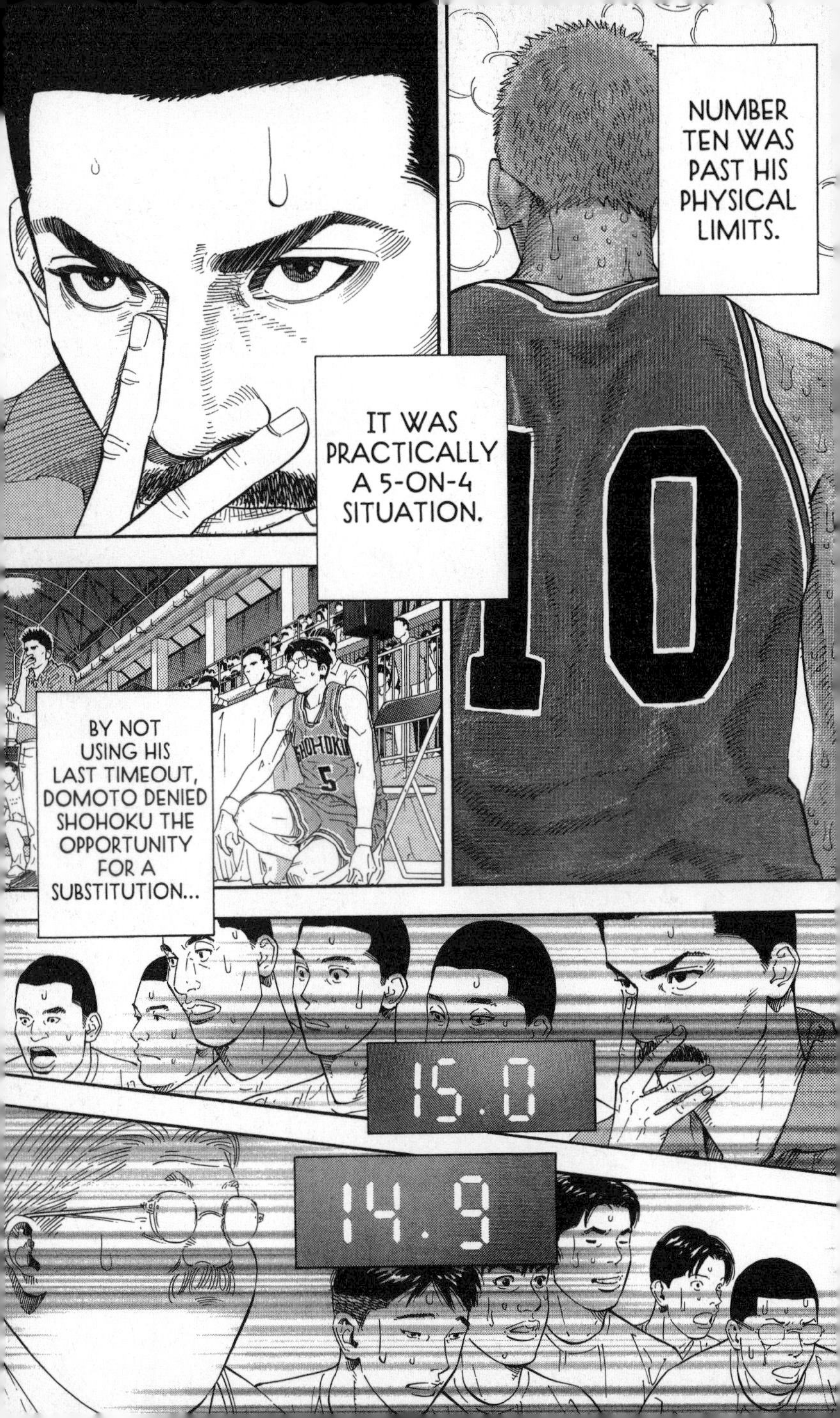
NUMBER TEN WAS PAST HIS PHYSICAL LIMITS.
IT WAS PRACTICALLY A 5-ON-4 SITUATION.
BY NOT USING HIS LAST TIMEOUT, DOMOTO DENIED SHOHOKU THE OPPORTUNITY FOR A SUBSTITUTION...
15.0
14.9

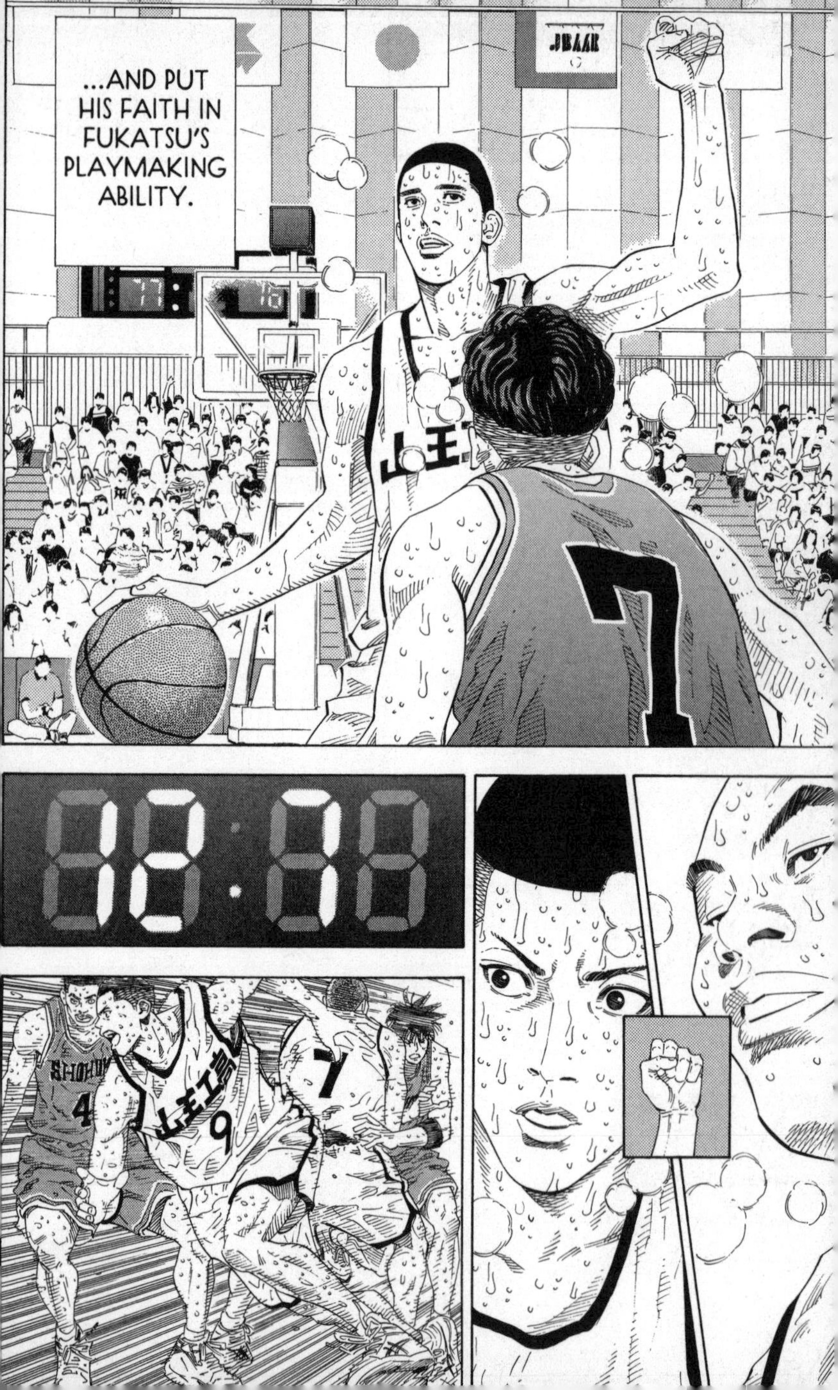
...AND PUT HIS FAITH IN FUKATSU'S PLAYMAKING ABILITY.

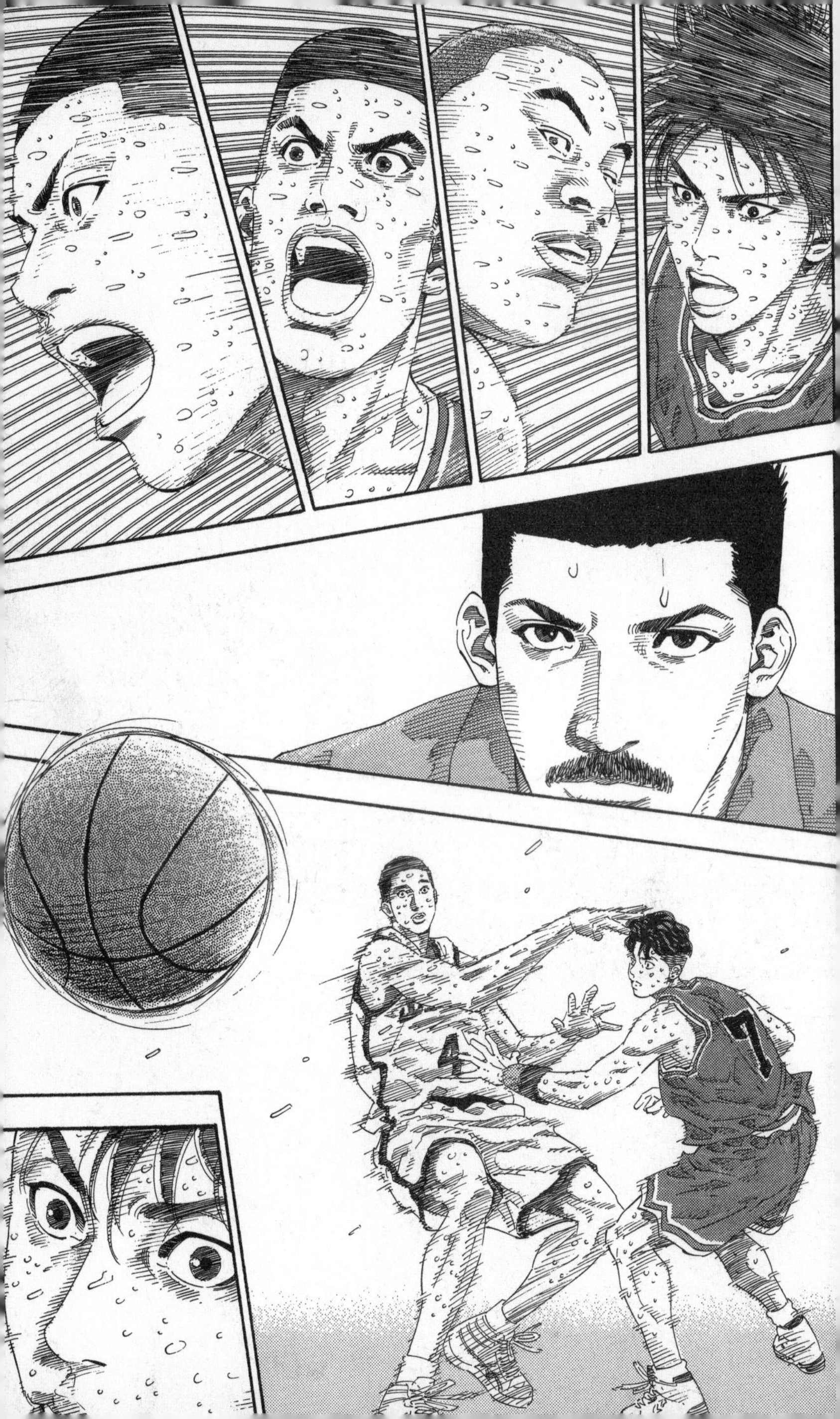

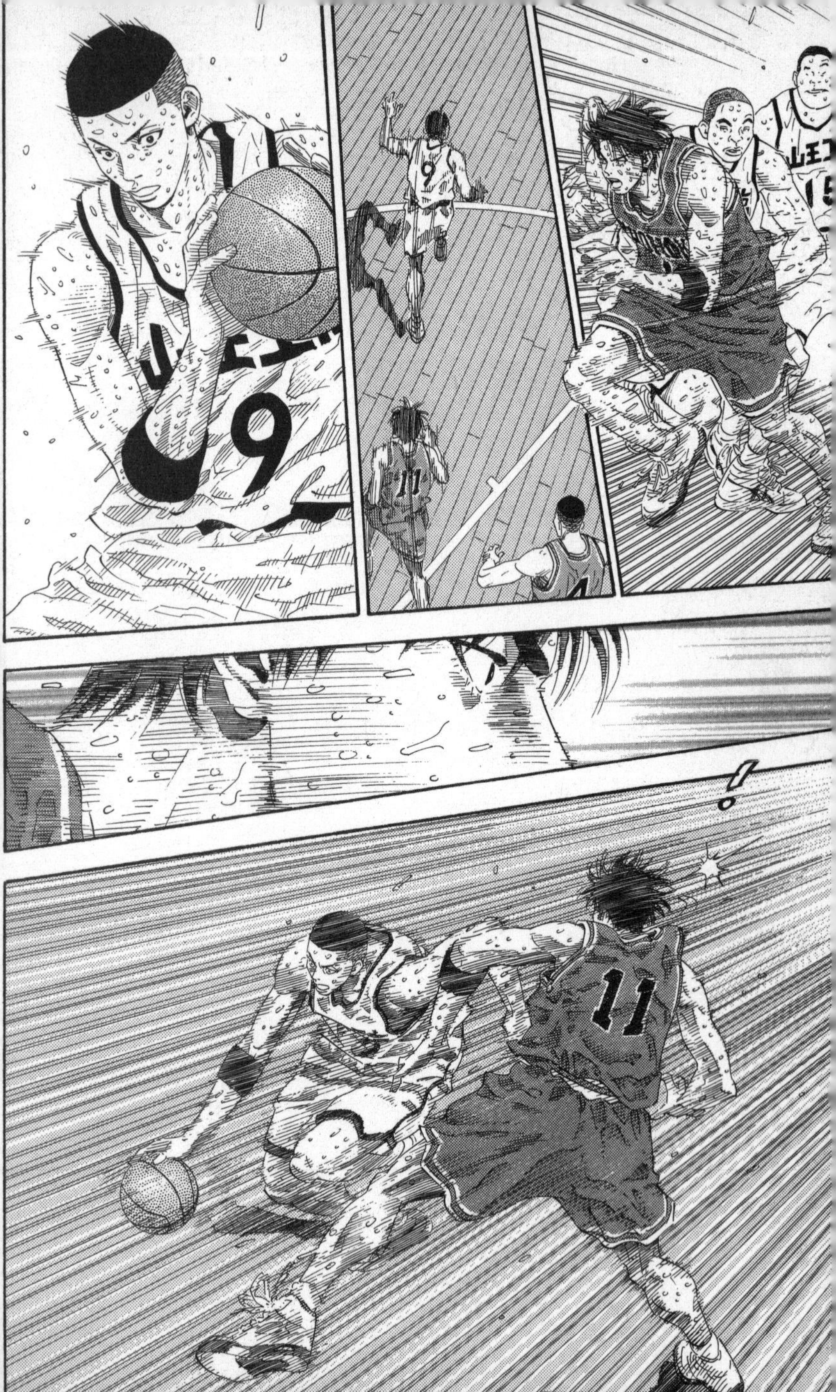
!

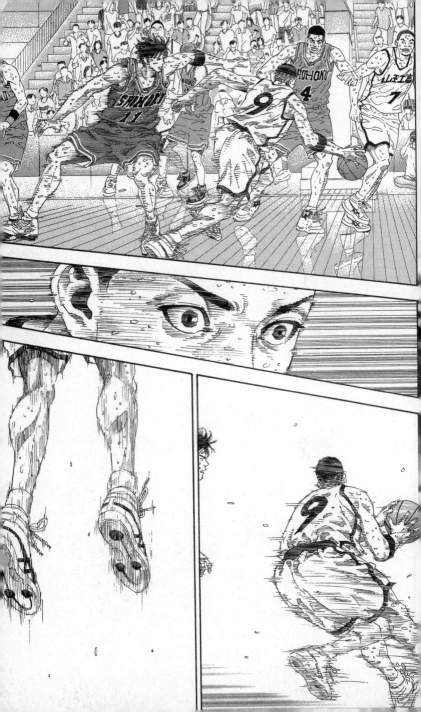

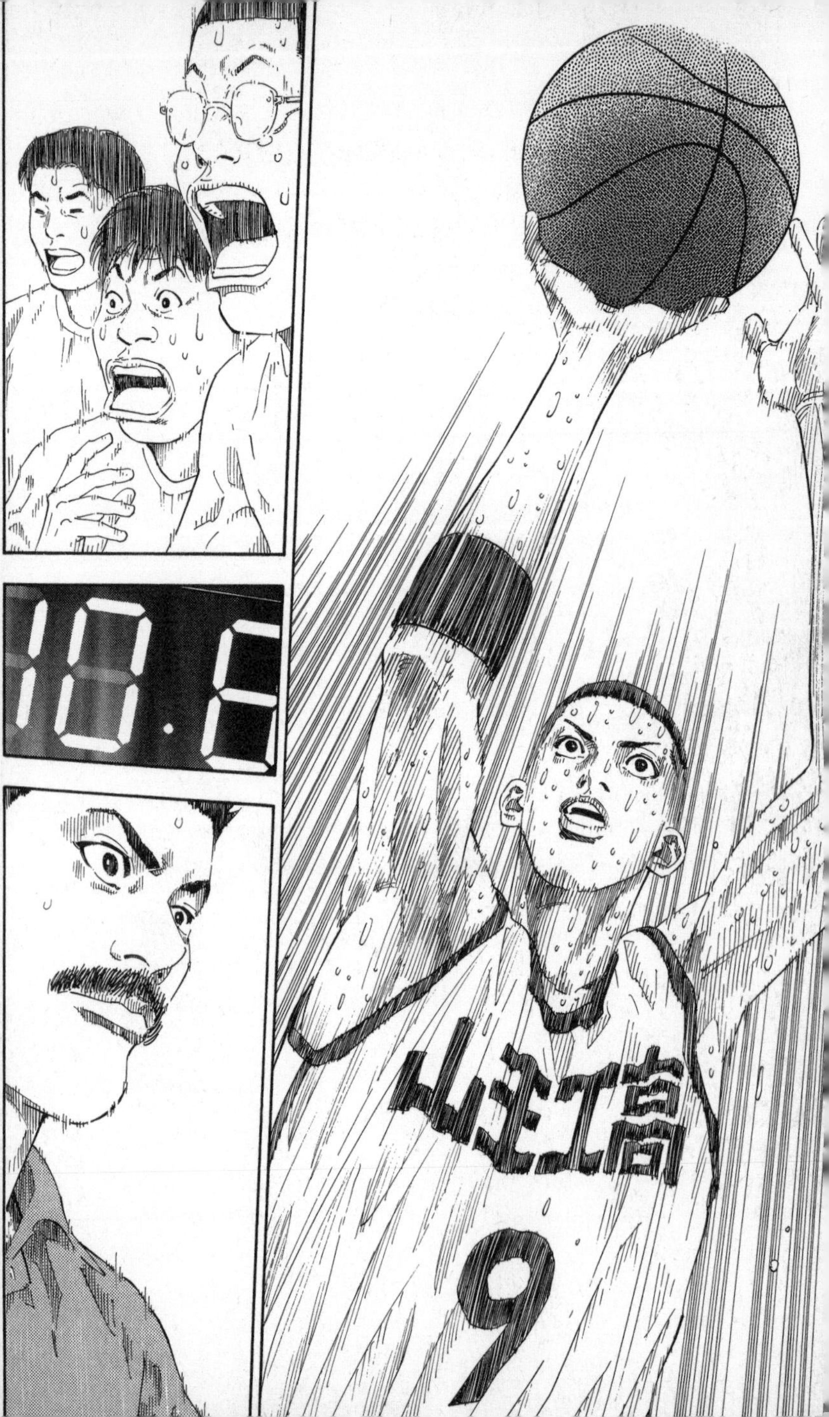
山王工高
9

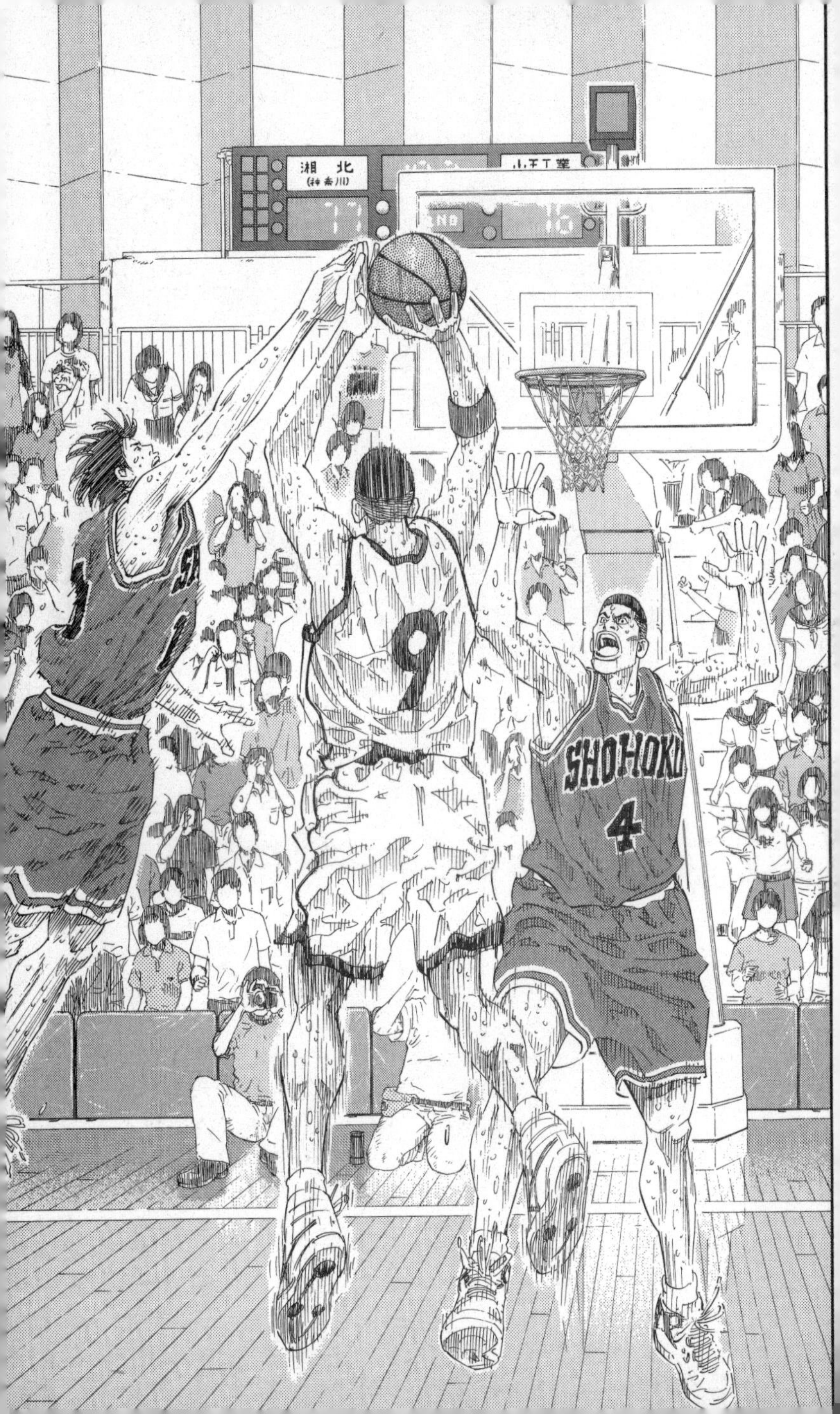
湘北
(神奈川)
SHOHOKU

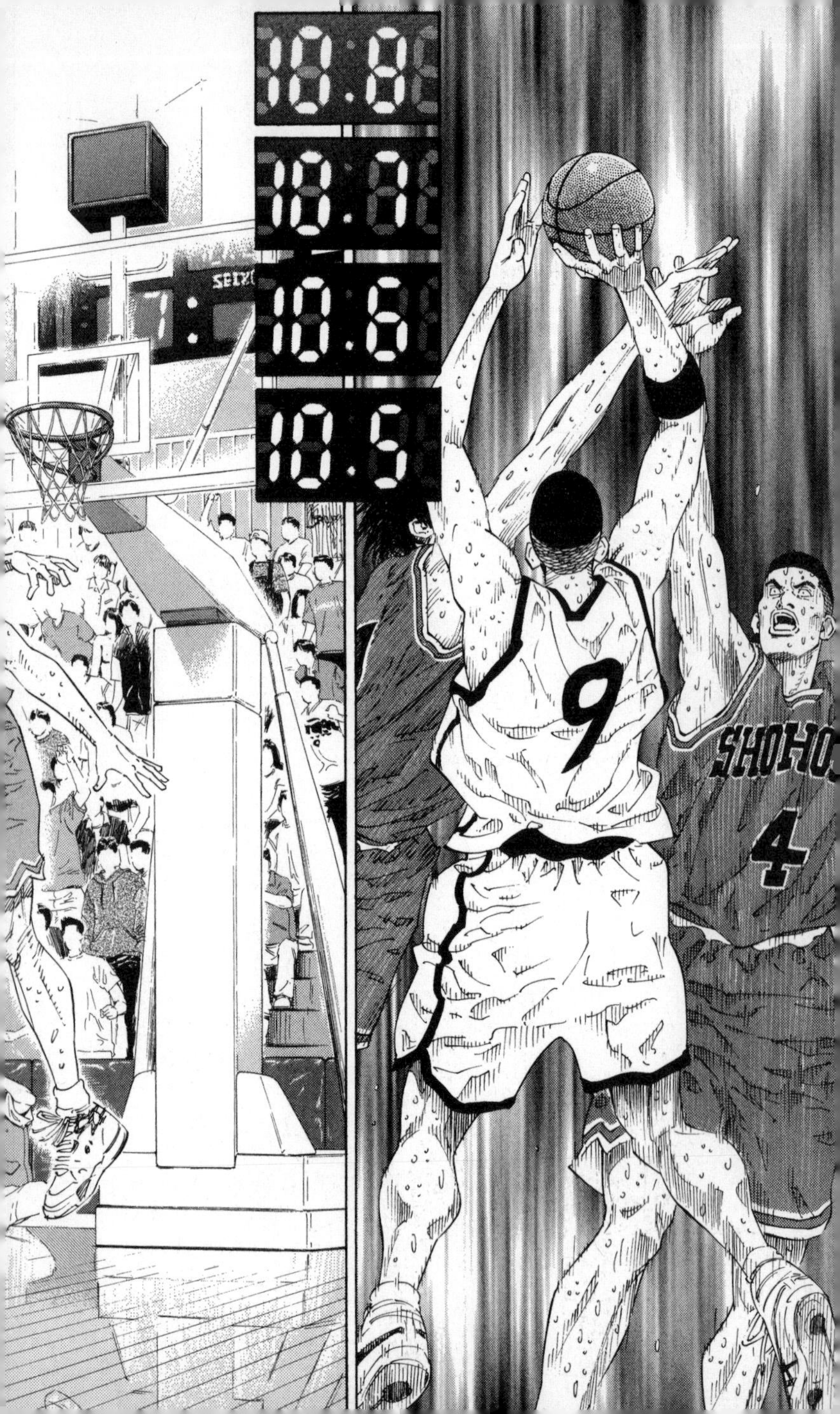
10.8
10.6
10.5
SEIKO
9
SHOHO
4

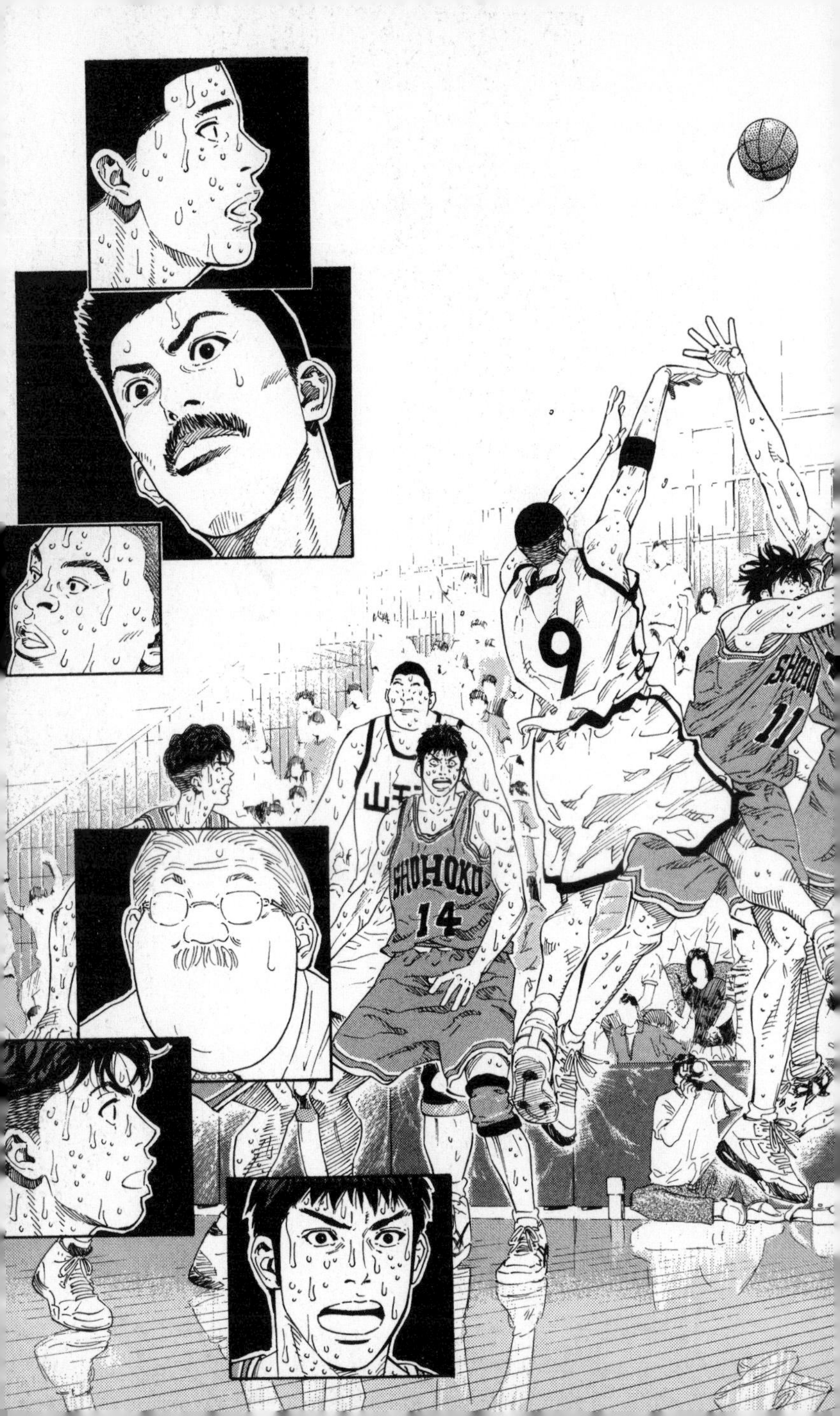
SHOHOKU

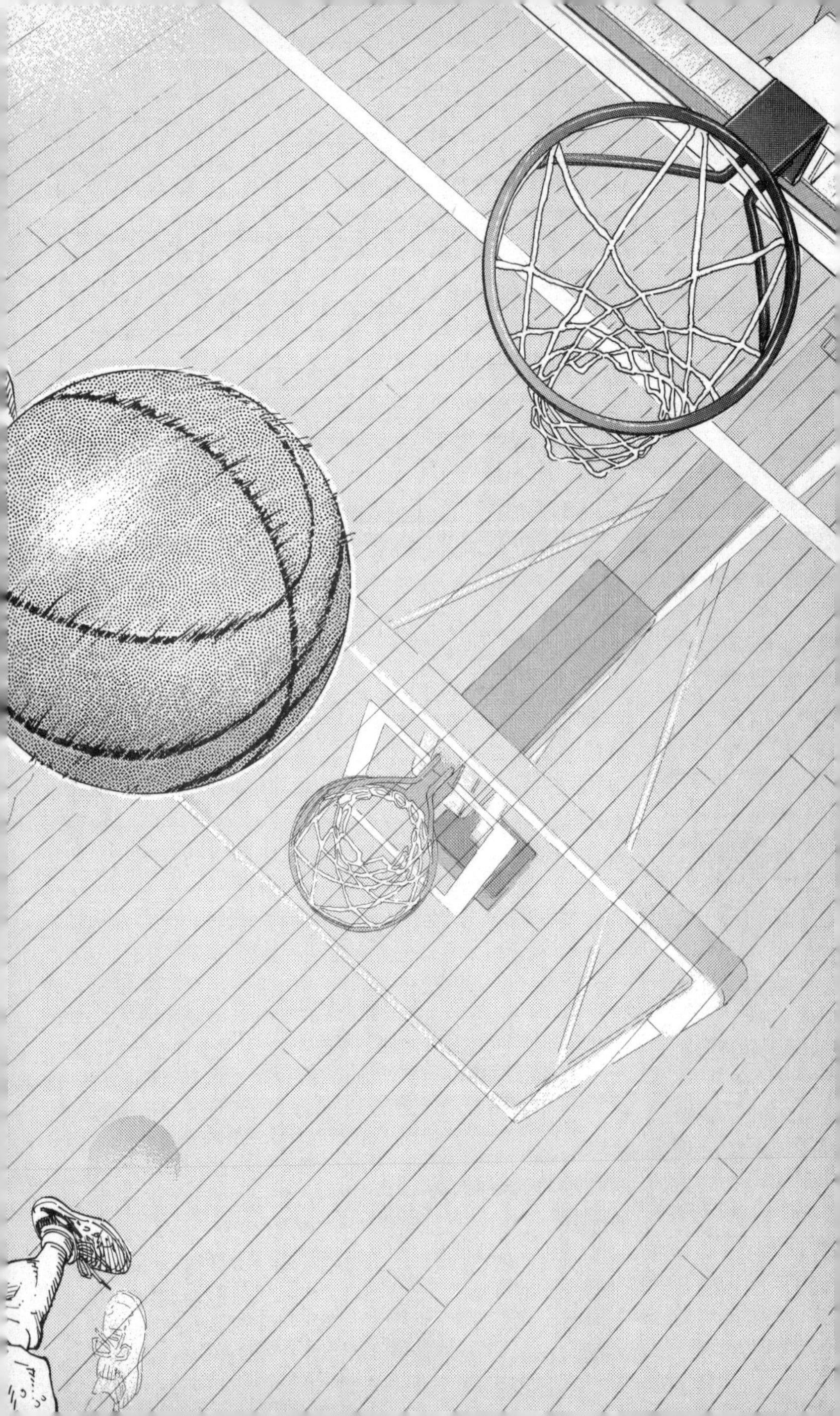

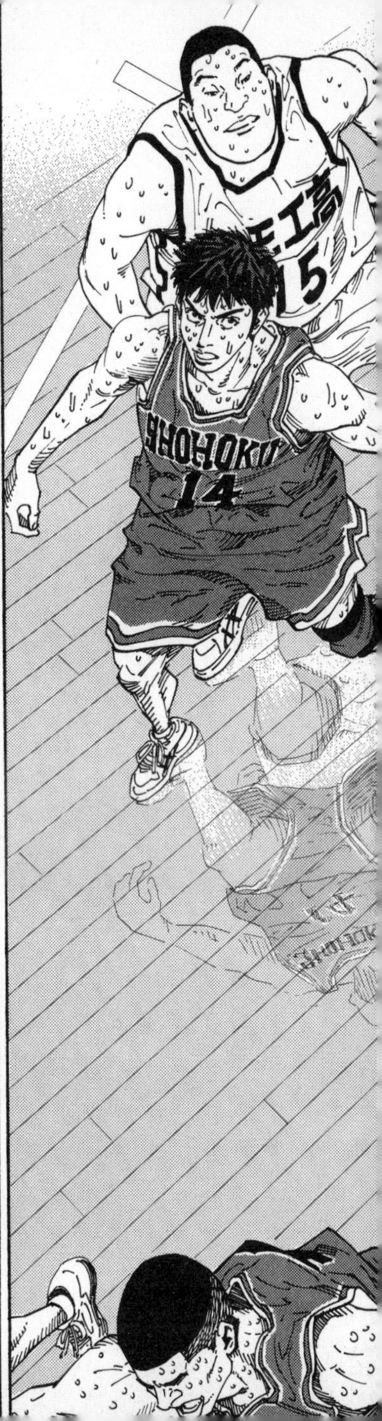
15
SHOHOKU
14
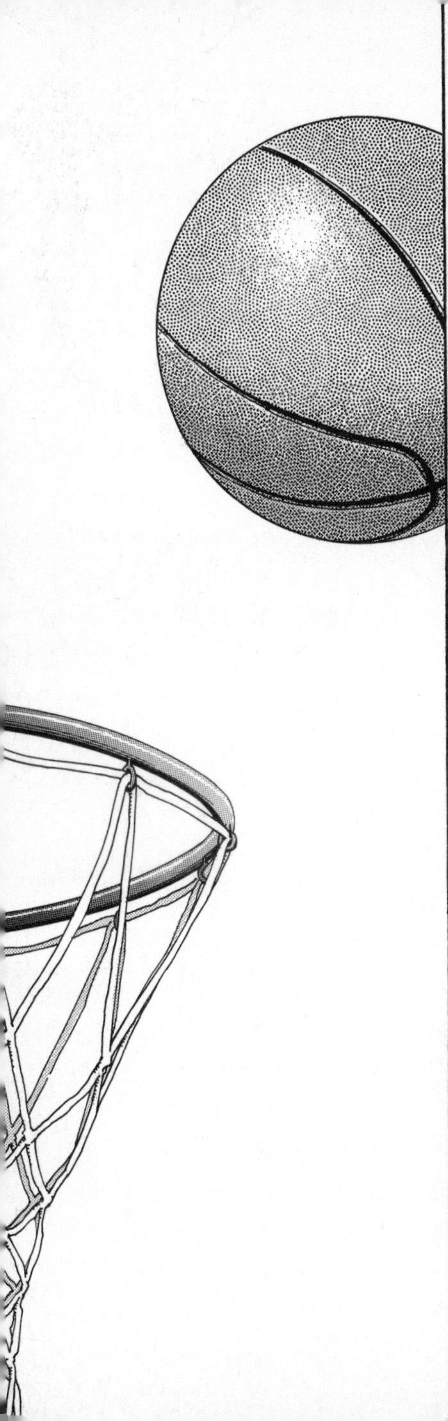

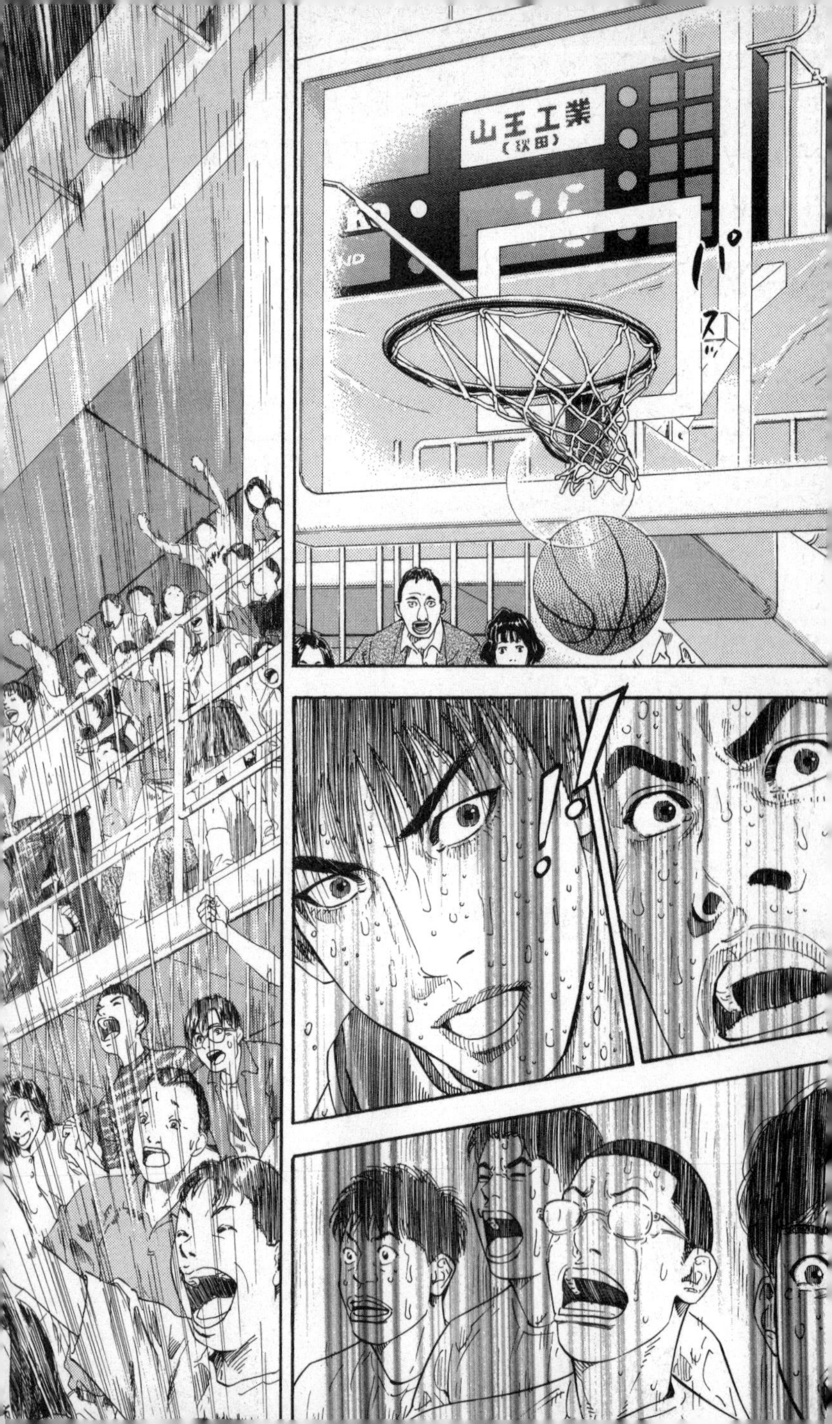
山王工業
(秋田)
パスッ
!!

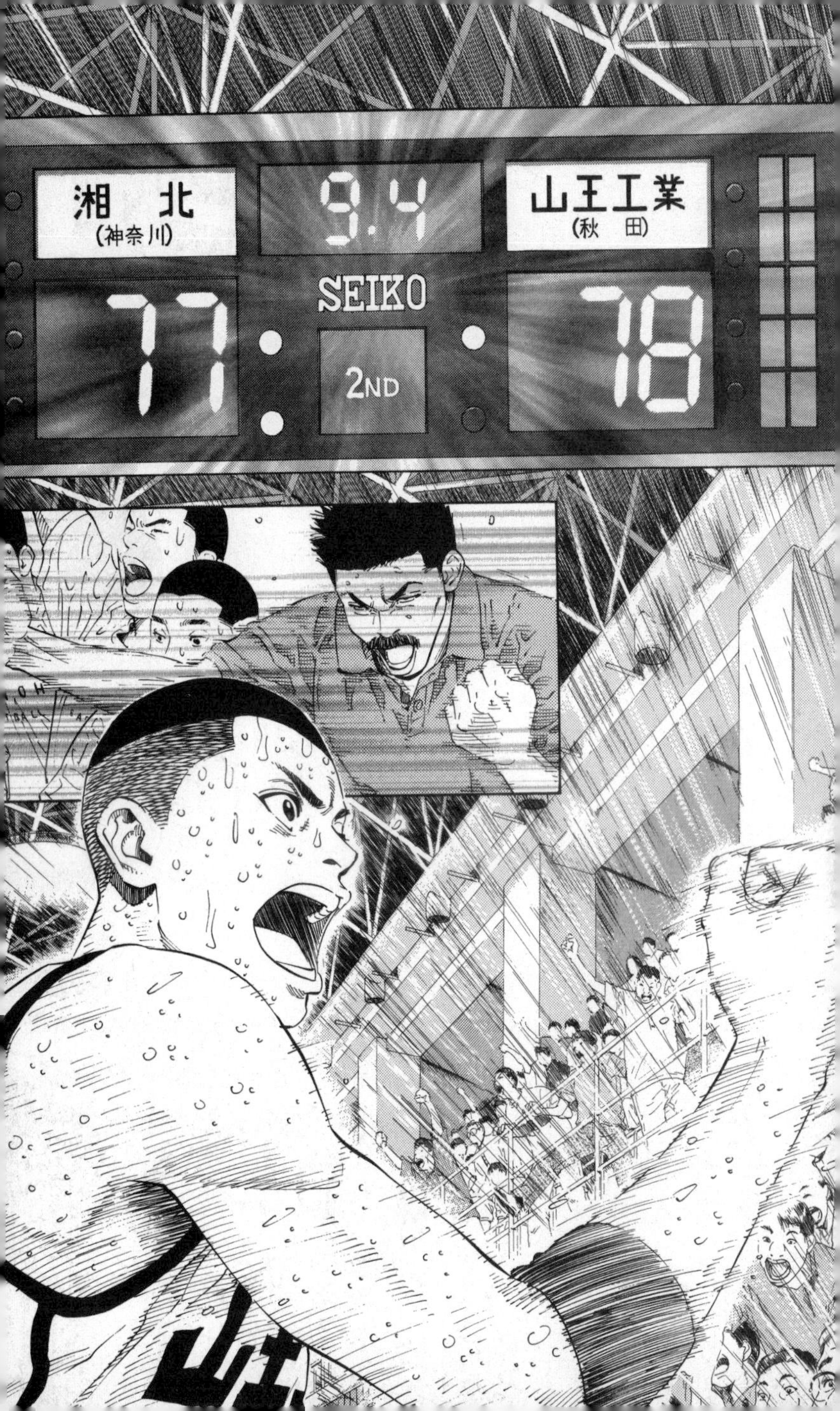
湘北
(神奈川)
9.4
山王工業
(秋田)
SEIKO
77
2ND
78

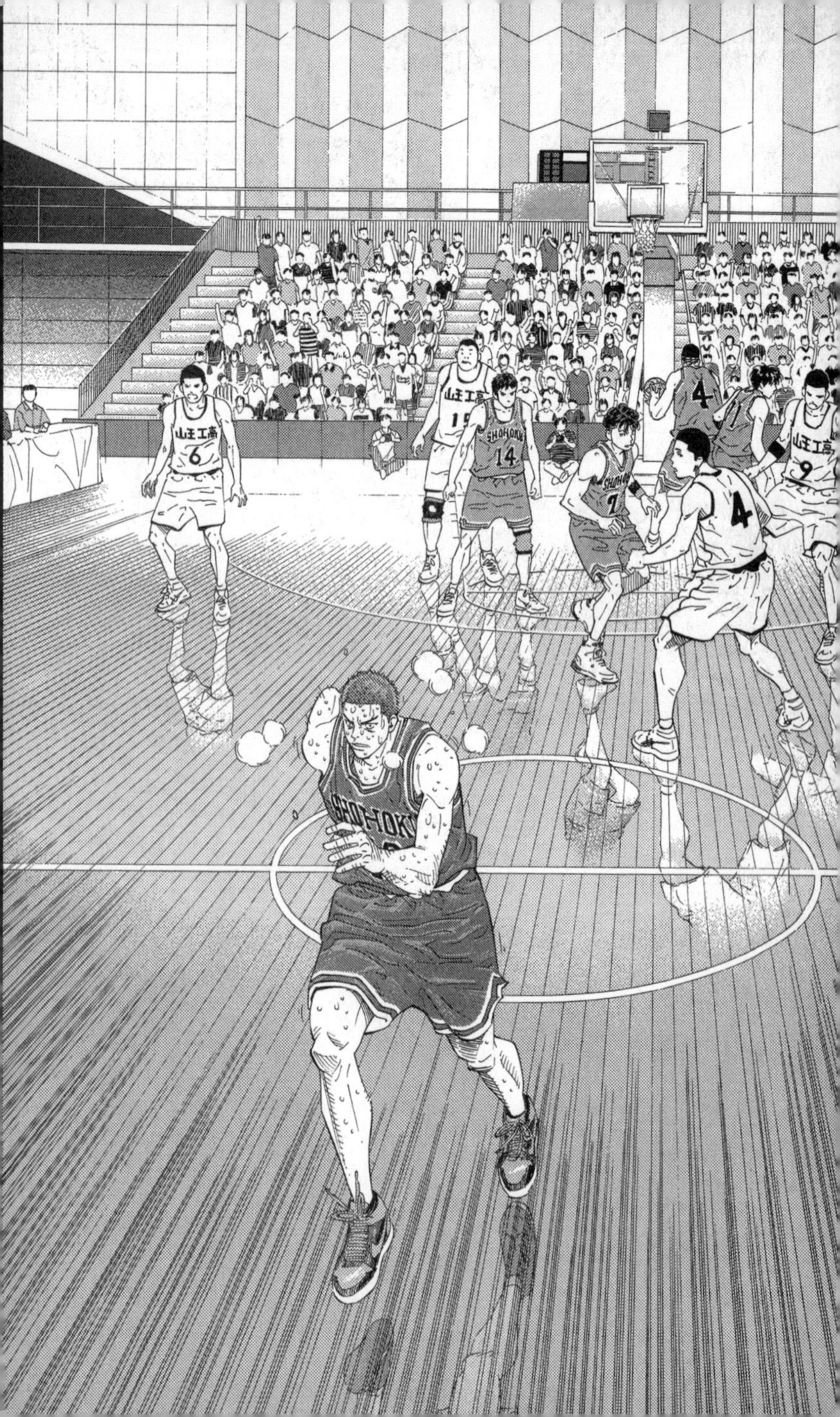
山王工高
SHOHOKU

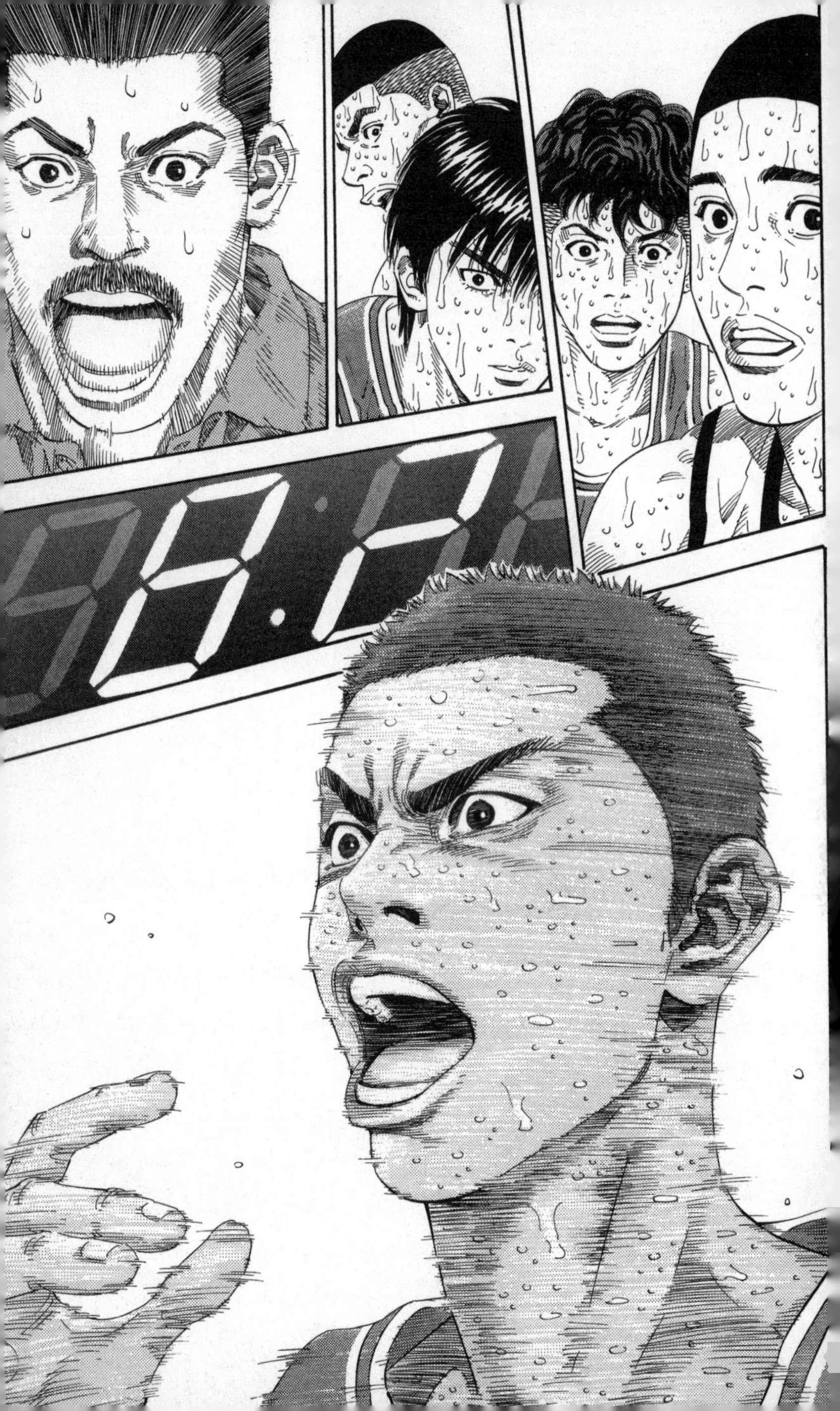

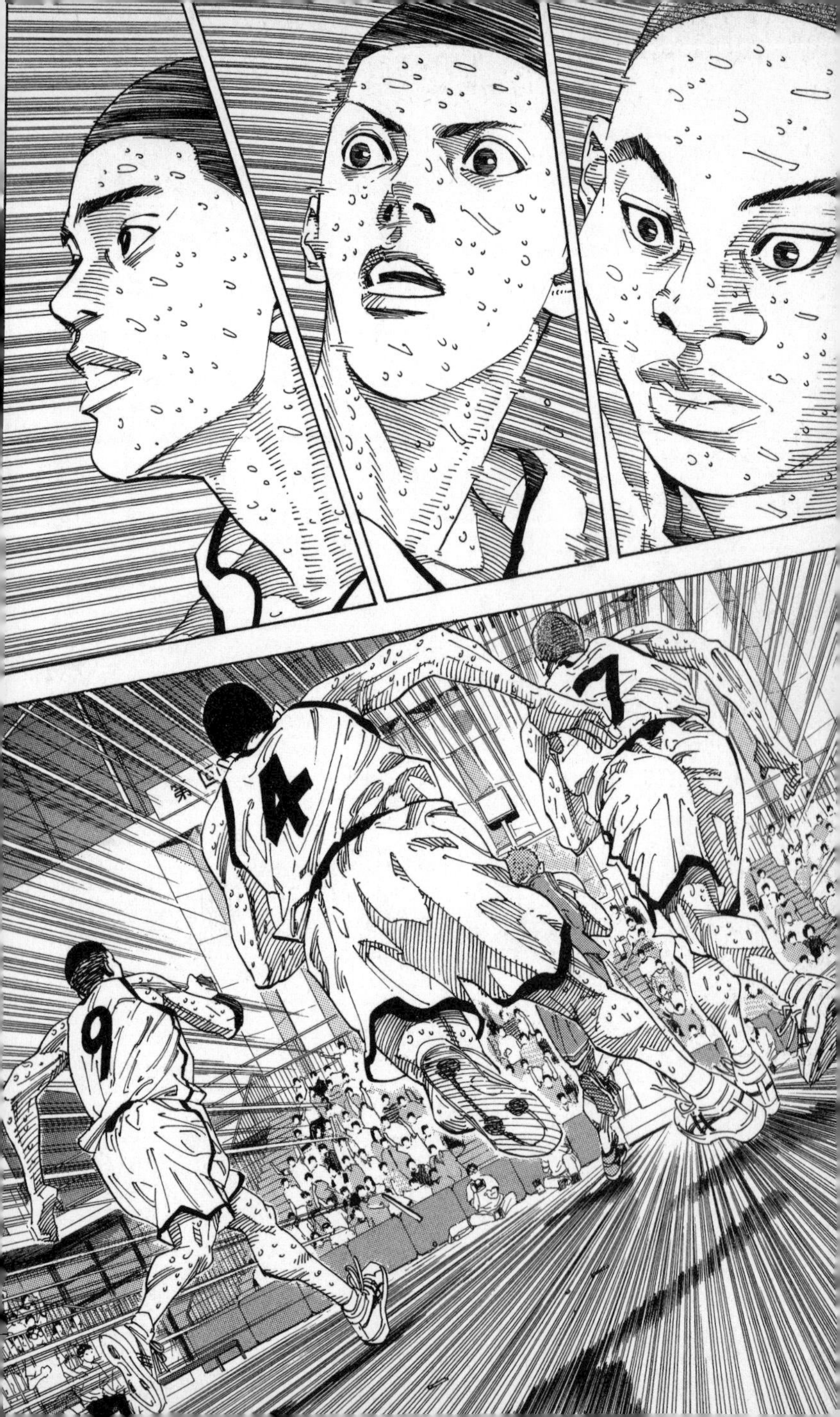

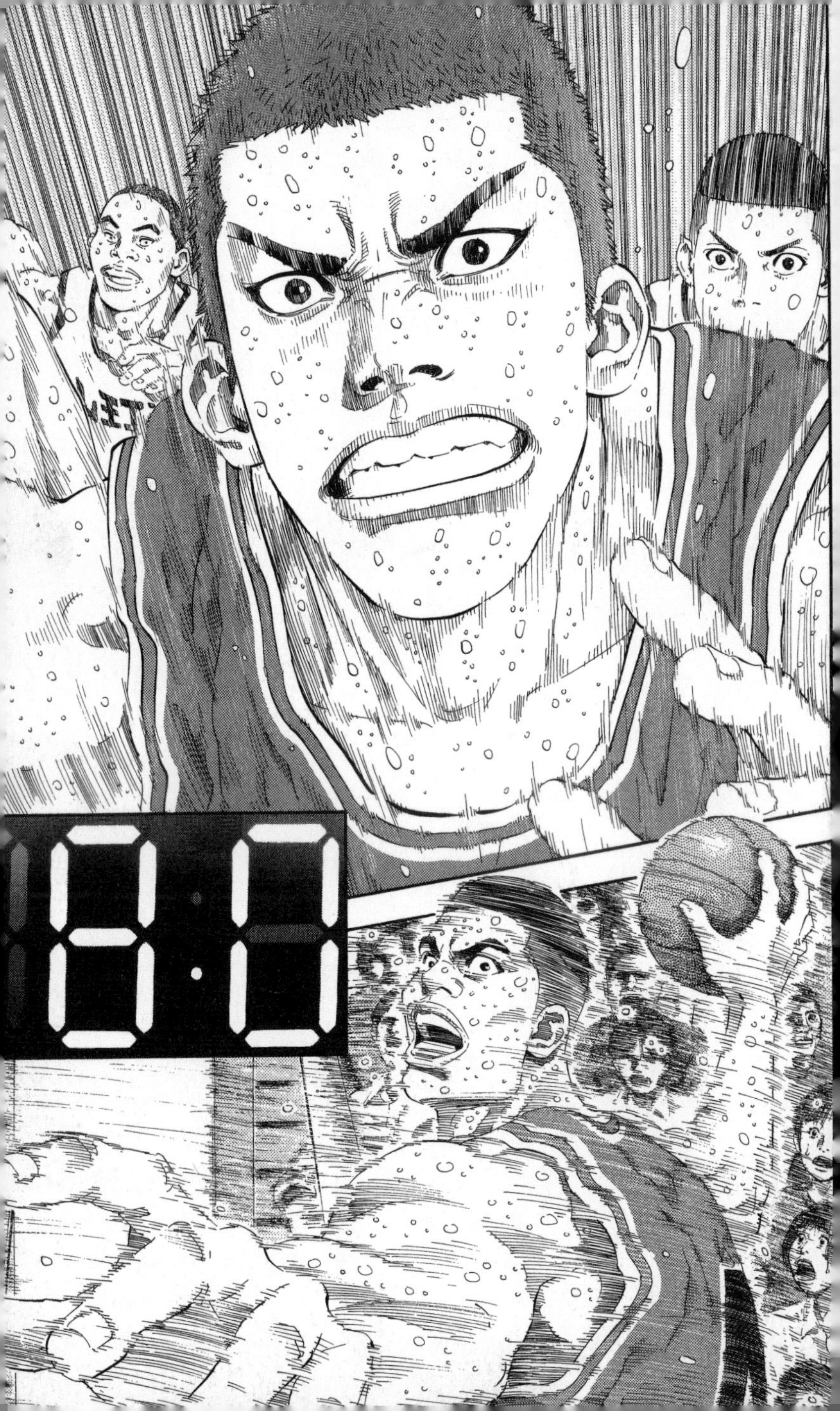

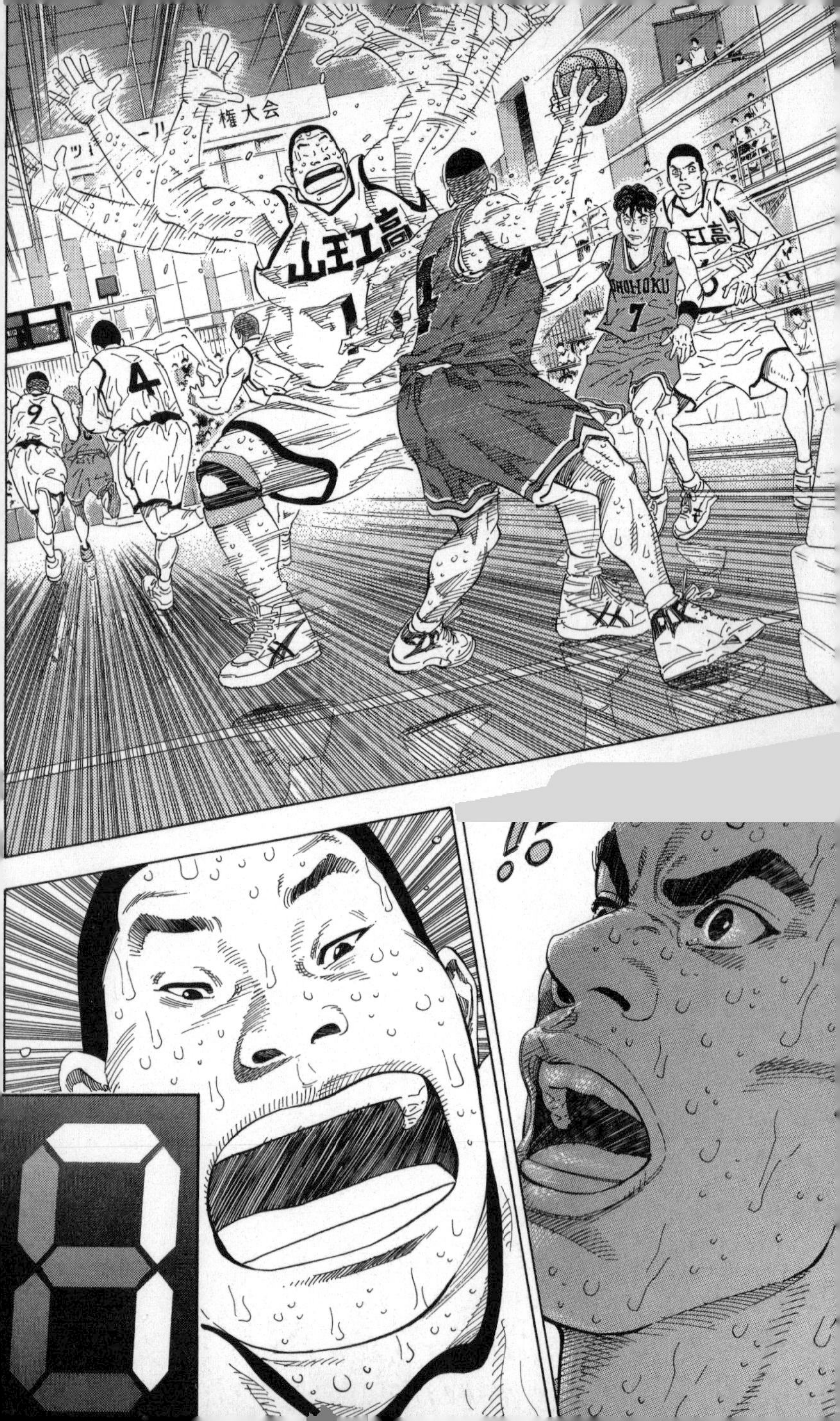
権大会
山王工高
!!

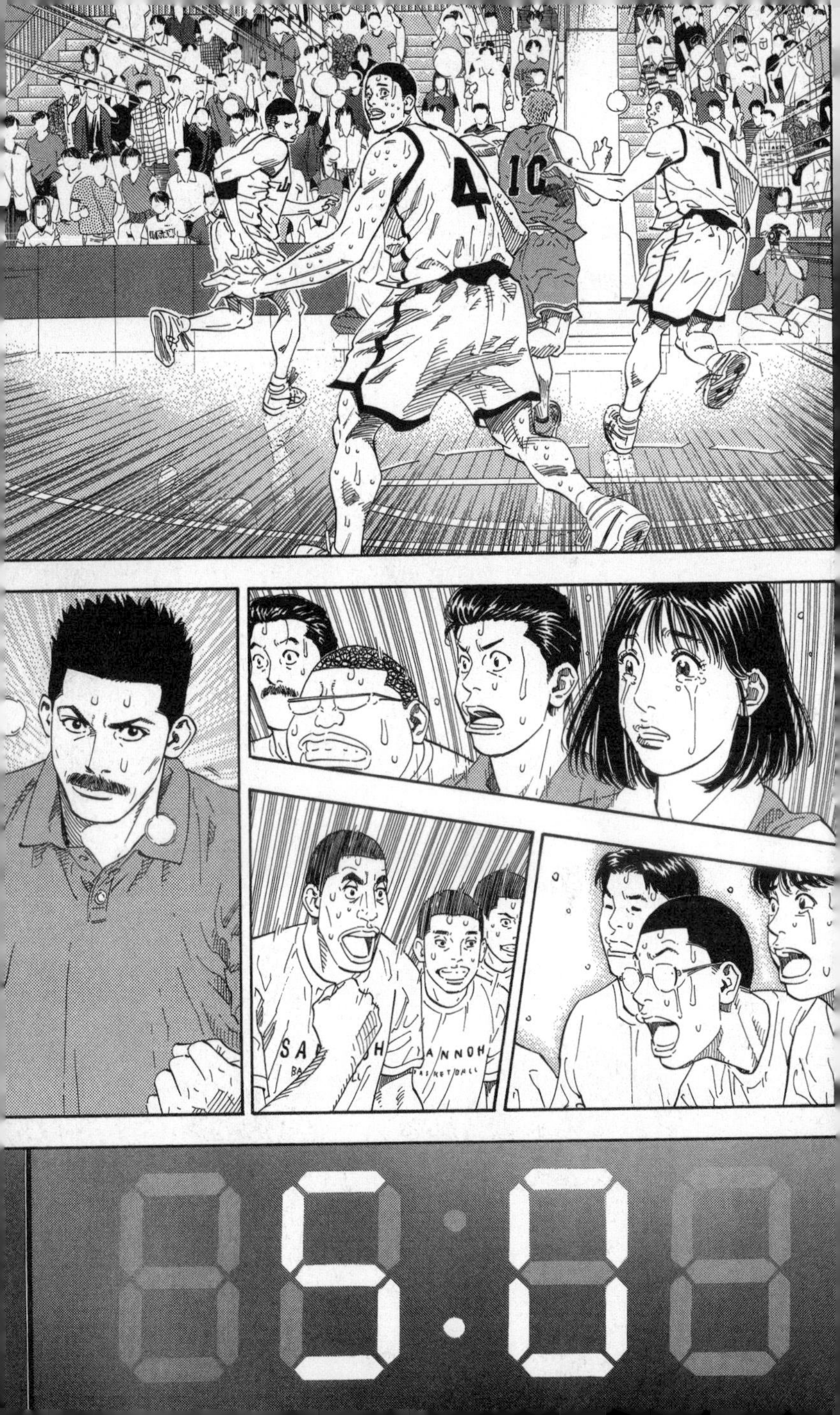

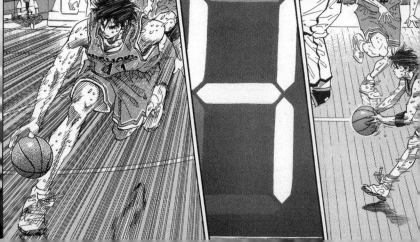

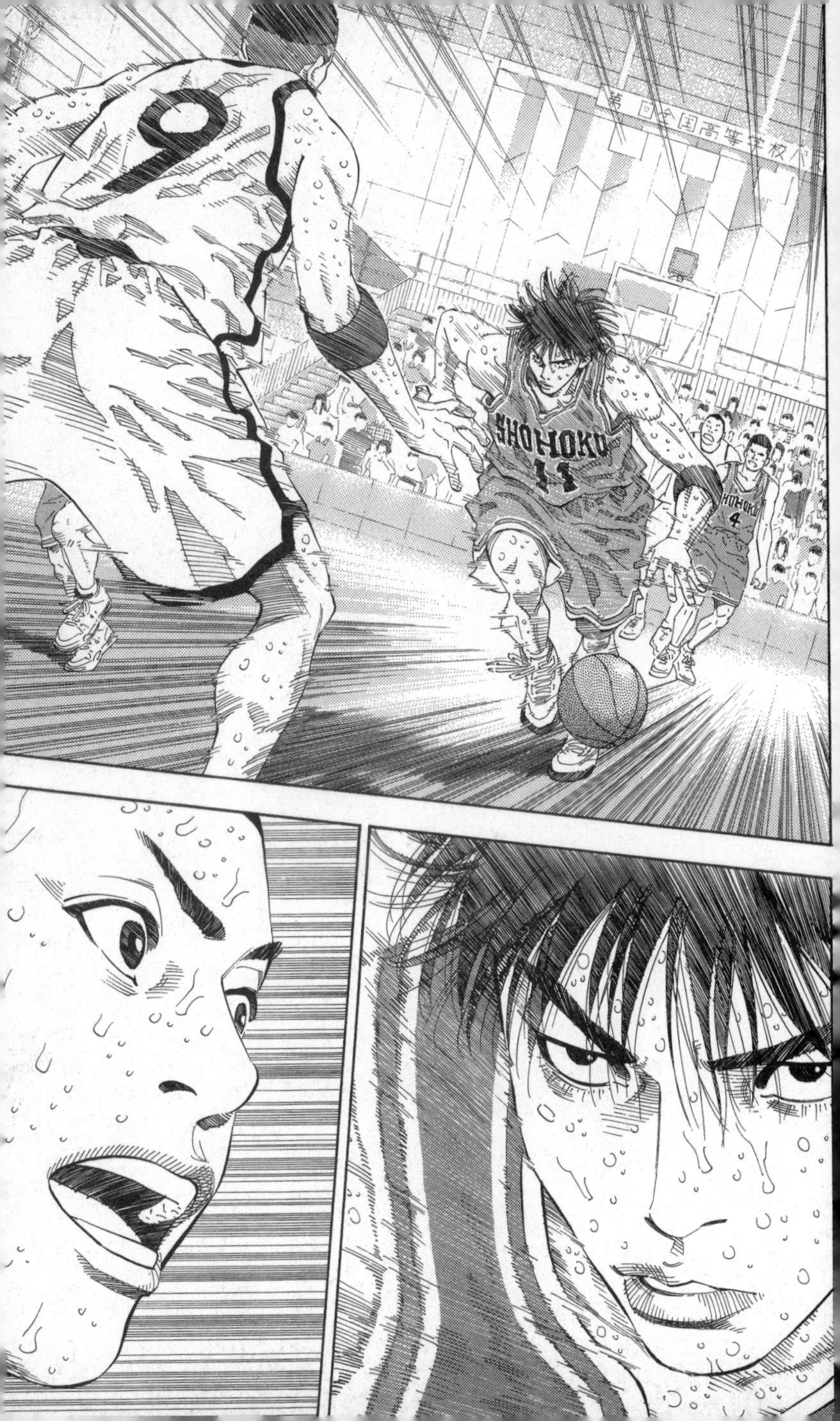
第 回全国高等学校バ
SHOHOKU
11
SHOHOKU
4

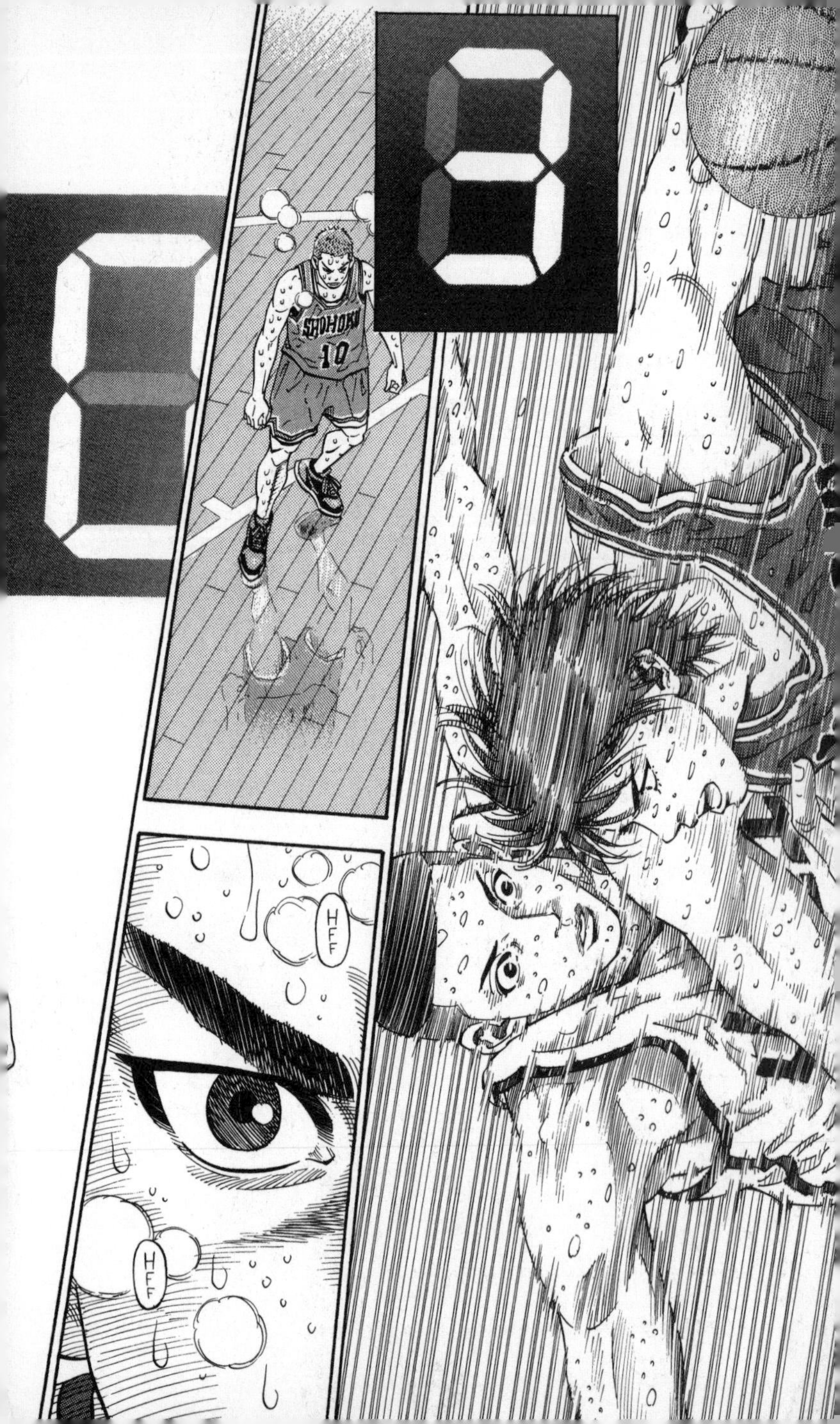
HFF
HFF

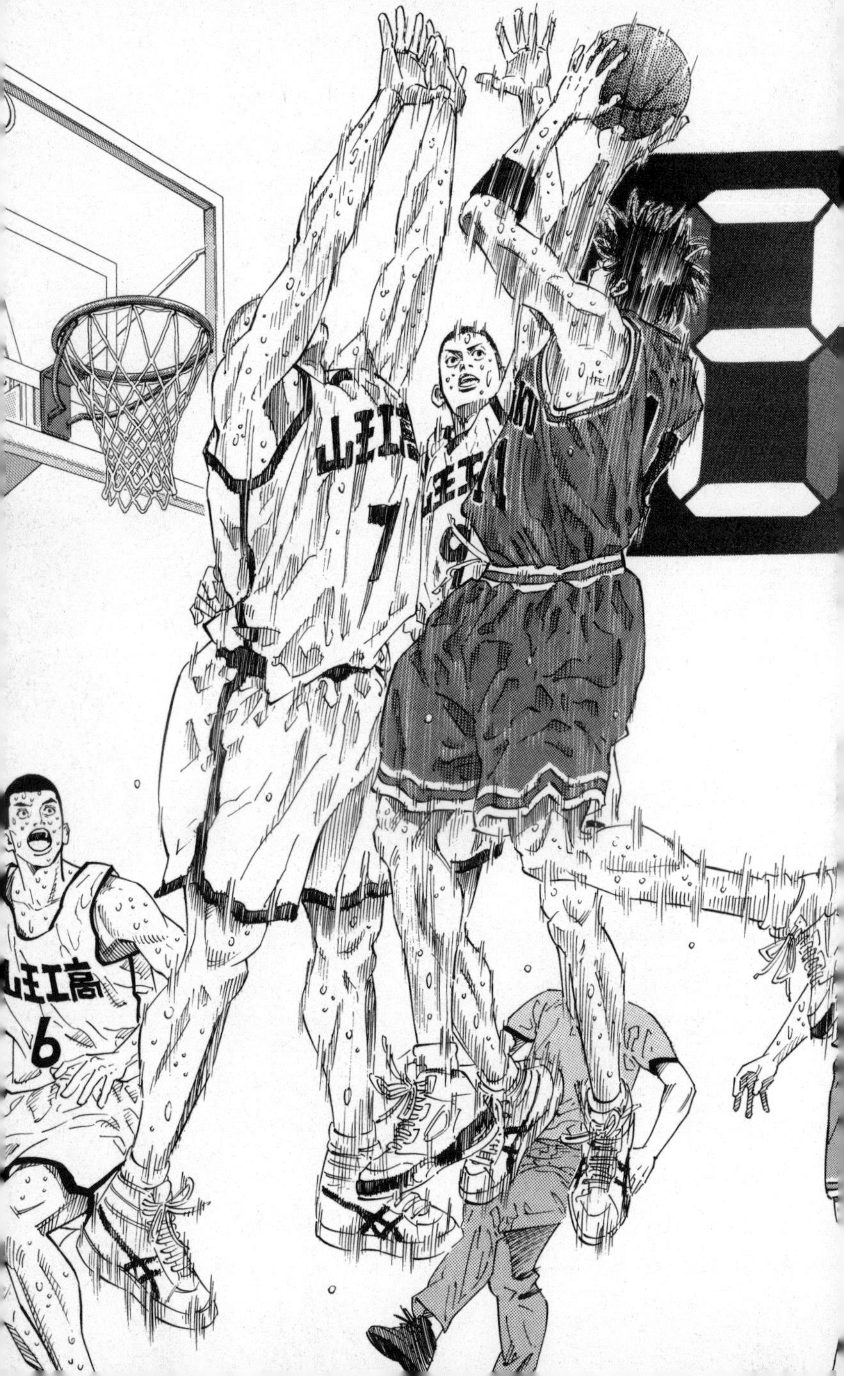
山王工高
6

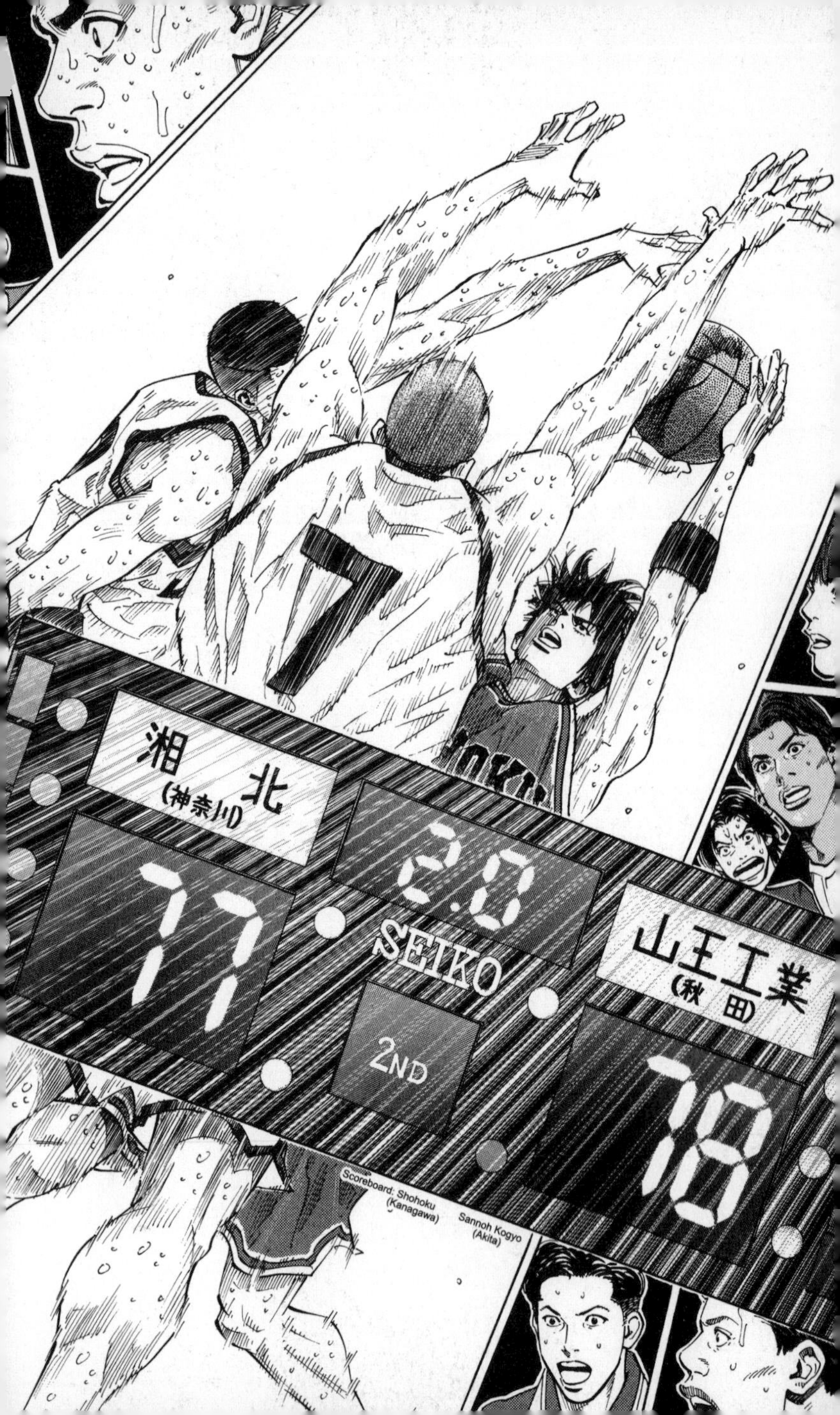
湘北
(神奈川)
77
2.0
SEIKO
2ND
山王工業
(秋田)
78
Scoreboard: Shohoku (Kanagawa) Sannoh Kogyo (Akita)

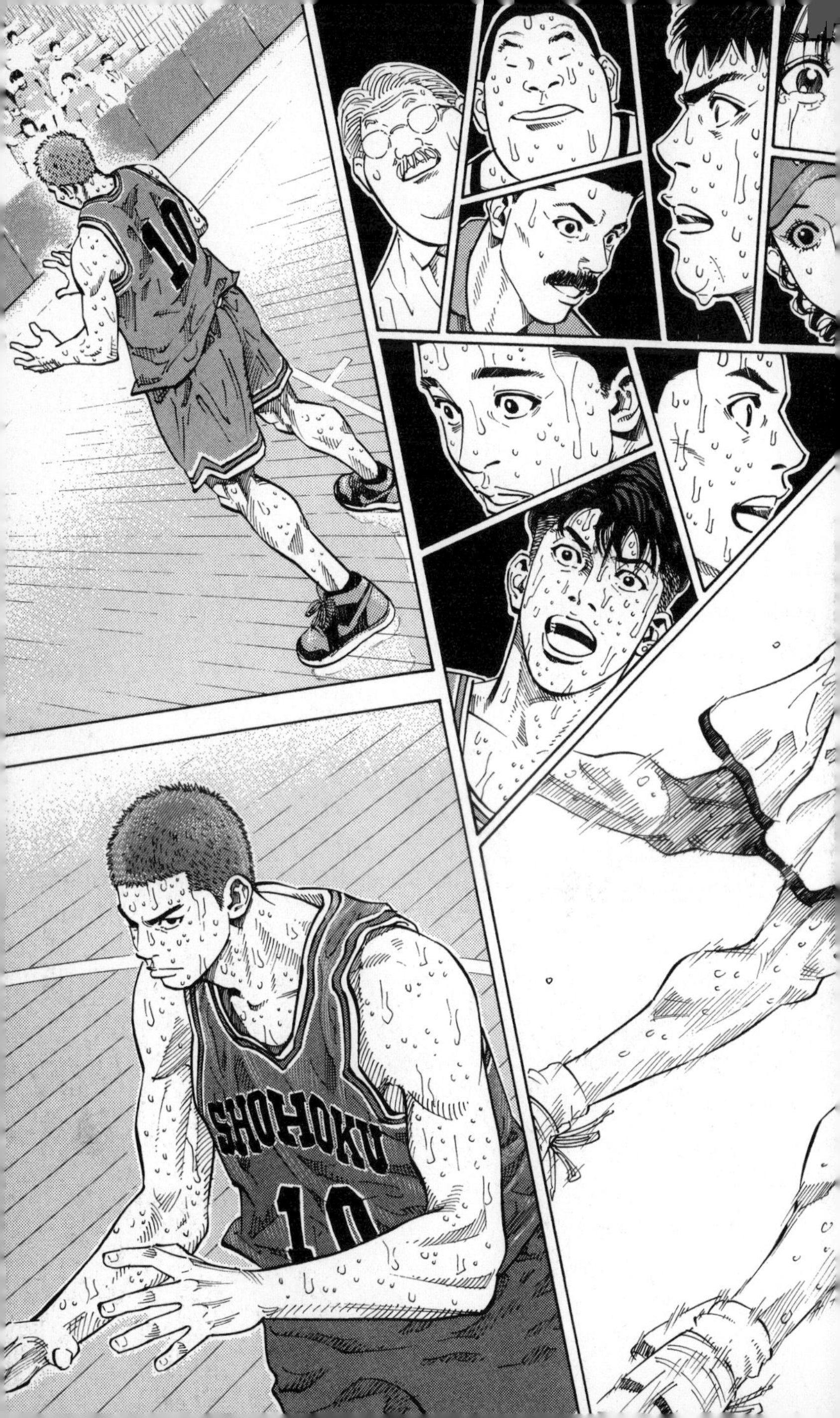
SHOHOKU
10

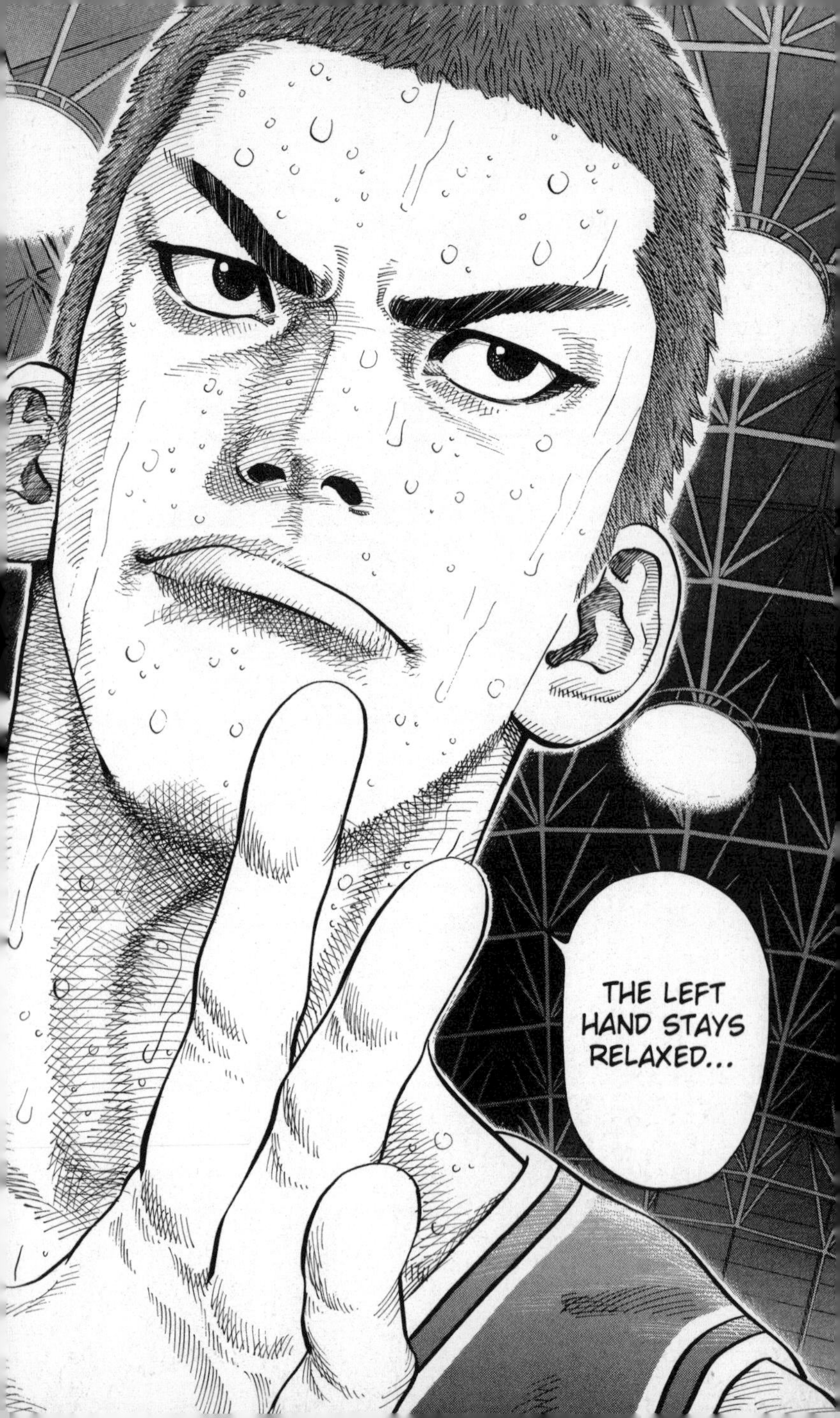
THE LEFT HAND STAYS RELAXED...

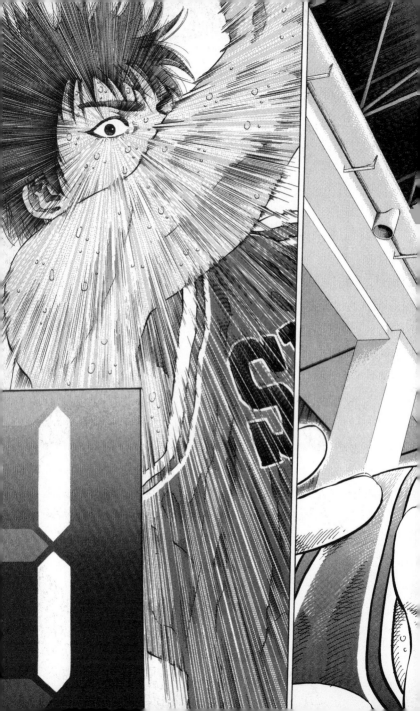

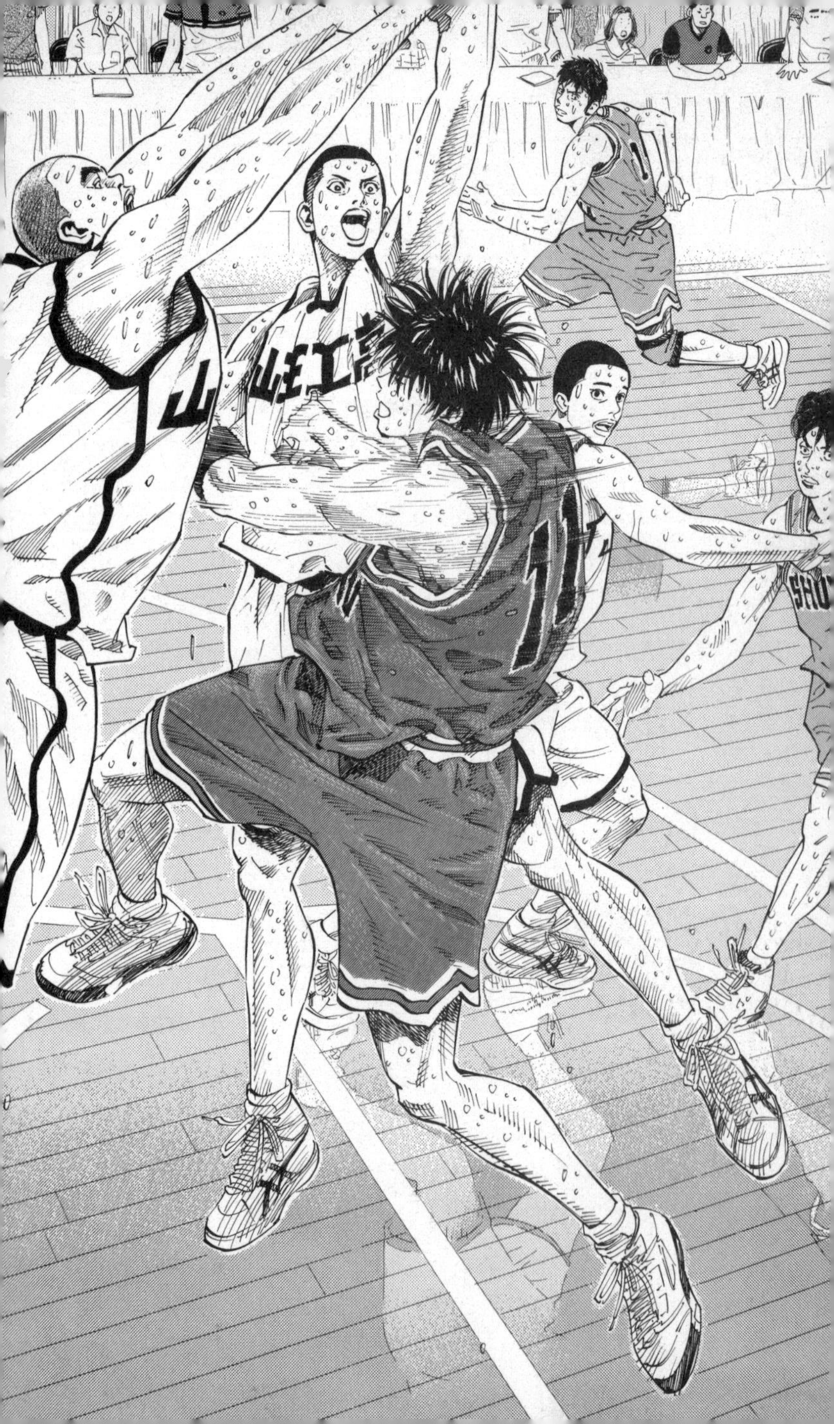

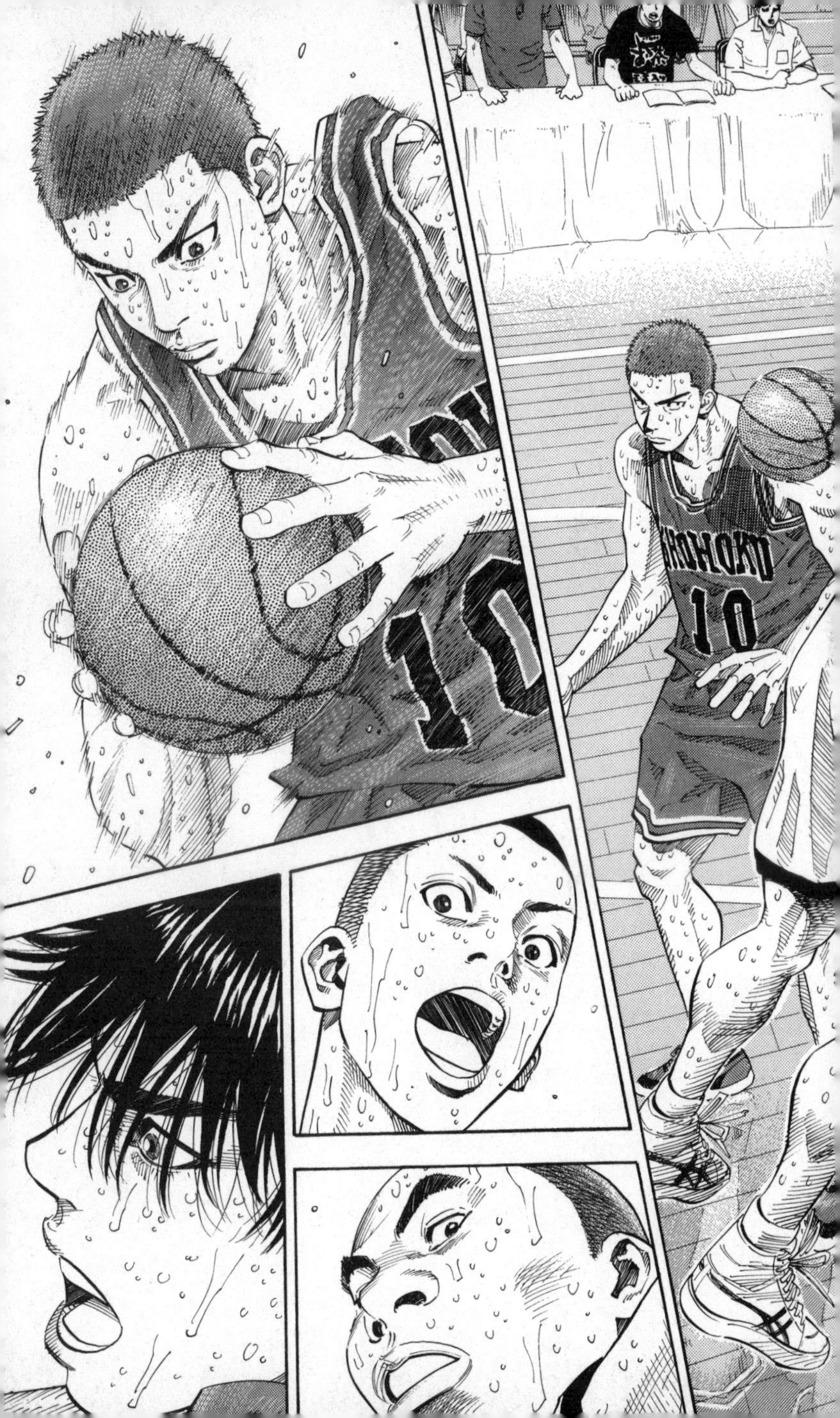

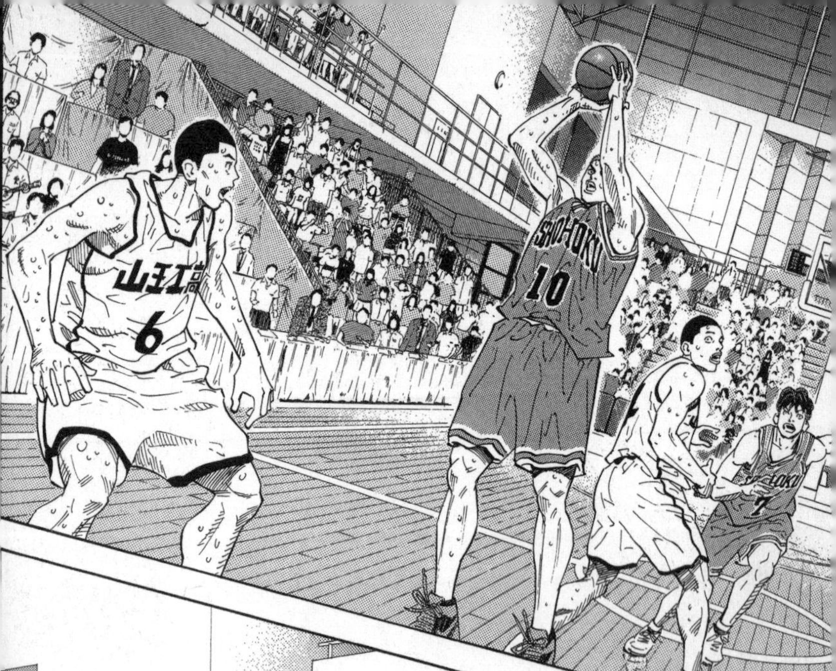
山王工高
6
SHOHOKU
10
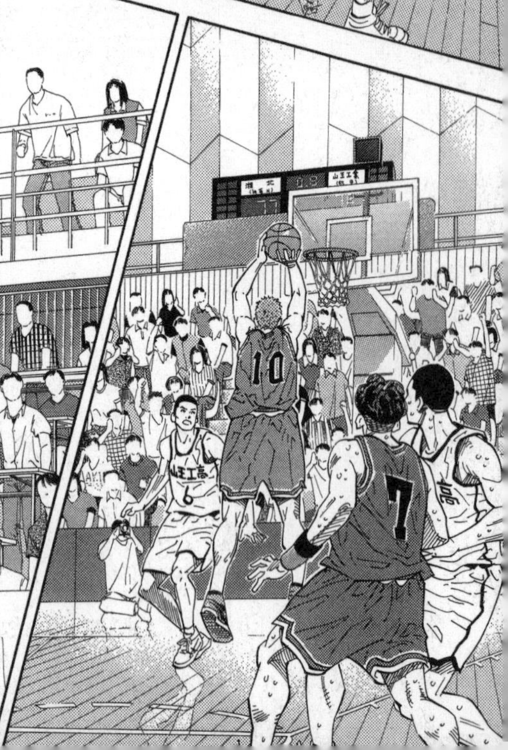
10
山王工高
6
7
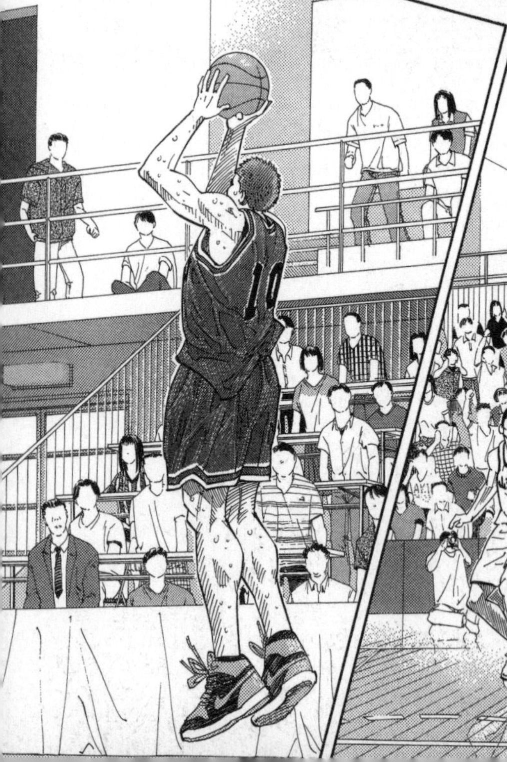
10

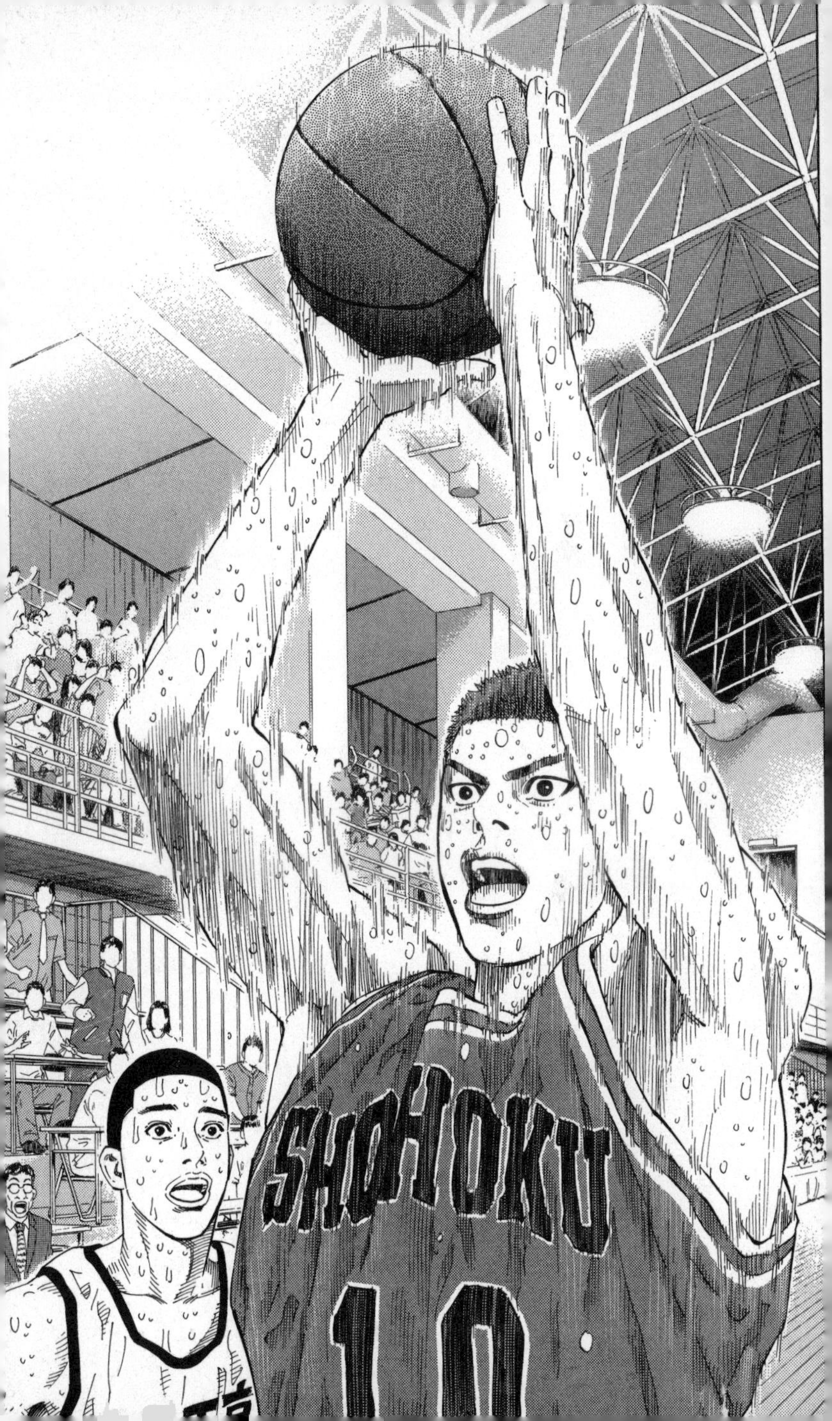
SHOHOKU
10

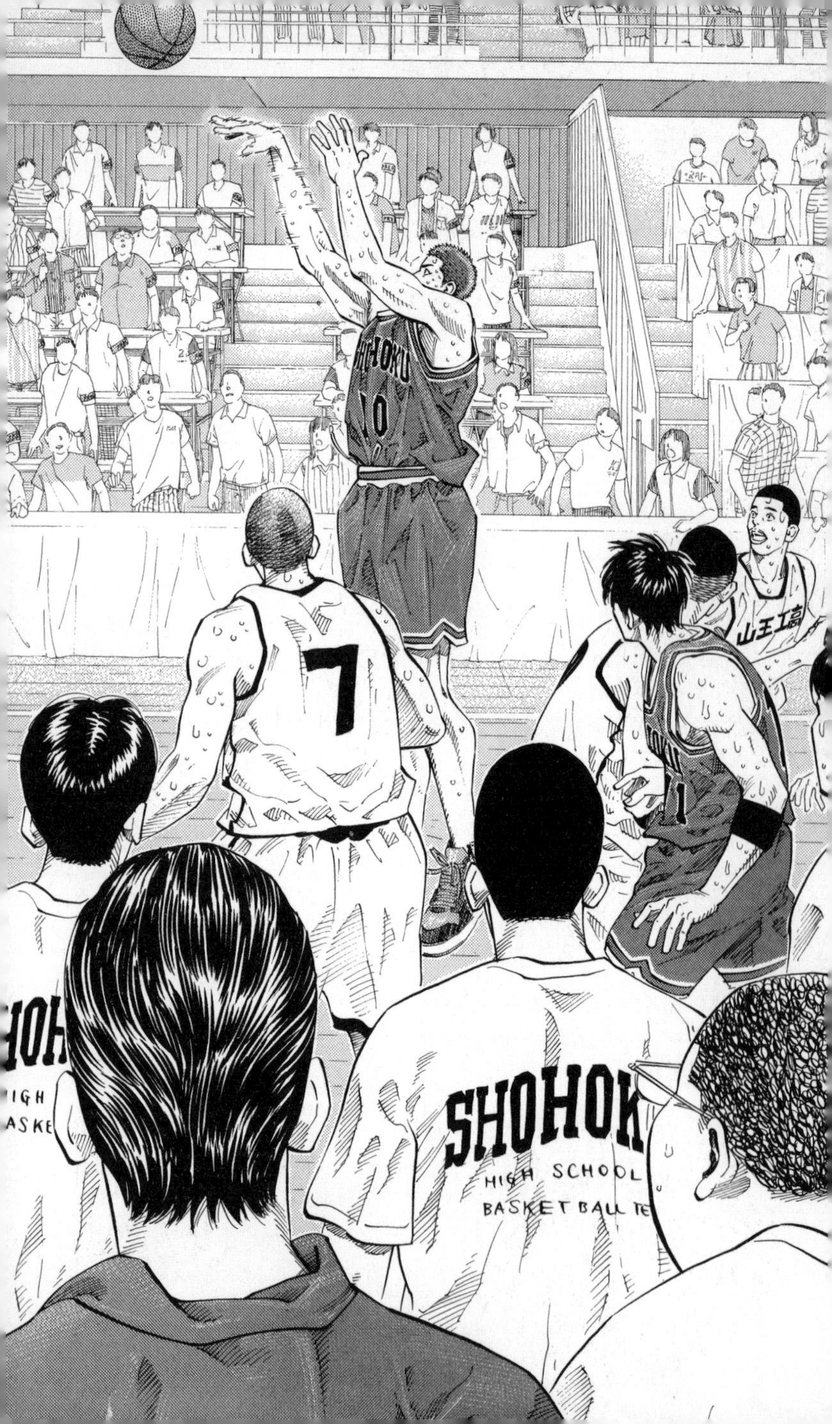
10
7
山王工高
SHOHOK
HIGH SCHOOL
BASKETBALL TE

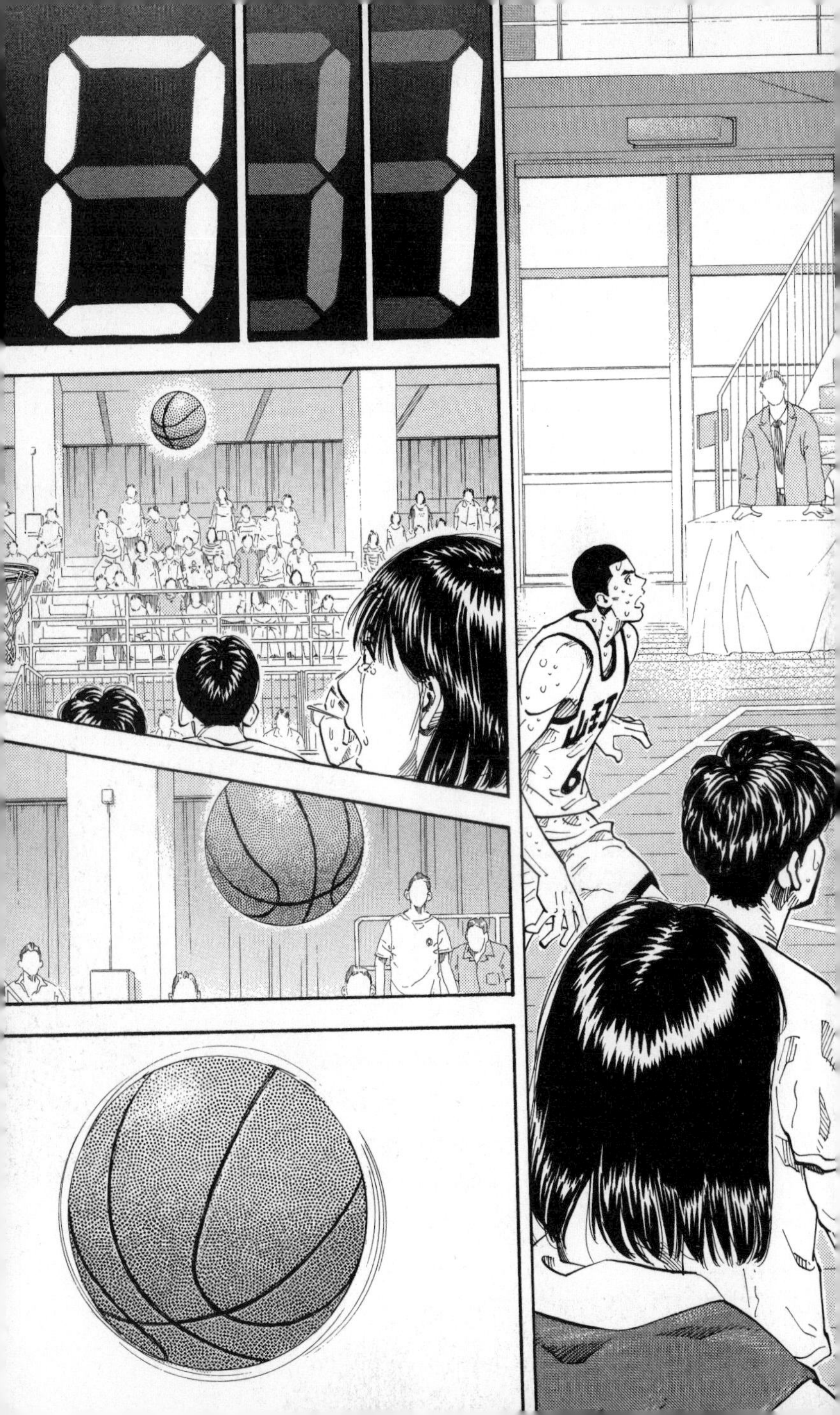

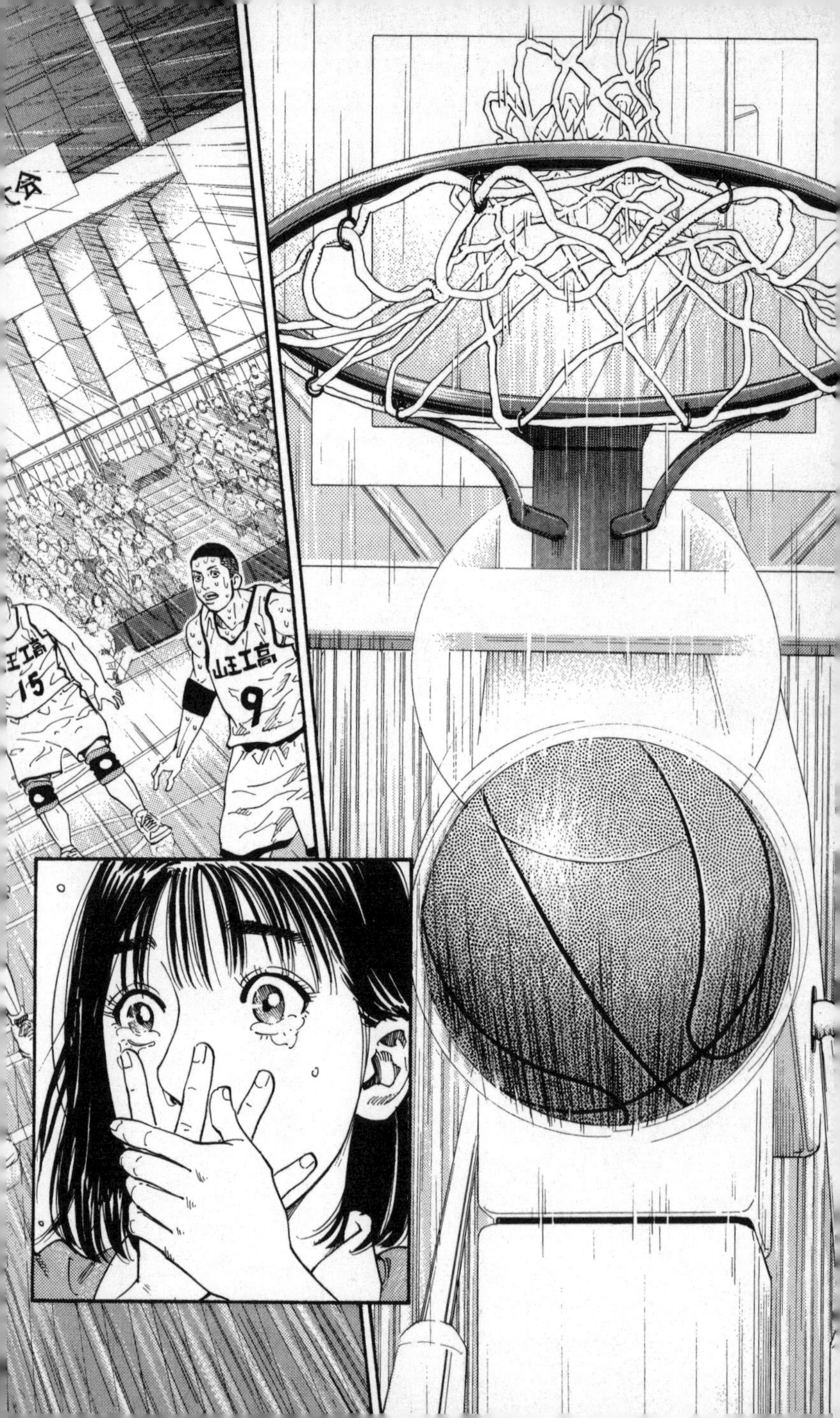
山王工高
9

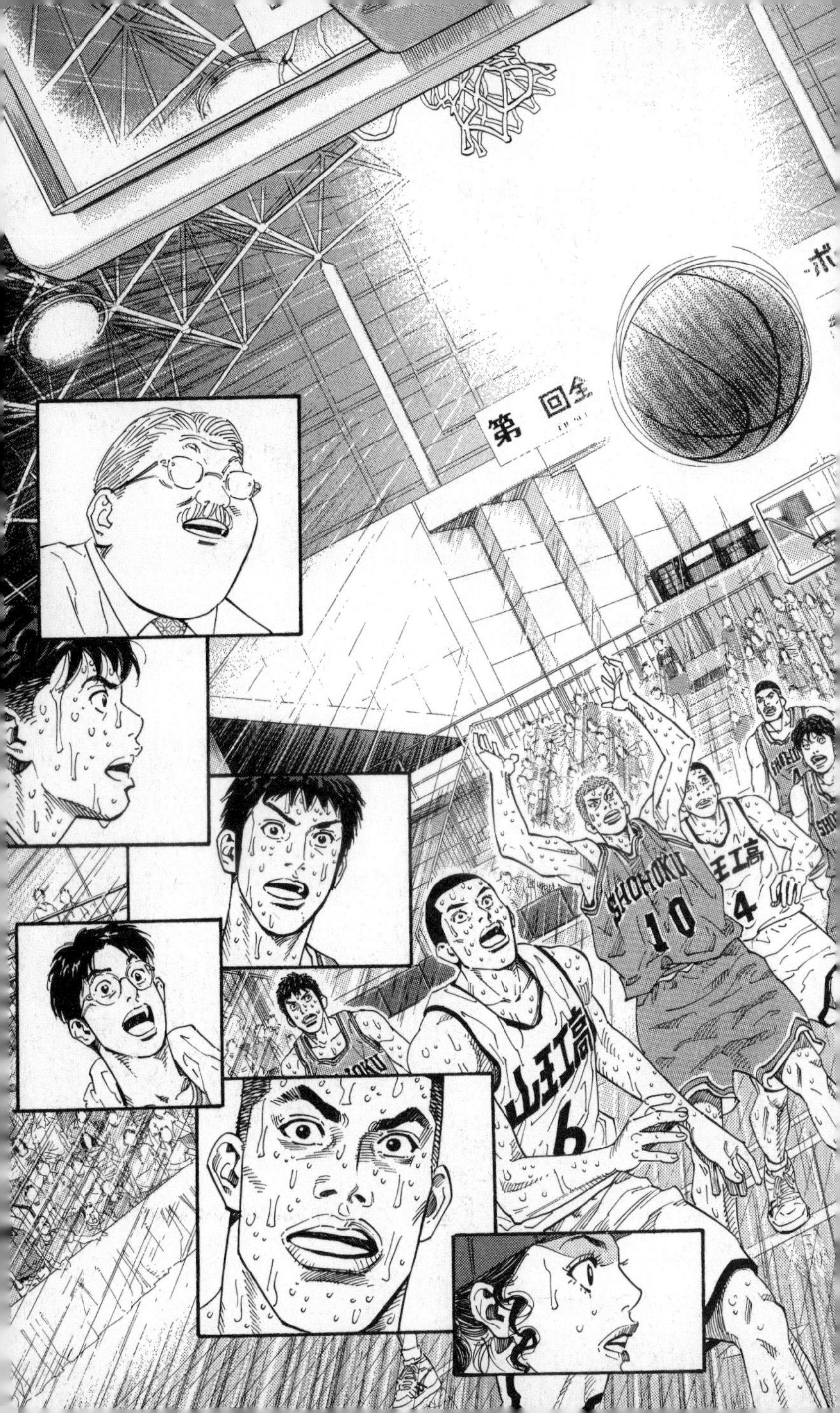
第 回全
SHOHOKU
山王工高

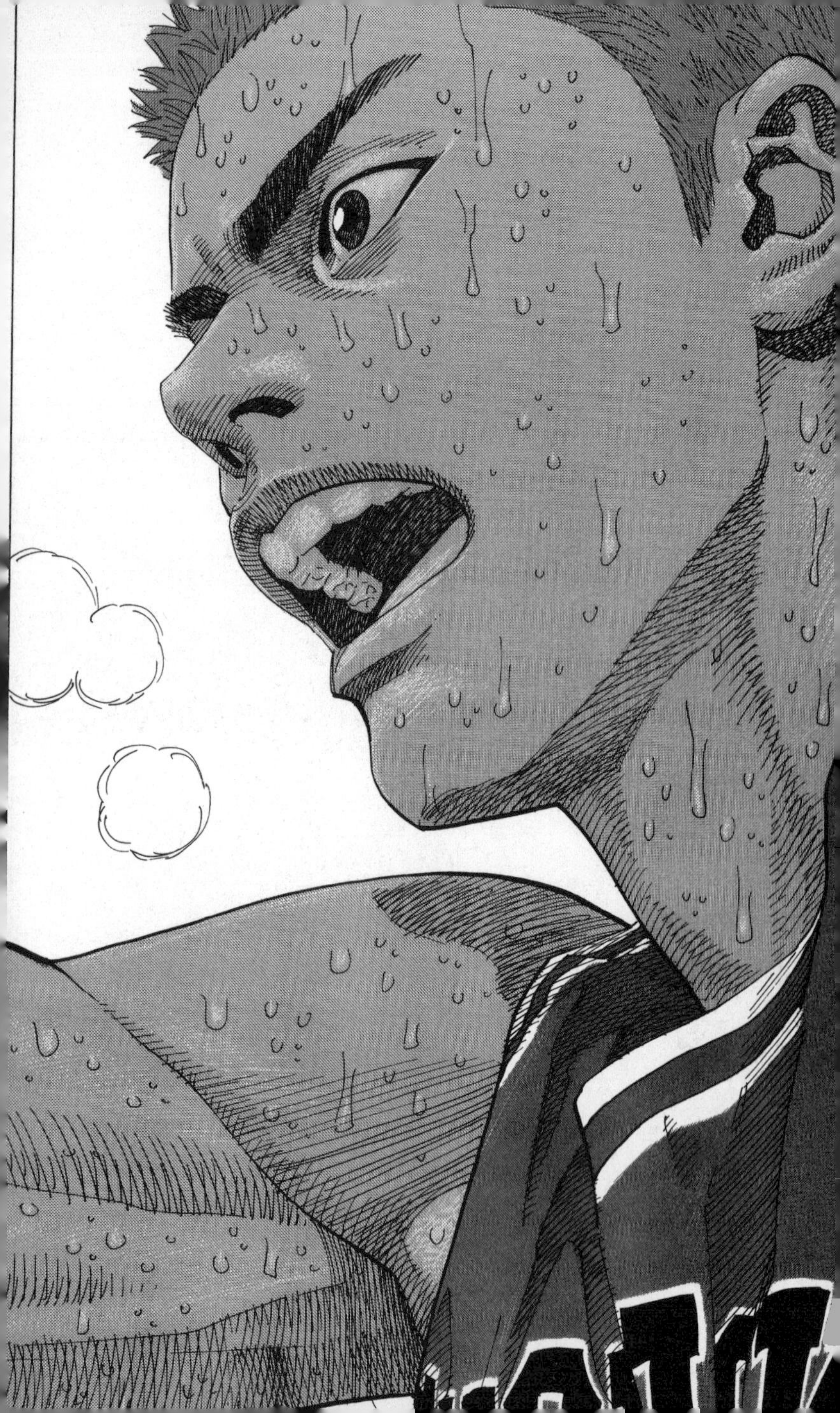

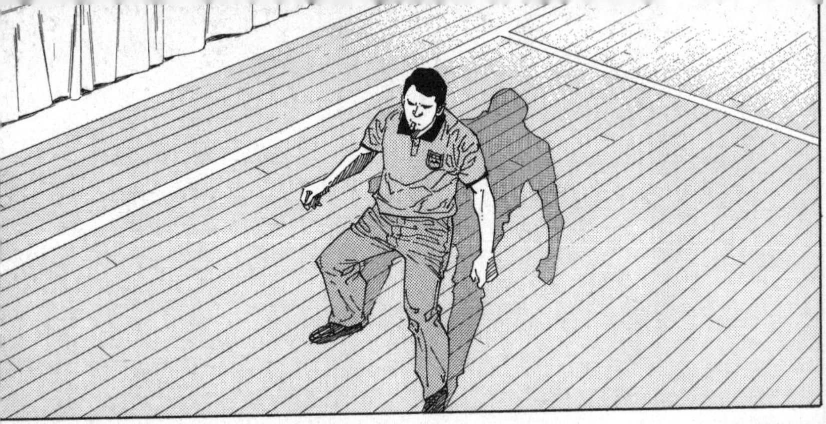

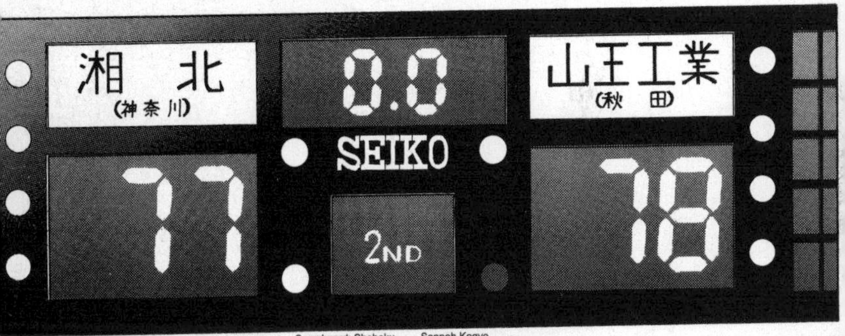
湘北
(神奈川)
0.0
山王工業
(秋田)
SEIKO
77
2ND
78

Scoreboard: Shohoku (Kanagawa) Sannoh Kogyo (Akita)

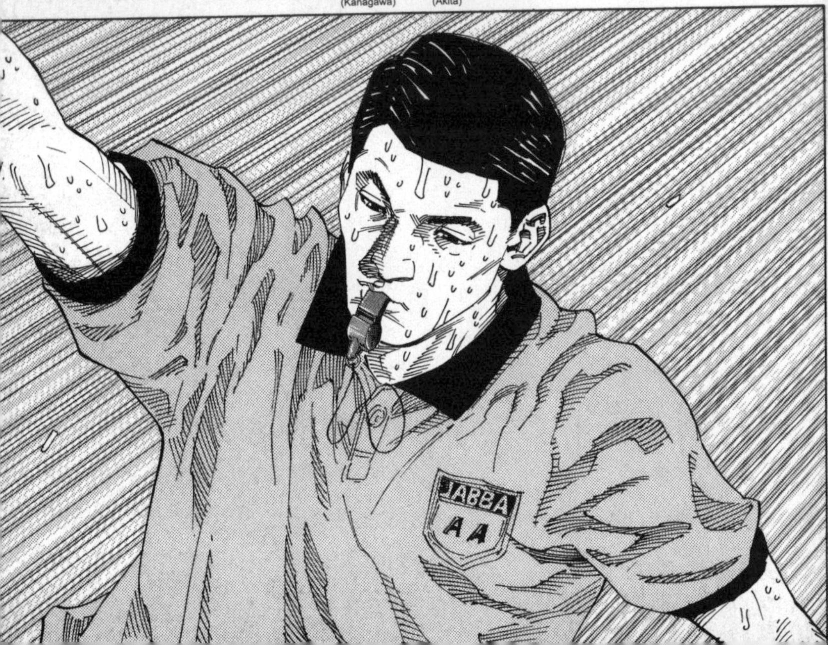
JABBA
AA

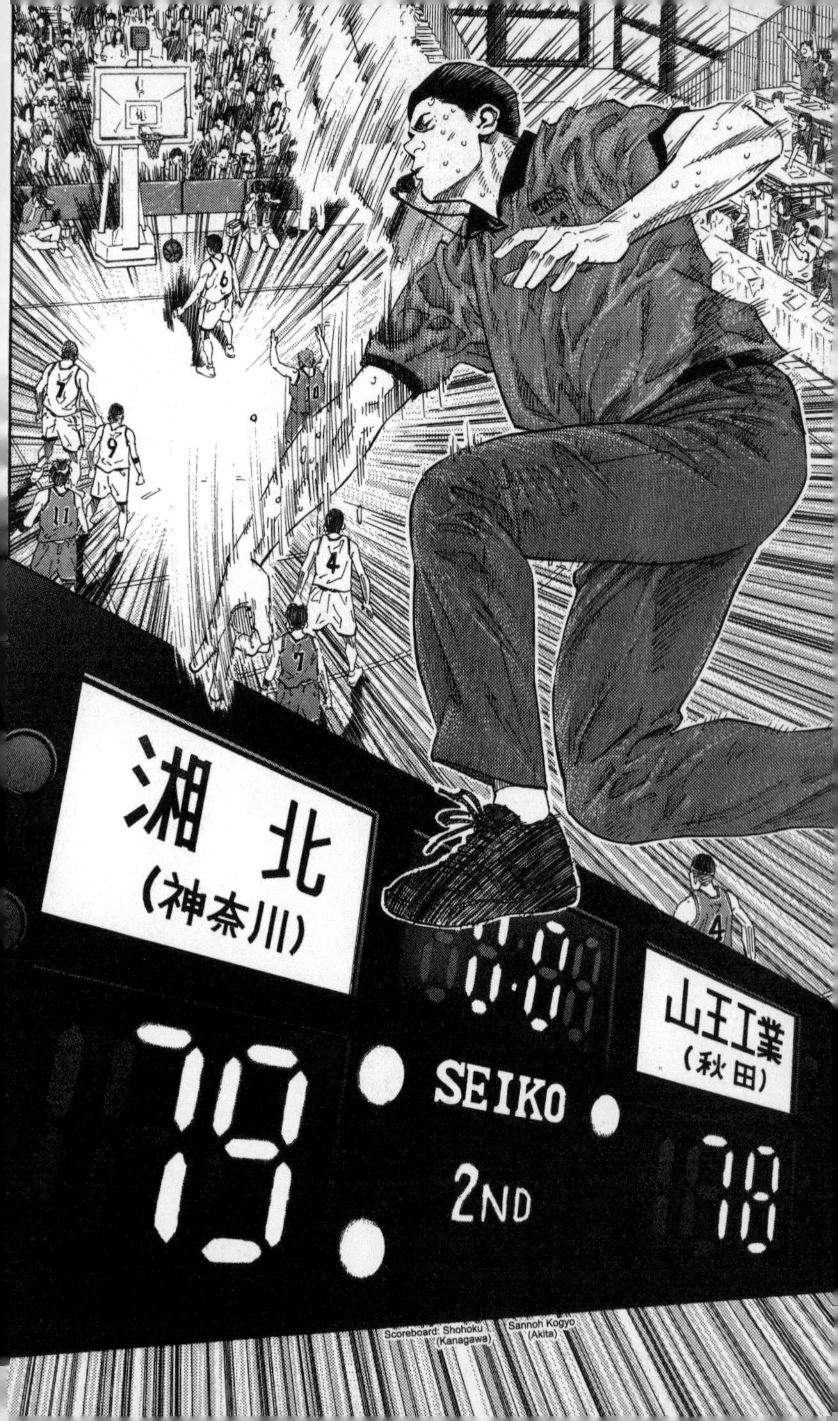
湘北
(神奈川)
山王工業
(秋田)
SEIKO
2ND
Scoreboard: Shohoku (Kanagawa) Sannoh Kogyo (Akita)

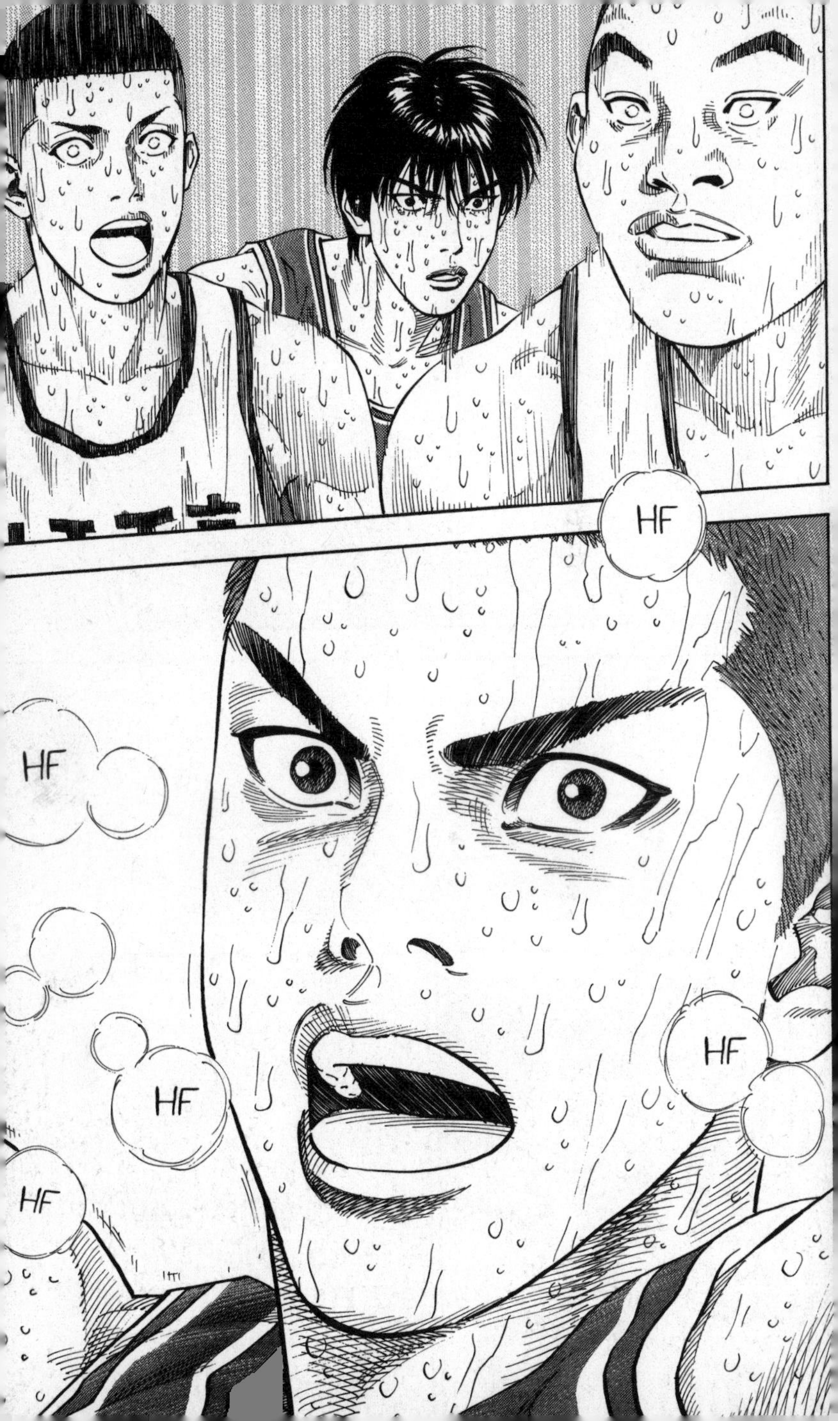
HF
HF
HF
HF
HF

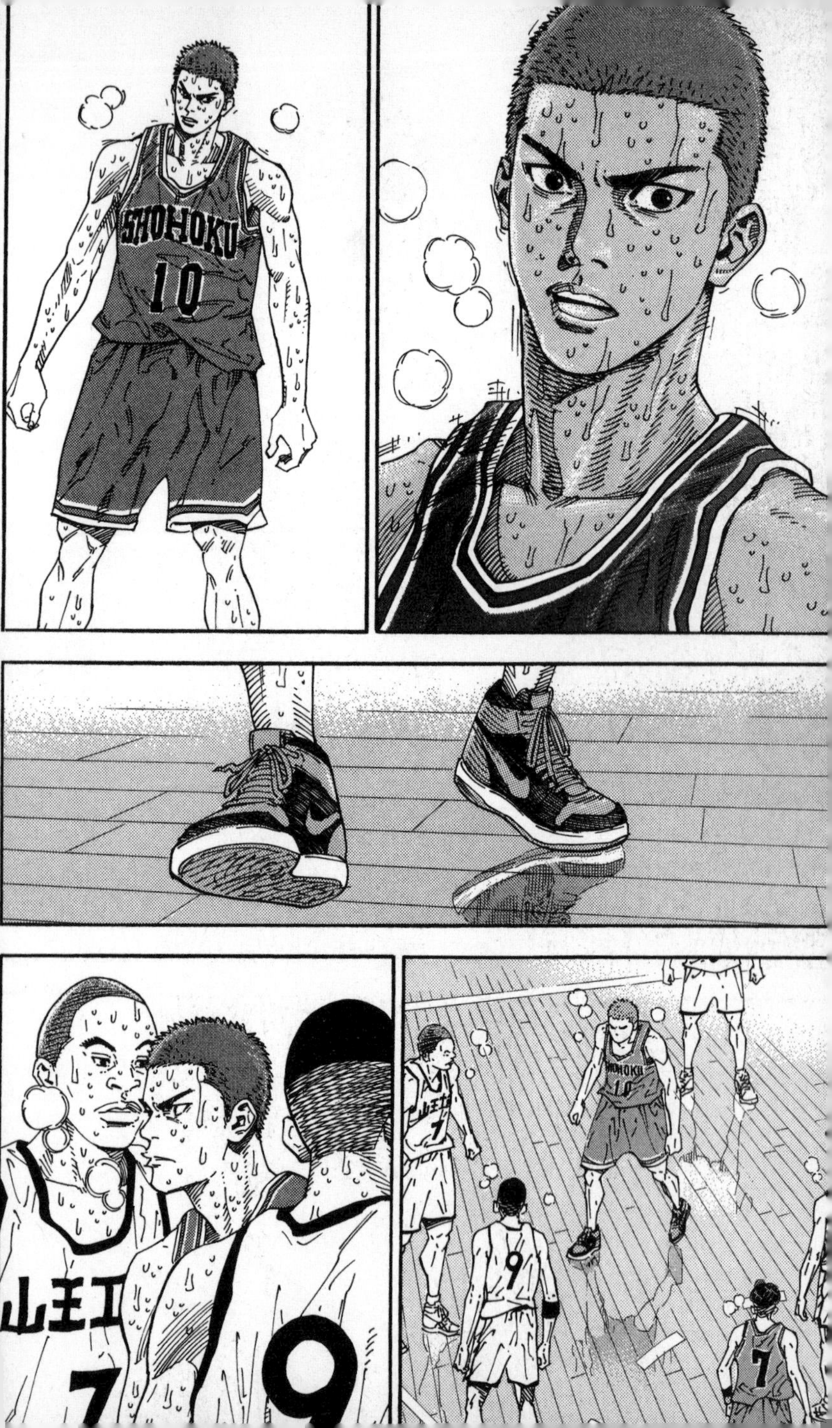
SHOHOKU
10
山王工
7
9

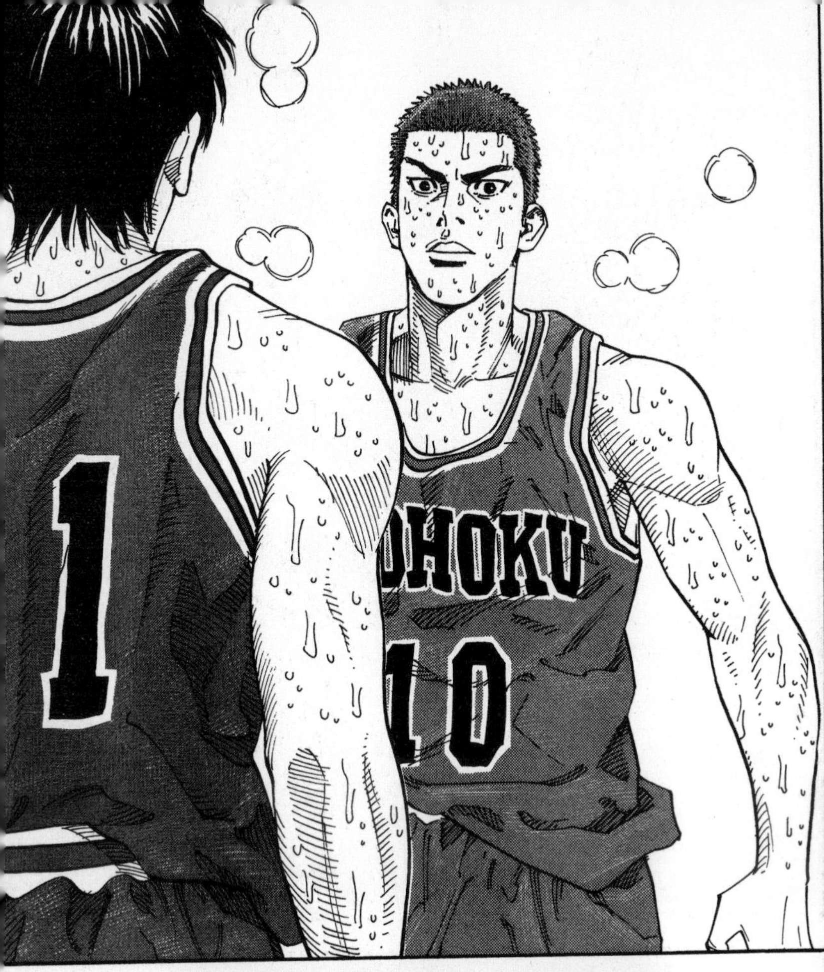
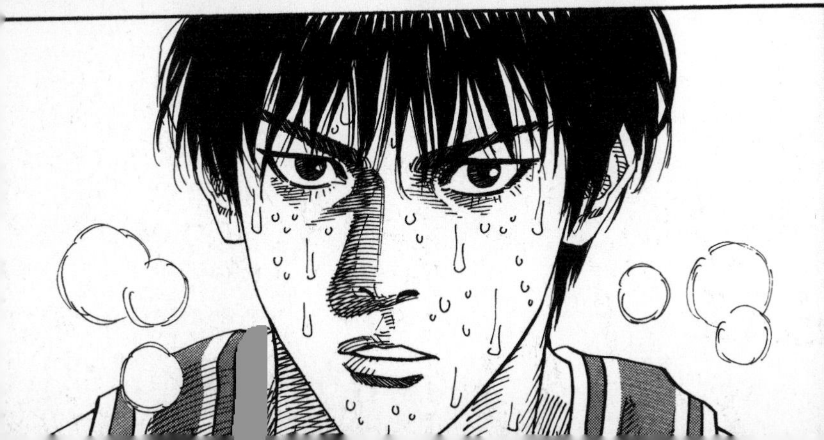

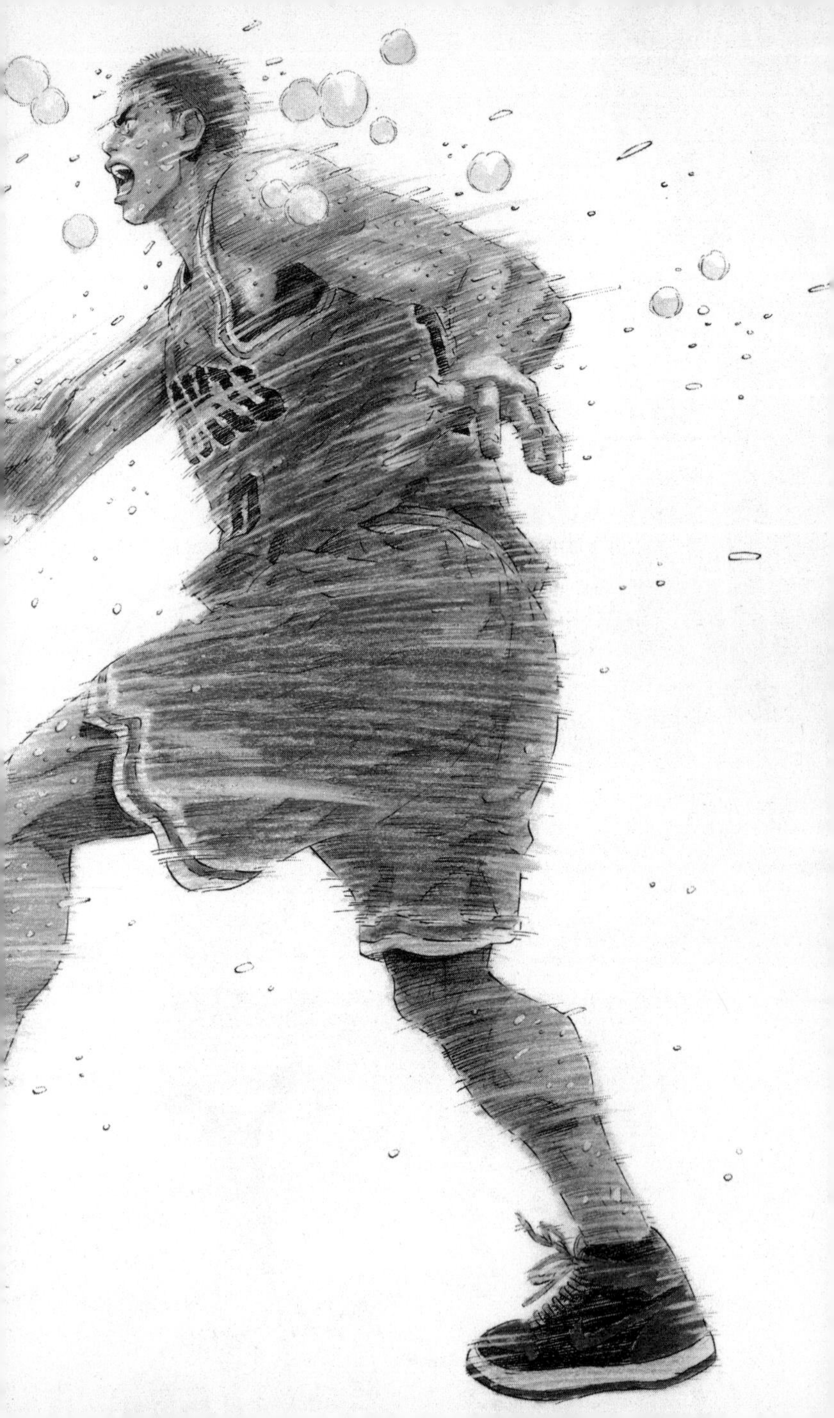

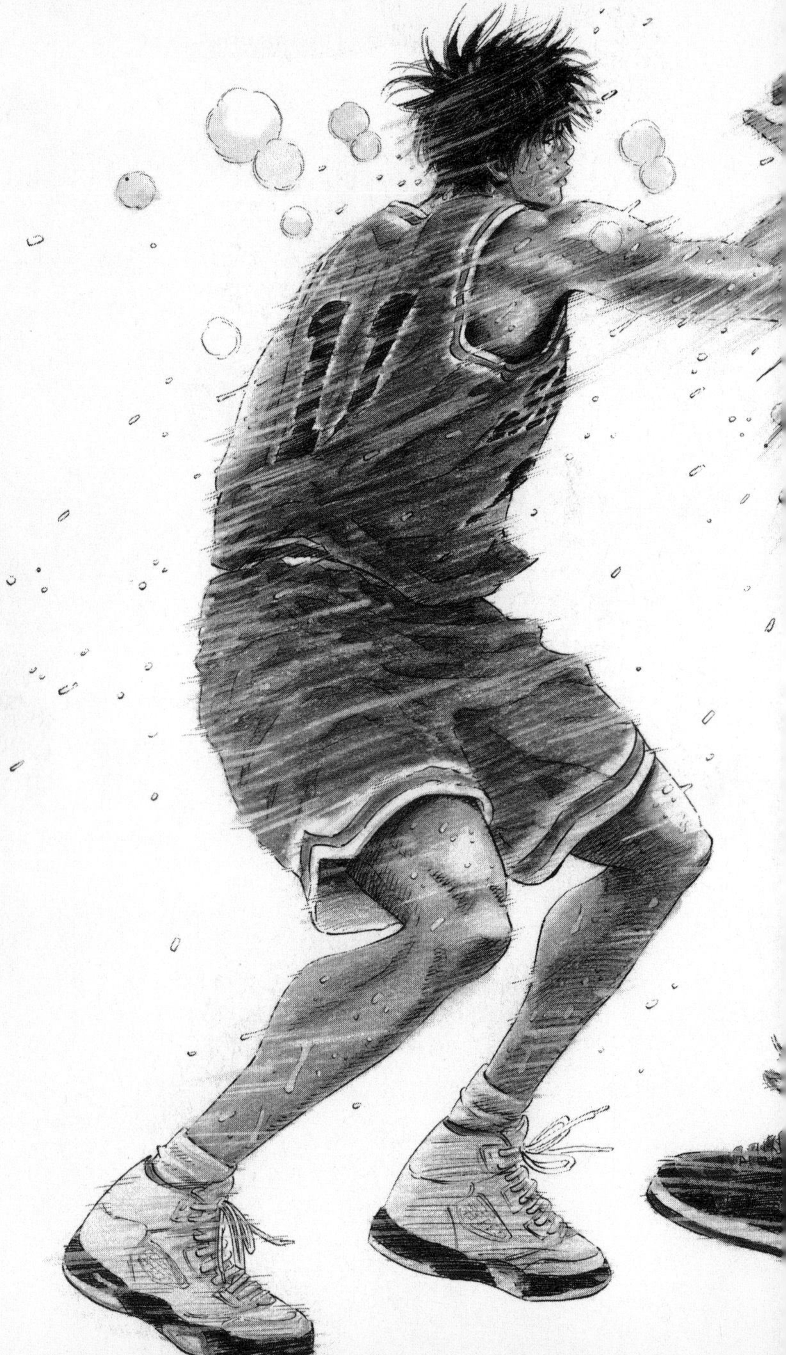

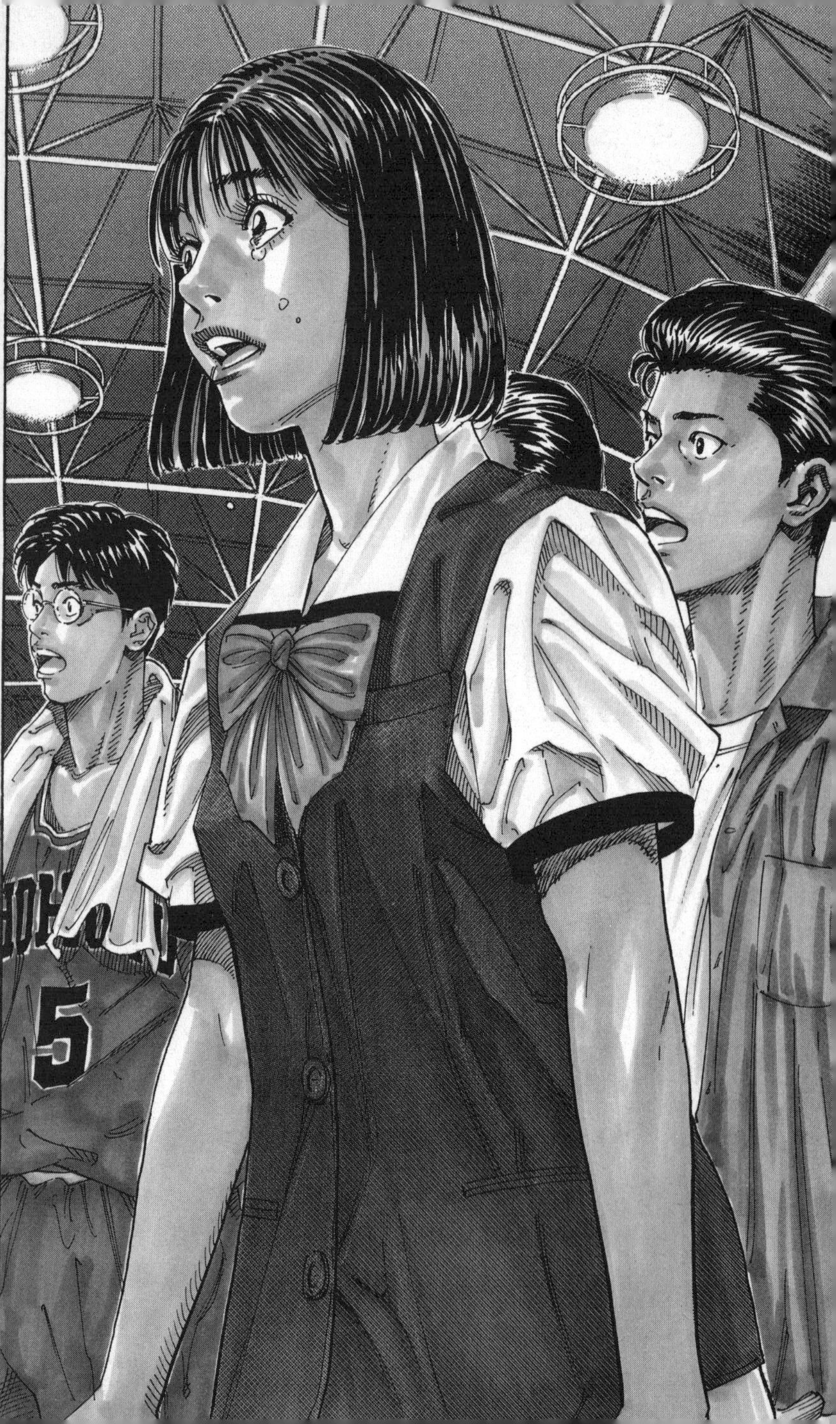

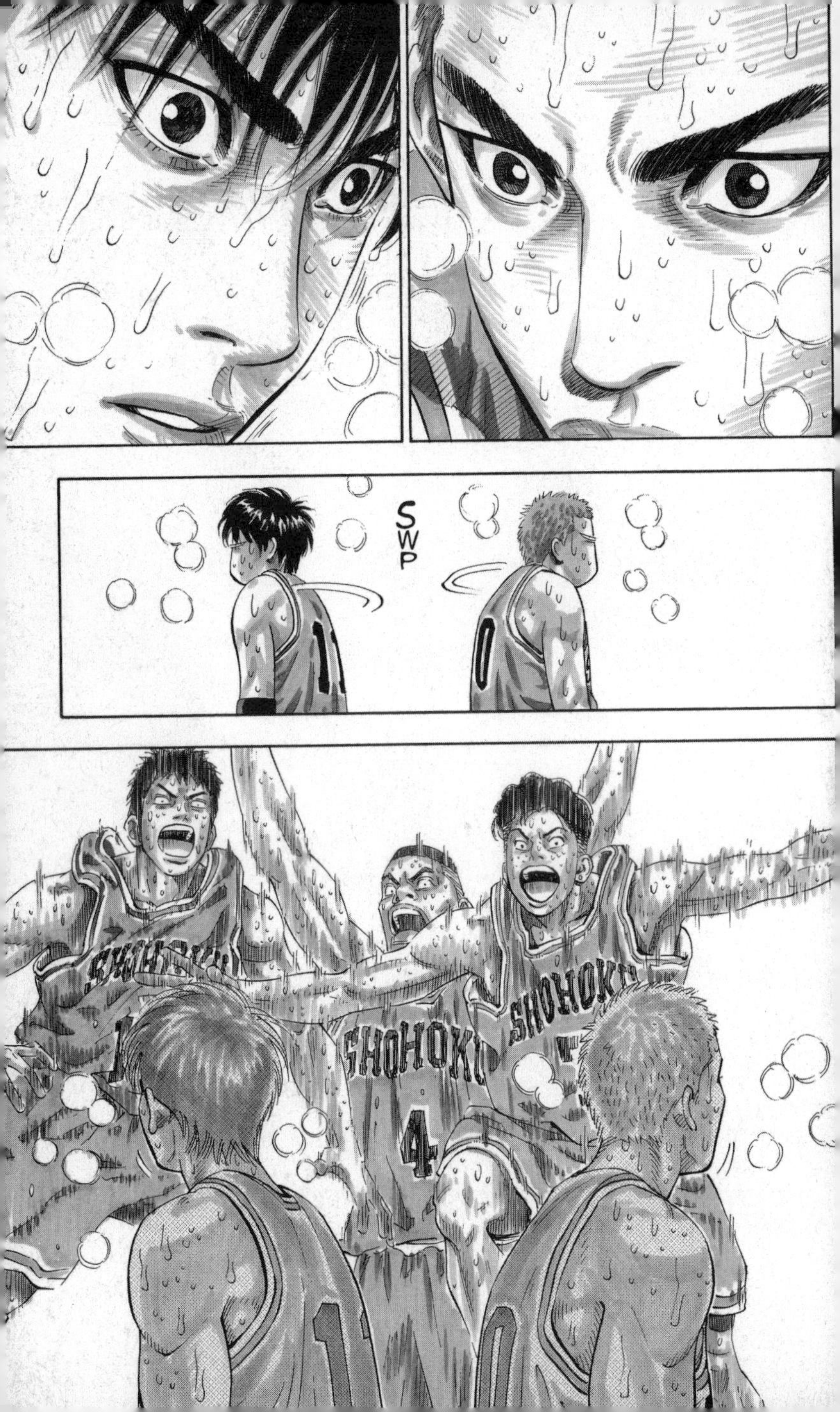
SWP

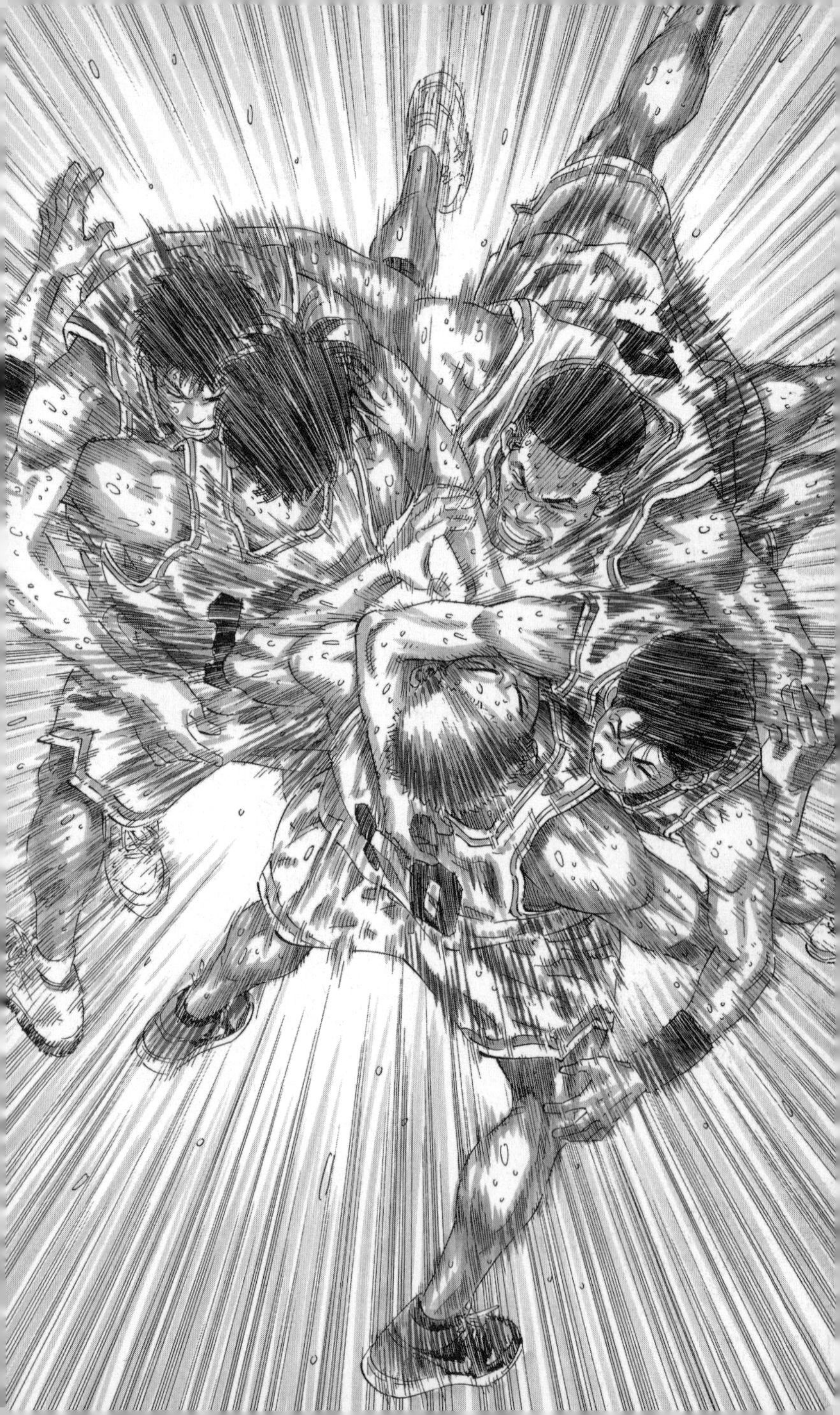

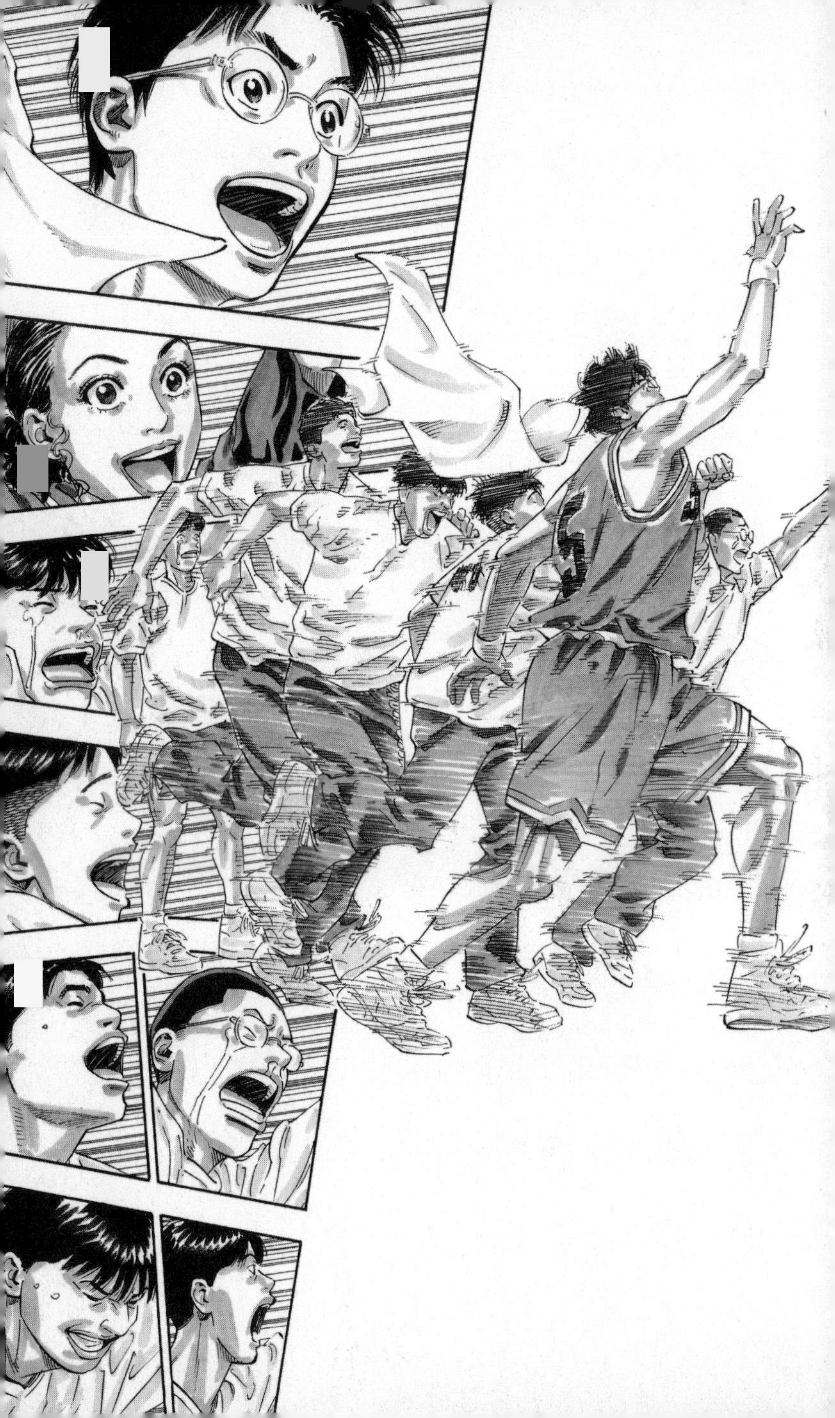

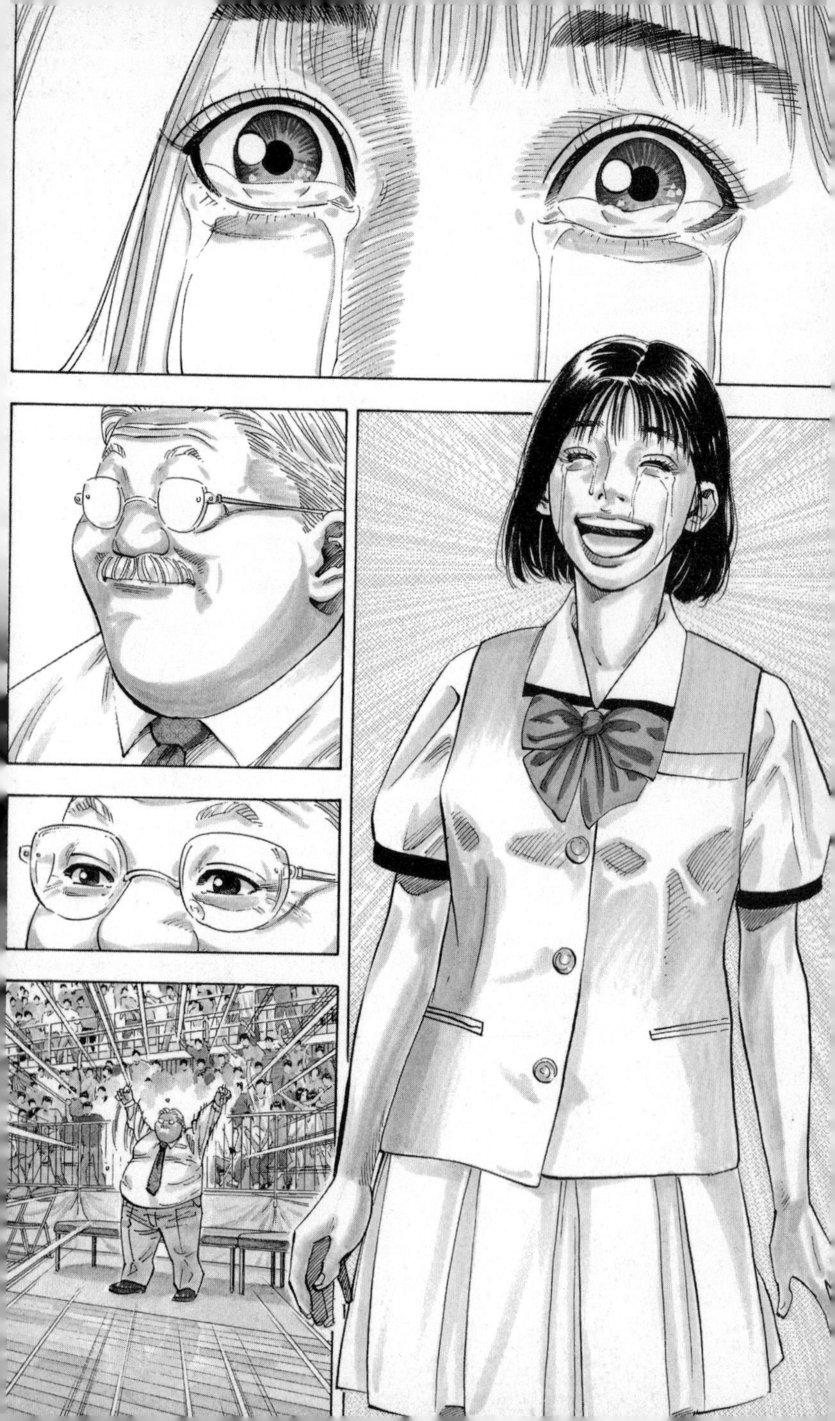

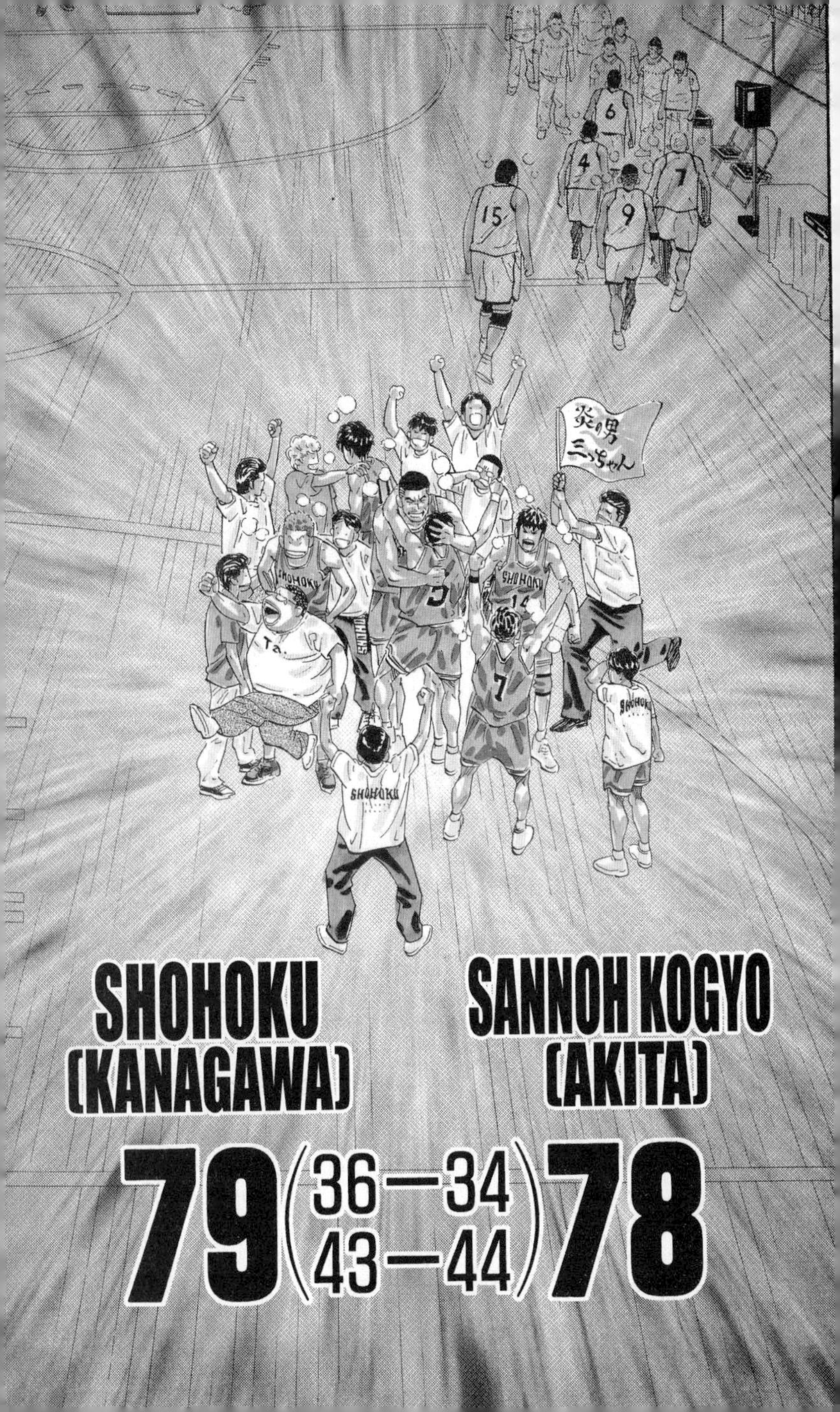
炎の男
三っちゃん
SHOHOKU
(KANAGAWA)
SANNOH KOGYO
(AKITA)
79 (36—34
43—44) 78

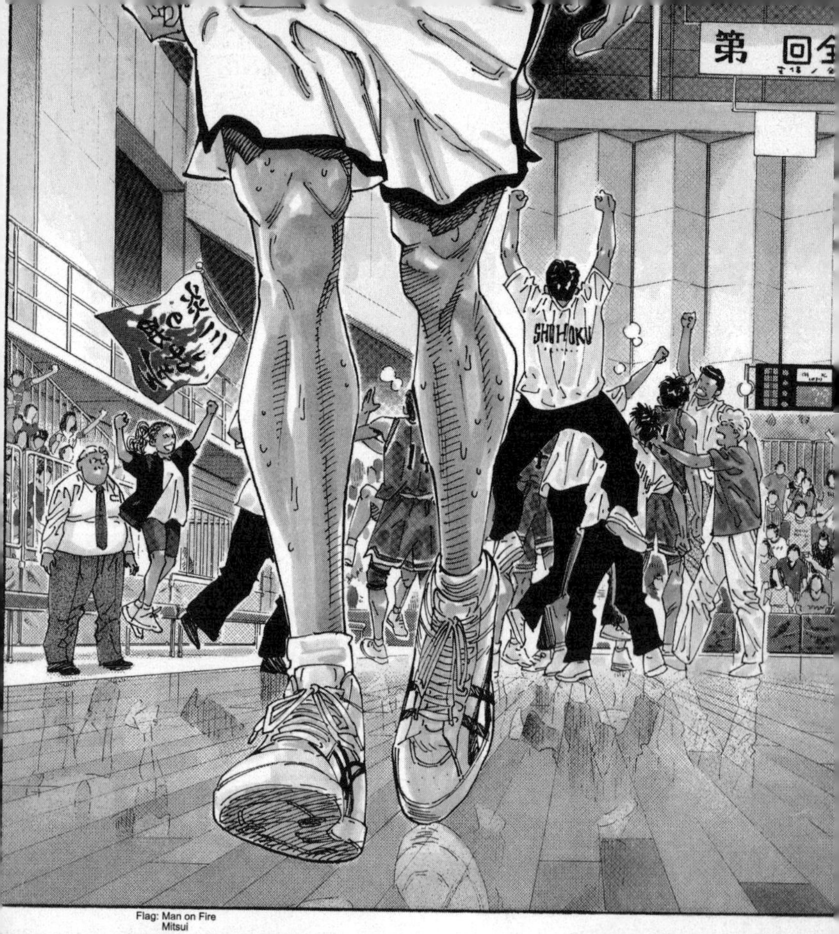
SHOHOKU

Flag: Man on Fire
Mitsui

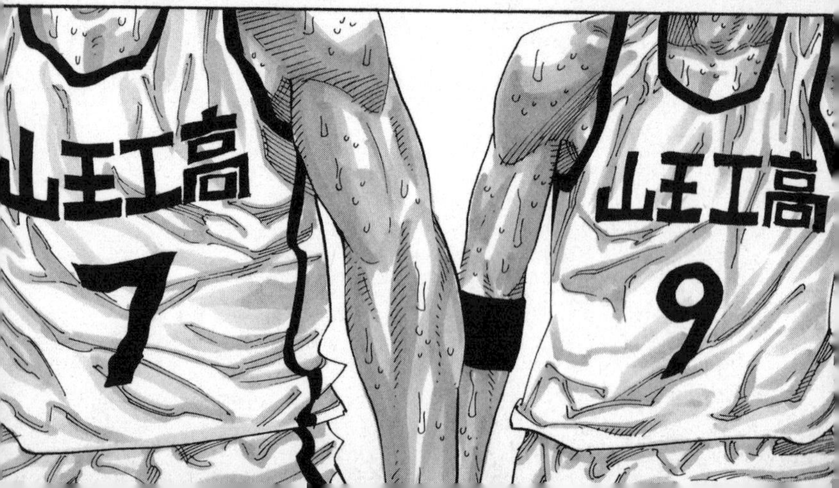
山王工高
9
山王工高
7

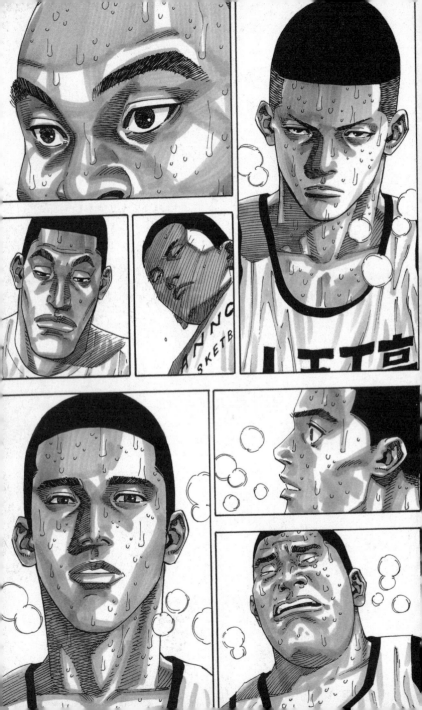

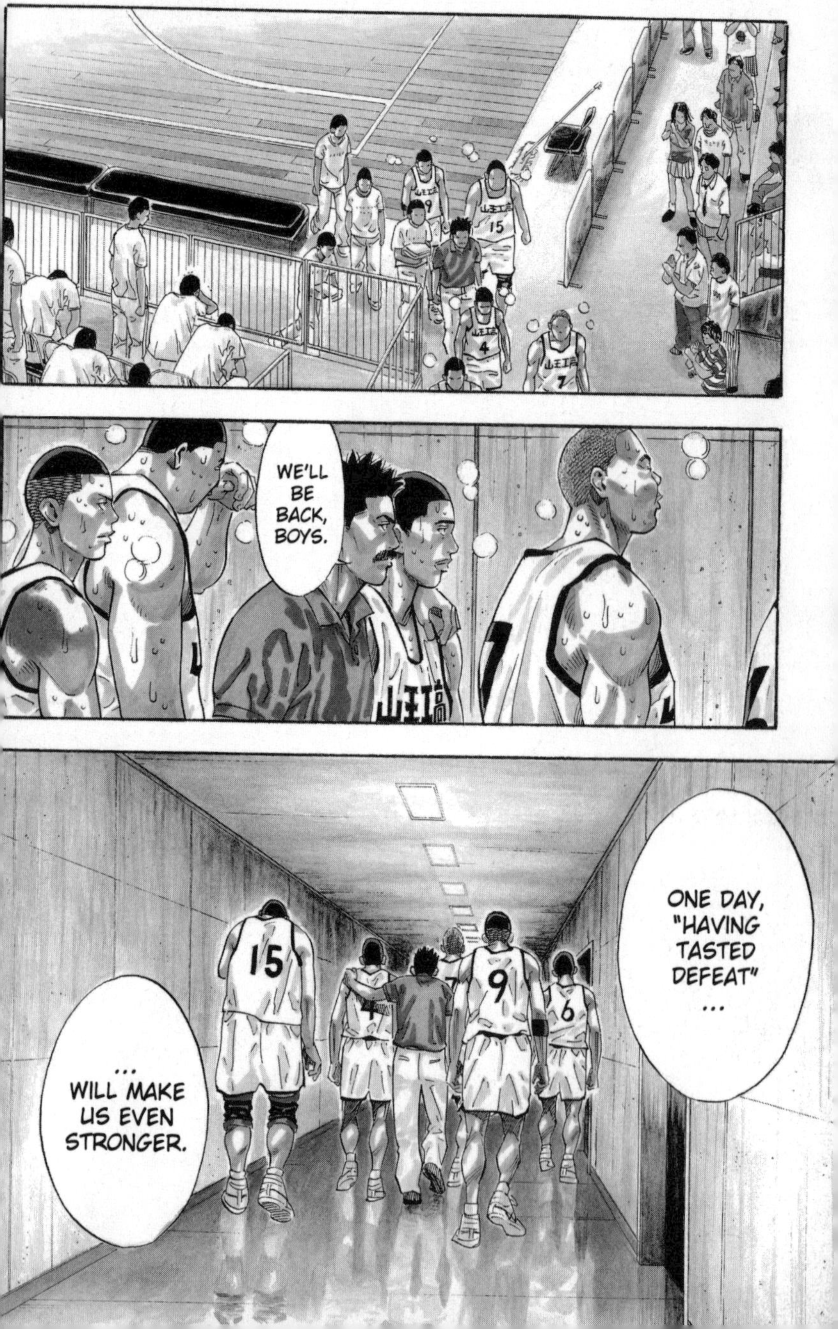
WE'LL BE BACK, BOYS.
ONE DAY, "HAVING TASTED DEFEAT" ...
... WILL MAKE US EVEN STRONGER.

READ THIS WAY

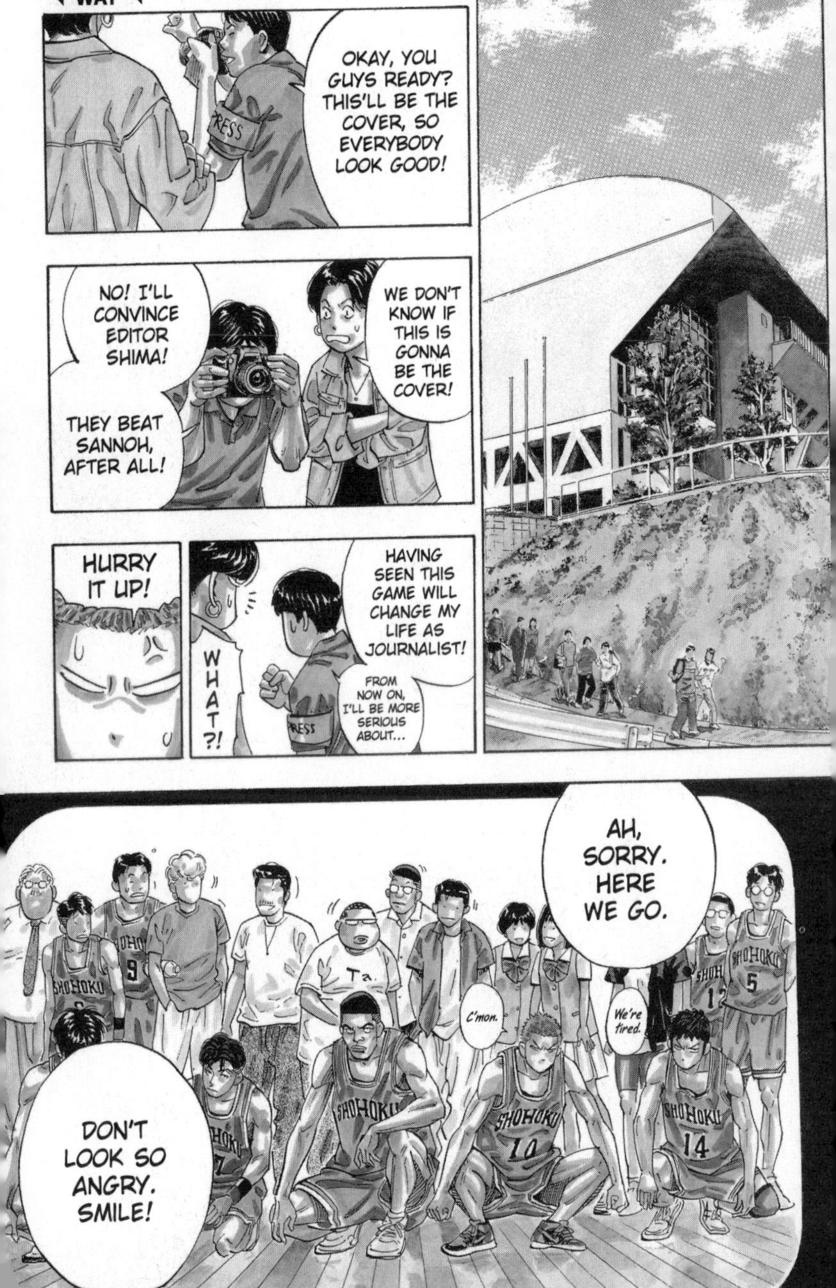
OKAY, YOU GUYS READY? THIS'LL BE THE COVER, SO EVERYBODY LOOK GOOD!
WE DON'T KNOW IF THIS IS GONNA BE THE COVER!
NO! I'LL CONVINCE EDITOR SHIMA!
THEY BEAT SANNOH, AFTER ALL!
HAVING SEEN THIS GAME WILL CHANGE MY LIFE AS JOURNALIST!
FROM NOW ON, I'LL BE MORE SERIOUS ABOUT...
WHAT?!
HURRY IT UP!
AH, SORRY. HERE WE GO.
We're tired.
C'mon.
DON'T LOOK SO ANGRY. SMILE!

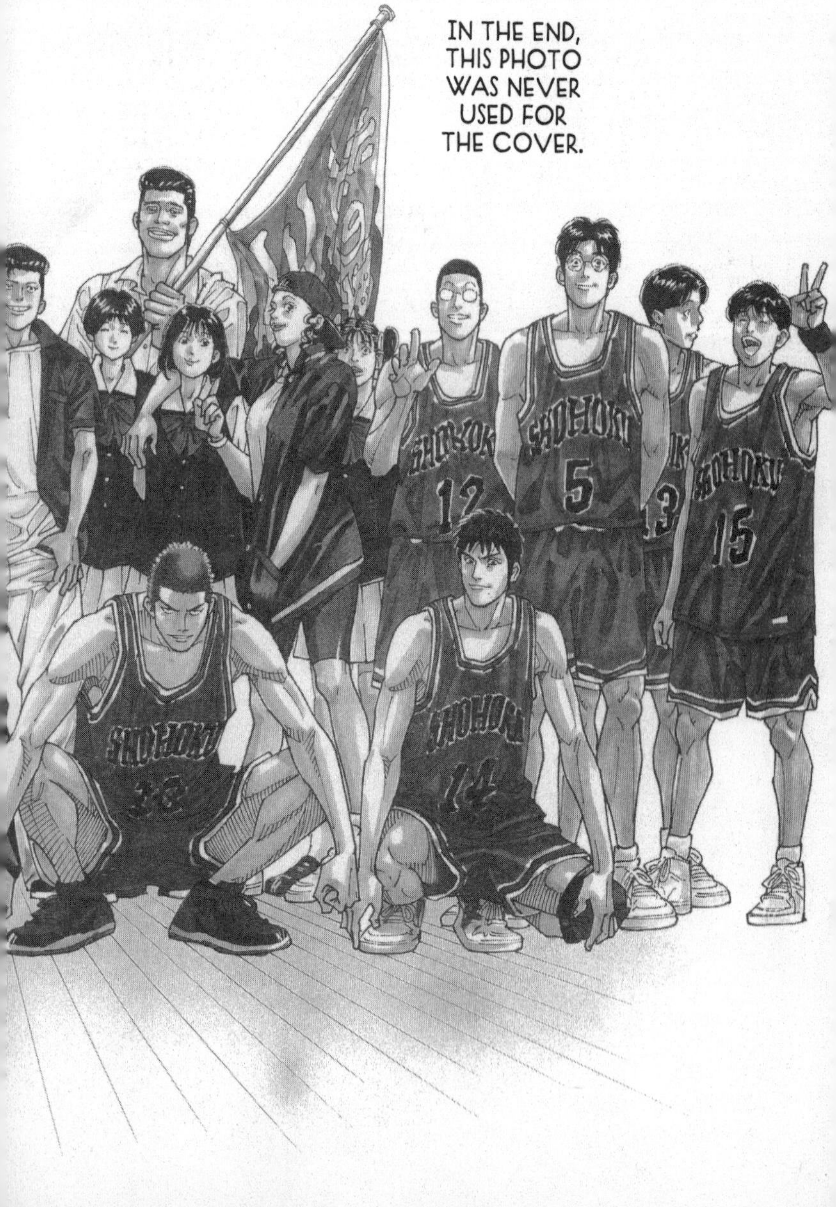
IN THE END, THIS PHOTO WAS NEVER USED FOR THE COVER.

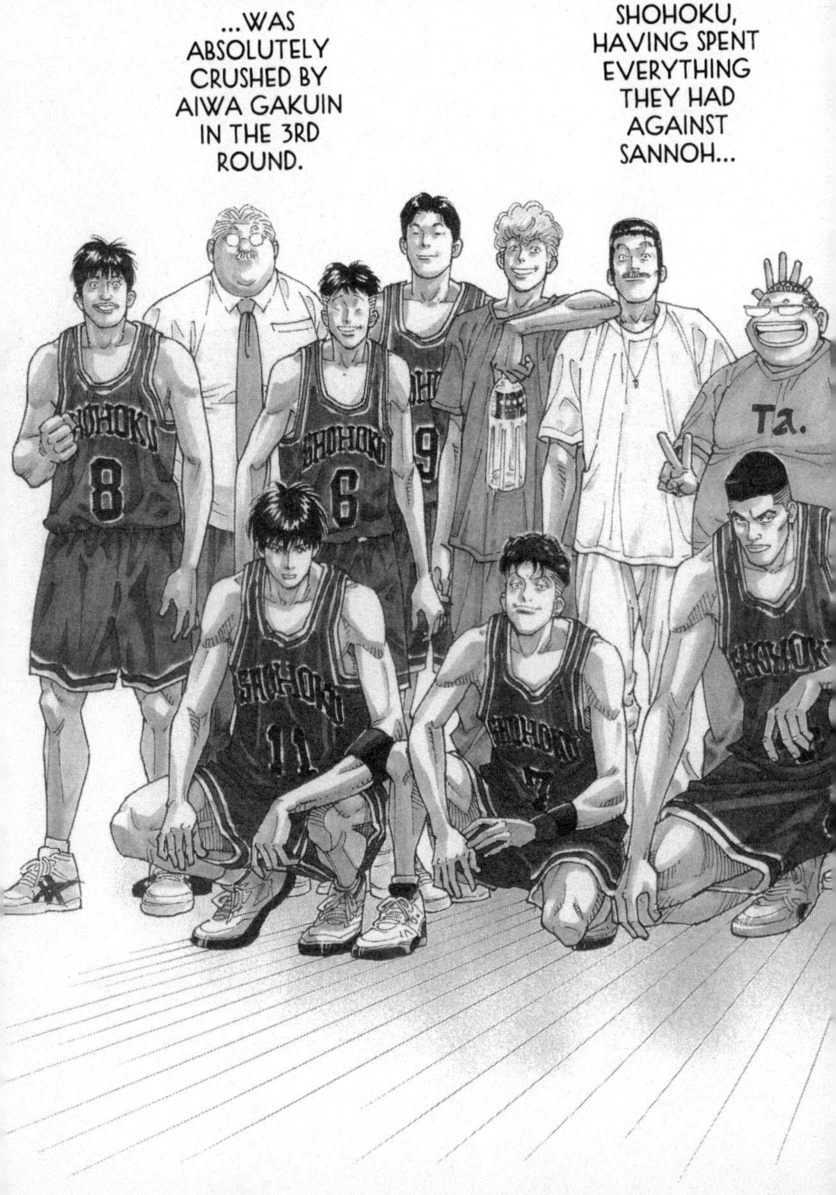
SHOHOKU, HAVING SPENT EVERYTHING THEY HAD AGAINST SANNOH...
...WAS ABSOLUTELY CRUSHED BY AIWA GAKUIN IN THE 3RD ROUND.

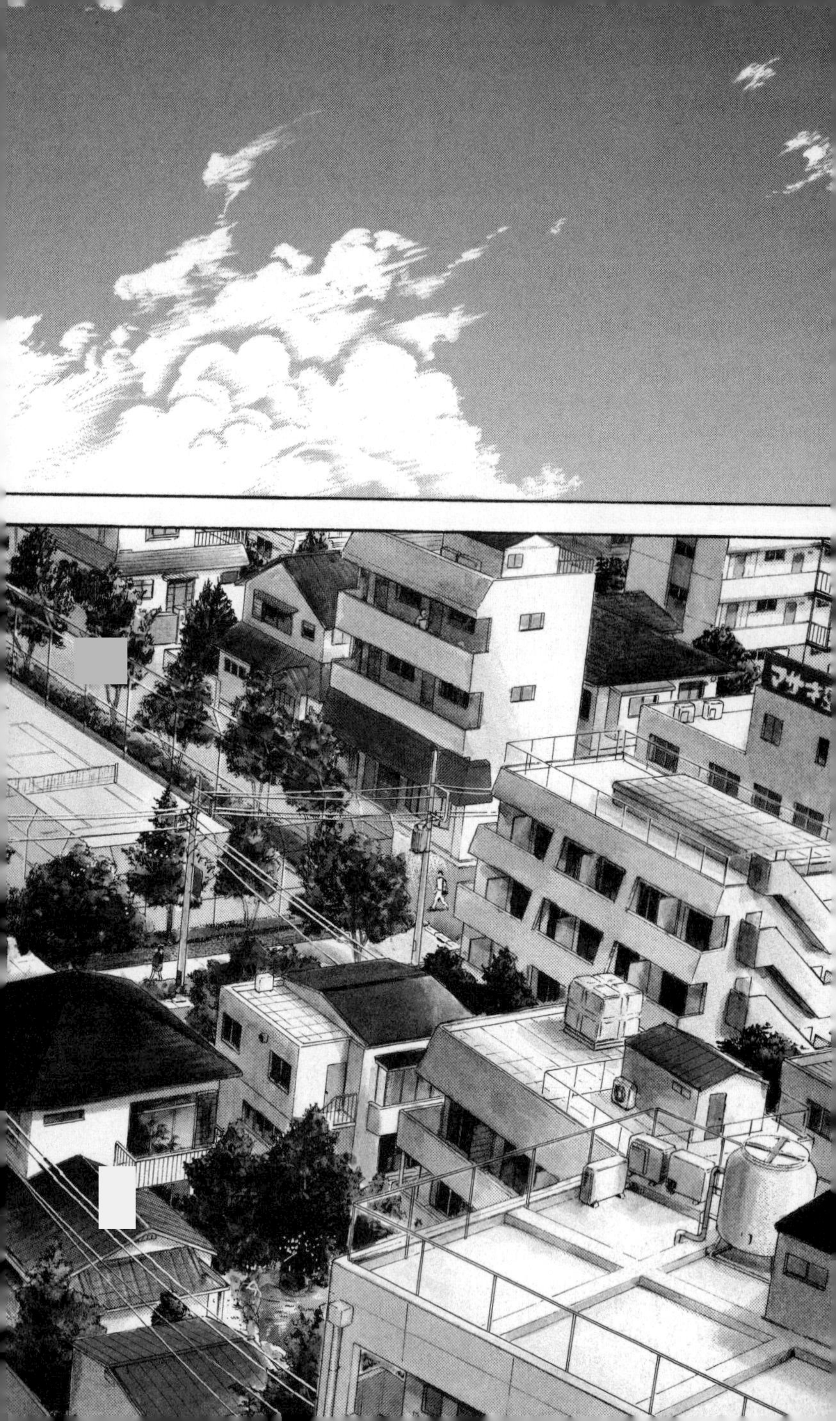

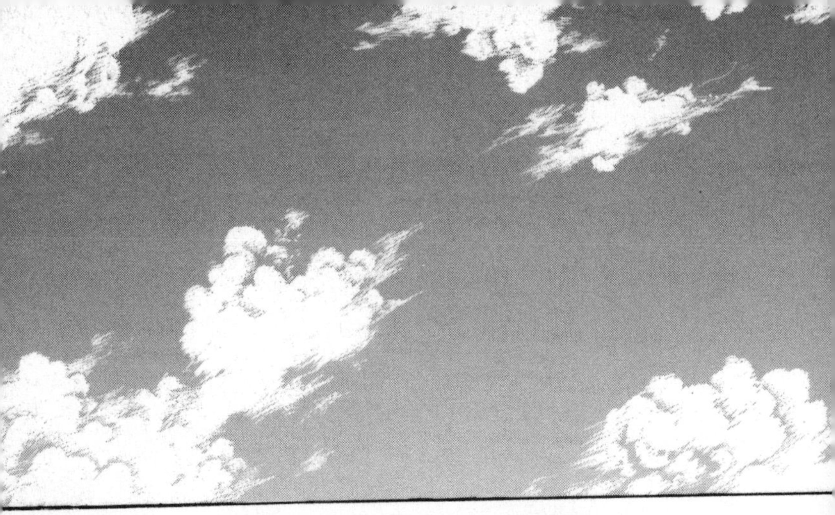
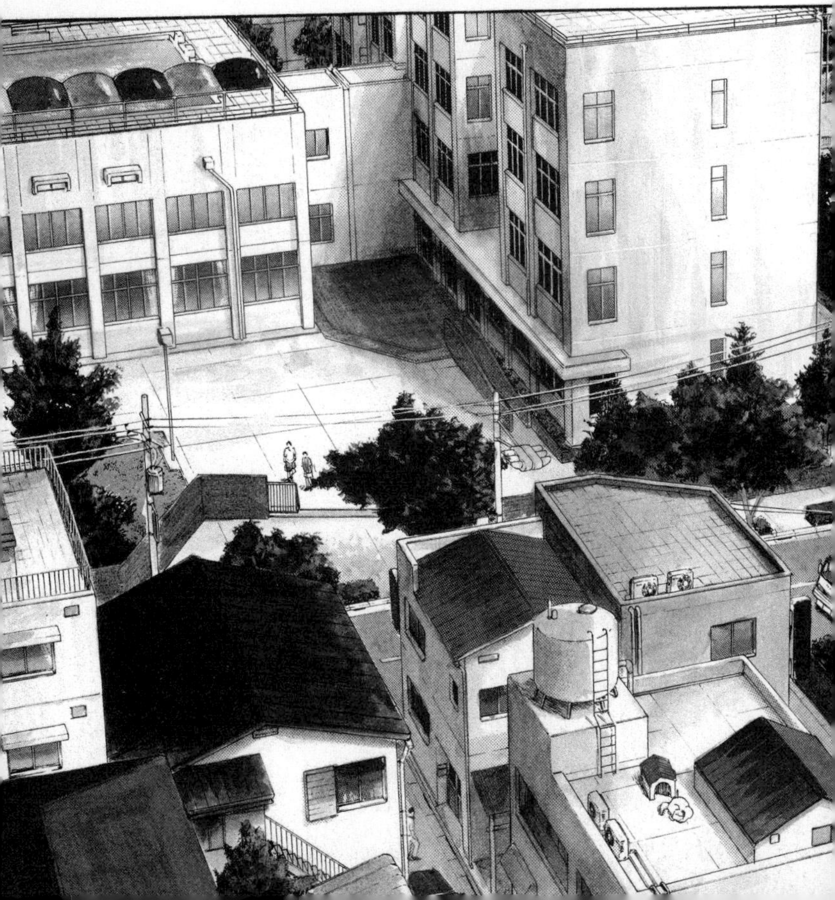

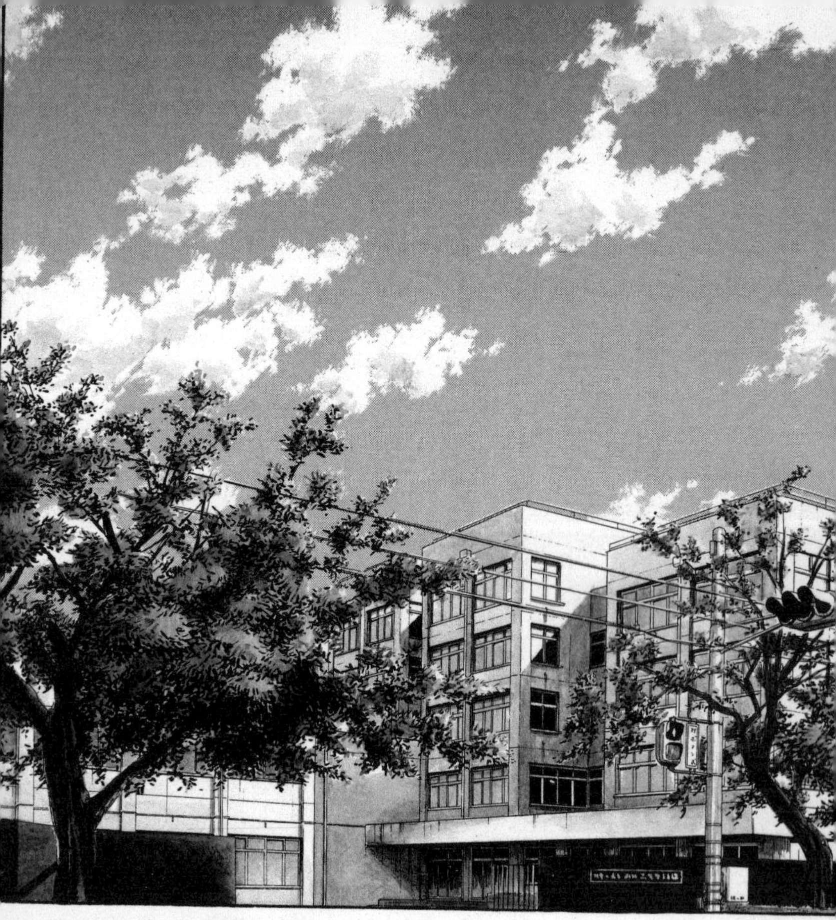

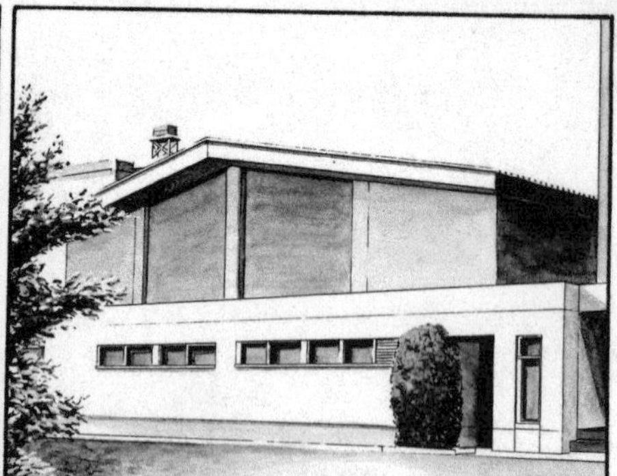

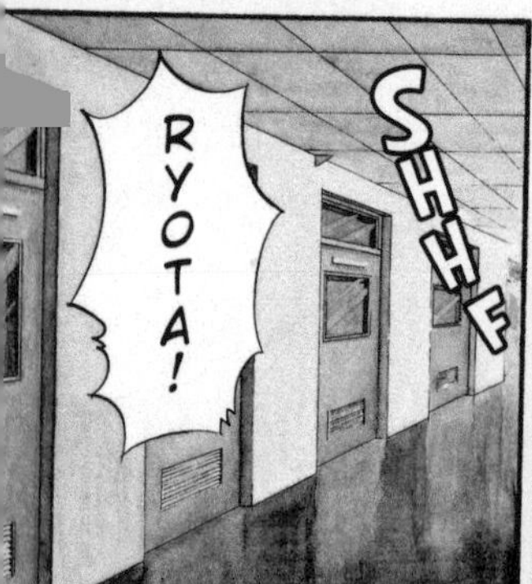
SHHF
RYOTA!

READ THIS WAY

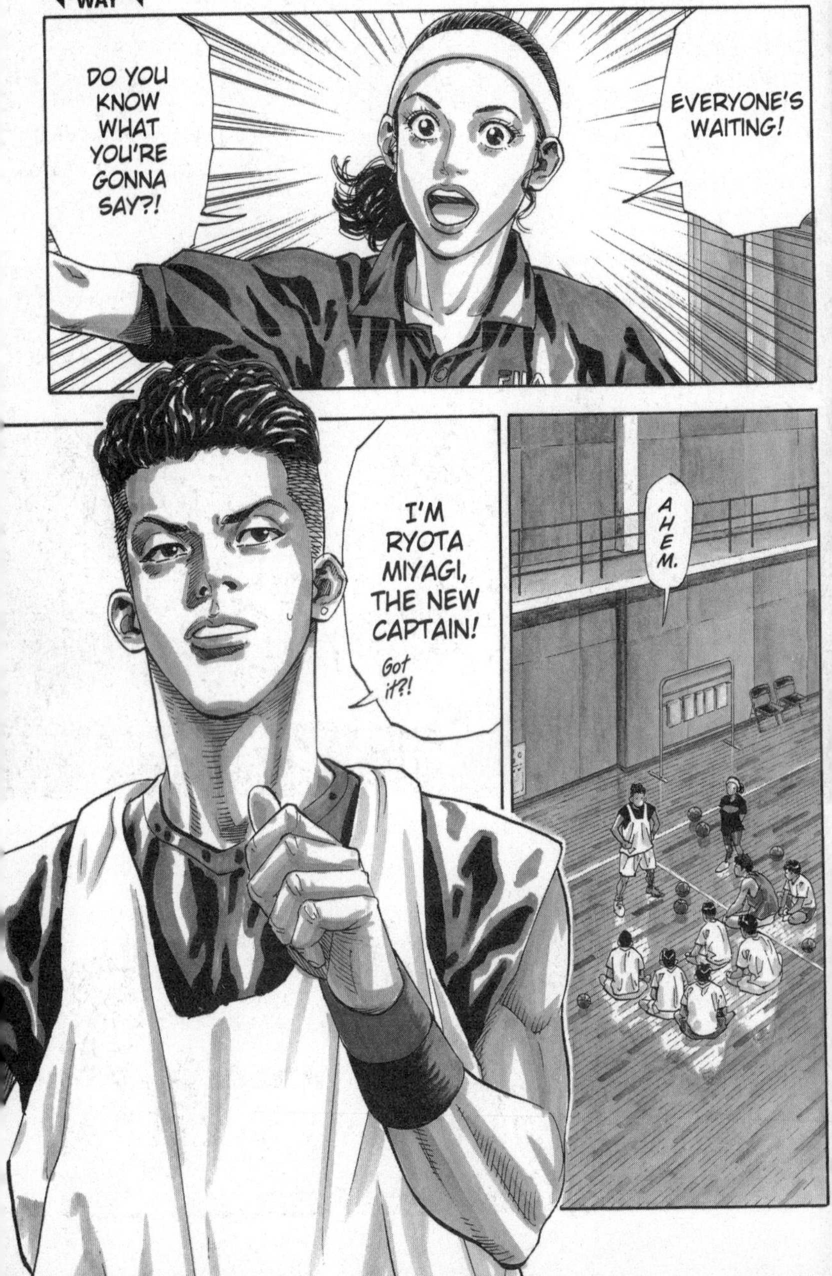
EVERYONE'S WAITING!
DO YOU KNOW WHAT YOU'RE GONNA SAY?!
AHEM.
I'M RYOTA MIYAGI, THE NEW CAPTAIN!
Got it?!

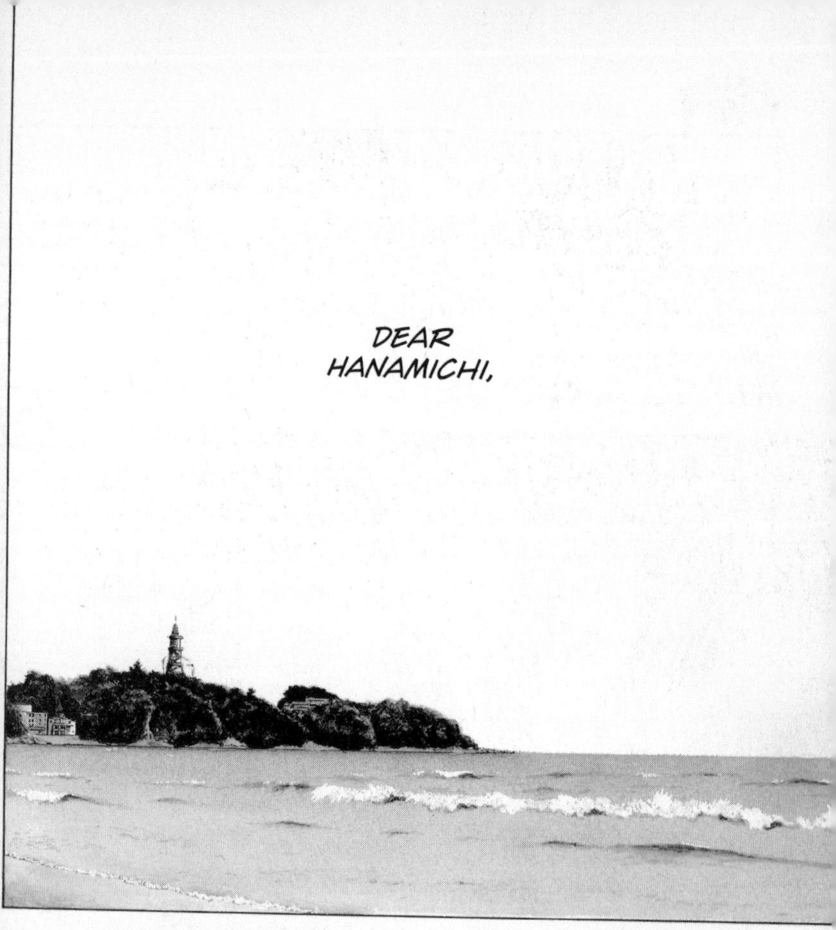
DEAR HANAMICHI,
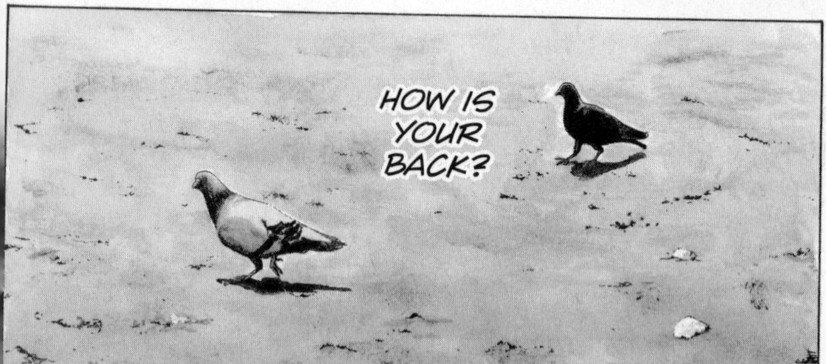
HOW IS YOUR BACK?

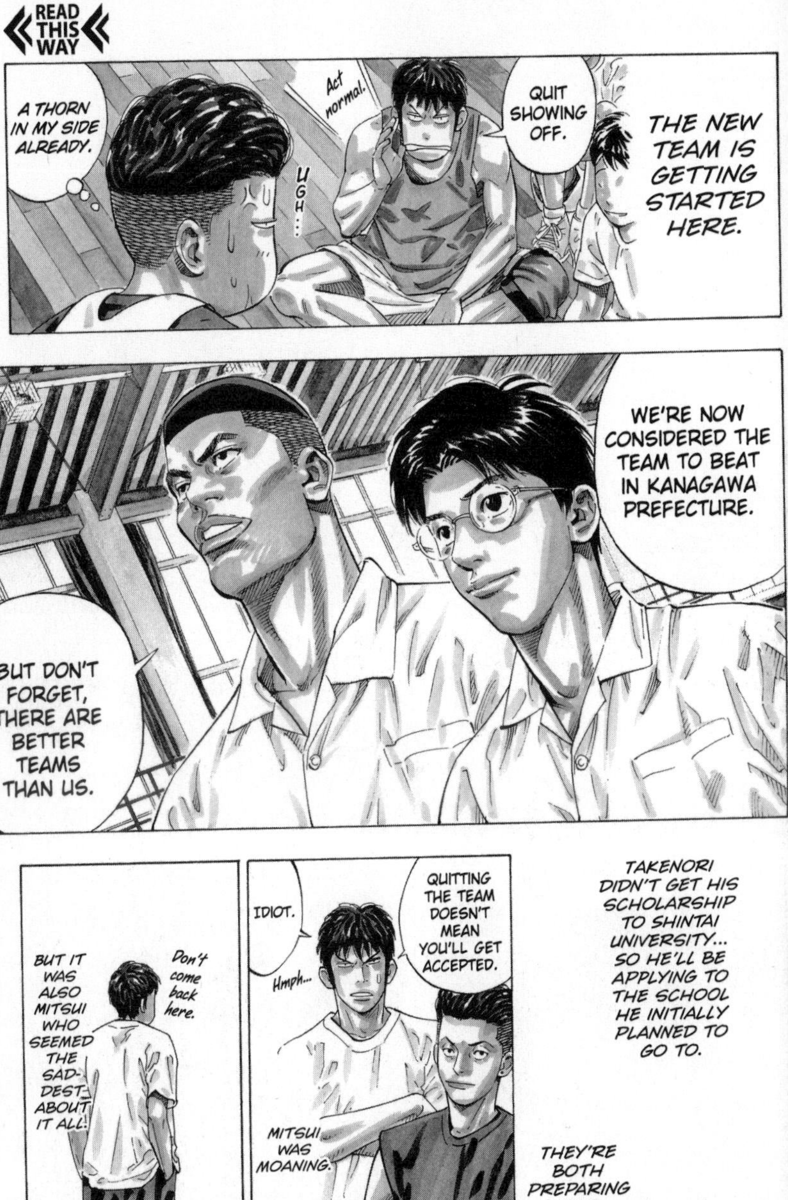
READ THIS WAY
THE NEW TEAM IS GETTING STARTED HERE.
QUIT SHOWING OFF.
Act normal.
UGH...
A THORN IN MY SIDE ALREADY.
WE'RE NOW CONSIDERED THE TEAM TO BEAT IN KANAGAWA PREFECTURE.
BUT DON'T FORGET, THERE ARE BETTER TEAMS THAN US.
TAKENORI DIDN'T GET HIS SCHOLARSHIP TO SHINTAI UNIVERSITY... SO HE'LL BE APPLYING TO THE SCHOOL HE INITIALLY PLANNED TO GO TO.
THEY'RE BOTH PREPARING FOR COLLEGE.
QUITTING THE TEAM DOESN'T MEAN YOU'LL GET ACCEPTED.
IDIOT.
Hmph...
MITSUI WAS MOANING.
Don't come back here.
BUT IT WAS ALSO MITSUI WHO SEEMED THE SAD-DEST ABOUT IT ALL!

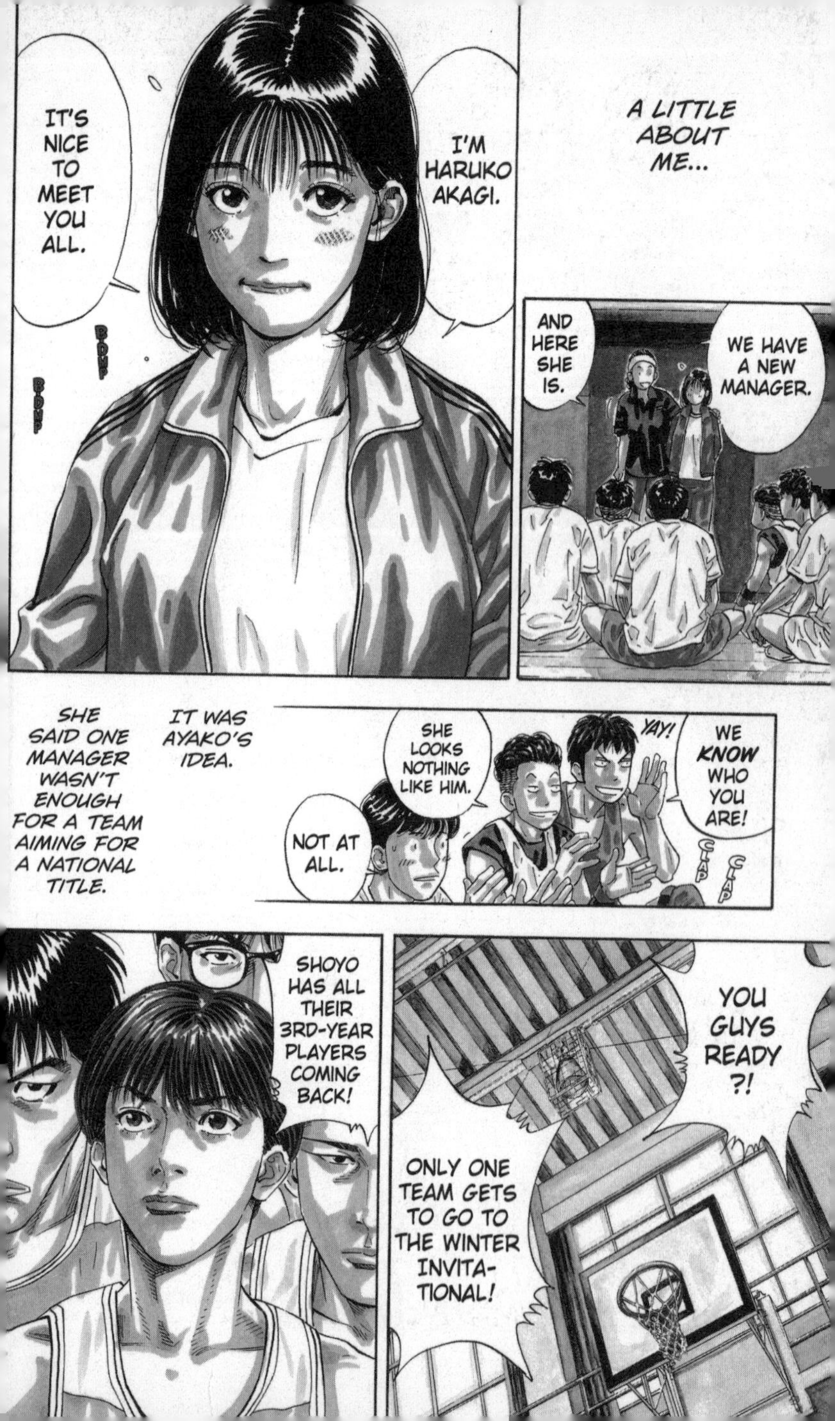
A LITTLE ABOUT ME...
WE HAVE A NEW MANAGER.
AND HERE SHE IS.
I'M HARUKO AKAGI.
IT'S NICE TO MEET YOU ALL.
BDMP
BDMP
WE *KNOW* WHO YOU ARE!
YAY!
SHE LOOKS NOTHING LIKE HIM.
NOT AT ALL.
CLAP
CLAP
IT WAS AYAKO'S IDEA.
SHE SAID ONE MANAGER WASN'T ENOUGH FOR A TEAM AIMING FOR A NATIONAL TITLE.
YOU GUYS READY ?!
ONLY ONE TEAM GETS TO GO TO THE WINTER INVITATIONAL!
SHOYO HAS ALL THEIR 3RD-YEAR PLAYERS COMING BACK!

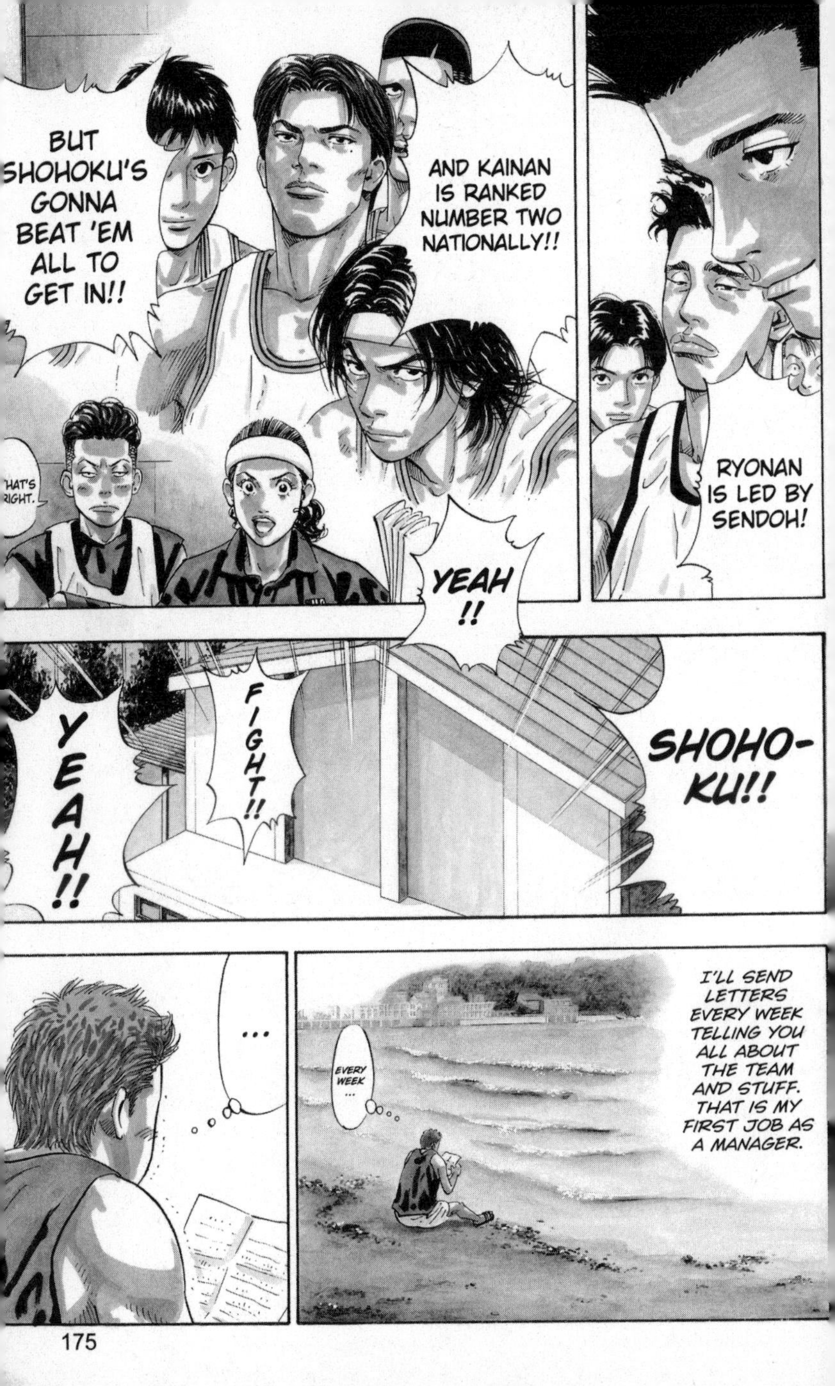
RYONAN IS LED BY SENDOH!
AND KAINAN IS RANKED NUMBER TWO NATIONALLY!!
BUT SHOHOKU'S GONNA BEAT 'EM ALL TO GET IN!!
THAT'S RIGHT.
YEAH!!
SHOHO-KU!!
FIGHT!!
YEAH!!
I'LL SEND LETTERS EVERY WEEK TELLING YOU ALL ABOUT THE TEAM AND STUFF. THAT IS MY FIRST JOB AS A MANAGER.
EVERY WEEK ...
...

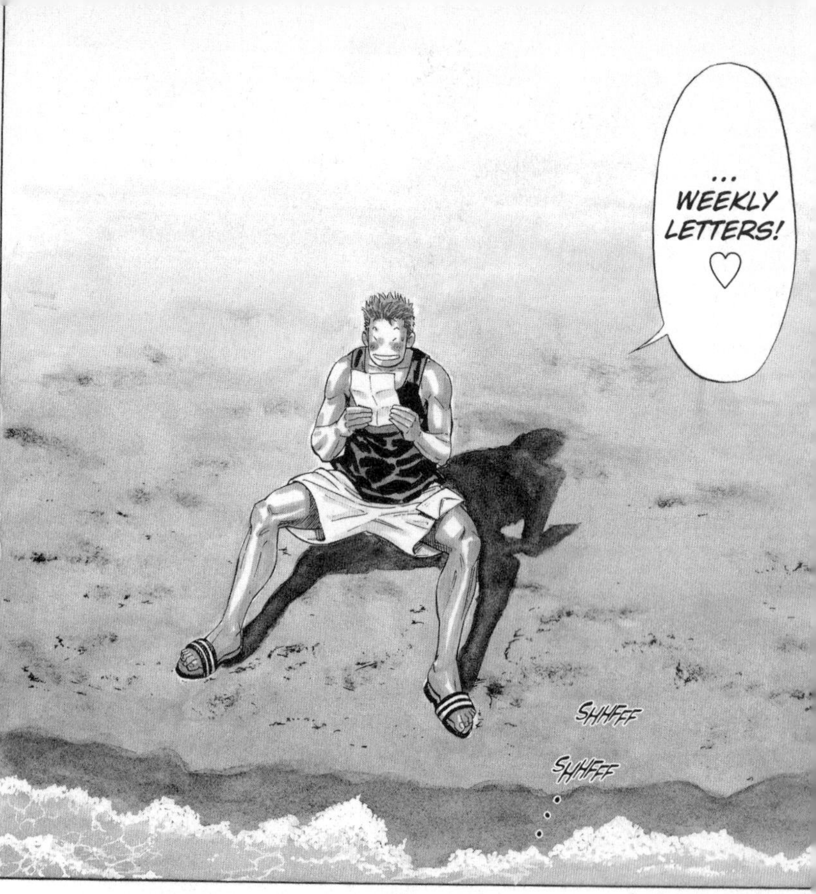
...WEEKLY LETTERS! ♡
SHHFFF
SHHFFF...
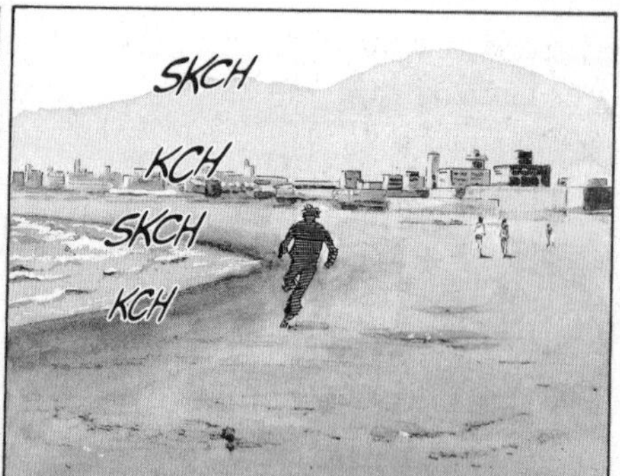
SKCH
KCH
SKCH
KCH
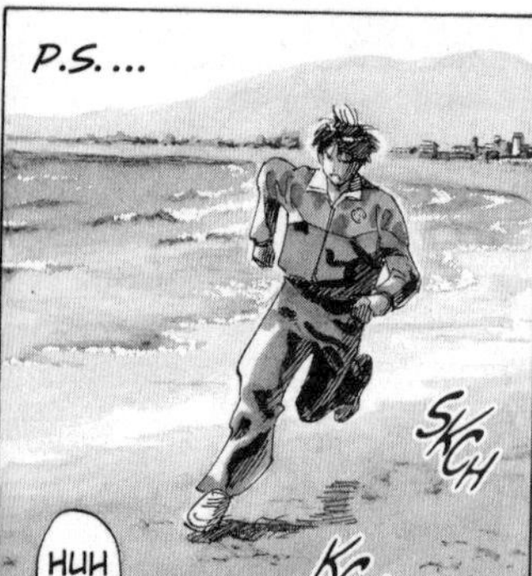
P.S. ...
SKCH
KCH
HUH?

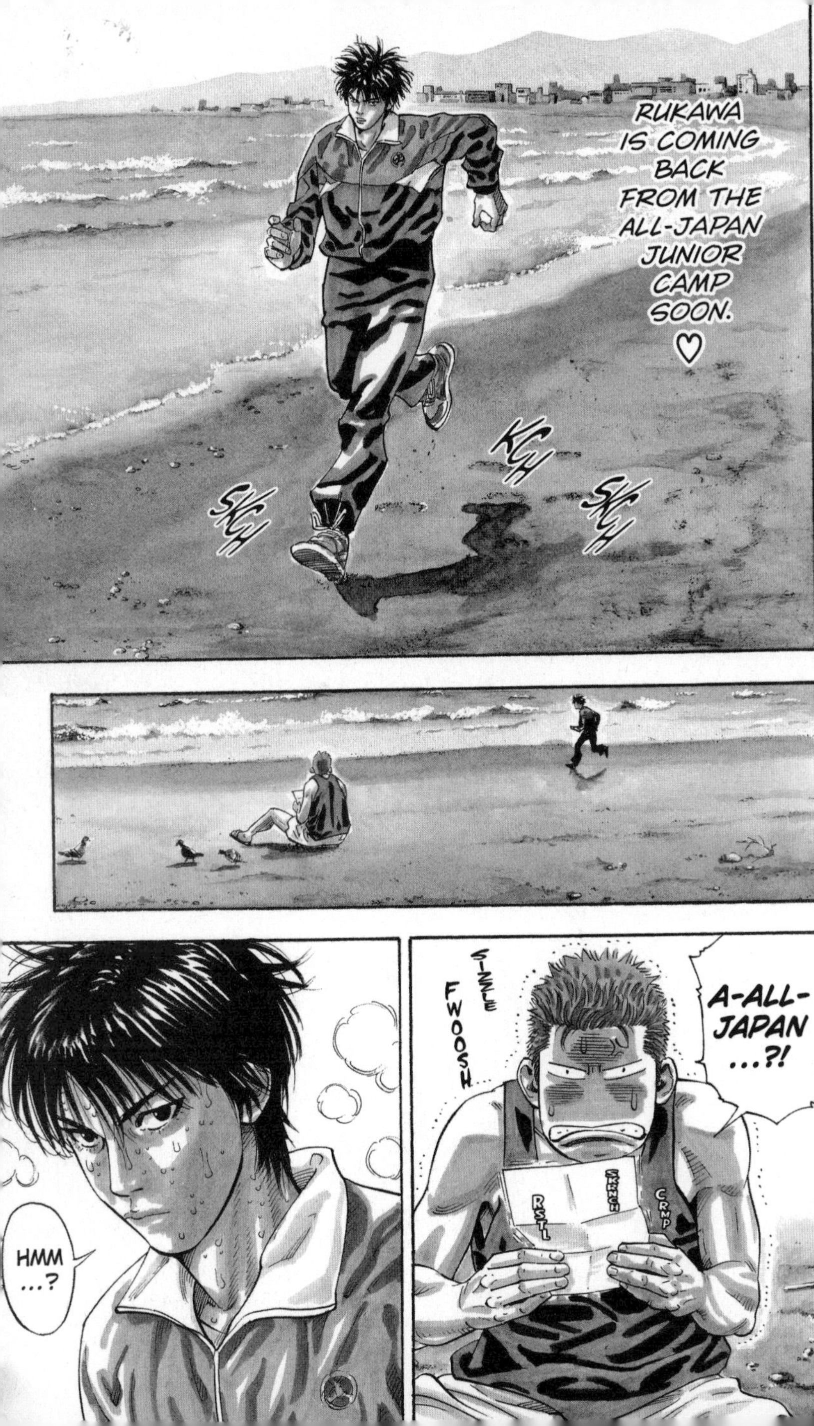
RUKAWA IS COMING BACK FROM THE ALL-JAPAN JUNIOR CAMP SOON. ♡
SKCH
KCH
SKCH
SIZZLE
FWOOSH
A-ALL-JAPAN ...?!
SKNCH
CRMP
RSTL
HMM ...?

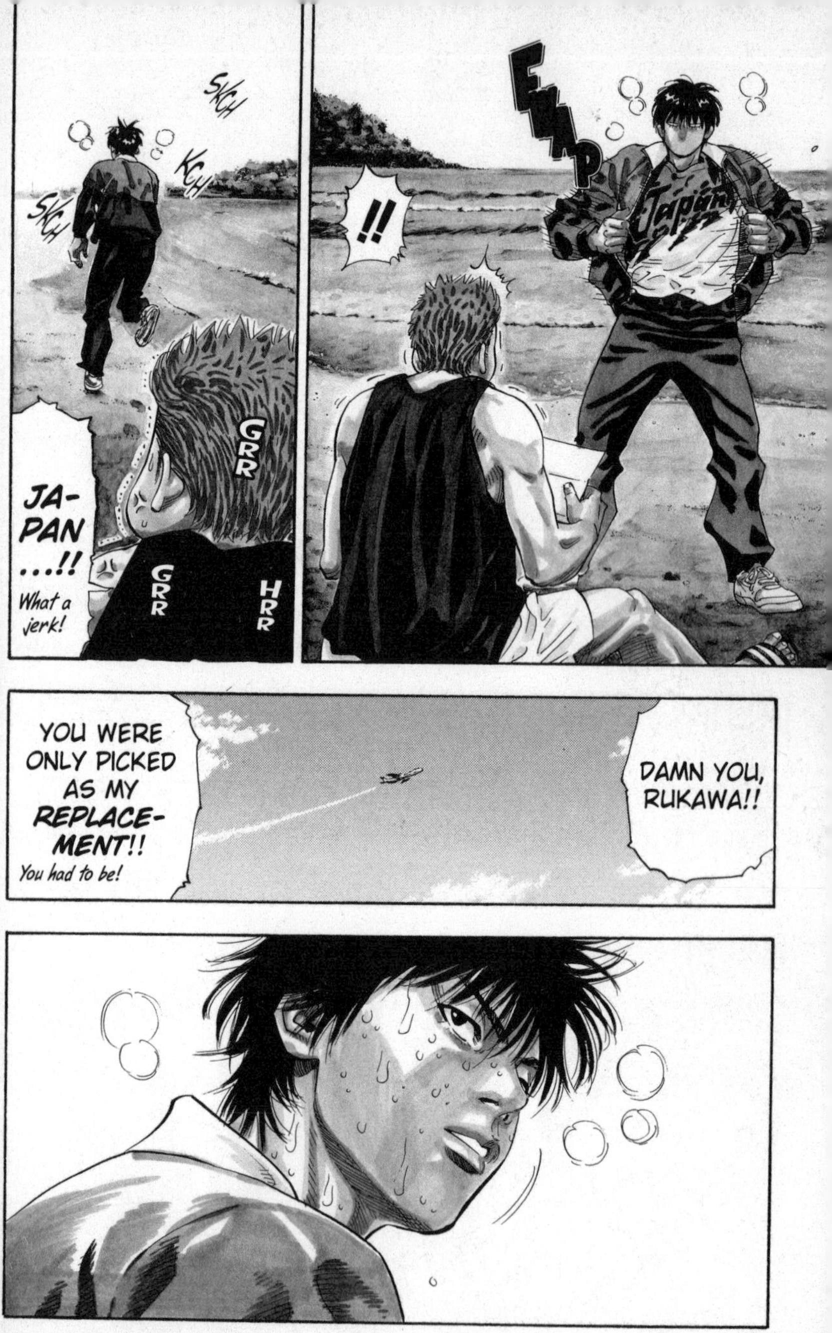
FWAP
!!
SKCH
KCH
SKCH
GRR
JA-
PAN
...!!
What a
jerk!
GRR
HRR
DAMN YOU,
RUKAWA!!
YOU WERE
ONLY PICKED
AS MY
*REPLACE-
MENT*!!
You had to be!

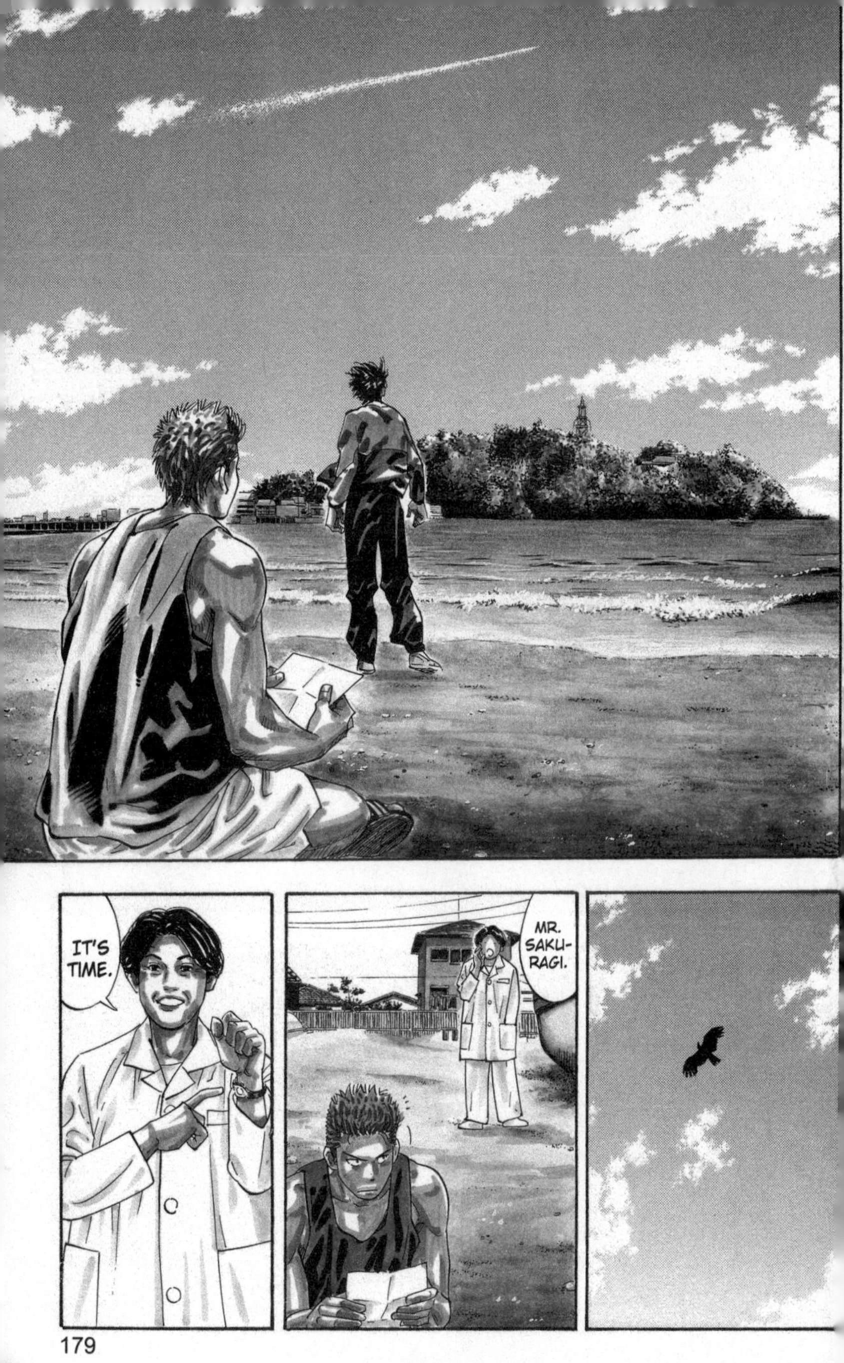
MR. SAKURAGI.
IT'S TIME.

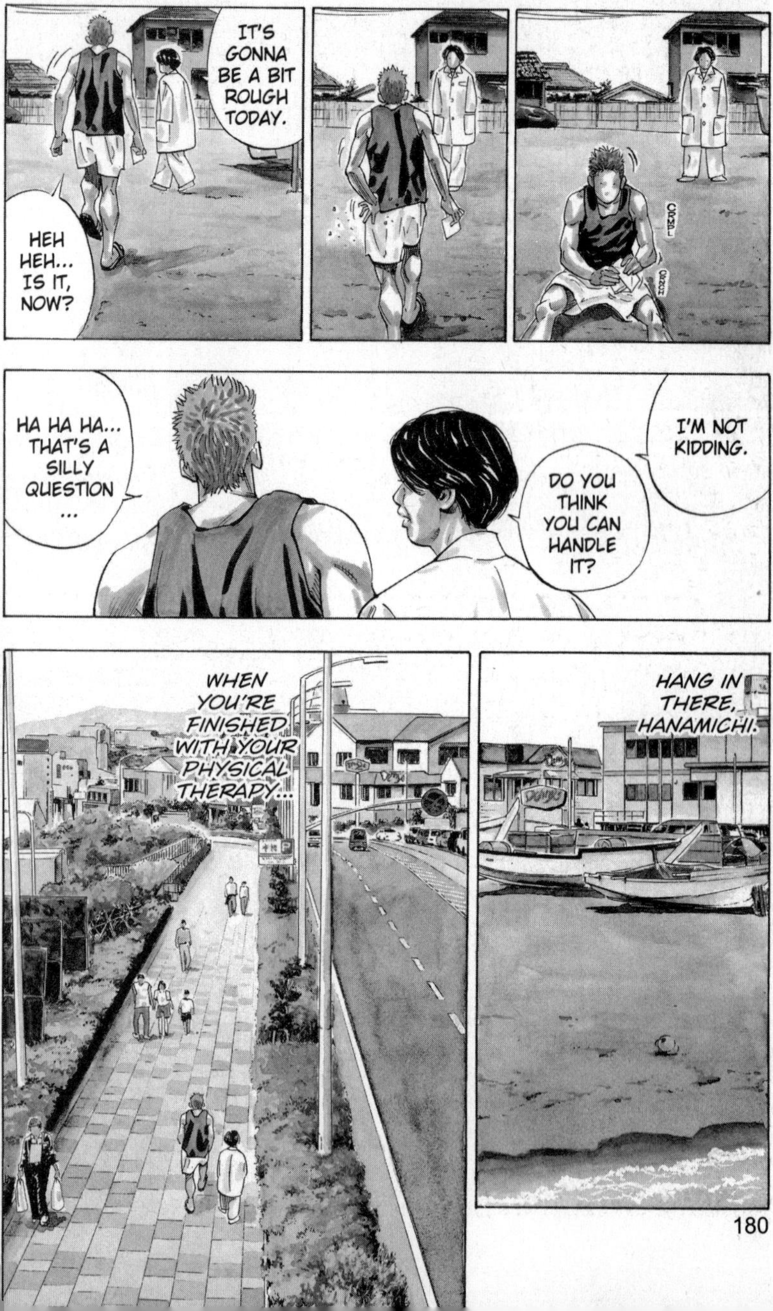
CRMPL
CRNCH
IT'S GONNA BE A BIT ROUGH TODAY.
HEH HEH... IS IT, NOW?
I'M NOT KIDDING.
DO YOU THINK YOU CAN HANDLE IT?
HA HA HA... THAT'S A SILLY QUESTION...
HANG IN THERE, HANAMICHI.
WHEN YOU'RE FINISHED WITH YOUR PHYSICAL THERAPY...

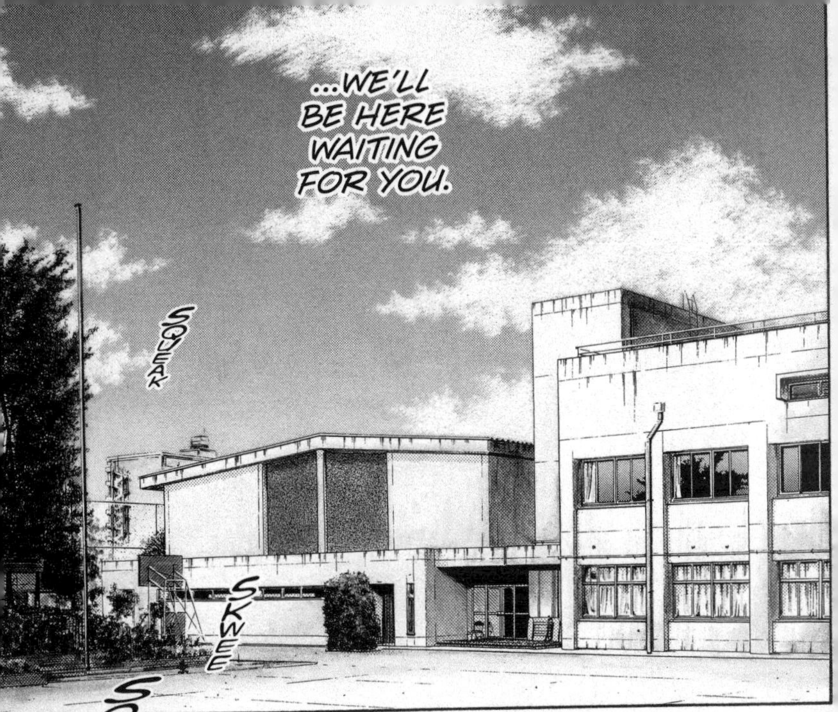
...WE'LL BE HERE WAITING FOR YOU.
SQUEAK
SKWEE
SQUEAK
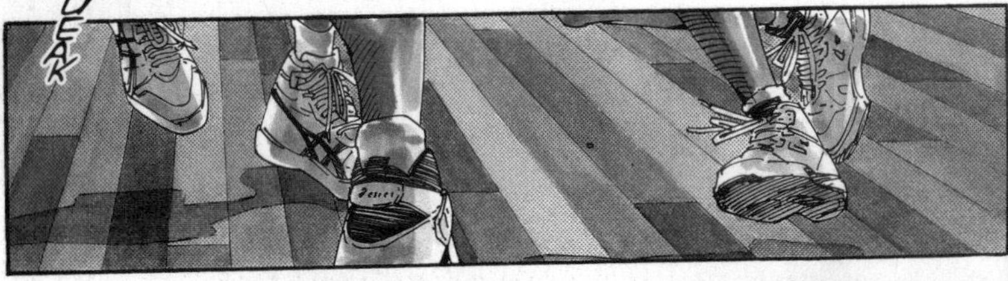
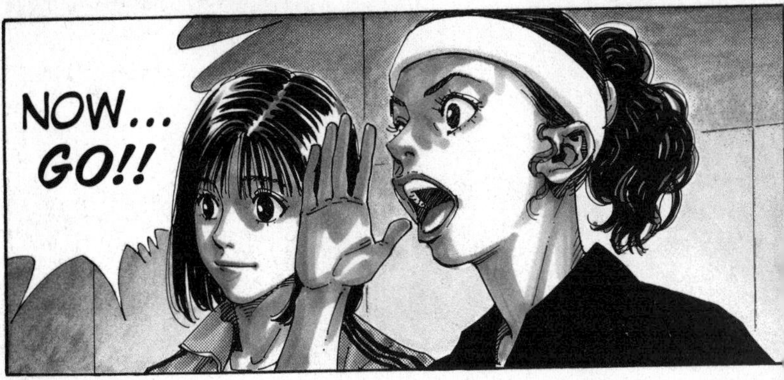
NOW... GO!!

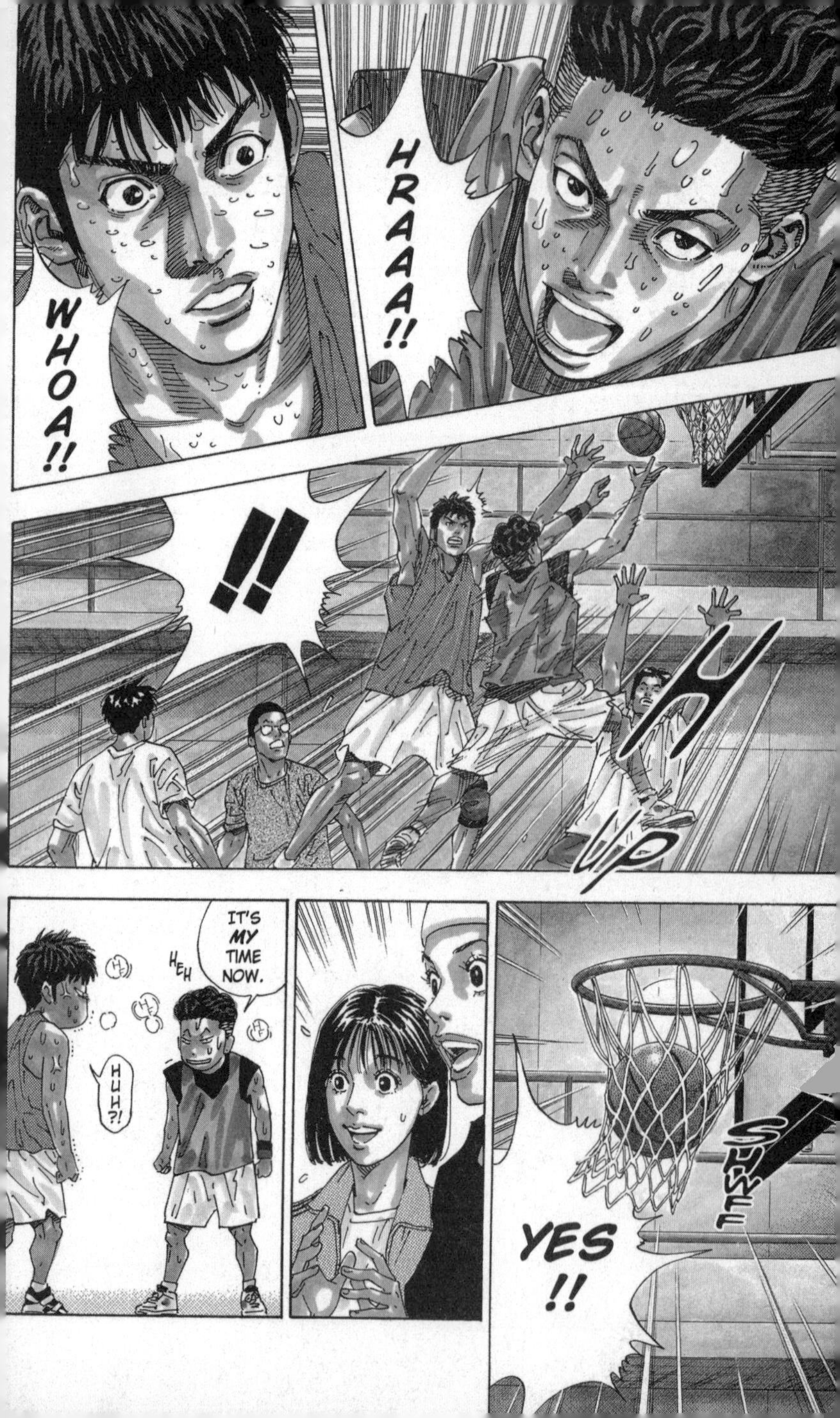

HRAAA!!
WHOA!!
!!
HUP
SHWFF
YES!!
IT'S MY TIME NOW.
HEH
HUH?!

READ THIS WAY

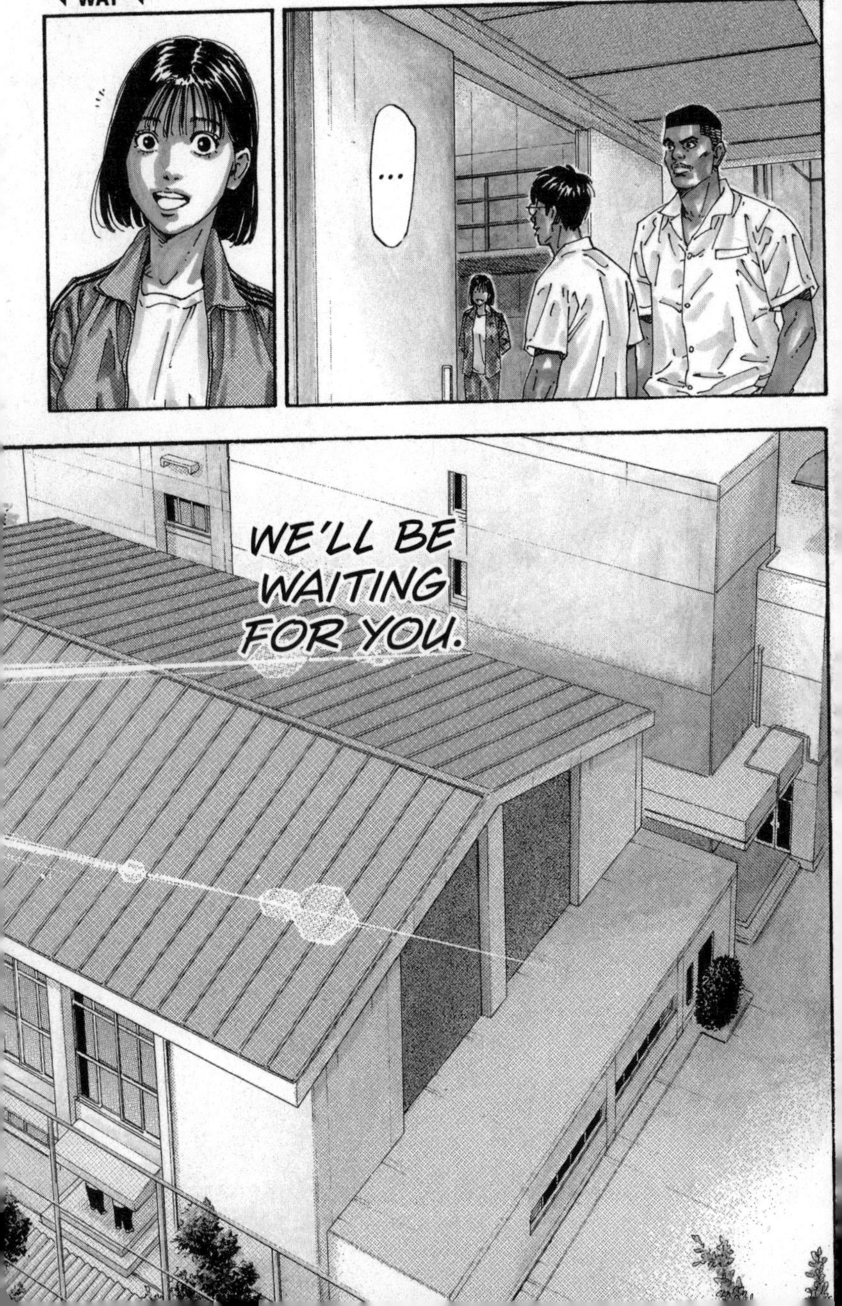
…
WE'LL BE WAITING FOR YOU.

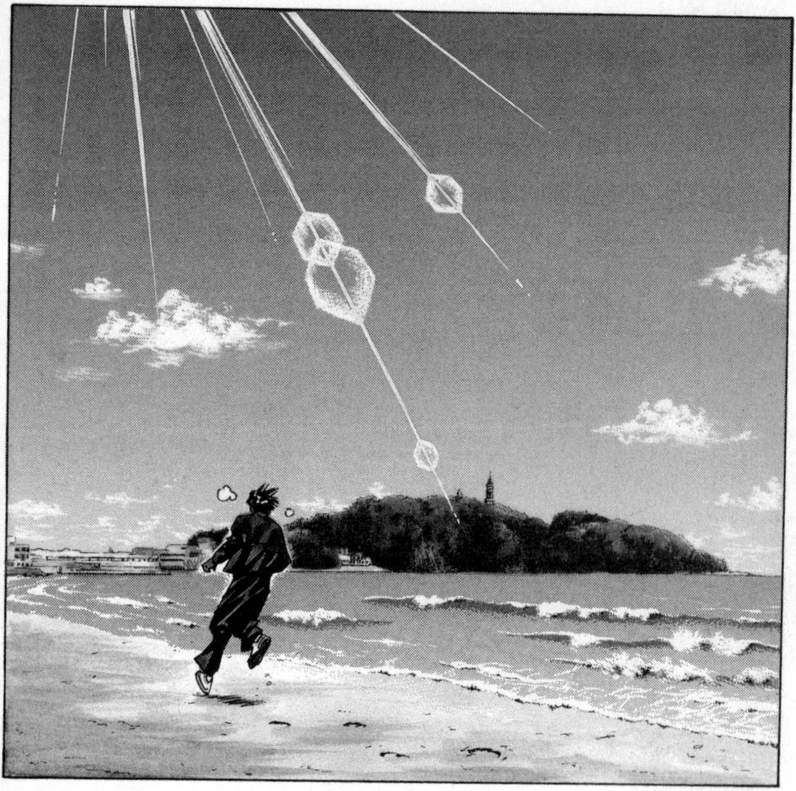
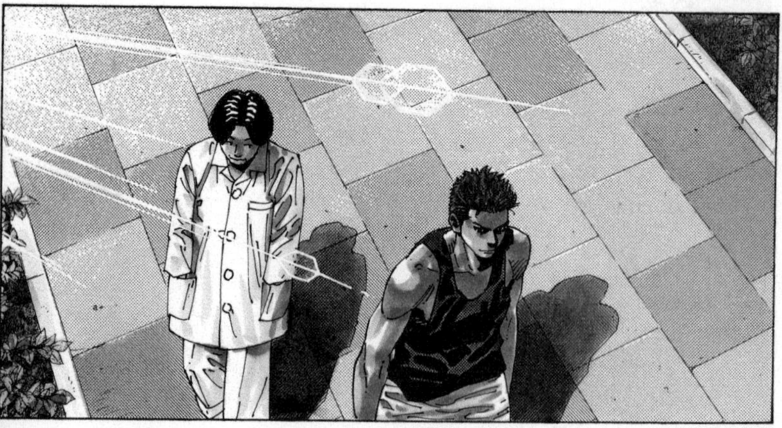

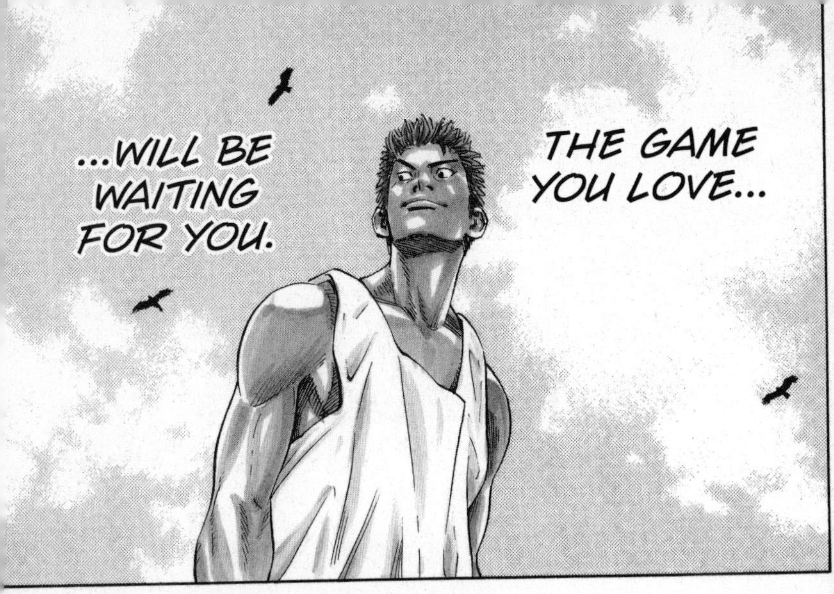
THE GAME YOU LOVE...
...WILL BE WAITING FOR YOU.

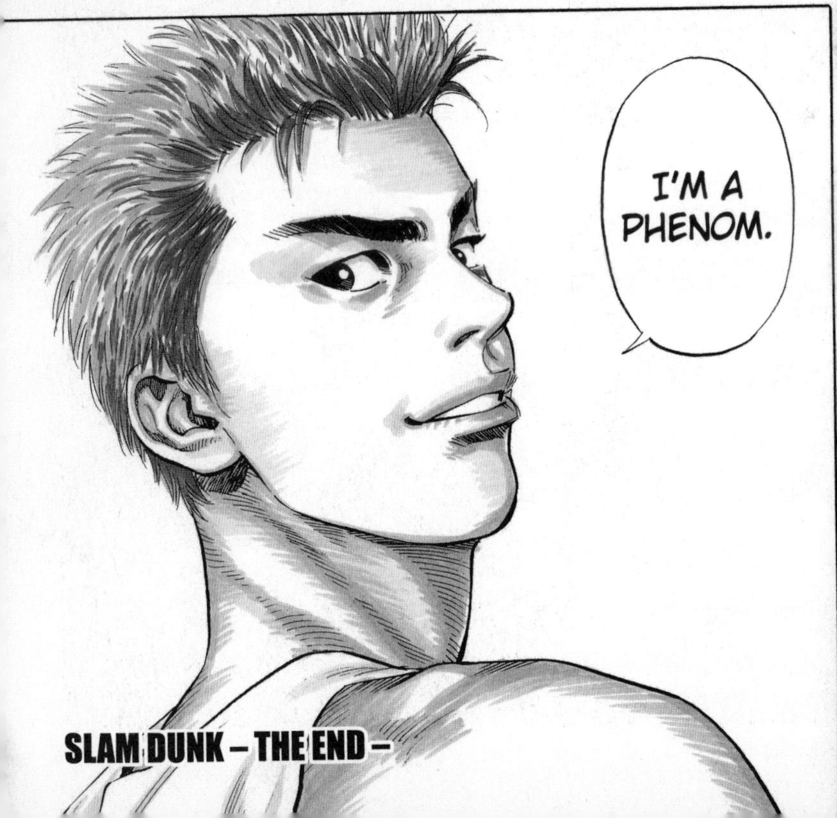
I'M A PHENOM.
SLAM DUNK – THE END –

Afterword

The question I was most frequently asked in interviews and letters was "Why did you choose to make a comic about basketball?"

Certainly, when the serialization started there were only a handful of basketball comics, and it wasn't a major sport in Japan. When I was working up the storyboards for it, an editor told me, "Basketball is a taboo in this industry." I think he meant I should be prepared for it to fail.

Yet writing a comic about basketball, at least for me, was very natural.

My debut comic was about basketball, and the first submission I made to a publisher when I was 19 was about high school basketball.

When I started seriously considering becoming a manga artist, what I was most into was basketball. I started in high school. That's why I think I naturally chose basketball as a subject. When I look back and think that I never even considered another subject, I wonder if I even would have become a manga artist if I hadn't come across basketball? I'm not so sure I would have.

Reading letters saying, "I learned to like basketball after reading your manga," really encouraged me. Those letters renewed my determination to create something better, to "write a better game." I cannot thank everyone who encouraged me enough.

Mr. Taizo Nakamura, Mr. Muneharu Machida, and Mr. Tomoyuki Shima of Shueisha have been invaluable both professionally and personally. I thank them from the bottom of my heart.

The lack of media attention the game receives despite the large number of people playing it irks me, but I am extremely grateful I was given the opportunity to write about a sport I love so much.

Takehiko Inoue

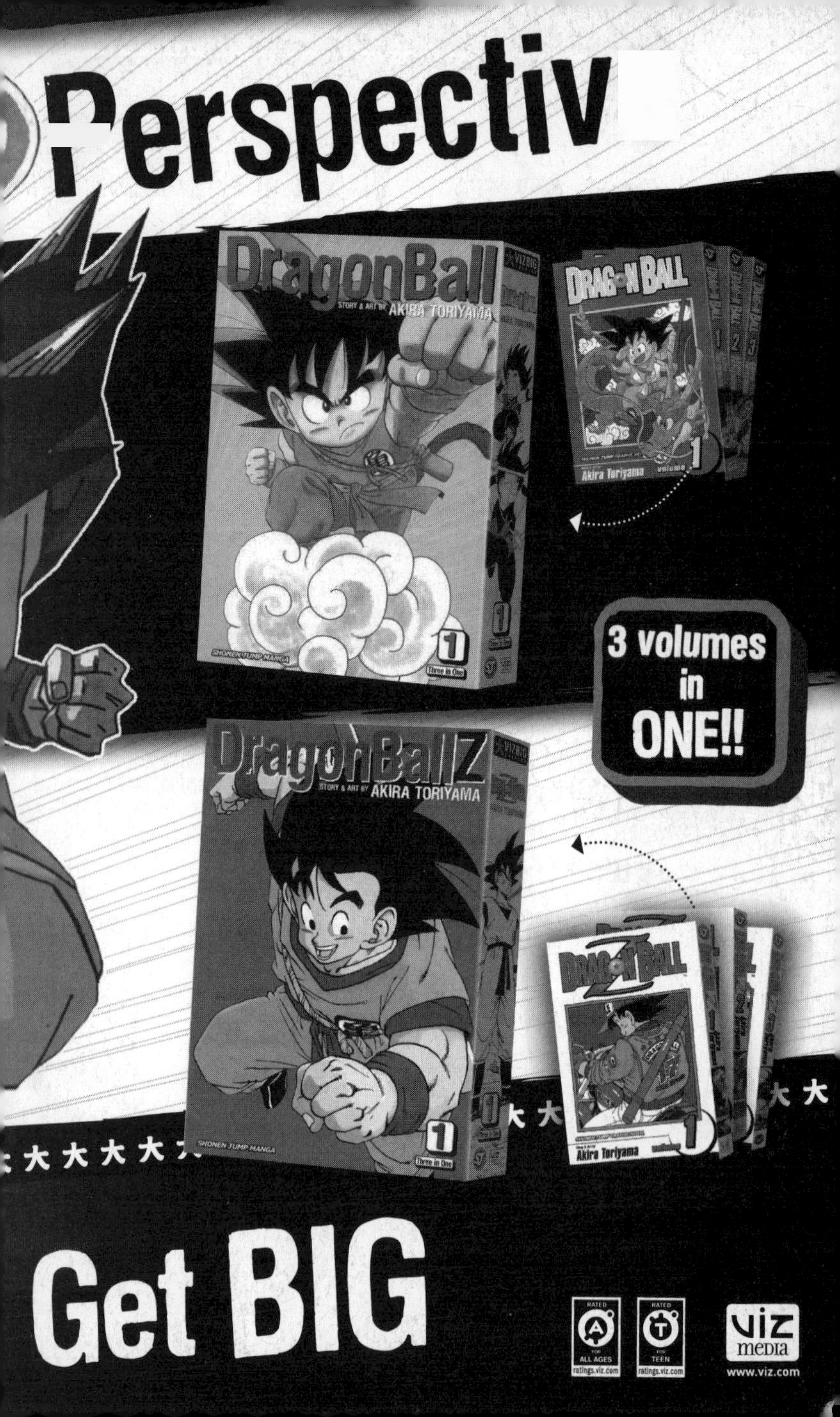
Perspectiv
DragonBall
STORY & ART BY AKIRA TORIYAMA
1
Three in One
SHONEN JUMP MANGA
DRAGON BALL
Akira Toriyama
volume 1
3 volumes in ONE!!
DragonBallZ
STORY & ART BY AKIRA TORIYAMA
1
Three in One
SHONEN JUMP MANGA
DRAGON BALL Z
Akira Toriyama
1
Get BIG
RATED A FOR ALL AGES ratings.viz.com
RATED T FOR TEEN ratings.viz.com
viz media
www.viz.com

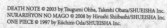

You're Reading in the Wrong Direction!!

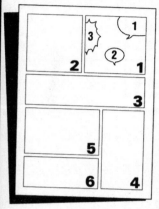

Whoops! Guess what? You're starting at the wrong end of the comic!

...It's true! In keeping with the original Japanese format, **Slam Dunk** is meant to be read from right to left, starting in the upper-right corner.

Unlike English, which is read from left to right, Japanese is read from right to left, meaning that action, sound effects and word-balloon order are completely reversed... something which can make readers unfamiliar with Japanese feel pretty backwards themselves. For this reason, manga or Japanese comics published in the U.S. in English have sometimes been published "flopped"—that is, printed in exact reverse order, as though seen from the other side of a mirror.

By flopping pages, U.S. publishers can avoid confusing readers, but the compromise is not without its downside. For one thing, a character in a flopped manga series who once wore in the original Japanese version a T-shirt emblazoned with "M A Y" (as in "the merry month of") now wears one which reads "Y A M"! Additionally, many manga creators in Japan are themselves unhappy with the process, as some feel the mirror-imaging of their art alters their original intentions.

We are proud to bring you Takehiko Inoue's **Slam Dunk** in the original unflopped format. For now, though, turn to the other side of the book and let the quest begin...!

–Editor